Lourdes

BODY AND SPIRIT IN THE SECULAR AGE

R

RUTH HARRIS

Lourdes

BODY AND SPIRIT IN
THE SECULAR AGE

VIKING

eet,

Penguin Books Ltd, 27 Wrights Lane,
London W8 5TZ, England
Penguin Books Australia Ltd, Ringwood,
Victoria, Australia
Penguin Books Canada Ltd, 10 Alcorn Avenue,
Toronto, Ontario, Canada M4V 3B2
Penguin Books (N.Z.) Ltd, 182-190 Wairau Road,
Auckland 10, New Zealand

Penguin Books Ltd, Registered Offices:
Harmondsworth, Middlesex, England

First American edition
Published in 1999 by Viking Penguin,
a member of Penguin Putnam Inc.

10 9 8 7 6 5 4 3 2 1

LIBRARY OF CONGRESS CATALOGING-IN-PUBLICATION DATA

Harris, Ruth, 1958–
Lourdes : body and spirit in the secular age / Ruth Harris.
p. cm.
Includes bibliographical references and index.
ISBN 0–670–87905–3
1. Mary, Blessed Virgin, Saint—Apparitions and miracles—France—
Lourdes. 2. Bernadette, Saint, 1844–1879. 3. Lourdes (France)
I. Title.
BT653.H37 1999
232.91'7'094478—dc21 99–29779

This book is printed on acid-free paper.
♾

Printed in the United States of America
Set in Sabon

For Iain and Michael

Contents

List of Illustrations

Every effort has been made to contact all copyright holders. The publishers will be glad to make good in future editions any errors or omissions brought to their attention.

The chapter heading engravings originally appeared in Henri Lasserre, *Notre-Dame de Lourdes* (Victor Palmé, Paris, 1878).

Photographic Acknowledgements

AKG, London: 22, 36, 37
Archives de l'Assomption, Rome: 13, 49, 50, 51
Archives de la Congrégation des Sœurs de la Charité et de l'Instruction Chrétienne, Nevers: 9, 31
Archives de la Congrégation des Petites-Sœurs de l'Assomption, Paris: 53, 54, 56, 61
Author: 5, 24
Monique Claude-Hermant: 6, 8, 14, 21
Desclée de Brouwer, Paris: 25
Office Central, Lisieux: 39
Mary Evans Picture Library, London: 40, 72
Iain Pears: 3, 4, 7, 12, 17, 26, 29, 30, 47
Le Pèlerin magazine, Paris: 59
Pascal Piskiewicz, Toulouse: 20, 23, 38, 42
Rex Features/Sipa Press, London: 74
Roger-Viollet, Paris: 16
Stiftung Leonard von Matt, Buochs: 11

Preface

I began thinking about Lourdes over fifteen years ago, when writing another work on French medicine towards the end of the nineteenth century. As I examined Parisian physicians' confident assertions that a new scientific age had dawned and that religious belief was to be swept away like cobwebs from a musty closet, I wondered how it was that Lourdes was living through its 'golden age' at the very same moment. The shrine – as vibrant and as assertive in its way as the increasingly secular capital – brought hundreds of thousands to prostrate themselves before the Grotto and to beg for the Virgin's intercession to cure the sick and dying. I knew that these two sides of France were intimately connected but, at the time, I too readily accepted the general verdict that Paris represented 'progress' and Lourdes 'reaction'. The passionate Marianism and concrete monumentalism of the shrine was repugnant to me; rather than the hushed majesty of a Romanesque church or the grandeur of a Gothic cathedral, Lourdes seemed to represent little more than kitsch for the Catholic masses.

Bur Lourdes would not go away, and became an intellectual concern central to my personal preoccupations. For several years I endured a condition (now alleviated) for which medicine had no diagnosis, and only a hit-or-miss treatment. What, I asked, do ailing people do when science can offer nothing? My work on Lourdes became part of a personal voyage, an act of sympathy with nineteenth-century pilgrims. Like us, they lived in an age that extolled the value of scientific rationality, and yet they knew its limitations all too well; in response they remained loyal to a spiritual world that championed the miraculous in spite of secular ridicule. Although I did not share their beliefs, their resistance to the promises of progress struck a chord as I faced the possibility that modern medicine might not be able to do much for me either.

Despite this growing desire to understand without judging, I remained timid, keen to stay within intellectual furrows already ploughed by other scholars and wary of assaulting the sensibilities of academic colleagues, many of whom found the subject unpalatable. As an historian, I was for a long time content to frame political and social questions that were safely conventional. For example, I wanted to see Lourdes in terms of a political counter-culture, hostile to the growing strength of the emerging secular republic; to oppose the way pilgrimage was so frequently represented as little more than a form of 'leisure', with Catholics from across France lured to the distant Pyrenees as much by the spa towns and mountain scenery as by the shrine. In the end both of these themes found a place in my narrative, but were soon thrust from the centre of my analysis by two central experiences.

The first grew out of getting to know the medieval and early-modern chapels dedicated to the Virgin in the region. The polychrome decorations in these old churches showed the ubiquity of shepherds and shepherdesses communing with the Virgin. Bernadette Soubirous's own encounter with the divine, lauded among Catholics precisely *because* it took place in the midst of the growing religious scepticism of the nineteenth century, suddenly came alive as part of an ancient, but still dynamic, tradition. Astride the great medieval pilgrimage routes, Lourdes was steeped in miracle tales and stories of the Virgin's mercy and power, and it was the continued strength of this tradition that meant the poor and illiterate were alerted to the possibility of the miraculous when they heard her tale. Avenues opened up into the richness of their religious imaginations, and I began to reposition Bernadette's experience between the older Pyrenean tradition of wondrous storytelling and the innovations of nineteenth-century Catholic spirituality. I also saw that it was the way Lourdes combined the two worlds that in large part accounted for its astonishing success.

Of even greater importance, perhaps, was going on pilgrimage myself. I undertook this with trepidation, doubting my ability to be of any use and half expecting to be repelled by the whole experience. Above all, I remember how angry I was when I left London, wondering why I had let work lead a non-Catholic like myself to this alien and frightening world. And yet, a moment later, I was taken up with the business at hand, directed to help a mother care for her adult son who was incontinent, paralysed, blind and deaf. As the pilgrimage progressed, my fear dissipated in the midst of yet another transformation. On previous visits to Lourdes I had been appalled by the pious commerce: the plaster Virgins, the plastic containers for spring water, the wall plaques, videos and cassettes of holy music on sale all around the sanctuary. Working with the hospital pilgrims meant that these judgements melted away; it was hard even to remember that such trading existed when their more pressing needs took over.

Mostly, Lourdes impressed and moved me; less frequently, some of the people there shocked and horrified me. Finally, the pilgrimage was vital to writing the book. Despite the great differences between my experience and that of the nineteenth-century pilgrim, at the core there was the same intense physicality, backbreaking labour, and centrality of pain and suffering. The body in pain was the focus of our collective and personal ministrations, a world that was rendered spiritual by ritual. This spirituality was invested in rites such as the Eucharistic processions and bathing in the pools, activities that seemed to have a timeless, unchanging character. In fact, they originated out of specific nineteenth-century conditions, and encapsulated a particular vision of body and spirit. This vision, and the religious imagination underlying it, became the central theme of this book, around which all the other elements of political and social history necessarily revolved.

What I saw at Lourdes touched me but did not convert me. Indeed, the open-mindedness and spiritual generosity of the group I went with only confirmed me in my Jewish secularism. The experience none the less completely changed my approach to the topic, and by writing a book that is neither a Catholic apology nor an anti-clerical tirade, I hope to offer a study that differs from previous accounts. This is no naïve claim to objectivity, but a statement of intent, however imperfectly realized: I wish to provide an historical context for believers and give non-believers a sense of where the appeal of Lourdes lies.

Obviously, this single volume covers only a small part of the story, and it is a work of history rather than a contemporary chronicle, seeking to investigate why Lourdes became such an extraordinary phenomenon. Some readers will no doubt be disappointed with my selection of topics. I have not even tried to capture the world of diocesan pilgrimage, preferring to focus on the main annual event of national pilgrimage that so dominated the years leading up to the turn of the century. By taking the story only up to 1914, I also miss out many of the themes that might interest Catholics today, but I was wary of writing the twentieth-century history when the documents on the key Vichy period are still unavailable. My narrative discusses not at all those who found Lourdes disappointing, as many undoubtedly did, for the documents provide only the most scattered evidence of such people. Others will want to know more about the cures, and will be disturbed that I come to so few conclusions about whether they are 'real miracles'. No doubt my approach in this important area was partly determined by the fact that, as I am not a physician, I was barred from consulting the medical records at the Medical Bureau. I have the feeling, however, that a greater amount of factual detail would not have substantially altered my conclusions. For my work tries to understand how pilgrimage and healing at Lourdes was organized and how individuals experienced their cures. It is their subjective assessment, rather than the 'objective' adjudication of physicians, that primarily interested me.

One of the greatest challenges has been to write for so many different audiences, to try to build a bridge between scholarship and the general reader. I have attempted throughout to weave my interpretation into the fabric of my narrative, rather than slowing it down with theoretical explanations. Yet I also want to acknowledge the wide variety of academic influences that have shaped my approach. For this book grows out of the last twenty years of historical work and is, at the same time, a critique of many of its tools and assumptions. For example, it owes a massive debt to social anthropology, which has investigated the importance of the rituals of pilgrimage, worship and sacralization. No one reading my work can fail to notice the impact of this field on my discussion of, say, the apparition site and the rituals surrounding it. My analysis of the 'folkloric' traditions of the Pyrenean world owes much to the passions of nineteenth-century ethnographers who sought to preserve in written form the oral and material culture of a world they believed to be moribund. They and their twentieth-century successors have helped me put the mythological and imaginative universe of the Pyreneans at the centre of my book.

But this approach has limitations. Social anthropology *generally* universalizes the particular and erodes a sense of time, looking at apparitions, pilgrimage, curing rituals across time and place, searching for the unifying themes that bind such human phenomena together. My study of Lourdes, in contrast, shows how essential is historical contingency – the specific actions, motivations and experiences of individuals and groups – for understanding how the shrine developed.

In other ways as well the work seeks to take advantage of recent theoretical directions, while pointing out inherent difficulties. The last twenty years have seen the rise and dominance of the so-called 'linguistic turn', a belief that historians should study representations of the past encoded in 'texts', be they documents, images or rites. Rather than studying the past per se, it is argued, historians must content themselves with these 'discursive constructions'. Despite the irritating and often obscure words that surround this field, this work has benefited from the sensitivity to texts that it promotes. No historian of Lourdes, with its pile of official documents, curative memoirs and narratives about the origin of the shrine, can avoid seeing the wisdom of the textualists' cautionary advice. Each type of document – above all the almost legendary story of the apparitions themselves – implies certain assumptions, highlights particular narrative devices and privileges aspects of plot and theme.

However, I wrote this book precisely because of a growing unease with the totalistic way the 'linguistic turn' reduces all human experiences to language. The Lourdes story provides a telling example of the limitations of such an approach by bringing to the fore the often inarticulate expressions of the body and of physical pain. Bernadette's silent body in ecstasy presented a corporeal reality that transformed the lives of witnesses in a way that a thousand words could not. The anguished cries of pilgrims offered a vision of physical distress that was as much a part of culture as the massive commentaries on the shrine itself. A devotee of discourse theory would no doubt argue that all we have is the textual evidence, and my attempt to examine such examples indirectly is philosophically naïve. I would counter by suggesting that history is contained as much in bodies as it is in texts. Pilgrims at Lourdes today, and people in many other contexts as well, carry within them the physical memories of the past in a way the notion of discourse does not satisfactorily recognize.

Such preoccupations also changed the way I look at healings at the shrine. The obvious approach to the tales of cures, so seemingly formulaic in nature, would have been to analyse them in terms of varieties of genre, style, form and influence that contributed to their construction. Such an interpretation would have led comfortably to the conclusion that they were literary representations of the periods and backgrounds of the writers. While this is no doubt true, I believe that there is a greater story to be glimpsed – if only dimly – of suffering and spiritual growth in the individuals involved. Even if the details of my analysis do not persuade, I hope that my quest will open up new ways of addressing aspects of historical experiences that seem beyond retrieval and hopeless of understanding.

Ruth Harris
Oxford
October 1998

Acknowledgements

One of the greatest pleasures of writing this book was the people who helped me along the way. I will never forget the intellectual generosity of Père Xavier Recroix, the chaplain of Garaison College, who shared his inexhaustible knowledge of the religious traditions of the Pyrenees, and introduced me to the beauty of the legendary and mystical world of the poor. I hope that some small measure of his love of their spirituality is conveyed in this volume. Monique Claude and Nadine Vivès provided hospitality and friendship, places that I could call home during my explorations around Lourdes and the region. Père Charles Monsch of the Assumptionists in Rome opened his archives with enthusiasm; his fearless dedication to unearthing both the 'bad' and 'good' of the history of his order was an inspiration to me. Perhaps some of his knowledge of nineteenth-century Catholic debates and his intellectual vitality has entered these pages. Sœur Gisèle Marchand at the Petites-Sœurs de l'Assomption helped me to put together the pieces of the pilgrimage puzzle and to understand better the personal motivations and spiritual yearnings of the leaders of her order. Sœurs Marie-Saint Jean and Bernadette Chauvier sent me the manuscript material from their Convent of Gildard, helping me to think through my thoughts on Bernadette Soubirous. Finally, but not least, were the archivists at the Archives de la Grotte at Lourdes. Père Rîme carted heavy boxes for my consultation despite a broken arm, while Mlle Thérèse Franque more recently provided me with thousands of pages of extra manuscript during the last stages of my research. All these people helped me as an outsider, even though they were not at all sure how I would tell the story of the shrine they esteemed and loved.

I am deeply indebted to all the people who went on pilgrimage, who lavished their kindness on me and encouraged me to consider issues far beyond the confines of my academic world. Their spiritual courage and faith impressed me, and it was their practice of pilgrimage that made me reflect anew on the historical project I had undertaken. Thanks are due to Maggie Parham, who urged me to bathe in the fountain's waters despite my fears, distrust and even anguish. The prayers of the women who immersed me in the freezing water of the pools showed me how this most physical encounter could be rendered spiritual, an experience that transformed my vision of the practices of healing at the sanctuary. I owe a special debt to Stephen Macklow-Smith for our conversations in recent years. Although we speak across a cultural and religious divide, his penetrating intelligence and unconcealed love of pilgrimage accompanied me throughout the writing of this book.

My colleagues in Britain, America and France were also of inestimable aid. Lyndal Roper's knowledge of the early-modern period helped me link my narrative more firmly to past traditions, while Nicholas Stargardt's eagle eye for intellectual confusion and unnecessary error saved me from many missteps. Their mutual enthusiasm for my work kept me going even in moments of despondency. Robert Nye's open-minded and critical reception of the work made me realize, yet again, how special his intellectual gifts are. His open regard for the work despite his early scepticism made me feel that I was on the right track. I thank Robert Gildea for applying his voluminous knowledge and critical acumen to the manuscript. Caroline Ford's plain-speaking made me understand that the work might provoke controversy. Fr Aidan Bellanger of Downside Abbey first put me in touch with the pilgrimage that took me to Lourdes and then kindly read the manuscript to weed out my theological inaccuracies; those that undoubtedly remain are my fault rather than his. Jacques Maître, whose work on psychoanalysis and sainthood is extraordinary, gave me one of the rare and valuable copies of printed manuscripts, a gift that saved me many hours in the library.

Penguin is a wonderful place to publish a book. I thank Ravi Mirchandani for commissioning the work, Kris Puopolo for working on it in the States, and Simon Winder for his acute editorial skills. His discretion and tactfulness meant that I was able to listen with ease to his criticisms, and to rewrite with renewed energy. Gill Coleridge is a fine agent who assured a smooth passage of the book everywhere.

Donna Poppy's skill as a copyeditor transformed the text at the final stages, while Cecilia Mackay's commitment to finding the best illustrations meant that something of the visual world of nineteenth-century Catholicism could be conveyed to the reader. Andrew Barker designed a beautiful book; Chris Miller and Renée Williams answered queries about the French.

The Guggenheim Foundation in New York generously provided time away from my duties at New College, while my colleagues there, especially Eric Christiansen and David Parrott, made it easy for me to concentrate. Finally, my greatest acknowledgement goes to Iain Pears, who shared every step of this journey with me and came to be touched by the story of Lourdes almost as much as I was. I cannot express in words the refined nature of his intellectual and emotional presence or the quality of the love that he brought to the completion of this work. As important as he is Michael Benjamin, our own small miracle, who keeps us laughing with delight.

Part One

The Lourdes of the Apparitions

Introduction

On 11 February 1858 the fourteen-year-old Bernadette Soubirous had the first of eighteen apparitions that made her and the small Pyrenean town of Lourdes famous the world over. She had only recently returned to her family after spending some time working as a shepherdess in a neighbouring village to spare her desperately poor parents the cost of her upbringing. Her father, François, had failed as a miller, and, while he now tried to earn a living as little more than a daily labourer, his wife, Louise Castérot, had to take in laundry and mending, and work in the fields. Even so, they barely scraped by, and their five children were badly dressed, undernourished and often cold.

That day her mother needed wood for cooking and could not afford to buy any; her second-eldest daughter, Toinette, and a friend, Jeanne Abadie, were sent to pick up what they could find. Bernadette went as well, even though her weakness from asthma meant she was unlikely to be of much help. The trio had to avoid places where they might be accused of stealing, and consequently headed for common land outside the town where the canal met the Gave de Pau, the river on which Lourdes stands; here there was a sandy area known as Massabieille, named after a nearby outcrop of rock, with a grotto at its base. When the two sturdier girls waded across the river to pick up some driftwood on the other side, Bernadette stayed behind, but, overcoming her fear of the cold, she eventually sat down near the Grotto to take off her stockings – she was the only one to have such a luxury because of her illness – so she could catch up with them.

First Bernadette heard a wind, but saw nothing move; then, as she bent down to take off the second stocking, she saw a soft light coming from a niche in the Grotto and a beautiful, smiling child in white who seemed to beckon to her. She was startled and instinctively reached for her rosary, but was unable to pick it up until the child produced one herself and began to make the sign of the cross; then she watched until the girl disappeared. No words were spoken by either side; the first apparition was over. No one else had seen, heard or felt anything, nor did they on any other occasion.

Bernadette told her sister what had happened, begging her to keep silent when she realized that Toinette had seen nothing. Toinette, however, was unable to keep a secret and told her mother. Both girls received a thrashing, and Bernadette was forbidden to go there again. She did her best to obey, but three days later she was back with a dozen or so companions. The girl in white appeared once more, and Bernadette tried to talk to her, telling her to stay only if she came from God. To make sure the apparition was not devilish, she threw holy water at it, and was relieved when the girl inclined her head gracefully until the bottle was nearly empty.

This communion was interrupted by Jeanne Abadie, who threw a stone as 'big as a hat' to try to knock the invisible girl from her perch. All but Bernadette jumped with fright; she remained so pale, immobile and seemingly paralysed that the others thought she might be in some sort of fit, and ran to the Savy Mill near by for help. The commotion they caused drew a crowd of onlookers, so that by the time Bernadette came round she was surrounded by a group of women amazed and moved by her demeanour. Indeed, they kept Bernadette's mother from beating her when, breathless and worried, she also arrived.

Once again Louise Castérot forbade Bernadette to return to the Grotto, and again Bernadette tried to obey, but events were fast passing out of her family's hands. Jeanne-Marie Milhet, a serving woman who had climbed the social ladder by marrying her employer, now intervened and used the fact that she employed Louise to do laundry to force a change of mind. Bernadette's third vision, on 18 February, was watched by this commanding woman and her friend Antoinette Peyret, who thought the apparition might be a revenant, the soul of Elisa Latapie, a famously pious woman who had recently died.

To find out, the pair came with paper and pen in case the apparition wanted to write its name, as it apparently would not talk. However, the girl in white laughed when Bernadette held out the writing equipment and instead spoke for the first time, addressing her, a poor girl, with remarkable politeness: 'Boulet aoue ra gracia de bié aci penden quinze dias?' ('Would you have the goodness to come here for fifteen days?') At this stage Bernadette refused to guess at the presence's identity, calling it merely *Aquéro*, the patois word for *cela*, an indefinable being, certainly not human but not necessarily divine.

By the next day the news was rapidly spreading, and the fourth encounter was witnessed not only by Jeanne-Marie Milhet, but also by Bernadette's mother, friends and, significantly, her Aunt Bernarde, her godmother and the most influential member of her mother's family. The day after that devotees from the Children of Mary came as well, for belief that the apparition might be the Virgin was already growing, even though neither it nor Bernadette had made any such suggestion. However, on neither of these two occasions did anything momentous take place; the apparition smiled silently, and Bernadette kneeled, pale and immobile. It was left to the growing numbers to make what they could of it.

After the sixth apparition, on 21 February, Bernadette had her first brush with the authorities, when Police Commissioner Dominique Jacomet brought her in for questioning. Jacomet was neither a cruel nor a brutal man; indeed, until his reputation was damaged in the aftermath of the apparitions, he was known as a good Catholic, popular for his selfless devotion to the poor during the cholera epidemic of 1855 that decimated the malnourished and sickly population. He was widely admired for his competence, intelligence and compassion, and, although the early cultists were angered by his behaviour over the apparitions, many continued to acknowledge his good qualities for years afterwards.

When he interviewed Bernadette, he was sure he was dealing with little more than a childish prank, but was concerned that it might still trigger an outburst of disorder. So he teased and provoked her, trying to force her into contradicting herself. His efforts failed, as Bernadette did not try to identify the white girl and stuck resolutely to her tale. By the time François Soubirous came to take her away, all Jacomet had achieved was to lay the foundations for her legendary stalwartness in the face of official persecution, and to provide the first written account of the apparition, described as having 'a white robe drawn together with a blue sash, a white veil over her head and a yellow rose on each foot . . . [with] a rosary in her hand'.

At least the interview made it seem likely she would not be seeing any more apparitions, as Jacomet threatened her with prison if she went anywhere near the Grotto again. But the effect of this warning also lasted only a few hours; on 22 February she was back, accompanied by fifty women and two gendarmes. She was now to be let down for the first time: *Aquéro* did not appear. The setback, however, was only temporary, and the next time she went the girl in white returned. Bernadette's trance was this time witnessed by Jean-Baptiste Estrade, the local tax collector, who later wrote an important (if inaccurate) account of the events. He came partly because the local priest, Abbé Dominique Peyramale, wanted first-hand testimony yet was concerned that going himself would encourage what might well turn out to be nothing more than a game.

Again, the importance of the occasion lay not with the girl in white, who did little, but with the audience, for the presence of Estrade and other bourgeois men showed how interest was spreading beyond women and the poor. Above all, through Estrade – who was instantly convinced that Bernadette was genuine – Peyramale himself was being slowly drawn in, despite his caution. His role was critical, for although tempestuous, he was also universally admired – he was known, literally, to give the poor the clothes off his own back – and his later support for Bernadette, and the fact that it was given so reluctantly, was of the utmost importance. It was he who communicated the religious aspirations of the poor to the bishop and later responded to the inquiries that came from around the world. He became Bernadette's protector and her family's patron, and was also a key figure in establishing the legitimacy of the shrine, even though his attempts to direct its evolution mired him in turmoil for the rest of his life.

At this stage he was still unconvinced, and watched while the apparitions continued to set out the instructions that constituted the 'mission' of Lourdes. On 24 February the white girl asked for penitence and prayers for the conversion of sinners and directed Bernadette to kiss the ground. The ninth apparition the following day was controversial, for the crowd saw Bernadette scratching the earth with her hands, drinking the dirty, salty water she found there, then tearing up wild cress and eating it. By the end she was a muddy, dishevelled sight, her appearance in striking contrast to her earlier serenity. Bernadette's aunts felt so humiliated by the performance that her Aunt

Bernarde smacked her as they left. They were distressed, but Bernadette was content; she had done as she was told, she said. She had, in fact, uncovered the fountain that was to become the focal point of pilgrimage.

The poor and pious went to fill bottles with the water she had found, but many believers were saddened, while the sceptics were jubilant. At this moment of confusion the authorities, this time the more imposing figure of the imperial prosecutor, Vital Dutour, tried again to frighten Bernadette into recantation. But, although a magistrate with the full majesty of the law behind him, Dutour failed either to catch her out or to stop her going to the Grotto. She went straight back the next day, and once more drank the muddy water. By the tenth apparition on 27 February around 800 people from Lourdes and the surrounding villages were there to watch.

The eleventh and twelfth apparitions on 28 February and 1 March saw only more gestures of prayer and penitence, but the thirteenth, the day after, contained another message, one of the most important of them all: 'Go and tell the priests to come here on procession and to build a chapel.' Bernadette immediately did as she was told and asked Peyramale for a procession the following Thursday. He was furious: how could he arrange a procession so quickly? Did she not know such things had to be authorized by the bishop? Bernadette was undaunted; when she remembered she had forgotten to mention the chapel, she went straight back to ask for that as well. With the message delivered, she had now provided the outlines of a mission that everyone in the Pyrenees could understand: prayer, penitence, bathing and drinking in a fountain, a procession and a chapel.

Peyramale's response when she repeated the request the next day – after two visits to the Grotto, as the apparition failed to appear on the first occasion – was to say that if the girl in white wanted a chapel, she should say who she was and make the wild rose bush in the niche blossom. Bernadette promised to relay the message, and the authorities ordered the gendarmerie near Lourdes to be in readiness to deal with the crowds. It was expected that 4 March, a market day when Lourdes was full of people and the end of the two-week period the girl had requested, would see momentous events. Onlookers jostled each other to find a place around the Grotto, and the length of the vision – forty-five minutes, the longest so far – suggested great things in store. And yet, nothing untoward happened; at the end of her encounter

Bernadette extinguished her candle and went home. Peyramale's request had been ignored; *Aquéro* had not named herself, the rose bush had not blossomed, there were not even any more messages. The apparition cycle had apparently ended in anti-climax; only Bernadette seemed unperturbed.

For the final resolution, town, priests and authorities had to wait another three weeks, until the day of the Annunciation, 25 March. In the interim Bernadette did not go to the Grotto and seemed unconcerned by the emotions she had aroused, but on the night of the 24th she awoke with a familiar urge to return. She arrived at about five in the morning but even so was not the first there; even Jacomet was already in place waiting for her. The girl in white appeared, and Bernadette pressed her to say who she was. After repeating the question four times, *Aquéro* finally put her hands together, looked heavenwards and spoke: 'Que soy era Immaculada Councepciou': 'I am the Immaculate Conception.'

The phrase was unconventional, even awkward sounding, and Peyramale disliked it, although he believed Bernadette's claim that she had never heard the phrase before. It was as if the apparition had said she was beauty rather than that she was beautiful, for the Virgin Mary was called the *Mère immaculée*, the *Vierge immaculée*, but never the Immaculate Conception. To use an event to describe a person sounded awkward, even discordant. Surprisingly, few suggested Bernadette had simply misheard or misunderstood the term during a sermon. Nor was anyone particularly surprised that the 'naming' occurred on the day of the Annunciation: the employment of sacred time seemed appropriate and inevitable rather than a suspicious coincidence.

The cycle of apparitions had reached its great climax, but was not yet over. At the Grotto once more, on 7 April, Bernadette was apparently unburnt when her hand touched the flame of her candle. This event became one of the most contested aspects of the visions, denoting for some a miracle, for others an hallucination or an explicable natural occurrence. Finally, on 16 July she saw the girl in white for the last time, bidding a private farewell from the far side of the river because the authorities had boarded up all access to the site to preserve order. Her distance from the Grotto on this last occasion prefigured her increasing marginalization. Bernadette's mission was over, and the direction of the sanctuary swiftly moved into other, more orthodox hands. While Lourdes developed into one of the greatest shrines in Christendom, the visionary whose experiences had called it into being spent the rest of her short life in a convent, hundreds of miles away.

This, in simplified form, is the story of Bernadette and *Aquéro*. The 'mythical' elements – Bernadette the shepherdess, Bernadette under interrogation, Bernadette and the priests, Bernadette and the awe-struck crowd, the sayings of the girl in white – were highlighted almost from the outset and give the story a fairy-tale quality that has proven irresistible to pilgrims, novelists and film producers alike. Like all good myths, it is largely true: the most diligent historical research has uncovered no lies, deceit or subterfuge. It is what is left unsaid that gives the story its timeless universality, but at the cost of expunging from the historical record the passionate struggles that enveloped this apparently straightforward, if mysterious, series of events.

For there was nothing inevitable about the success of Lourdes; indeed, its beginnings seemed far from promising. The young visionary came from a poor and even disreputable family, could not speak French and was probably already sick with the tuberculosis that eventually killed her in 1879. All the attributes that later became legendary – her poverty, simplicity and ignorance – were at first held against her by the clergy and the educated. The apparition relayed the most minimal of messages, while the most important words she did utter – 'I am the Immaculate Conception' – were decidedly discordant to the pious ear. Lourdes in 1858 was poor and benighted, buried in the Pyrenean foothills and virtually unknown to the rest of France. The local authorities were hostile and did their best to repress the shrine before it had even begun. Nor was it at all certain that the Church would lend its support: keen on their prerogatives, wary of attack and sceptical of the 'superstitious', many in the French hierarchy were far from comfortable with the outburst of popular devotion that followed the visions.

Yet Lourdes prospered against all the odds, and very quickly: by the time Bernadette died in her convent in Nevers, hundreds of thousands were going to the shrine every year, as rich and poor alike, women and then men, concluded that she had indeed been granted a genuine encounter with the Virgin. Far from being a liability, she proved an ideal recipient of divine favour, stoically loyal to the details of her revelation and all but spotless in her personal behaviour, despite the tremendous pressures brought to bear on her. The initial antagonism of the local authorities, rather than deterring believers, goaded them into a stubborn resistance, and later hints of imperial favour fostered the shrine's development. The timely opening of a railway line in 1866 also helped, as the coming of the trains meant that Lourdes was now, for the first time, relatively accessible from the rest of the country. Even the collapse of Louis Napoleon's empire seemed somehow to bring benefits: in the chaos after the Franco-Prussian War and the Commune, those wanting to restore the monarchy – a real possibility in the early 1870s – chose Lourdes above all other sites for pilgrimages of national penitence. Even when that campaign failed and France was finally confirmed as a secular republic, the shrine still continued to grow, for it had by then become the pre-eminent sanctuary of the sick and of the miracle cure.

Nor was Lourdes a fly-by-night phenomenon. Rather than dying with the nineteenth century and the struggles between Church and state that typified that era, it continued to prosper in the twentieth. In 1908 more than one and a half million pilgrims came to commemorate the fiftieth anniversary of the apparitions; a similar number came in 1950 when the Assumption of the Virgin was declared a dogma of the Catholic Church; almost five million were coming every year in the early 1990s, now arriving from all over the world on package charter flights.

The way the shrine triumphed over adversity explains the temptation for many to see its success as the result of divine providence. But none of this was inevitable, for Lourdes could have developed in countless different ways. Why, for example, did Bernadette become the *unique* seer, while other visionaries – sometimes with stronger reputations for piety and virtue – were repressed and almost written out of the history? What historical circumstances made Lourdes of interest to important elites in Paris, so foiling the attempts of the local authorities to suppress this 'superstitious' wave? What appeal did Bernadette – poor, simple, even sometimes considered slow-witted – have for a nineteenth-century audience? Why did Lourdes achieve priority over other shrines in France where children had also seen the

Virgin? What motivated those who organized the pilgrimage hospitals and the special 'white trains' that carried the sick to their destination? How did Lourdes engage the loyalties of so many just at the moment when science and secular thought seemed so close to intellectual supremacy everywhere?

These themes and others provide the basis for an account of the shrine up to the First World War. Lourdes in these early decades is a story about France, about the struggles of Catholics in the aftermath of revolutionary turmoil, the capacity of the Second Empire to adjust to, and even profit from, religious movements, and the inability of the Third Republic to suppress them. This work concludes with the First World War because in some sense 1914 closes what might be called the 'golden age' of the sanctuary. By that time all the essential elements of the pilgrimage phenomenon had been established in the midst of a hostile political climate; in this period also Lourdes became a focal point in the wider debate between science and religion, and between anti-clericalism and clericalism. Although these polemics simmered on – and reappeared with ferocity during the Vichy period – their venom had weakened by the 1920s. With the changed political and social landscape that the close of the First World War brought, Lourdes also lost some of its prominence as a topic of controversy.

At first glance Lourdes seems to epitomize packaged piety and rampant consumerism, the mass mobilization of crowds and new techniques of indoctrination. From this perspective it appears as a vibrant manifestation of 'modernity'. The concept, however, hardly does justice to the complex reality of the pilgrimage phenomenon, for Lourdes differed greatly from the mass political and leisure movements of the nineteenth century. At the heart of pilgrimage lay the lure of the miraculous and the individual encounter with the supernatural, a vision of community and of selfhood entirely at odds with secular creeds. Despite the crowds, the mind-numbing chanting, the harrowing train journeys and the transparent anti-republicanism of many participants, Lourdes celebrated service to the sick and the special mercy of Mary's intercession. In this special spiritual vocation lay both its unique character and enduring attraction.

Indeed, Lourdes is more commonly associated with anachronism and superstition, a dying world trying to resuscitate itself with the techniques, but not the spirit, of the modern age. In this schema it can be fitted all too easily into an historical framework that mechanically opposes religion, reaction and the Old Regime on the one hand, with modernity, progress and the republic on the other. But these dichotomies, in some sense the heirs to the anti-clerical battles of the nineteenth century, do little to promote an understanding of the meaning and attraction of the sanctuary. More dangerously, they suggest a vision of social and cultural change that is unilinear and unidimensional, with one set of beliefs simply stripped away and another imposed upon a neutral, or even willing, surface.

The nineteenth century is generally seen as the era in which such a transition occurred, when France became a secular and republican nation. But Lourdes suggests this conventional interpretation needs rethinking; the shrine's massive appeal alone indicates how much religion remained a crucial part of 'modernity', itself a notion that requires reconsideration. Nor should we see Lourdes as representing 'tradition within modernity', an island of old belief in a sea of surging innovation. The number and variety of pilgrims, as well as the ability of proponents of the miraculous to argue effectively with the advocates of scientific rationality, makes the phenomenon of pilgrimage more than an instance of antiquated survival.

Understanding Lourdes requires a different approach and central to this, I believe, is a more sympathetic approach to the sustained appeal of the miraculous in religion, a topic which, on the whole, historians of the modern era have been wary of examining. While medievalists happily dwell on the supernatural – recounting narratives of saintly women sucking the pus of the sick, visions of nursing from Christ's breast and Eucharistic ecstasy – historians of the nineteenth century are usually ill at ease with, if not actually repelled by, the equivalent phenomena in their own period. The magical incantations of the peasant world, the pious murmurings of female devotees of the Sacred Heart and clerical communion with the Virgin, let alone miraculous cures, are usually seen as little more than superstitious remnants on the road to extinction. Relegating the study of such religious phenomena to the Middle Ages and early-modern period is one of the ways that historians have maintained a division between our 'modern', 'rational' age and the 'irrational', ecstatic world that supposedly preceded it. The distinction allows them to erase any acknowledgement of the sustained attraction of religious mystery and adherence from more recent history. Such studies as are conducted tend to see these practices in terms of 'survival', an orientation that either ignores or belittles the constant evolution, and vitality, of belief that was manifestly present.

It is hardly surprising, then, that mainstream historians have left Lourdes to Catholic scholars, unable to approach such a phenomenon with the same anthropological pleasure that the flickering remains of peasant folklore and popular devotion – small scale, communitarian and an object of nostalgia – arouse. While the rituals of emerging republicanism, from Bastille Day to the Tour de France, draw scholars eager to track signs of secular 'progress', Lourdes retains a regrettable air of reaction, representing for many a world that *should* have been killed off by the Revolution. Yet, when the limitations of such preconceived ideas are abandoned, the spiritual aspirations of the period shine through as critical for an understanding both of the shrine and also of France itself.

The story of the apparitions reveals the religious universe of a small community on the edge of France and its belief that the supernatural world – both punishing and beneficent – was closely watchful of the affairs of humankind. God and the Virgin were omnipresent, but there were also lesser creatures – fairies, witches and devils – who capriciously intervened in daily life. Nor were such beliefs confined to the poor, for the Lourdes story shows how genteel Catholics inhabited the same miraculous realm as the shepherdess, the seamstress and the serving girl. They lived in a shared world of myth, magic and transcendence: the story of the lone shepherdess communing with the Virgin was a tale that placed Bernadette's epiphany within a familiar oral tradition, joined to the landscape of the *bourg*, the common and the wilderness beyond the valley.

I have attempted in this book to capture this living, dynamic tradition, to recover the mythological and imaginative universe that the Pyreneans created in their encounter with the Virgin Mary. They judged Bernadette's visionary experience against the traditions of earlier centuries, but their beliefs were hardly the superstitious remnants of a bygone age. They were potent enough to appeal to urban, educated Catholics around the world, to influence virtually all subsequent Marian apparitions, and to transform the veneration of the Virgin in contemporary Catholicism.

If the story of the apparitions mingled differing religious cultures, then the pilgrimage movement that grew around it was attached, almost from the outset, to the fortunes of international Catholicism. The linking of the Virgin of the Grotto and the Virgin of the Immaculate Conception epitomized the alliance between the Vatican and the faithful which gave that movement much of its force. For what separated Bernadette's apparitions from similar occurrences across the Pyrenees in previous decades and centuries – the sighting of the Virgin had been a celebrated if infrequent event in the mountains for at least 500 years – was the saying of the words 'I am the Immaculate Conception.'

The apparition thus seemed to confirm the dogma promulgated only four years earlier by Pope Pius IX. Enunciated in the wake of the revolutions of 1848, when Pius was forced to flee radical rebellion at home, this new article of faith confronted the onward march of secularism with a defiant assertion of belief in the miraculous. The dogma, which placed Mary as the first and only woman in creation to be delivered from the Original Sin that Eve had brought upon humanity, was received with great enthusiasm by the faithful, who seemed to revel in the way it created an even greater chasm between Catholics on the one hand and Protestants and freethinkers on the other. The apparition's statement thus brought together the disparate worlds of rural piety and the Vatican, and provided a tremendous comfort to a papacy beleaguered by the hostility of liberal, rational and democratic movements.

That the apparitions occurred in France was also significant for the Church. Home of the revolutionary tradition, and of policies that had dispossessed it of property, prestige and influence, France was seen as the seedbed of anti-religious sentiment. The Napoleonic Concordat of 1801 enabled the Church to become once again the religion of the 'majority of the French', but at the price of the episcopate and clergy becoming salaried employees of the state. Its lands sold, its clergy impoverished and dangerously diminished, its relics scattered or buried to save them from the destructive fury of revolutionaries, the Church attempted valiantly, but only slowly, to claw back its position in the years of the Restoration and the July Monarchy.

Despite this bitter legacy – which was to have an important impact on the way Pyrenean churchmen were to promote Lourdes – there were signs of regeneration, above all in the burgeoning Marian piety of the period. The nineteenth century was the 'age of Mary', a cult that brought together both clerical and popular religion and built on traditions that belonged as much to the landscape and to local pride as to Christianity. Mary was protectress of village fields, crossroads and regions; she was hope, consolation, grace, pity, aid and comfort, her generous intercession solicited in the smallest mountain chapel and the most majestic Gothic cathedrals. Nineteenth-century Catholics built on these age-old roots: the Children of Mary, congregations of pious girls and women devoted to emulating the Virgin in all her guises, was founded in parishes across France. They took a special role in the activities of the Month of Mary in May, when the contemplation of the mysteries of the rosary was a duty, and the processions in honour of the Virgin an often dramatic demonstration of devotion. Massive churches were built in her honour at Puy, at Fourvière in Lyon, at Notre-Dame de Lorette in Paris, while bishops across the land promoted sumptuous ceremonies to crown existing and new statues. Catholic houses – from the richest to the poorest – were adorned with porcelain images of the Virgin, while, in later years, pious families displayed reproductions of Our Lady of Lourdes, artefacts of modern industrial production that none the less testified to a ubiquitous and profound belief.

Apparitions were the most extraordinary displays of Mary's solicitude for a sinful nation. The year 1830 brought the apparitions of Catherine Labouré in the rue du Bac in Paris, visions that heralded the dogma of the Immaculate Conception and produced the miraculous medal, a representation of the vision, which sold in the millions and comforted the sick and dying of the cholera epidemic of 1832. She appeared in 1842 in Rome to a Jewish Alsatian named Alphonse Ratisbonne, making a miraculous conversion that clerics publicized widely. In 1846 a luminous Virgin predicted destruction and disaster in an isolated commune in the Alps when she appeared to two shepherd children at La Salette, causing enthusiasm and controversy in equal parts among both laymen and clerics. Lourdes in 1858 brought messages of penitence and redemption, an apparition cycle that seemed to unite the Catholic world in a stroke.

France's defeat by Prussia and the disaster of civil war in 1870–71 brought still more examples of Mary's concern. In the midst of Prussian bombardment near Pontmain, children saw an apparition of the Virgin in the starry night, enjoining them to prayer, and found that their village was spared. In conquered Alsace, especially in Neubois, the Virgin's apparitions strengthened the resistance of the Catholic population to Prussian, and Protestant, domination. The apparitions at Pellevoisin in 1876, which enjoined the faithful to wear a scapular with the sign of the Sacred Heart, the symbol of the Bourbon dynasty, were also taken up by monarchists disappointed by the failure of their campaign for Restoration.

This long list suggests that Lourdes was only one element in a larger pattern of Marianism, one that investigators have sought to comprehend ever since. It is certainly true that children and women seemed more privileged, and that the languages of the illiterate, the patois of the poor, were as favoured as the elegance of French, suggesting a preference for a popular Catholicism that reflected nineteenth-century tastes. But there were almost as many exceptions as there were rules, and each apparition provided an intriguingly specific constellation of local, regional and often political concerns to round out the spiritual messages. In fact, the only consistent thread joining them together was the fervour for Mary they demonstrated.

Lourdes certainly benefited from, and added to, this enthusiasm, but it was crucially transformed and enlarged by fierce political polemics that helped to launch the national pilgrimage during the 1870s. In particular, it was affected by the continuing difficulties of a papacy coping with the loss of its temporal domains to the newly unified Italy. Pius's response to this calamity was obdurate: he refused to recognize the new state and retired into the Vatican, proclaiming himself a prisoner. French Catholics hailed his intransigence as a martyrdom, and applauded his temerity and defiance in proclaiming the dogma of papal infallibility in 1870 at the moment when his temporal fortunes were at their lowest.

In France the Pope's plight was intimately linked to the campaign to restore the Bourbon monarchy after the defeat by the Germans and the civil war in 1870–71, a double cataclysm that monarchists saw as a punishment for the country's unwillingness to defend the papacy against the Italian nationalists. Their reaction was to advocate a two-pronged assault, intending to restore the Pope's position on the Italian peninsula at the same time as he re-established the alliance between throne and altar within France. In this programme a newly organized national pilgrimage to Lourdes became a vital way for Catholics across the country to show their solidarity and strength. The campaign failed when a majority of French voters opted for a republic in 1876, but, despite the defeat, travel to Lourdes continued as *the* leading spiritual and philanthropic event of a Catholic counter-culture opposed to the anti-clerical campaigns of the new secular republic.

Animating this vast but disparate movement were aristocratic women and members of new female orders who joined with activist priests to promote a vision of pilgrimage that brought rich and poor together in Catholic solidarity. Their ethos – which produced the new rituals surrounding the sick – blended religion and politics, as they celebrated the France of Saint Louis and the Bourbon ascendency, sought to re-invent the theocratic rituals of the Middle Ages, and promoted their vision of the most 'Baroque' of Counter-Reformation devotions. Not only did they want a restored monarchy in the 1870s, they later laboured against republicanism with an ardour that seemed to confirm their opponents' conviction that Lourdes was part of some clerico-monarchical conspiracy. The movement also became increasingly anti-Semitic, its leadership joining in the anti-Dreyfusard chorus of the 1890s, dedicated to excluding all enemies, be they Jews, Freemasons or republicans.

Despite the way Lourdes engaged the sympathies and loyalties of such right-wing groups – conjuring up images of theocratic clerics, reactionary aristocrats, and society ladies battling passionately against republican emancipation – national pilgrimage was more complex than the caricatures of anti-clerical opponents suggested. It was a movement of intense ambivalence, peddling the race hatreds of the era and also celebrating a vision of maternal protection, mercy, service and firmness reinforced by a suffering Christ capable of miraculous healing. People prayed in an ecstatic manner as if determined to offend secular sensibilities, bathed in soiled water to the horror of hygienists, and were cured at the moment of Eucharistic procession as if they were participating in medieval Corpus Christi celebrations. It was a movement that valued and gave status to women, acknowledging many of the tasks that they did in private, as they consoled, fed and nursed. Adherents sought to demonstrate publicly the physical and spiritual bonds between people of different ranks, catering to the sick and poor like servants. In contrast to a republican vision of the individual with rights, they stressed the importance of organic bonds uniting people of different ranks under God. They rejected positivism, the reigning ideology of the Third Republic, which justified a lay approach to social and political questions through an appeal to a particular scientific method. So important was their alternative vision of a Christian collectivity that they were willing to risk death – a regular if infrequent occurrence on the white trains and at Lourdes itself – to show the superiority of faith over the transient remedies of science.

The extravagant gestures and rituals during pilgrimage typified a Church increasingly reliant on women, and fuelled anti-clerical claims that the 'backward' sex took refuge in obscurantism when faced with secular awakening. At the same time the Church was accused of deliberately catering to the 'sentimental' and 'meretricious' tastes of female worshippers, women consumed with a passion for Mary, the Sacred Heart, the infant Jesus and any other kind of 'mawkish' devotion. Such characterizations had political implications because the case for denying women the vote in France rested largely on a conviction that they would bring about clerical domination.

There is no doubt that women did appear at Lourdes in larger numbers than men, that they invested their devotions with passionate emotionalism and that they were more likely to be the recipients of cure. From the earliest moment, Lourdes put women and young girls into the limelight, as visionaries, enthusiastic witnesses and as the first worshippers at the shrine. For the sceptical, such 'susceptibility' to the miraculous was proof of their gullibility, an anti-clerical stereotype that dismissed the spirituality of Lourdes by pinning on it an 'anti-modernist' tag. I will take issue with this derogatory portrayal by showing how the Church provided a realm for spiritual reflection and practical activism that the secular republic was rarely able to match. It is in this context that the appeal of pilgrimage and the lure of the supernatural for nineteenth-century women must be understood.

The apparent opposition of the miraculous and scientific rationality at Lourdes was not as straightforward as first appears, however. The sanctuary physicians who set up the Bureau des Constatations médicales (Medical Bureau) in 1883 to vet claims of cure hoped to use modern medical diagnosis to strengthen religious belief rather than undermine it. As the 'miraculous mood' intensified at the close of the nineteenth century – with the crippled jumping to their feet and joining Eucharistic processions, or shouting out in joy as they were cured in the glacial water of the pools – the Medical Bureau was seen as a means of distinguishing between the cure of hysterical and 'real', 'organic' ailments. In this way, it aimed to identify the 'true' miracles that could convert the sceptical by rejecting the false claims that might bring the shrine into disrepute. But in promoting the Medical Bureau, the shrine made a Mephistophelean bargain with positivism. On the one hand, the Church gained a measure of scientific sanction for the miraculous; on the other, it ceded some of its authority, no longer willing, it seemed, to pronounce without medical approval.

Whatever the ambiguities of the Medical Bureau's intervention, Lourdes did provide examples of remarkable healings that the scientific world could neither dismiss nor explain. By the end of the century the greatest non-Catholic physicians of Paris and other Continental capitals had flocked there to see for themselves; they did not believe in supernatural intervention, but were convinced of the therapeutic efficacy of the shrine and the need to investigate it. As a result Lourdes became embroiled in arguments about the role of suggestion, the 'subliminal unconscious' and mediumic power. In this way Lourdes and the nature of the miraculous became as much a part of the *fin de siècle* search for the 'self' as Freud's psychoanalytic investigations.

Books about Bernadette and the shrine began to appear almost from the moment the apparitions came to an end, and it has proved a topic capable of generating some remarkable pieces of writing, both of history and of novels. Part of the reason why Lourdes was so successful lay in the ability of one of its early chroniclers to generate a stunning narrative that answered the spiritual yearnings of an era. Henri Lasserre, in his *Notre-Dame de Lourdes* (1869), produced the most romantic of stories. His tale, which pitted Bernadette and 'the people' against the officials who sought to repress the apparitions, provided an all but ineradicable narrative of naïve weakness and faith triumphant, of state villainy and scepticism confounded. And, while increasingly his work was attacked for its inaccuracies, and Lasserre himself was virtually excluded from the shrine because of the bitterness aroused, his melodramatic flourishes and epic rhetoric meant that throughout the nineteenth century – and perhaps even today – it was difficult to see Lourdes except through his eyes. Because Lasserre contributed so much to the history of Lourdes, part of my own account will analyse his success and the ensuing struggle with other historians for possession of the 'truth'.

Lasserre's greatest opponent was Léonard Cros, a Jesuit determined to shatter Lasserre's 'literary' version and produce a history based more soundly on testimony and documents. He gathered as many official papers as possible, interviewed scores of surviving witnesses in 1878 and procured many written testimonies thereafter in an effort to conserve memories before the participants died. His interpretation saw the reluctant officials as the virtuous doubting Thomases rather than as nefarious schemers, and the over-enthusiastic 'people' themselves as perilous to the true cause of the Grotto. Also, he revealed the moral inadequacies of Bernadette's family, condemned the actions of the local clergy and dismissed the celebrated 'miracle of the candle' of the seventeenth apparition. In the second of his three-volumed history he fully explored the world of the *petit peuple*, seeing them as dangerously credulous, and spent much time on the episode of the 'false visionaries' who followed in Bernadette's wake. It is not perhaps surprising that his *Histoire de Notre-Dame de Lourdes* (1927) was not published during his lifetime, nor that its posthumous appearance evoked very mixed reactions.

These rival accounts were central to the struggles that attended the sanctuary in its early days. By the centenary of the apparitions, the Benedictine scholars René Laurentin and Bernard Billet sought to end historiographical dispute once and for all by providing a truly 'scientific' history stripped of the rancour of the past. The monumental works they produced did indeed quell all serious controversy over the facts: Laurentin's six-volume *Lourdes: Histoire authentique des apparitions* (1961–4) judged the veracity of witnesses, dated texts, and finally fixed a chronology of the apparitions that is difficult to gainsay. Although he favoured witnesses who confirmed *his* interpretation of Bernadette's personality, his work none the less deftly balanced the various accounts and confronted contradictions bravely, without trying to brush them aside.

Laurentin's massive work with Billet, *Lourdes: Documents authen-*

tiques (seven volumes, 1957–66), provides an exacting documentary parade that runs from Bernadette's childhood in the 1840s through to her departure to the convent of Nevers in 1866. However, any insights into the spiritual world of the Pyrenean poor – especially the epidemic of visionaries – are secondary to their primary goal of illuminating the really important event, the apparitions themselves. Like Cros before them, their aim was to reserve a space for the divine within a rigorous 'scientific' history. No amount of documents, however, can 'prove' that Bernadette saw anything at all. Silent and invisible to everyone but the young shepherdess, the apparitions were believed because of the ardent faith of the visionary and her witnesses. Presenting the troubles of Bernadette and the faithful, the drawn-out negotiations for the establishment of the sanctuary, the saintly apprenticeship of the visionary, do not in themselves confirm the appearance of Notre-Dame de Lourdes, although the way Laurentin and Billet have written the story suggests that they do.

As with all the past histories, I am sure that my own account will also fail to please many people. For while I hope that nothing will offend the faith of believers, I cannot engage with the question of whether or not Bernadette Soubirous saw the Virgin Mary: it is not a matter an historian can decide. Instead, my aim is to counter the reigning forgetfulness about the shrine's origins among historians and Catholics alike. Pilgrims prefer their stories of Bernadette and the apparitions stripped down and 'picturesque'; they are unwilling or unable to assimilate the reality of poverty, conflict and political polemic that shaped the development of the sanctuary. Many dismiss with a wave of the hand the clerical and anti-clerical struggles of the nineteenth century – in a gesture of annoyance they consign these 'unseemly' tales to a mental dustbin, seeking to discard the virulence of Lourdes's earlier right-wing profile. Such a yearning to forget, however, unjustly denies the curious ways that the 'good' and the 'bad' of the Lourdes tradition were so inextricably bound together. What is now treasured at Lourdes – above all, the attention to the sick, which I am convinced is genuinely loving – had its roots in the same political and spiritual universe that so violently detested Jews, Freemasons and the republic.

Lourdes also provides an unparalleled opportunity to delve into the nineteenth-century vision of the 'self' by examining reactions to the psychic experience of the miraculous. Those cured on pilgrimage left behind a unique body of accounts describing the overwhelming power of the supernatural and revealing how the process of cure engaged all the emotional and physical resources of the individuals concerned. The memoirs of these women – they were almost always female, and were often poor and ill educated – reveal fantasies of love and attachment, resistance and anger, which contributed to their attempts to organize and put into words an existential experience that was the most transformative event of their lives.

For at the centre of the history of Lourdes lies physical pain. Omnipresent if often inarticulate, neither suffering nor its alleviation were easily contained within the defining power of language. The way paralysed people began to walk again after years of incapacity and suffering makes the historian confront the body not as a philosophical or linguistic abstraction but as an intensely corporeal reality, one on which the pilgrimage movement itself laid ever greater stress. In this sense there was a paradox at the heart of the sanctuary, for the more physical pilgrimage became – with its emphasis on disease and dying – the more spiritual it became as well, as if the assembled at Lourdes were obliquely aware of an attempt to transcend the mind–body divide of contemporary society. Appreciating and trying to understand their quest requires an imaginative capacity to think anew about the body and spirit in the secular age.

I

Town, Region, Family

For nearly all writers Lourdes was defined by its location: a town at the edge of the country, nestling in the valleys of the Pyrenees, scarcely affected by the buffeting of the nineteenth century. For Lasserre, this gave the region a romantic tinge, and he transformed it into the embodiment of a world of mountain stoicism maintained by religion and tradition. Louis Veuillot, a Catholic polemicist and political firebrand who was later of critical importance for the shrine, portrayed Lourdes as the essence of French provincial society, not utterly unenlightened but scarcely on the cutting edge of either fashion or progress:

> a little town in the Hautes-Pyrénées, very old, passed through rather than known . . . a small market town, neither sleepy nor lacking in what people these days call 'enlightenment' . . . There are large houses, fine inns, cafés, a [literary] circle with its supply of newspapers . . . a newspaper, *Le Lavedan*, the paper for the Argelès Arrondissement, politically moderate, but reluctant

to credit anything not vouched for by the police commissioner and authorized by the sub-prefect.[1]

He saw Lourdes almost as a theatre set, waiting for the drama to begin, a view that, one hundred years later, Laurentin unwittingly reinforced by likening it to Camus's Oran before the plague:[2] the image is of people living almost in a time-warp, their humdrum lives soon to be transformed utterly by momentous events. Though a century apart, both subscribe in various degrees to a vision of stasis conjured up by *pyrénéisme*, that most romantic of nineteenth-century movements, which mystified the hard, bleak life of the mountains, made its very distance from the cosmopolitanism of Paris into its greatest virtue and ignored the ever deteriorating economic conditions of the first half of the century.[3] The Virgin, it was often argued, decided to appear to Bernadette because she somehow represented a world uncontaminated by materialism and secularism, and it is this image of purity in poverty that almost all sympathetic writers sooner or later employ.

Viewed from Paris, Lourdes did indeed seem to be little more than a small speck on the edge of the map of France. Even getting to it was difficult until the coming of the railways: Bordeaux to Bagnères-de-Bigorre took at least thirty-two hours by coach, and one traveller claimed after the experience that Dante should have used the vehicle in his inferno to punish sinners.[4] What the voyager saw when he or she arrived was, above all, the mountains, the forbidding, rugged peaks that tower above the Pyrenean piedmont where Lourdes nestles between Tarbes to the north and Argelès to the south. Lourdes itself was less than remarkable, its most prominent feature the medieval fortress, the traditional seat of the counts of Bigorre, which in 1858 quartered idle soldiers. To the west of this monument was the Gave, which powered the mills, provided the town's water and washed up the debris that Bernadette was collecting on the first day of the apparition cycle.

To the east of the fortress was the town itself, which contained little to catch the eye of even the diligent tourist. The main road was the rue Saint-Pierre, which ran from north to south and was dominated by a small cluster of public buildings – the parish church, the town hall and police station – all of which faced the maison Cénac, where Jacomet and Estrade lived. At the southern end it opened on to the place Marcadal, which contained the main café frequented by the notables. On the northern edge of the town, going towards Tarbes, was the Hospice–Ecole des Sœurs de Nevers, where Bernadette took her catechism lessons and later lived until she left for the mother-house in Nevers (see illus. 1).

Although a market town essential for the local economy, Lourdes had not made many advances in the first part of the century and remained a 'parish of the second class', even though it had five clergymen – Abbé Peyramale, three vicars and Abbé Pomian, Bernadette's confessor.[5] Above all, it had lost out to Argelès in the competition to be the seat of the sub-prefect, an administrative function that would have increased its prominence. Moreover, it had no water supply suitable for developing a spa: instead, the Lourdais had to watch Cauterets and Bagnères grow prosperous on this increasingly lucrative business.

The importance of the town was greater than it appeared, however, for its significance had always lain in its position at the intersection of seven different valleys of the Lavedan – indeed, this was the reason the fortress had been built in the Middle Ages. By the nineteenth its location made it a natural stopping-point for travellers, and by mid century these were becoming numerous. Those who came to the Pyrenees sought the sublime in the mountains and the exotic in the population, drawn by the descriptions of ethnographers and literary luminaries like Vigny, Sand, Baudelaire and Flaubert.[6] The locals, with their infinitely various local costumes and languages, were deemed the 'Indians' of France and colourfully represented as the indigenous peoples of an unadulterated race.[7]

Such descriptions, which tended to depend on a contrast with northern urban centres, disguised the region's long involvement in wider national and international currents and made it seem far more isolated than was actually the case. The chateau itself was a brooding reminder of Lourdes's often bloody and tumultuous past. The town had been razed when trying to resist Huguenot armies in the sixteenth century.[8] Between Spanish and French territories and the target of competing secular jurisdictions, the region had known Charlemagne, Simon de Montfort, the Black Prince, Du Guesclin, Jeanne d'Albret

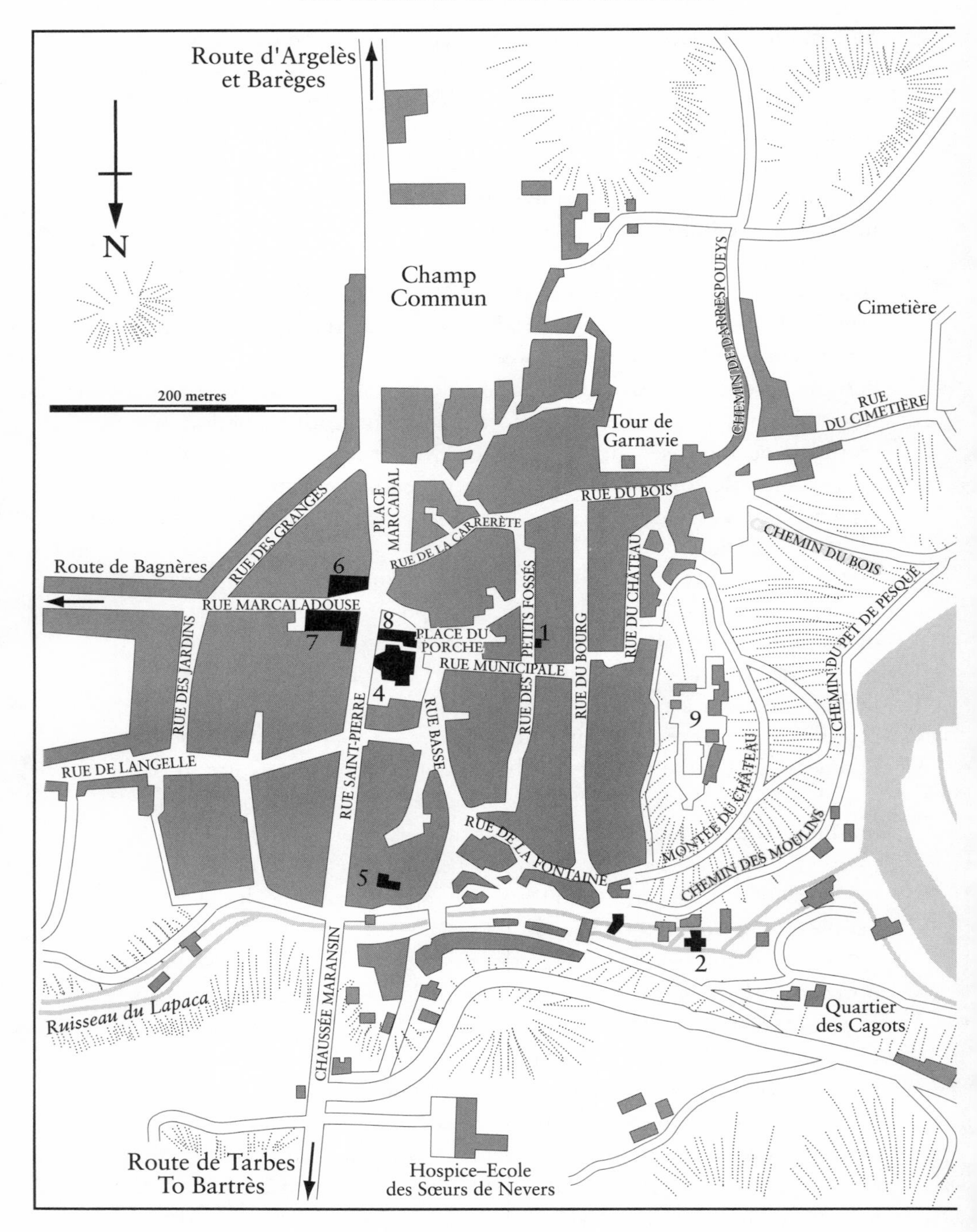

Route d'Argelès et Barèges
N
200 metres
Champ Commun
Cimetière
Tour de Garnavie
CHEMIN DE DARRESPOUEYS
RUE DU CIMETIÈRE
RUE DU BOIS
CHEMIN DU BOIS
PLACE MARCADAL
RUE DES GRANGES
RUE DE LA CARRERÈTE
Route de Bagnères
RUE MARCALADOUSE
PLACE DU PORCHE
RUE MUNICIPALE
RUE DES PETITS FOSSÉS
RUE DU BOURG
RUE DU CHATEAU
CHEMIN DU PET DE PESQUÉ
RUE DES JARDINS
RUE SAINT-PIERRE
RUE BASSE
RUE DE LANGELLE
RUE DE LA FONTAINE
MONTÉE DU CHÂTEAU
CHEMIN DES MOULINS
Ruisseau du Lapaca
CHAUSSÉE MARANSIN
Quartier des Cagots
Route de Tarbes To Bartrès
Hospice–Ecole des Sœurs de Nevers
1
2
4
5
6
7
8
9

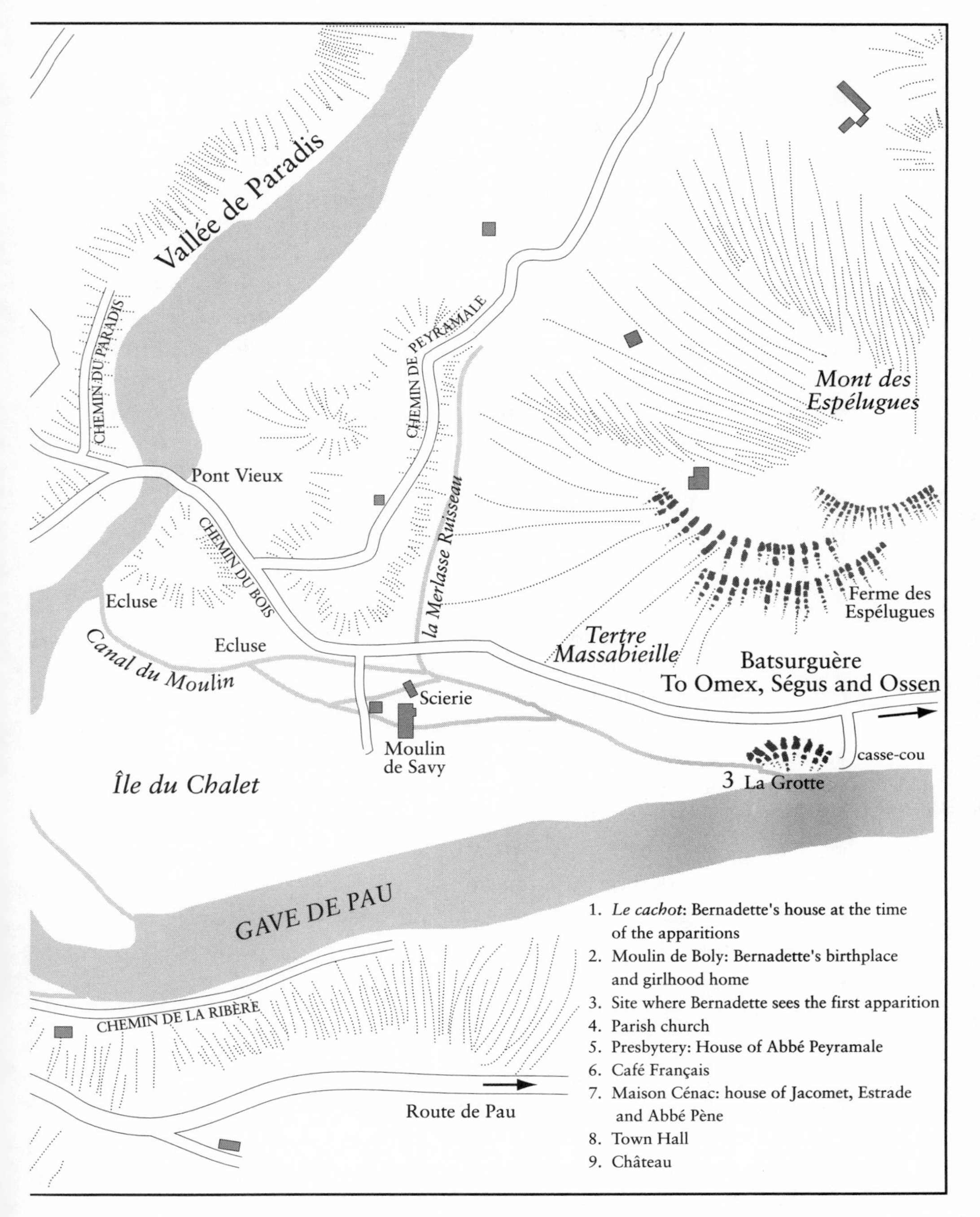

1. Map of Lourdes at the time of the apparitions, 1858

and Henri IV. The Revolution forced the town to pay attention to national quarrels,[9] while the Peninsular War under Napoleon sucked the local population into the struggle with Spain.[10]

Even though it missed out on the vogue for 'taking the waters', Lourdes drew some benefit from the growth in tourism, which was one of the few new activities with the potential to replace trades, such as metallurgy or textiles, that were being squeezed by new industrial processes. None the less, in 1856 it had a population of no more than 4,000 people,[11] of whom 120 were notables – men in the liberal professions, *rentiers*, physicians and so on – with a similar number of small tradesmen. The largest section of the population consisted of the manual workers – the shepherds, farmers, millers and forestry workers, as well as the quarrymen who exploited the marble, stone and slate found in the mountains; their accidents and injuries were to figure in the earliest miracle tales of the Grotto.[12] Finally, at the bottom of the social hierarchy were the day workers, men with no fixed employment who sought a crust from whatever was going. François Soubirous, Bernadette's father, belonged to this group.

For Lourdais such as the Soubirous, life was a harsh struggle to keep body and spirit together, as the Pyrenean economy collapsed under pressure from agricultural scarcity and disease mainly brought on by a 40 per cent increase in population between 1801 and 1846.[13] The land produced wheat and corn as well as rye and potatoes, but cultivable fields were scarce and increasingly subdivided; and, while sheep and cows were pastured on common land or in the forests in the good months, shepherds found it ever more difficult to provide the feed their animals needed to survive the winter. It was precisely at this moment that common pasturage was subdivided or sold, and the forests – the source of firewood and building materials – were subjected to tighter controls; the importance of this for the story of the apparitions will appear later on.[14]

Bernadette's parents' generation was the worst affected: there were food shortages twice a decade until 1850, and the crisis between 1853 and 1857, just before the apparitions, pushed grain prices to their highest point in half a century.[15] The result was disease: diet-related illnesses such as goitre, chest complaints, eye diseases and pellagra, as well as the cholera epidemic of the 1850s, which struck Bernadette and Lourdes.[16] The department of the Hautes-Pyrénées was notable for the poor quality of its military recruits, the ailing and diseased soldiers a testimony to the ill-health of the population in general. It is not perhaps surprising that under such circumstances the poor welcomed a miraculous fountain that might ease their pain.[17]

The plight of the Soubirous family illustrates the cycle of indebtedness, dispossession, malnutrition and disease that afflicted so many. They were forced first to leave two mills and reduced to living in the *cachot*, the old Lourdes prison, picking up what work they could. Bernadette, struck down in 1855 by cholera, became permanently asthmatic and weakened, a perfect example of the impact of epidemics on the fragile health of the poor.[18] The children were the victims of the region's poor diet: one of the boys nibbled the wax from the church candles to fill his empty stomach,[19] while Bernadette was treated by her mother to an occasional slice of wheat bread because she was unable to digest the unpalatable *milloc*, or mashed corn, which was the staple of the poorest.[20] It was at this stage that her father was arrested for stealing a bag of wheat from an employer.[21]

Rather than existing in a bubble of unchanging stability, therefore, Lourdes and the Pyrenees in general were in the midst of a crisis in the 1850s, and an explosive situation was perhaps averted only by the mass exodus of artisans and smallholders, who generally ignored the attractions of northern France and instead used eighteenth-century Béarnais–Basque links to go to Argentina and Uruguay.[22] The preference indicates one of the defining features of Pyrenean identity: few in the mountain regions had much understanding of the concept of a frontier and they had little sense of being French. That this should be the case was not surprising, for the 1659 treaty of the Pyrenees with Spain had more to do with international relations than with the life of the mountain dwellers; exactly where the boundary ran was not even properly established until after 1853.[23]

As a result the Pyreneans went back and forth as though the Spanish frontier scarcely existed; not only did muleteers, brigands, counterfeiters and shepherds brave the cold and the avalanches, large numbers of agricultural workers and artisans regularly left for months at a time to find work – from the French side into Spain in the eighteenth century, the other way round in the nineteenth, for however poor the French Pyreneans were, their neighbours over the mountains were now even poorer. In addition, the boundaries of language bore no relation to those established by statesmen: in the west, Basque dominated on both sides; the peoples of the east spoke Catalan; and in the centre, where Lourdes was situated, a wealth of Béarnais dialects flourished, Gascon languages that made the acquisition of Spanish relatively simple. Bernadette's patois thus linked her to a common Pyrenean heritage even as it marked her off not just from the rest of her nominal country, but from inhabitants of other valleys. There were comical instances of miscomprehension when she recounted the words of the apparition, as speakers of other patois heard a different meaning in the messages.[24]

Not only did Pyreneans have little notion of Frenchness, what sentiments they did have were often hostile, for they had traditionally enjoyed considerable independence in a region in which feudalism had taken hold only superficially and where the hand of the state had never gained a strong grip. Villagers maintained local languages, costumes and customs against the regulating tendencies of bureaucrats well into the second half of the nineteenth century,[25] and disdain for the state found expression in various forms of illegality that were essential to family and community survival. Breaking – or rather ignoring – the law was virtually the norm; rather than the great and wily *contrebandiers* of legend, for example, the majority accused of smuggling were the poor, especially women and children, caught carrying salt and other household necessities across the border.[26] The Hautes-Pyrénées were third in national tables for the number of young men who evaded military service, with many encouraged by their families to emigrate rather than to go into the army.[27] It would take the railway link, the sanctuary and republican institutions – the ballot box, barracks and schools – to confer a truly French identity on a place like Lourdes, and even then local families retained strong links with emigrants to the New World in the same way that Sicilians remained tied to brethren in New York.[28]

The tradition of 'honourable illegality' that led to smuggling and evading military service appears in the history of the shrine when the Lourdais and surrounding villagers defended 'their' Grotto from the officials' overweaning interference. For the Grotto of Massabieille was on common land – it was precisely for this reason that Bernadette went there in the first place – and was considered part of the collective patrimony of the poor; the apparitions, in this sense, sanctified the conception of collective ownership. This perception of communality mingled the spiritual and economic almost indistinguishably; the quarrymen, for example, would lay a path to enable more people to approach the Grotto and honoured the Virgin by doing the work for free.

At the same time, however, the Lourdais also believed in their right to build the chapel the Virgin had requested, seeing in this divine instruction a dispensation of providence.[29] Like the poor in neighbouring spa towns who saw mineral springs as collective property and sought to live off the tourists,[30] the Lourdais saw the benefits the Grotto might bestow and were keen to establish their right both to protect the site and to exploit its potential. For the Virgin had appeared among them, who were so desperately poor; there was nothing impious in making the best use of her gift. It was, perhaps, out of this original attitude that the mingling of spirituality and commercialism that so dismayed later commentators developed.

The Grotto was in the line of battle because of its proximity to the communal forest, the greatest cause of friction between Pyreneans and the state in the first half of the nineteenth century. Covering a third of the mountains, the forest was crucial for survival – providing fuel, building materials and grazing – and a new code in 1828 to limit the amount and kind of wood that could be taken was bitterly resented.[31] While the concern of the government was to control the depredations of a growing and starving population, the effect on the poor was devastating. The result in the early 1830s was the War of the Demoiselles, in which Pyrenean men attacked the forest guards who had become their enemies. Dressed in white, the rebels hid their identity by behaving like the *demoiselles*, or fairies, the dainty denizens of the forest. Light of foot and punishing to those who had wantonly offended the delicate balance between nature and people, the Demoiselles joined the struggle for communal rights to a vision of the supernatural nature of the forest.[32]

Although it peaked between 1830 and 1832, this rebellion was followed by an interminable war of attrition, centred on the Hautes-Pyrénées, which continued unrelentingly through the 1850s.[33] While the earlier, more violent conflict had been waged by men, women and children dominated the later stage, carrying off faggots of wood in a persistent campaign that continued despite fines and imprisonment.[34]

After the apparitions, the poor of the region around Lourdes often linked their ventures into the forest with prayer at the Grotto: the two activities were similar in nature, for both evaded authority, staked their claim to proprietorship and demonstrated spiritual loyalties.

One day, I was passing the rocks of Massabieille when I saw some women and children and a young man, on their way to or from the woods. They went into the Grotto to pray. Just then two gendarmes arrived. The women and the young man tried to escape by crossing the canal that serves the mill. They had gone a fair distance through the deep, rapid streams – when they spotted another gendarme ahead of them. They came back to the Grotto and probably gave their names to the two gendarmes there.[35]

The Spiritual World

Because the apparitions occurred at the very peak of this crisis, it is tempting perhaps to see them as nothing more than spiritual consolation in the midst of escalating misery. There is no doubt that the poor did indeed find reassurance in the Virgin's visitation, but it must be emphasized that there was no causal link between the social and economic crisis – a general phenomenon throughout the region – and the supernatural encounter, which occurred in a particular place. On the contrary, these social and economic realities were significant not because they somehow *caused* the apparitions, but rather because they formed the material lens through which the fantastical and mythological was viewed and then interpreted. Poverty, scarcity of food, conflict with authority, these were all themes that would permeate the many tales – ribald, subversive and holy – that surrounded Bernadette's divine encounter.

Lourdes was anything but a spiritual backwater. The location that made it a crossroads for tourists in the nineteenth century meant that it also straddled some of the great pilgrimage routes to Rocamadour, Montserrat and Compostela[36] (see illus. 2). The populace was nurtured on a steady diet of pilgrim stories from the Middle Ages, tales that marvelled at the Virgin's beneficence and the possibility of miracles. Pyreneans in general lived in a cosmological universe that cannot readily be reduced to a simple dichotomy between popular and orthodox, pre-Christian and Christian influences. Religious belief permeated all aspects of daily life, with the well-to-do as ready to entertain the possibility of the magical and legendary as the poor and illiterate. For example, the letters of Adélaide Monlaur,[37] a genteel young woman who wrote avidly to her male cousin describing the apparitions and the rumours that circulated among the excited populace, gave credence to the tale that a dove was seen flying near the entrance to the Grotto.[38] She therefore unwittingly associated the apparitions with the Holy Spirit, a Celtic symbol of feminine purity as well as wandering souls common to the region.[39] Nor did churchmen automatically throw off their Pyrenean beliefs once ordained; Peyramale discreetly recounted to his brother how, soon after the apparitions, he was escorted through the woods by a pack of gentle wolves, sent by providence to protect him on a cold and snowy night after ministering to the faithful in a distant parish.[40]

For although instructed in the religion of the Counter-Reformation, the people of the region held on to a magical and religious outlook in defiance of official teaching[41] and, in a world of mountain villages and harsh climatic conditions, sacralized the landscape in ways that combined older beliefs with Christian worship. Thus, women placed bouquets at the bases of menhirs and on the tables of dolmens to pray for fertility;[42] they mixed magical incantations into revised versions of Latin prayers to make them more effective against illness and black magic.[43] Legends evoked a world of wondrous supernatural creatures: giants fighting in the high valleys and mountain tops, fairies – little white ladies who also figure in the Lourdes story – living in the fountains and grottoes, and demons lurking dangerously at crossroads and on bridges.[44] The pagan cult of trees and waters was no more, but special trees and fountains none the less acted as magical intermediaries between the population and Christian saints,[45] while the Virgin Mary and her appearance was, as will be seen, associated with certain flowering and healing bushes.[46] All over the Pyrenees villagers celebrated the festival of Saint John the Baptist (and the summer solstice) by rolling in the dew and worshipped at local fountains without dispensation from their priests. The ceremonies of washing and bathing so important in Bernadette's message, therefore, also had particular resonance.[47]

Alongside these often hidden, if pervasive, acts of worship, villagers

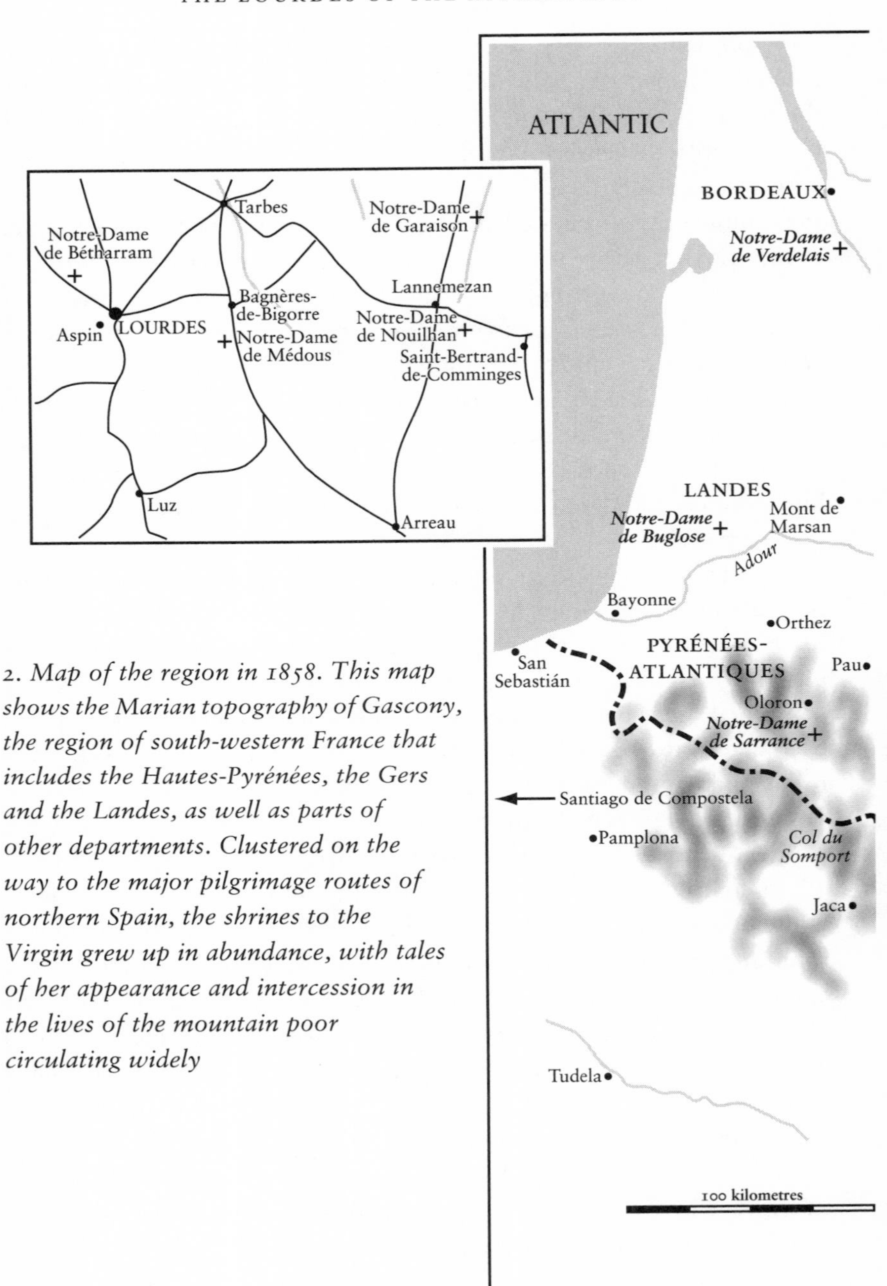

2. *Map of the region in 1858. This map shows the Marian topography of Gascony, the region of south-western France that includes the Hautes-Pyrénées, the Gers and the Landes, as well as parts of other departments. Clustered on the way to the major pilgrimage routes of northern Spain, the shrines to the Virgin grew up in abundance, with tales of her appearance and intercession in the lives of the mountain poor circulating widely*

Tulle
Périgueux
Brive
Saint Flour
Libourne
Aurillac
Dordogne
Notre-Dame de Rocamadour
Figeac
Cahors
Rodez
LOT
FRANCE
AVEYRON
Notre-Dame de Ceignac
Agen
Notre-Dame de Bon Encontre
LOT-ET-GARONNE
Millau
Garonne
Montauban
TARN-ET-GARONNE
Albi
Aire
Notre-Dame de Brugières
TARN
Auch
GERS
Notre-Dame de Canuzac
TOULOUSE
HAUTE-GARONNE
Castres
Béziers
Notre-Dame de Saint Bernard
Carcassonne
Narbonne
Saint Gaudens
LOURDES
Notre-Dame de Vignes
Saint Girons
Pamiers
AUDE
Foix
Notre-Dame de Celles
Saint Béat
ARIÈGE
Perpignan
Notre-Dame de Héas
Notre-Dame de Bourisp
Vielha
Ax-les-Thermes
PYRÉNÉES-ORIENTALES
ANDORRA
Puigcerda
La Seu d' Urgell
Figueras
Tremp
Gerona
SPAIN
Vich
Montserrat
Lérida
BARCELONA
MEDITERRANEAN

took part in religious ceremonies and associations typical of the south of France and southern Europe more generally, their piety recalling something of the flamboyance of Spain.[48] Captain Adolphe d'Angla, stationed at Lourdes with his men and highly sceptical about the apparitions, spoke disparagingly of the locals' religious temperament: 'In the outward forms of worship, they like pomp and show, as all southerners do.'[49] This scornful evaluation, however, underestimated the importance of such rituals to the communal identity of the poor and misunderstood the conviction that only in solidarity could collective disaster be avoided.[50]

Such was the view expressed by villagers who defied the authorities during the Revolution and continued to make their annual pilgrimage to Notre-Dame de Médous, convinced that in fulfilling this ancient vow they had, for yet another year, protected their villages from calamity.[51] Joining together the youngest and the oldest, pilgrimage confounded the priests, who were often unable to control the feasting, dancing and even love-making that were part of the days of adventure.[52] Village feasts, and other festivities in the name of patron saints, were celebrated with the same popular abandon, despite brief interventions from priests to remind the people of orthodoxy. Carnival remained one of the most important events of the rural calendar, a period of abundance and licence prior to the privations of Lent. It was an eruption that symbolically 'turned the world upside-down', allowing the poor to mock their betters, be they rich, powerful or priestly.[53] In later years, when the raucous and undisciplined aspects of such devotions disappeared at Lourdes, the 'pomp' remained, as the crowds, costumes and display became institutionalized at the new sanctuary.[54]

At the heart of Pyrenean religious life was the love of the Virgin, and in the twenty-five kilometres between Coarraze and Pau there were forty shrines dedicated to her.[55] During local and regional pilgrimages entire parishes would descend, barefoot or on their knees, to make individual and communal supplication to the ancient statues in these chapels and churches.[56] All over the Pyrenees, between the thirteenth and seventeenth centuries, shepherds and shepherdesses had direct contact with the Virgin, either through visions or the miraculous discovery of images. At Notre-Dame de Sarrance a shepherd followed a straying bull that swam across a river to kneel before a previously unknown image (see illus. 3 and 4).[57] At Notre-Dame de Héas

3. and 4. Details of two eighteenth-century wooden reliefs, Notre-Dame de Sarrance

shepherds stole a famous statue from Spain and built a chapel in the most isolated part of the majestic Cirque de Gavarnie. Although the image was retrieved by the original owners, miracles none the less continued to take place at the spot: a fountain was discovered and later two white doves showed the shepherds where to find another precious statue.[58] At Notre-Dame de Bourisp a shepherd followed a steer into the forest and found it licking a statue of the Virgin with its tongue.[59] At Notre-Dame des Nestes a calf found an image of the Virgin in a bush, and once again a chapel was built near by to mark the place.[60]

Two significant elements characterize such tales. The first is the importance of the beasts that found the miraculous images. The mainstay of the Pyrenean economy, herd animals lived on the border between domestication and wildness. Unlike the fowl of the *basse-cour*, which were enclosed and closely watched by the women of the household, cattle were allowed to wander and thus could discover images that human eyes could not find. There was, in addition, the fertility symbolism that could underpin the tale of the discovery, as in the example of the bull which lovingly caressed the female statue, blending Christian and Mediterranean pagan symbolism in one potent narrative.

As important as the animals were the shepherds themselves. Despite the prominence of bulls and calves in the legends, shepherds were generally described as tending sheep, an iconographic device that simplified the reality – they herded donkeys, cows, sheep or any other animal – in favour of an evocation of biblical imagery.[61] Their actual status within Pyrenean society, however, was far more ambiguous. They were seen as representing vigilance, and indeed the contact between the human and supernatural worlds occurred when they went in search of straying animals. Their knowledge of the stars, of the weather, and of the flora and fauna of the mountains indicated their expertise. They were as solitary as hermits[62] but less holy, though still potentially in touch with cosmic elements. Their poverty-stricken and isolated existence also hinted at a dangerous wildness, a way of life not subject to the rules of ordinary society.[63] Both folklore and official documents attested to the potential violence of the shepherds' life, as they terrorized the farming population by marauding on their lands.[64]

These fiercely independent individuals discovered images with similar qualities, resisting, in league with the common folk, the patronage and authority of the Church. For example, the statue of Notre-Dame de Sarrance was taken to the cathedral at Oloron but escaped, swam back across the river and returned to the stone where the bull had found her.[65] Notre-Dame de Héas stayed in her remote place and even produced a miracle to sustain the loyal masons who built her chapel: every three days miraculous goats would descend from the neighbouring mountain peaks to bring a delicious milk to the workmen, rewarded because they had not sought to 'civilize' the image but to bring the church to the wild.[66] When a disastrous landslide threatened to cut her off in the seventeenth century, worshippers vainly tried to move the image to the church at Luz; she miraculously returned to her favoured spot.[67]

Rather than leading the devotion that surrounded such places, priests often sought to superimpose orthodoxy or to repress them entirely. With Bernadette's apparitions, Church and authorities conformed to this tradition through their initial hostility and scepticism, and the official warnings seemed to increase the early cultists' ardour and their devotion to the Grotto as a place of prayer and pilgrimage.[68] In 1858, as in the past, the Virgin's power was tied to a sacred, natural space: the Grotto, the spring and the distance of both from the parish church were enough to alert the villagers to the possibility of genuine apparitions.[69]

Bernadette was likely to have known such tales of miraculous discovery and healing fountains, especially those of Bétharram and Garaison, the pilgrimage sites nearest to Lourdes and the most famous of the region. Bétharram is situated only a few kilometres from the Benedictine monastery of Saint-Pé and the Grotto at Lourdes. In its founding legend, shepherds were guarding their flocks at the base of the mountain when a ray of light in the bushes showed them the way to a statue of the Virgin. The inhabitants of nearby Lestelle sought to place the statue in a niche on a bridge over the Gave, but, as usual, the statue went home. So they tried once more and locked her in the church of Lestelle, but she escaped again, and so they built a chapel at the special site.[70] Bernadette reportedly visited Bétharram, and stories tell how her treasured rosary was probably bought there. While in the imposing seventeenth-century church she presumably prayed before an altar, which showed a rendering of the Virgin appearing to shepherds in the mountains (see illus. 5).

Most important of all, perhaps, was the story of Anglèze de Sagazan, a twelve-year-old shepherdess who saw the Virgin at Garaison in the early sixteenth century. Although further away than Bétharram, the shrine's renown was greater, for it stood at the intersection of the Pays des Quatre Vallées, between France and Spain, the Bigorre and the Comminges, Toulouse and Bayonne. Local faith was nurtured there by a constant stream of pilgrims coming to and from Saint James of Compostela, Notre-Dame de Montserrat, Saint Bertrand de Comminges and Notre-Dame de Rocamadour. The stories they told were as old as the twelfth and thirteenth centuries, often reverently reconstructed and creatively transformed in later periods. The story of Anglèze explained how, near the fountain of Garaison, the Virgin Mary appeared, ordering her to tell the leaders of neighbouring Monléon to plant a cross at the site and begin to build a chapel. Here was a tale of an innocent, ignorant, pious girl, who spoke nothing more

5. Altarpiece showing the apparition c. *1620, Notre-Dame de Bétharram*

than patois and successfully petitioned the authorities to undertake a costly religious venture. Garaison became a pilgrimage centre, and Anglèze herself went to live in a convent.

Anglèze's story was strikingly similar to Bernadette's own, despite divergences in detail.[71] Like Bernadette, Anglèze was the poorest of the poor. Anglèze was the only one privileged to see Mary, while everyone could hear her; Bernadette alone could hear and see the white girl. The Virgin at Garaison miraculously transformed scarcity into plenty, rather than healing the sick as at Lourdes, for Anglèze's black bread was changed into the finest white loaf, and a chest at her home was miraculously filled with the same refined fare[72] (see illus. 6 and 7).

Mid-nineteenth-century contemporaries repeatedly noted the marked similarities between the two stories (see illus. 8 and 9). However, rather than seeing the parallels as evidence of fraud, or even as the product of a particular Pyrenean cultural legacy, they interpreted them instead as further proof of a genuine sacred presence in the

6. The apparition of Notre-Dame de Garaison.
This seventeenth-century rendering already embellished the stark and unadorned quality of Anglèze de Sagazan's early sixteenth-century narrative. Here the impoverished shepherdess is shown with accessories that she would never have possessed – a dainty parasol and even a small pannier – as the large and imposing figure of the Virgin appears. Humble villagers stand awestruck near by, hearing the voice of the Virgin but not able to see what Anglèze beheld

Grotto. Here as before was the example of a young girl, ignorant and poor but also pious and innocent, visited by the divine in time of scarcity. Bernadette's story had no reference to food, but legends of food miracles grew around her, again drawing on clear New Testament precedents and referring more specifically to the region's hunger:

Another time, the wet-nurse was at a loss as to how to make dinner when the corn flour had run out, and asked Bernadette to go to the mill and ask the miller for some flour. Bernadette is said to have replied: 'Don't worry, give me what flour you have, I'll make the dinner with it.' The flour increased, and there was more after the dinner than before.[73]

7. The first apparition of the Virgin to Anglèze de Sagazan. This nineteenth-century version of the apparition of Notre-Dame de Garaison is part of a larger series of panels depicting the mission of the Garaison Fathers, who came to evangelize the region in the seventeenth century. They returned again in 1836 and flourished under the patronage of Mgr Laurence, the Bishop of Tarbes and Lourdes, during Bernadette's apparitions in 1858. Here a Virgin in neo-classical pose confronts a more sentimentalized version of the country shepherdess and directs her to relay her messages to the priests

The continued centrality of communal pilgrimage, carnival, legends and apparitions suggests that the more severe and regularized religion of the Counter-Reformation had made no impact at all on the Lourdais or the Pyreneans more generally.[74] In fact, every one of the thirty-two parishes visited by Mgr Laurence in 1856 in the diocese of Tarbes and Lourdes had Confraternities of the Holy Sacrament and of the Rosary,[75] centres of orthodox and clerically led devotion. In 1841 the Children of Mary, devoted to the Virgin in all her incarnations, was founded in Lourdes, as in so many other parishes across France,[76] and had 130 members by the time of the visions.[77]

8. Anglèze de Sagazan, late sixteenth-/early seventeenth-century painting, Eglise de Monléon-Magnoac, Notre-Dame de Garaison
9. J.-M. Soubirous, Bernadette Soubirous, *undated, Couvent de Saint-Gildard, Nevers*
Nothing demonstrates better the unconscious association between the two visionaries than these renderings. The late sixteenth-century painting of Anglèze is virtually reproduced by Bernadette's brother, Jean-Marie, in his painting of his sister's visionary pose. Although said to be drafted after a photograph by Paul Bernadou, one of Bernadette's earliest photographers (see ch. 5), the iconographic style is much closer to the anonymous sixteenth-century depiction

Belonging to such a group and wearing the blue sashes and flowing white dresses was only a dream for a girl like Bernadette – who did not even know her catechism – although she was admitted after her visions. But for all her ignorance and marginality, Bernadette, her family, neighbours and friends respected the rituals of the Church and embraced religious observance. In their impoverished world daily prayers were said, weekly mass attended, and the yearning for a Christian life and the sacraments expressed.[78] Bernadette left her work at Bartrès to prepare for her first communion in Lourdes, an indication of the importance she and her family placed on this central rite of passage. And, while Lourdes possessed a number of sceptics about the apparitions, it had very few freethinkers. The town was a Christian, deeply religious society scarcely touched by secularism or doubt. That people managed to hold together so many different kinds of belief is an indication of their capacious religious sensibility.

Bernadette and Her Family

At the centre of the story of the apparitions is Bernadette and her family. Genealogical tables of the Castérot and Soubirous clans begin Laurentin's 'pre-history' of the apparitions, a preoccupation with birth and death certificates, marriage licences and family trees that betrays an almost antiquarian fervour.[79] Bernadette's contemporaries would have understood this passion, for at the heart of Pyrenean life were kinship relations, and the household – as system of honour, patronage and material survival – was crucial for laying claim to a position within the community. Nothing illustrates this interweaving of material and psychological needs better than the story of the Castérots, the tenants of the mill at Boly, flung into desperation by the sudden death of their father in 1841 as the result of an accident (see illus. 10). The widow, left with five children – and a son only ten years old – began an immediate search for a son-in-law to marry her eldest daughter, Bernarde. Her aim was to get the mill working again without the extra cost of a paid worker and, hopefully, to continue paying off the premiums that would make them proprietors, rather than tenants, of a business they had been trying to acquire since the eighteenth century.[80]

The mother and daughter set their sights on François Soubirous, still a bachelor at thirty-four. But rather than choosing the first-born, the organized and strong-willed Bernarde, he preferred instead the docile, blonde Louise, the younger sister, whom he married in church

10. The mill at Boly, c. *1900*.

in early 1843. Bernadette was born a year later, the *héritière*, or head of the household's next generation, her birth of such significance that the entire matriarchal line – ranging from her grandmother to her four-year-old Aunt Lucile – was there to witness it.[81] During her early years she was to live amid her maternal family, her father's authority undermined by her grandmother and her Aunt Bernarde, as keen on her prerogatives as the first-born child as Bernadette herself would be.

For to understand Bernadette, we must understand the unique Pyrenean system of inheritance. Since medieval times at least, the Pyrenean *casa*, or household, was the primary economic, social and symbolic unit, with the eldest child of either sex holding the name, honour and property of the household, and having a decisive role in determining the activities and marriage prospects of younger children.[82] This institution continued into the nineteenth century despite all attempts to impose the partible inheritance system of the Napoleonic code. Although a rising population forced some changes, families in much of the Pyrenees, and especially in the Bigorre where Lourdes is situated, still instructed notaries to try to keep both the household and the position of the eldest intact.[83] Thus, Bernadette was born, and initially brought up, with certain expectations: she would have had the right to stay at home; to order her siblings to work in service or act as shepherds; and, at marriage, her husband would have come to live with her, rather than the other way round.

Such hopes, and her young life, were transformed by misfortune. When her mother burnt her breast in an accident, tired, it seemed, from a new pregnancy, Bernadette was sent out to be nursed by Mary Laguës, in the village of Bartrès just a few kilometres away. This separation apparently weighed more heavily on Bernadette's father than on Louise; François, witnesses remembered, found excuses to visit his first-born in Bartrès as frequently as possible.[84] For five francs a month[85] Marie Laguës nursed Bernadette and apparently loved her, showering her affection on a baby who had replaced the son she had just lost. Bernadette was around two years old when she was weaned, a separation perhaps hastened by the fact that Marie Laguës was again pregnant herself.

Life at the mill at Boly, however, was slowly deteriorating. For François Soubirous sought only to keep up the payments on the rent rather than trying to purchase the mill as his in-laws had wanted; both he and his wife seemed relieved when relations deteriorated so much in 1848 that Louise's mother and her children moved out to live in Lourdes. Finally free of supervision, they gave themselves over to a gentler life; they entertained clients, drank more freely, and worried less over their business affairs than had Louise's mother.

In the following years the business declined, and then collapsed. The quality of the flour they ground decreased, and, with it, the quality of their clientele. Disaster followed on disaster; François was blinded in one eye while trying to work one of the millstones. The couple had increasing difficulty in paying the rent, and had to give up and move out. Even a chance inheritance did little to repair their fortunes; François used it to start up at another mill and raise some livestock, but this venture also failed.[86] From now on their social descent was sharp and ignominious. François became a *brasseur*, a labourer, while Bernadette was sent to work as a waitress in her Aunt Bernarde's *cabaret*, looking after her children, working in the house and serving at the counter.[87]

Although this descent was partly due to ill-fortune, partly to the dire economic conditions described earlier, several acquaintances tended to think the Soubirous had brought their problems on their own heads, declaring that François was a fully fledged drunkard and that Louise also drank, if not as much.[88] Others were more charitable and decided that, despite the family's somewhat irregular behaviour, they were *braves gens* who simply could not stem the tide of ill-fortune. Many, however, thought of them as good-hearted but weak and ineffectual.[89]

> François was an idler, a drinker, and so was his wife; they got nowhere because of it, but, apart from that, they were good people . . . Mother Soubirous was not worldly or a gadabout, but because they were millers there was always someone who was going to the mill who would pay with a bottle of wine while she made the fritters. I have seen her tipsy and heard her say indecent things at such times.[90]

Historians also differed on how to assess the evidence: the Jesuit Cros took a stern nineteenth-century view, and saw the inevitable descent of a 'family fallen from grace', which deserved little better and whose predicament made Bernadette's saintliness all the more miraculous.[91] In contrast, Laurentin in the early 1960s represented the family's poverty as a 'passion', explicitly evoking the torments of Christ; moral failings were largely overlooked, and the more negative testimonies undervalued.[92] Both authors, however, saw Providence at work in the choice of such a family.

Wherever the responsibility for their dire circumstances lay, public knowledge of their fall became inevitable in 1857 when the Soubirous had to move into the notorious *cachot* (see illus. 11). This lodging was so dark, dank and malodorous that only the poorest of Spaniards were prepared to live in it.[93] That the family should have sunk to the level of such people was perhaps the ultimate humiliation, as André Sajous, a relation who helped them in their misery, explained:

> The room was pitch dark and not wholesome . . . In the courtyard there was a privy that overflowed and made the place stink. We had to keep the dung there . . . I used to put the Spaniards who came to dig during the winter there; they slept on the flagstones with a blanket, often without straw bedding.
>
> Soubirous asked my uncle for the downstairs room; he had the income

11. The cachot

from it; at the time there were no lodgers. My uncle told me that evening. We said, 'Since they're on the street, we have to put them up.' It made me angry! They had four children; I had five. My wife was a good woman and I knew she'd feed them out of my money . . .

It was a wretched set-up: two small beds, one to the right of the door, the other on the same side closer to the chimney. They had one small trunk for all their clothes. My wife lent them some shirts; they were covered in vermin . . . My wife got it when she shared a bed with Bernadette. She often gave them maize bread, but the children never asked. They would rather have died before they asked.[94]

With her family reduced to this most miserable state, and her father even arrested on suspicion of stealing grain during the famine of 1856/7, Bernadette was sent back to Marie Laguës's house in Bartrès, this time to be a maid-of-all-work and shepherdess. Time and again, she has been portrayed in hagiography as the humble shepherdess, a pious girl who attended to the bleating lambs that surrounded her, thus doing in reality what Christ did in metaphor (see illus. 12). Such

12. J.-S. Hartmann, Bernadette à l'agnelet, *1936*

portraits imply some closer affinity to the supernatural by virtue of her simplicity, piety and proximity to nature.[95] The truth, however, was very different: far from being a rural idyll, it seems her life was toilsome and grim, even by the standards of the region.[96] She ate poorly – unable to digest the corn-mash bread that was her daily fare – did the housework, watched the children and tended the flock. Material hardship was matched by psychological torment at the hands of the woman who had once been so kind to her.[97] As a baby Bernadette brought comfort by replacing a child who had recently died, but as a girl she annoyed, Marie Laguës never forgiving her, in Laurentin's view, for 'having taken the milk of her dead baby'.[98]

Such woes compounded her social degradation: although the *héritière*, Bernadette had to accept jobs normally suited only to younger siblings, a blow to her expectations that Pyreneans even today will acknowledge as central to her psychology.[99] The first apparition took place three weeks after her sympathetic father helped her to come back home; the visions occurred, therefore, at a time of a rupture, within weeks of coming back to her family, as well as to humiliating and miserable poverty.

By conventional standards, her spiritual life seemed similarly impoverished. Marie Laguës sought unsuccessfully to teach her the catechism in French, a language she did not understand. Nor did her unending work permit her to go to school in Bartrès.[100] Her instruction in Catholic theology was virtually non-existent, as her confessor at Lourdes, Abbé Pomian, discovered: she was a '*tabula rasa* in doctrine! She didn't even know the rudiments, such as the mystery of the Holy Trinity.'[101] But even though she knew only the Our Father, the Hail Mary and the Creed,[102] she prayed with fervour; she had a rosary from 1856 and, like others in the Bigorre, seemed taken with this devotion: 'When she was very little, she had a rosary, she did go to school a bit, but what with poverty and work, not enough to learn anything, and so the rosary was her reading.'[103] Aunt Bernarde's comment suggests the importance of the rosary for the illiterate; certainly Bernadette relied heavily on it for reassurance when she confronted the apparitions.[104]

Like many children, she made altars for the Virgin in May, the Mois de Marie, and prayed no doubt before the white porcelain Virgin on the chimney breast in Bartrès, a youthful but maternal figure, clad in classical robes with arms folded across the breast. Her knowledge was perhaps expanded by sermons, by the iconography of the chapels and by the limitless tales of supernatural intervention in the lives of Pyrenean people. However, while her ignorance sometimes shocked those who came to interrogate her, it fitted perfectly with traditions of Marian appearance in the Pyrenees. Her pious simplicity was seen by many as proof of her innocence and hence fitness to be the recipient of divine messages.

There is no doubt that the early apparitions – before the crowds, threats and interrogations began – represented the most joyous moments of Bernadette's life, and few contemporaries, even those who refused to believe her, ever doubted her sincerity. After every experience she returned to family, work and childhood activities with no evident change of personality, so that, despite her often enigmatic reticence, she reassured by the stability and reliability of her account: she stuck to her story, and those few changes that did appear over the next twenty years often happened in moments of distress, distraction or illness. This resilience was maintained despite constant tests by doubters, and there are so many anecdotes of this sort that it is hard to separate them from the conventional narratives of sainthood with which they are clearly linked.[105]

Bernadette was a devout girl forced to defend herself against a formidable number of enemies and detractors. Important women were initially ranged against her: her mother reportedly smacked her for her early account of the apparitions, while the mother superior at school tersely told her to stop her pranks.[106] Then the authorities bore down on her, particularly Police Commissioner Jacomet, who, according to one highly spiced account, insulted her.[107] On top of this she also had to contend with the scepticism of Abbé Peyramale, who saw her as an unlikely vehicle for the transmission of divine messages. Then came a never-ending stream of believers, sceptics and the curious who wished to talk to her, catch her out or have their own faith strengthened. She did not even escape when she was finally enclosed in the nunnery, as there too historians and clerics sought ways of gaining access to put ever more questions to her.[108]

Those who doubted her were met with an unyielding persistence: observers were repeatedly struck by the way such an ignorant and seemingly slow child answered difficult questions with spirit and often canny peasant humour.[109] Nor did she succumb to other entrapments: although frequently offered tempting presents, ranging from a fresh apple to a golden rosary, she politely but firmly refused everything in a fashion her abject poverty made extraordinary. Instead she promised to pray for her well-wishers at the Grotto and act as a mouthpiece for the entreaties of others. It was on the shoulders of this girl, seemingly so simple and yet so strong, that the wondrous burden of the apparitions fell.

The Apparition Site

Very different from the site as it appears today, or even as it was ten years after the apparitions took place, the Grotto in its original state was wild, unkempt, a place that both children and the poor knew well. Certainly it was then some way out of the town, nearly a kilometre to the west over rugged, boggy and stony country, and across the river. It could be approached from two directions. One, the easiest, involved walking out of Lourdes through the old gateway, across the Pont-Vieux and along the chemin du Bois before turning right to cross three branches of a canal that supplied the Savy Mill with water for its millstones. The mill, on the île du Chalet, was owned by the Nicolau family, who jealously guarded their property against scavengers like Bernadette, lessening their surveillance in winter when the poor needed dead wood to survive.[110] The western junction of the canal and the Gave was about 200 metres away: the Grotto was at this point, on the far side of the canal.

The other route was more dangerous; staying on the chemin du Bois rather than crossing on to the île du Chalet led along the side of the mont des Espélugues and over the outcrop of Massabieille, or *masse vieille* ('old mass'), in the direction of Omex and Ségus, villages whose population participated in events during and after Bernadette's apparitions. From here, an extremely steep and very dangerous path called the *casse-cou* (literally 'breakneck') led down to the Grotto itself. Hollowed out of Massabieille, the Grotto was uneven, of irregular height, with part of its base submerged under water (see illus. 13). It had all kinds of cavities but above all an oval niche in which a wild rose bush grew. Bernadette explained that when she appeared, the Virgin stood on a rectangular rock and placed her feet on this plant.

The area around the Grotto brought together many different elements of Pyrenean life, beliefs and legends in a place of illegality, pleasure and scavenging. Farmers illicitly pastured their cows there at night, hoping no one would notice. Children escaped there to fish for trout, bathe in the water and look for nests or wild strawberries.[111] From at least the beginning of the seventeenth century the pigs of Lourdes grazed there, and a few years before the apparitions they took up daily residence on the humid, grassy and sandy place near

13. The Grotto of Massabieille, 1858

the Grotto's mouth.[112] Until 1858, when the apparitions put an end to the custom, the Lourdes *porcatier*, Paul Layrisse, known as Samson, 'went through the streets around eight in the morning (five o'clock in the summer) blowing a horn [to collect the pigs] . . . there were between 140, 120 [*sic*] and 150 of them . . . they put their pigs out at night and it was easy to get them back; they went home by themselves'.[113] The site was, therefore, a marginal and even filthy place, covered in 'blood and pig hair',[114] of which the respectable Elfrida Lacrampe, daughter of the proprietor of the Hôtel de Lourdes, said, 'When you wanted to say someone was badly brought up, you used to say, "He must have been educated at the banks of Massabieille." '[115]

Apart from its malodorous general reputation, the Grotto also had its own particular legends. Before Bernadette, people were known to cross themselves when passing by to fend off some 'devilish spell'.[116] A tale current just before the apparitions also suggested that something harmful inhabited the place:

Some time before this extraordinary business, a woodcutter was coming from the forest with a load of wood on his back and passing Massabieille when it began to rain. He put down his load and went down into the Grotto for shelter, but a moment later he heard the plaintive cries and groans of someone in great suffering. He was so afraid that he had to leave, he said he'd rather get drenched to the bone than stay there.[117]

Across the Pyrenean chain, caves were seen as housing all manner of witches, demons and fairies, inclined towards evil or mischief, many with particular personalities and ancient lineages that survived well into the nineteenth century.[118] Villages were often identified by the malevolent creatures that lived near them: one way of insulting a neighbouring settlement and demonstrating solidarity with one's own was to identify the 'other' as the werewolf, witch or demon of their locality.

While fears of evil emanated from the place, there was also an equally large number of prophecies of divine visitation that surrounded it. People could remember old testimony of dying priests who predicted something supernatural coming from the wood, while still others cited grandfathers who predicted divine apparitions.[119] Twentieth-century historians like Laurentin dismiss these predictions as too convenient, retrospective embellishments that added nothing to the 'authentic' history of events.[120] However, it was precisely this kind of legend-making – either before or after the events – that gives an essential clue to the mythological prerequisites for divine visitation and provides the context for understanding why the local population were prepared to believe that Bernadette had indeed seen something, and that the girl in white was the Virgin Mary.

2

The Apparitions and Their Interpretation

At the beginning the task confronting Bernadette and the community was the urgent need to interpret the apparitions. Were they a manifestation of divine grace or the incursion of diabolical influence? Was Bernadette trustworthy or playing on people's gullibility? Did her trance-states and gestures indicate hysteria, possession or ecstasy? These were questions that witnesses, officials, physicians and clergy asked the more urgently as only the poor, illiterate and insignificant Bernadette saw anything at all. Her audience therefore had little choice but to scrutinize her manner, her body and the messages she delivered, to try to glimpse the truth at second hand.

So well known was her family's poverty that there were some who at first refused even to enter into the process of evaluation, assuming her tale was a fabrication to hide an act of petty thieving. D'Angla, the captain of the gendarmes, remarked, 'But I was convinced that the girl had just stolen some wood, and I didn't believe in her visions, I didn't, I thought, "If God wanted to perform a miracle, he wouldn't use a little thief." '[1] Jacomet's wife, more generous but no less doubtful, thought Bernadette had been surprised by guards while stealing wood and in her fright had mistaken a screech-owl for some kind of apparition.[2] For them, her reputation as a poverty-stricken scrounger made her claims to miraculous visions ludicrous. The first reports of the apparitions brought a variety of disapproving responses from the adult world. Her mother was fearful that her stories would bring even more misfortune on to the family, while at school the nuns scorned her and told her to stop her *carnavalades*.[3] The first apparitions were during Carnival, and in making this remark the nuns suggested that Bernadette was trying on some elaborate and impious joke in tune with the days of feasting and subversion.

Not everyone shared this scepticism. On the contrary, the process of testing that ensued was complex, for not only did different currents of 'folkloric' belief mingle and compete with each other, but also other forms of knowledge and faith were projected on to her gestures and words. Varying types of devotion – especially towards the Virgin – as well as other kinds of theological conviction, medical theorizing and even moments of spiritualist speculation were all brought to bear on the problem. The resulting evaluation was never neat and tidy; older concepts warred sometimes uneasily with ideas that seemed to have an exclusively nineteenth-century pedigree. Equally, both individuals and the community as a whole dismissed seeming contradictions and sometimes unconsciously changed Bernadette's testimony to suit their own tastes and expectations. The visions were also often recast in more reassuring moulds by the literate and more orthodox, but even they – and later the Church – were never completely able to strip the story of its essential ingredients; nor indeed did they desire to do so. The allure of the Virgin in a grotto communicating to a poor shepherd girl was an integral element of the miraculous tale that ultimately seemed to move all believers.

Bernadette and the Evidence

To begin with, there was little to go on; the apparition did not even speak until the third vision, so the only clues to its identity lay in its appearance and movements. *Aquéro* seemed benevolent, for not only had she helped Bernadette reach for her rosary during the first vision, she also remained unperturbed by the holy water the young girl sprinkled upon her during the second. Her appearance, however, was inconclusive. On the one hand she had beautiful bare feet – a positive sign, for devils were betrayed by their cloven feet or cats' paws, and Bernadette's insistence on their lovely shape and colour was significant later in convincing a sceptical Jesuit.[4] On the other hand she bore little resemblance to orthodox notions of what the Virgin should look like: Bernadette did not see a mother with the infant Jesus in her arms, but a whitened image of youth, albeit resplendent and beautifully clad. Above all she was small, as was Bernadette herself, and very young. She described *Aquéro* as *uo pétito damizélo*, a little girl, and nothing disturbed commentators as much as this insistence.

Until pressed to demand that the apparition name itself, Bernadette herself seems to have been remarkably incurious about its identity: she relayed messages from the priests and others, and conveyed back its words, yet asserted herself scarcely at all, seemingly content just to be in the young girl's presence. After the second vision, the business of sifting the evidence shifted to onlookers, beginning with Jeanne-Marie Milhet and Antoinette Peyret, who considered the possibility that the vision was a revenant, a tormented soul returning from purgatory.[5] This was an obvious possibility to explore, for errant souls were known to come back from their netherworld to plead for masses and indulgences to speed their way to heaven.[6] While the Church had an orthodox repertoire of beliefs and practices, actively promoted in the nineteenth century, Pyreneans added their own customs and often lived in a close relationship with the recently dead, hoping to satisfy their yearnings and fearing retaliation if they did not. Revenants appeared as luminous apparitions in the night or as birds in accordance with Celtic legend. They communicated with the living by leaving marks on linen that only disappeared when the masses for the dead were said and prayers offered, and they occasionally processed around the village on the night of All Saints, hungry for the food left out for them. Legends spoke of the remorse experienced by the living over thoughtless acts of miserliness towards the dead. One father saw his ghostly daughter shunned by her fellows who were decked out in their grandest funerary clothes. Grabbing his best sheet, he wrapped her in it and thus enabled her to depart with them. Another woman heard of her daughter's disappointment at wearing a torn shawl to the grave; the mother had the body exhumed and clad her in 'a handsome white shawl that she had knitted herself', and was relieved when the ghost reappeared no more.[7]

Jeanne-Marie Milhet hoped to identify Bernadette's apparition as Elisa Latapie, one of the most pious women in the community, who had died the previous October. Latapie had left fifteen hundred francs to complete the chapel in the local prison and had also died in a holy fashion, as Abbé Peyramale recounted in a letter to his bishop. The manner of her death was a most edifying spectacle, her faith an inspiration. She left nothing to chance in her preparations and was especially concerned with the details of her funerary 'toilette':

> She asked to be dressed in a white dress of coarse calico, her Congregationist robe, and she wanted her hat on, without ribbons or lace; she was probably afraid that when dead she would be loaded with ribbons that she had never worn [when alive]. She wanted to be in death, in her tomb, as she had been in life.[8]

At the funeral Peyramale personally ordered 'the greatest pomp and show' and expected miracles at her tomb, an indication of his personal belief in her saintliness.

Given the fame of this 'good death',[9] it is not perhaps surprising that Jeanne-Marie Milhet and Antoinette Peyret thought that Latapie might be Bernadette's apparition. The simple white robe of her burial was seen as a clue, as was the blue sash suggesting the Children of Mary that she had headed in Lourdes. Nor did her choice of Bernadette seem surprising, as young girls and women were frequently the confidantes of revenants.[10] Bernadette's description suggested that the soul of Elisa Latapie also required some form of release, so the supplicants came with paper, pen and inkpot, as well as holy water, for revenants were commonly asked to write their wishes.[11] This practice suggests that the feats of automatic writing performed by spiritualist mediums had their origins in much older beliefs or, alternatively, that this urban fashion had permeated the Pyrenean countryside and was overlaid on local practices.[12] Although the documents on the apparitions never mention local seances, the 1850s and 1860s saw a craze for the *spiritisme* of Allan Kardec, the most famous advocate of the new 'science' on the Continent.[13] Enthusiasts made lively contributions to the debates immediately following the apparitions, seeing Bernadette as a powerful medium with heightened psychic powers, or trying to determine the impact of the spirits of the fountain in engendering her visions.[14] Their emotional investment in the debate underscores the way such nineteenth-century spiritualism built on Christian notions of wandering souls and older classical ideas of local genii, and the overlapping nature of these apparently dissonant systems of belief.

The apparition, however, laughed gently at the suggestion that she write her name and instead spoke: 'Would you have the goodness to come here for fifteen days?' Such extraordinary wording, spoken in patois, used the formal form to a humble young girl, with the request softened by the phrase 'would you have the goodness', the common local expression of politeness. The significance of such courtesy was not lost on the better-off and more literate women, who acknowledged that their own higher social standing had brought them no favours. Bernadette was no longer the inferior, but now required deference as the only one with access to the apparition. Jeanne-Marie Milhet took Bernadette back to her own home, though she kept her only briefly: Aunt Bernarde swooped down and retrieved her niece, a move that showed her authority within the family and her position as its defender. This brief battle for possession began to spread word of the occurrences, and on the next market day – a time when hundreds came into Lourdes – the town buzzed with the news.[15]

By this stage the apparition had survived two tests: she was neither diabolical nor a wandering soul from purgatory. Although these tests were significant for building up general belief in the reality of Bernadette's experience, other factors, directly relating to her body, were of much greater importance. Partly this was because the nature of the apparitions – with a single visionary and simple messages – provided little else for the populace to assess. Bernadette's apparitions were, in this vital sense, in stark contrast to the apparition in the isolated Alpine commune of La Salette in 1847. This sighting of the Virgin occurred when a boy and girl tending livestock in the uplands of their village encountered a light that turned into a beautiful, if initially frightening, lady shimmering in white. She spoke in French at first, claiming to have important news and explaining that she was trying to stay the hand of her son, who was preparing a terrible punishment. Confused by the meaning of the words, one of the children, Mélanie Calvet, turned to her companion, Maximin Giraud, and the apparition began to speak in terrifying terms in their native patois, predicting disaster for the irreligious behaviour of the population.[16]

At first glance the similarities seem striking: both apparitions occurred in poor, upland frontier regions with messages delivered in the semi-wilderness to obscure, poverty-stricken children who went to the priests and notables of the community to relay the Virgin's words. Both diverged from earlier patterns by the conveying of 'secrets', a nineteenth-century innovation that seemed to establish some kind of personal relationship between the Virgin and her poor and dispossessed messengers.[17] Bernadette was told three at an unspecified moment during the apparition cycle and never revealed them, while her counterparts at La Salette tantalized the Catholic world by refusing to divulge their confidences to anyone but the Pope.

The differences, however, were as important as the similarities. The lady of La Salette was large and maternal, not petite and girlish. While both were magnificently luminous, white creatures of the wilderness, the girl at the Grotto was gentle and joyful, and only sometimes sad, while the lady at La Salette wept bitterly for humanity. At La Salette she spoke at length in an apocalyptic tone, while at Lourdes the presence mixed an unadorned message of penitence with hope and simple devotion. The Virgin of La Salette presaged calamity unless 'the people' repented and converted:[18]

> If you have wheat, you must not sow it; all that you sow, the beasts will eat; what grows will turn to dust when you thresh it. There will come a great famine. Before the famine comes, the children below seven years of age will be taken with a trembling and will die in the arms of those who hold them; the others will do penitence by famine. The walnuts will go bad; the walnuts will rot.[19]

Rotting potatoes the previous harvest, and the dire spring and summer that followed, seemed to confirm this terrifying prophecy, which clerics saw as punishment for the sins of irreligion. Still others, like the ethnographer Arnold Van Gennep, gave an ingenious and equally plausible interpretation of the Virgin's rhythmic chant, claiming to discern the 'seven plagues of Egypt set forth in the catechism' in the patois of the Alpine region. He also noted that this imprecation served as the basis for individual pilgrimage in search of cure for feverish or trembling children, as well as inspiring collective procession to ensure the good harvest of cereals, nuts and the vine.[20]

In sum, at La Salette it was the text that required deciphering, while at Lourdes all the interpretive effort of necessity revolved around Bernadette's body. Her physical reactions, rather than her words or the messages relayed – except for the mystery of the term the Immaculate Conception – provided the proof both of her sincerity and, even more importantly, of the authenticity of her experience. From the beginning her bodily poses struck observers. Accounts note how she crossed the swift-moving Gave barefoot, a significant act denoting humility. I have described how she fell to her knees and searched for her rosary, crossing herself when the apparition 'enabled' her to do so. Annalists from the seventeenth and eighteenth centuries similarly described Pyrenean women who, especially on pilgrimage, walked barefoot or on their knees, clutching their rosaries and inclining their heads.[21] In fact, the emphasis on the rosary was a relatively novel affair in this region, a product of the Counter-Reformation that was associated with feminine piety.[22] In the local Marian shrine of Garaison the seventeenth-century paintings of pilgrims in procession show only a few men with rosaries in their hands, while all but the poorest of women clutch one (see illus. 14).

Another issue was whether Bernadette's body showed any taint of possessive, convulsive or hysterical experience. Newspapers described how she appeared tired and burst into 'a short, broken, nervous laugh';[23] another described how her 'hands began to tremble and [the] nervous twitching . . . sets in';[24] while still a third described how her 'lips shook convulsively', before the onset of ecstatic immobility.[25] These kinds of symptoms were once again attested to by three physicians called in to examine her to see if she required confinement:

14. La Procession du village, *1699, Notre-Dame de Garaison*

they stated that at the moment of the fourth apparition, on 19 February, 'convulsive laughter comes and goes on her lips'. Even more harshly, they remarked that 'later she was to be seen prostrating herself on the ground and, in the height of her delirium, biting the dust'.[26]

It might be that newspaper editors, representing 'enlightened' opinion, expressed a reflexive hostility to popular feeling, suggesting the likelihood of mental illness with these remarks. The physicians were called in as experts, to see if Bernadette was a candidate for administrative incarceration on the grounds of mental illness. They prepared their report for Prefect Baron Oscar Massy, the highest civil authority in the department, soon to be demonized by the poor for his opposition to the Grotto. Like the journalists in the newspapers, they had not observed Bernadette's visionary experience at first hand, and their tone was also sometimes harsh and dismissive. At the same time they hedged their bets admirably, noting Bernadette's fragile and asthmatic constitution, but not suggesting any permanent psychic derangement. While they were convinced that she did not wilfully deceive, they none the less wondered whether 'she might have been the victim of a hallucination'.[27] Underlying their descriptions was the possibility of emotional excess and physical uncontrollability, states that would have undermined her claims without requiring her permanent confinement.[28]

Most observers, however, saw harmony rather than disorder. Poorer witnesses interviewed by the Jesuit historian Cros maintained that, although they were sometimes only a few yards away, they saw nothing twisted or awkward on her face or in her body. Literate opinion in 1858, including some notables and a lone priest who attended, saw only beauty and spirituality in her physiognomy and pose. Even the unconvinced, like Captain d'Angla, affirmed that during her ecstasy there was 'nothing repugnant, nothing grimacing, it was a beautiful sight'.[29] More common were exclamations of delight, summed up by Estrade, who described Bernadette as 'an angel of prayer, reflecting in her face all the raptures of heaven'.[30]

Such opinions did not mean that all observers were willing to take Bernadette on trust and, just as she had tested the apparition, so the audience, in turn, tested her: one Eléonore Pérard stuck a big pin with a black head in Bernadette's shoulder without producing any reaction.[31] Similarly the popularly accepted, if later contested, 'miracle of the candle' also indicated a special anaesthesia. Her invulnerability to pain and injury suggested Bernadette's holy other-worldliness at the moment of her apparitions. What is striking is that both were the sort of tests conducted on subjects under investigation for either demonic influence or hysterical tendencies. The famous seventeenth-century witch of Loudun, Urbain Grandier, was subjected to similar prickings,[32] while the Parisian neurologist Jean-Martin Charcot also used large needles to show the anaesthesia of his hysterical patients in the 1880s, thus transferring this aspect of theological examination into modern medical practice[33] (see illus. 15).

Bernadette seemed to differ from these pathological or diabolical examples because of her capacity to perform sensible tasks while in her trance. For example, she shielded her candle from the wind, relit it when it went out, and passed it to a neighbour when she went down on her knees. In ecstasy she seemed pained when some careless observer touched the rose bush in the niche or scraped the surrounding vegetation. Sometimes she became angry, other times she sighed, fearful that the apparition would be knocked off her rocky perch.[34] She awoke from her ecstatic encounters with no ill-feeling or tiredness, rubbing

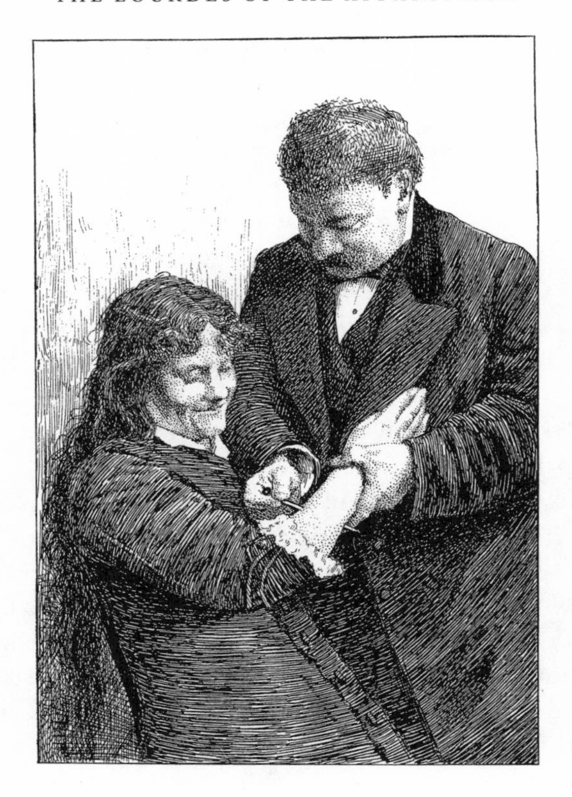

15. Paul Régnard, 'L'Anesthésie hystérique', engraving from his book Les Maladies épidémiques de l'esprit, *1887*

her eyes to adjust them to the relative darkness after the glowing light of the apparition.[35] The influence of the apparition was thus utterly benign. All these indications persuaded observers, especially when she was compared with the later visionaries, whose emotions seemed unbalanced in comparison and their gestures unworthy, if not obscene, in their extravagance.

During her ecstasies Bernadette seemed to communicate both intensely and intimately with the apparition, a contact initiated by the recitation of the rosary. As early as the seventh apparition on 23 February, her particular physical attitude attracted the attention of Emmanuélite Estrade, who was just a few paces away; she later recalled that:

After grasping her rosary, she crossed herself, and began to recite it . . . In one hand she was holding the rosary, in the other a lighted candle. She must have started to recite the first decade of the rosary, when her prayer seemed momentarily interrupted, giving way to a smile (to which nothing can be compared) that spread over the face of the blessed young girl. She was staring at the hollow in the rock. By the movements of her lips and the muscles of her throat, we could easily see that she was talking. Sometimes, she stopped talking as if to listen to what her beloved Vision told her, then continued. At times she accompanied the movement of her lips by head movements, sometimes negative, sometimes affirmative [by nodding and shaking her head].[36]

While these conversations were impressive, other physical responses were even more striking. Most important of all was the immobility that so panicked her friends during the second apparition on 14 February:

Bernadette was on her knees, very pale, her eyes wide open and fixed on the niche; her hands were joined, the rosary was between her fingers, and tears streamed from her eyes; she was smiling and her face was beautiful, more beautiful than anything I have ever seen. I was pleased and afraid, and all day my heart was touched when the thought came back to me . . . tears were flowing continuously . . . I put my hand in front of her eyes every now and then and wiped away the tears. The smiles continued until the mill.[37]

In her ecstasy Bernadette's tears were no longer normal but 'clearer than water',[38] like those of the Virgin herself and almost the stuff of which miracles were made. Her hands, pressed together in prayer, were thought to take on the same position as that of the apparition. All of this was deemed extraordinary because Bernadette, although not unattractive, was sickly, worn and lice-ridden, yet her experience seemed to transport her to another spiritual and physical plane. In the presence of the apparition she was even momentarily cured of her illnesses: 'As soon as the Blessed Virgin appeared to Bernadette, her coughing stopped, her breath seemed to die away; her lungs which, a moment before, had breathed the air so laboriously, now seemed no longer to need it.'[39] This evanescent healing, rather than being interpreted as psychosomatic in origin, was seen as clear evidence of heavenly balm poured on earthly ills.

Bernadette and the Crowd

Bernadette's ecstasies quickly became a public event, and witnesses' reactions would shape subsequent developments as much as the visionary herself. Their many responses were as important to the authentication process as any of the 'tests' employed by Bernadette with her holy water, Jeanne-Marie Milhet with her pen and inkpot or Eléonore Pérard with her big black pin, opening up a window on to both individual and collective psychology.

Although the early apparitions were witnessed by only a few poor girls, growing numbers, first from Lourdes and then from the surrounding villages and valleys, began to assemble to watch the later appearances. However, even as late as the ninth apparition on 25 February the crowd was still fairly small at around 350 people. It was after this point that the numbers seemed to take off, as the observers grew from over 1,000 on 28 February to 3,500 on 3 March, finally reaching over 7,000 the next day, when the crowds waited in eager anticipation of the miracle that did not come. They sought to squeeze themselves into the small space around the Grotto and, indeed, the overflow was so great that people had to stand on the other side of the river.[40]

In the early days the poor came before the rich, women before the men. The young ladies of the Children of Mary arrived to join the women of the poorer classes, and when Estrade arrived on 23 February he still felt uncomfortable among the impoverished throng.[41] By the twelfth apparition, on 1 March, she was accompanied by both her parents, there to support their daughter before the multitude. Abbé Antoine Dézirat, the only priest present at one of the apparitions, also came, as did the light infantry from the Visens annex, soldiers curious like everyone else, who helped make way for the visionary among the crowd.[42] By 4 March the crowd finally included a larger contingent of well-to-do men, while 'outsiders' – villagers from near by – came in groups, some even staying up all night to try to get a good place. People stood, heaving and crushed, on rocky escarpments, sat in the boughs of trees, and directed each other to behave correctly so as not to disturb Bernadette or the apparition.

Bad behaviour was punished by the apparition's absence. The failure to turn up on 3 March, for example, was, the apparition later told Bernadette, 'because there were people who wanted to see the countenance that you would have in my presence and they were unworthy. They spent the night in the Grotto and they profaned it.'[43] The apparition required suitable respect: childish pranks, noise and pushing made her retreat, and hence there were renewed efforts to keep silent, pray and behave decorously.

By repeating these reprimands, Bernadette ultimately achieved the right atmosphere, despite the ever growing numbers. When observing her at the Grotto, the mood of the crowd became increasingly solemn, with individuals crying, standing with bowed and uncovered heads, and kneeling on the ground. Bernadette and her apparitions had brought different ranks of society together, moving some to reflect on the seemingly spontaneous creation of a Christian collectivity that erased class and status:

> Our meadow was covered in people on foot, on horseback, in carts or carriages. It was an imposing sight, really striking. A religious silence prevailed everywhere, the devout contemplation of faith and prayer. At a given signal, everyone, the soldiers on surveillance duty and the civil servants alike, took off their hats, bowed their heads, crossed themselves, and prayed, following Bernadette's example. All ranks of society mingled there: barons, counts, marquises and dukes merged with the crowd of countrymen and workers from the towns.[44]

This report may have inflated the number of the well-born and elevated their rank, but it none the less supports the view that the crowd bore witness and, through its emotional reactions and moral transformation, reinforced belief in the apparitions. The public nature of Bernadette's experience was considered key to her veracity. Frère Marie Léobard, the schoolteacher in Lourdes, explained how Bernadette had not sought to deceive by having her apparitions in her room or in some place hidden from view. Instead, she had exposed herself to public scrutiny so that people could easily examine her.[45] In so doing, she had diverged in one important way from Pyrenean tradition, although her first, unobserved contact was in the normal fashion. While her youth, poverty and ignorance all fit squarely within that heritage, as did her mission to go to the priests and have a chapel built, the public nature of the remainder of her ecstasies was more unusual. Normally visions occurred 'off-stage', in a field, mountain valley, deserted chapel, dark street or at home in the manner that Frère Léobard condemned as encouraging fraud and charlatanry.[46] One priest briefly heard that Bernadette had had other visions in the *cachot* where she lived,[47] although it is unclear whether this actually happened, or whether the stories circulated because such an event was expected.

Because of the often private nature of the event, clergymen of the fifteenth and sixteenth centuries required tangible proofs of Mary's appearance. Apparitions left footprints or bloodstains; shepherds, as mentioned, produced miraculous images, while others had holy crosses imprinted on to them by the Virgin.[48] Bernadette provided no proof of this kind, so Peyramale, fulfilling the traditional role of priestly sceptic, ultimately requested that the girl in white should prove herself by making the rose blossom[49] (see illus. 16). For in the Pyrenees the Virgin showed a proclivity for hawthorns and wild roses, as she had reputedly dried the laundry of the infant Jesus on a hawthorn hedge, an act that miraculously made it bloom.[50] Between the Roussillon, Catalonia and Euskadi (in the Basque country), twenty-eight shrines to the Virgin Mary appear in or near a wild rose or among the hawthorn bushes. Moreover, in this region thorny plants were healing tools, used in small surgical operations to lance abscesses and wens. The Virgin of Espinars in Coustouges, found in a hawthorn bush, was reputed to have special healing powers in this domain.[51] Symbols of Christ's passion, the thorns were necessarily part of redemption, the crucifixion reinvoked in the blood-red of the rose, and his purity echoed in the early whiteness of the hawthorn.

But even though Peyramale's request was neither outrageous nor novel, neither Bernadette nor her apparition complied: 'The lady smiled when I said that you were asking her for a miracle. I told her to make the rosh bush flower, and she smiled again.'[52] The response implied that Peyramale was naïve, and instead directed attention back on to Bernadette herself. With only the evidence of her appearance available, individuals in the crowd engaged in a series of projections

16. Abbé Dominique Peyramale (1811–77)

and identifications to make sense of it.[53] Witnesses repeatedly referred to her immobility and translucent pallor, describing her body as like a waxy surface ready to take impressions.

Some saw Bernadette as the mirror of the divine apparition: in her smiles were the Virgin's smiles; in her sadness, a divine *tristesse*; in her gestures of piety, heavenly movements. As one observer commented: 'If you had seen her face during the apparition, you would indeed have said, "Here is a true virgin."'[54] This mimesis extended itself to the crowd, which began to copy the same movements, spreading a sense of religious awe through its ranks. Witnesses saw in Bernadette sadness and joy, and in return experienced 'pleasure and fear at the same time',[55] a strikingly ambivalent attitude that irritated and enraptured simultaneously. Time and again witnesses linked this reaction to the perceived play of light and darkness on Bernadette's countenance, as if 'a grey cloud passed across her face'.[56] Although they tried to resist being emotionally flooded, observers explained how they wept and were for ever transformed: 'She had a smile that went to people's hearts; at least, she made me cry.'[57]

But Bernadette was not just a reflection; in the depositions of the poor, in particular, she was associated with two preoccupying themes, those of death and of childhood. Laurentin believes that these reactions pointed to the eschatology of the apparitions, which, through uniting birth and death, held out the promise of resurrection. Such a theological interpretation, however, neglects the specific cultural tone of their remarks, which hinted at more mundane associations of holiness and purity. For example, the pious and genteel Marie Tardhivail insisted on the particular whiteness of Bernadette's face, which was not 'pale, tinged with blue, livid . . . but translucent',[58] suggesting the luminosity of candles: 'You would have thought it was made of wax, an angel, she was white as a candle.'[59] This holy light was celestial and earthly at the same time, representing the angels in heaven and the glow of church candles. Innocence was captured in the images of babies sleeping in their cribs, with Pierre Callet, a *garde champêtre*, remarking that 'She seemed like a child dead in its cradle.'[60] But such images of death were less terrifying than they initially appear. Bernadette's immobility suggested an innocent serenity, a moment purged of sin, an idea reiterated by Catherine Labayle, who described her as 'white, as if she had died in a bed'.[61] In this second guise Bernadette was a corpse at peace, laid out and ready for her eternal journey.

Less frequently other witnesses also saw Bernadette as a child with her mother. For Fanny Nicolau, 'it seemed the Blessed Virgin was acting like a mother, when she hides so that her child will look for her',[62] a vision of playfulness, even mischief, that was a widespread popular appreciation of the apparition's charming, if somewhat mercurial character. Marie Tardhivail, more soberly, saw 'a gentle urging towards the object and, at the last moment, a movement like that of a child towards its mother',[63] a picture of loving intimacy. For witnesses and later historians, Bernadette either copied or interacted with a maternal figure, and this conventional picture of a mother–child relationship became one of the most important and deeply rooted projections in the story. However, it was completely belied by the evidence – Bernadette's description had no maternal qualities at all.

Indeed, the hide-and-seek analogy of Fanny Nicolau suggests more a vision of a playmate and companion than a tender mother and child.

While gestures and impressions of prayer, beatitude and innocence were expected, other movements seemed more extreme and perplexing, especially her behaviour during the apparition that led to the discovery of the fountain, when she drank, then spat out the water, and ate some weeds she found growing near by. What was remarkable during this strange performance was Bernadette's entire insensibility to those around her: 'She acts as if she were alone – alone with someone up there . . . And yet, she passes through a serried throng . . . People push and shout to make way for her.'[64] Her agitation contrasted strikingly with the immobile serenity of her earlier experiences and was greeted with dismay.[65] Perhaps more than anything else she did at the Grotto, this performance alarmed middle-class observers. On 27 February, Peyramale castigated her: 'I'm told you ate grass, like the animals', a statement in line with the view of others that such gestures were grotesque.[66] These movements, however, probably had strong if unconscious resonances for observers, as Bernadette's body linked earth, water and the power of the feminine supernatural.

The unending commentary on her body in ecstasy was an attempt to articulate what some acknowledged could not be expressed through language. Her physical gestures and expressions seemed to draw on that aspect of shared culture that went beyond words. Like the everyday acts of walking, gesturing, crying or sitting, her extraordinary manifestation of religious experience fitted into a form of communication and understanding that was physical rather than verbal; it was not what she said, but the nature of her trance, the movement of her hands and the quality of her tears that persuaded. In a sophisticated but semi-literate culture such signs were all important, as those who accepted their authenticity believed Bernadette because they 'knew' that divine visitation was possible and revealed itself through unusual sensory experience. Like the suave odour of the uncorrupted bodies of saints, Bernadette's physicality convinced them as much, if not more, than the verbal messages that she relayed.[67]

The White Lady

If Bernadette's message and appearance reassured, her description of the apparition continued to produce consternation, especially among the literate and privileged. By her account, the figure was very small, no bigger than her own diminutive one metre forty (small even by the standards of this malnourished region) and, according to early interviews, perhaps even shorter. She was also very young, and Bernadette said she resembled a local child of about twelve who appeared regularly in white costume.[68] Occasionally Bernadette seemed unwittingly to identify with the apparition by remarking that *Aquéro* was no bigger than herself, a statement she repeated until her death, despite the disappointment and even irritation of questioners.[69]

She initially described the apparition as a *jeune fille*, a description that she was forced to abandon by the onslaught of commentators who refused to accept such an unorthodox description. The first newspaper report described the apparition as a *dame*, a lady, and the word *demoiselle*, or unmarried girl, virtually never appeared in print thereafter.[70] Well-meaning interpreters continually increased the apparition's age, with estimates ranging between fourteen and twenty. Priestly and pious opinion preferred the convention of Mary at the time of the Annunciation, and hence advanced the age to between the fifteenth and seventeenth year;[71] Lasserre accepted another priest's insistence that she was around twenty years old, a mistake that spread wherever his book was read.[72] Finally, other influential attempts to force Bernadette's image into more familiar Marian iconography included the statue erected in the Grotto by the Lyonnais sculptor Joseph Fabisch in 1864, and now the standard representation of the Virgin of Lourdes. Although the bequest from two women that financed his work specified he take Bernadette's description into account, Fabisch none the less managed to transform her words into the conventional idiom of nineteenth-century academic art.[73] The result angered Bernadette considerably by being both too big and too old (see illus. 17), and throughout her life she dismissed the many images that sought to re-create her vision with uncharacteristic irritation.

From the beginning, those who questioned her clearly had in mind

17. Joseph Fabisch, Notre-Dame de Lourdes, *1864*

something far removed from her own description. During his interrogation Jacomet suggested that the apparition must resemble two elegant and sumptuous local beauties (see illus. 18 and 19).[74] One was 'the beautiful chocolate-seller', Marie-Rosella Pailhasson, the thirty-year-old wife of the pharmacist and famous for the amount she spent on clothes. The other was the eighteen-year-old Marie Dufo, the fiancée of Romain Capdevielle, the editor of the local newspaper *Le Mémorial.* Here again the emphasis was on her impressive figure and clothes, as well as the refinement of her presentation.[75] However, the svelte simplicity of the apparition was entirely at odds with the corsets and crinolines of the Second Empire fashion, and Bernadette indignantly rejected the comparisons.

Obviously disturbed by Bernadette's description, Cros also tried to reconcile the various possibilities with her testimony, and noted that

18. Mme Marie-Rosella Pailhasson,
'La Belle Chocolatière' (1827–86)
19. Mlle Marie Dufo (1840–1928)

the conventional age of Mary at the time of Annunciation was around fifteen years of age. At first glance this fitted with Bernadette's account that the apparition was her own size or smaller, for she also was at the beginning of her fifteenth year. But he also realized that, whatever her age, Bernadette looked no more than eleven and, moreover, had described the apparition as *bien mignonnette*, an expression that sought to capture her tiny delicacy; she was a little girl, not even an adolescent.[76] As will be seen, this description may well have had an important lineage that contemporaries may not have wished to explore.

The smallness of the apparition is less surprising if one considers that, across the Pyrenean chain and more specifically in the Bigorre and Béarn, the most sacred and ancient representations of the Virgin were generally tiny. In Bétharram and Garaison, the former representing a Virgin and child, the latter a *pietà*, the images were no more than 59 or 63 centimetres respectively[77] (see illus. 20 and 21). Only a very few statues – from the Romanesque through to the

20. Vierge allaitant l'enfant, *seventeenth century, Notre-Dame de Bétharram*
21. Pietà, *sixteenth century, Notre-Dame de Garaison*

Baroque – are larger than a metre, a characteristic of religious statuary that includes the Virgin of Montserrat and the more stately, but still eminently portable, Virgin of Rocamadour (see illus. 22 & 23).

Most of these images show a Madonna and child, and so diverged sharply from Bernadette's non-maternal vision. Not far from Lourdes, however, an apparition only ten years earlier showed how a vision of diminutiveness and extreme youth could be tied up with an ancient and holy image. In Nouilhan in 1848 young visionaries of the community sought to revitalize their ancient chapel and honour 'their' Virgin, attributed to a fourteenth-century discovery legend. Attempts to reconsecrate the chapel after its destruction in 1793 finally came to a head in 1848 after the eruption once again of the War of the Demoiselles and an invasion of the neighbouring valley by the National Guard. After the bitter suppression of the riots, a twelve-year-old girl saw a pale child of no more than two and a half under a holly bush,

22. La Moreneta (The Black Madonna), *twelfth century, Notre-Dame de Montserrat*
23. La Vierge noire, *twelfth century, Notre-Dame de Rocamadour*

completely dressed in white: all who investigated the matter agreed that the apparition corresponded in size and demeanour to the Madonna of Nouilhan, no more than 55.5 centimetres in height.[78]

Bernadette's apparition, therefore, could have been associated with the smallness of the Madonna images that frequently formed children's conceptions of the Virgin. This impression is supported by the visionaries who succeeded Bernadette, ten-year-old boys like Jean-Marie Laborde, who described how 'at the back of the hole' he saw 'something white, like a little woman. She was the size of the virgins you see in the church.'[79] Similar experiences were recorded in northern Spain, where child visionaries saw a Virgin Mary like themselves.[80] While seemingly rooted in the imagination of the poor, this mystical tradition found its most literate and famous expression in Saint Theresa of Avila's autobiography, in which she described her vision of the Virgin as *muy niña*, a child of no more than seven years: 'The beauty I saw in Our Lady was very great . . . dressed in white, in a very splendid light . . . Our Lady seemed to me very like a young child.'[81] The similarity of expression is extraordinary, and suggests that this vision of the Virgin as child-like innocence was more strongly rooted than the dismayed Lourdais with religious education would allow. Cros thought that Bernadette's description, 'she is very tiny and dainty', was a literal translation of Theresa's expression *muy niña*, one that conveyed the charm and youth of the great mystic's impression.

Although her apparition bore little resemblance to orthodox Marian imagery, its similarities with mythical creatures of Pyrenean folklore were much more marked. The site of the apparition was inhabited by the fairies, the *dragas*, *damizélos*, *hadas*, *fadas*, *encantadas* – the term varied as the patois changed across the Pyrenean chain – who inhabited the forests, bushes, fountains and, above all, grottoes of the region. By first calling the apparition *uo pétito damizéla*, Bernadette chose the term used to describe fairies, the little women of the forest.

Like their Celtic counterparts, Pyrenean fairies appeared sometimes as serpents or cats, but more often as enchanting little women, only a little bigger than dwarfs.[82] Dressed in luminous white, they were beautiful, capricious creatures linked to cosmic forces: 'Flowers grow where they walk; they stir up and calm storms as they will, and heap kindnesses upon those who do them sincere homage.'[83] But while they could sometimes do evil – occasionally stealing food and even children – their intervention in human affairs was more generally benign.[84] Usually they demanded only affordable favours, namely meals for New Year's Eve, often rewarding those who were good to them. Mostly they spent time washing, and they were famous for the whiteness of their clothes and the laundry that they laid out to dry near fountains outside their well-appointed grotto abodes. They used golden rods to beat linen, making a noise in the night as they worked. They were known to replace dying children with ones who were sound and healthy, to marry men and become good household managers and mothers, only to be obliged to depart when the enchantment was broken by a brutish or heedless husband who called them by their name.[85] Such tales, which were told in different versions across the Pyrenees, reiterated tirelessly the need to refrain from this name-calling. Perhaps such a fear explains Bernadette's reticence in identifying *Aquéro*, for all supernatural creatures demanded, it seemed, this respectful reticence.

Bernadette did not see a fairy, for her apparition was clearly differentiated from the little ladies of the forest by her golden rosary and blue belt. But both the poor and well educated were none the less alerted to this possibility: M. A. Clarens, the director of the Ecole supérieure de Lourdes, for example, recognized the parallels, since *Aquéro* also appeared in a grotto and, with her smallness, beauty, snowy whiteness and especially the yellow roses on her feet, showed several fairy-like attributes.[86]

The parallels were not merely in appearance, however, for saints could behave like fairies and fairies like saints. The Pyrenean vision of the Virgin showed her willingness to engage in the daily affairs of men and women with severe punishments or quick rewards. Bernadette's apparition was also mercurial, for she did not always turn up on time, leaving the visionary bereft and accused of fraud.[87] She could be severe, exacting a penitential devotion that the transgressor would never forget. For example, Jacques Laborde, a cabaret owner and a tailor, known for the way he ignored his religious duties and questioned Bernadette's sanity, was punished swiftly for cursing after the wild rose bush caught his cap. That very night he came down with a terrible diarrhoea and had to wash all his sheets, an act often seen in peasant society as a rite of purification.[88] From that time forward Laborde went to the Grotto every morning, his joined hands holding the rosary. 'When on my way to Lourdes of a morning, I often met him coming down, humbled, eyes lowered. He went like this to the Grotto every morning. One could see from his humble demeanour that he was doing penance.'[89]

In the eyes of the poorer Lourdais the Virgin was not the sentimental character of nineteenth-century images of piety, but rather the strong, sometimes harsh mother of peasant society.[90] She hit back hard when slighted or insulted and demanded speedy fulfilment of proper religious observances. An indication of this mentality can be seen in the way they transformed orthodox devotions, much to the annoyance of the clergy. In the June before the apparitions the bishop of Tarbes and Lourdes, Mgr Laurence, wanted to stop the way the standard 'Hail Mary' was followed by a mixture of supplication and a talisman to ward off potential suffering: 'Whoever wears this prayer on their person will not die a sudden death.' Many suggested that great punishments were in store for those who did not recite these inventions with proper care at the moment of death.[91] Thus, the Virgin of the poor required appeasement as much as veneration, and in this resembled the Virgin of Garaison, who 300 years earlier smacked Anglèze de Sagazan despite her piety and humility.[92]

While Bernadette's lady could be harsh, she could also be infinitely merciful, in keeping with her image as divine mother and as mercurial fairy. From this early moment, before the clerical commissions and medical consultations that were later to surround Lourdes and make it famous, the poor were convinced of the Virgin's miraculous intercession. Catherine Latapie-Chouat, from a distant and poorer branch of the Latapie clan, bathed two paralysed fingers in the fountain within days of its discovery and was immediately cured.[93] She recovered the use of her hand – able again to take up her household duties – and then gave birth almost painlessly, a significant parallel with the Virgin whose unique freedom from Original Sin had spared her the agonies of childbirth. There were other miracles that never entered the annals of the shrine, but were equally potent signs to early worshippers: one man recounted how after eight years of childlessness his wife finally gave birth to a child after going to the Grotto.[94] Another story of a dying child told of a physician who sent away the parents in order to save them the final torment of the infant's death rattle. Left alone with the child, the grandmother placed around its neck 'a bit of the wood of the rose bush': the child took hold of the object and was cured.[95]

Such miracle tales account for believers' enthusiasm, but they do not explain why Lourdes became more than just a local shrine such as the largely unknown sanctuary at Nouilhan. So far I have concentrated on the way Bernadette's body, more than the apparition's words, carried conviction among the theologically untutored. For the poor, the statement 'I am the Immaculate Conception' was simply another, and conclusive, confirmation that the apparition was the Virgin, manifesting herself in one of the many guises they had venerated since

24. La Vierge immaculée, *seventeenth century, Hospice–Ecole des Sœurs de Nevers, Lourdes*

the Counter-Reformation[96] (see illus. 24). For the clergy and the educated, however, it was crucial.

Men like Peyramale believed that the words explained the whole purpose of the apparitions, and enabled them to see the events as the culmination of a theological tradition that stretched back to the Middle Ages.[97] Lourdes, in this view, was the latest in a series of miraculous events within living memory that had pointed the way to the promulgation of the dogma of the Immaculate Conception in 1854. In France the most important of these had been the vision of Mary that Catherine Labouré, a Sister of Charity, saw in 1830.[98] The miraculous medal produced as a result (see illus. 25) sold in the millions across France

25. The miraculous medal of Catherine Labouré, c. *1832*

and was credited with curing cholera and helping women in danger of dying in childbirth.[99] It showed Mary stepping on a snake, the symbol of Original Sin, with her hands radiating miraculous rays. Although mistaken, a belief that Bernadette's apparition had taken the same pose persuaded many priests of the truth of her vision. It was of little import that she always denied this assertion and insisted that, apart from a few moments, her Virgin had appeared with hands lightly touching at breast height.[100]

This reluctance, even refusal, to accept her description of the pose mirrored the clerical and elite rejection of her account of the Virgin as a little girl. It is one more piece of evidence indicating the way orthodox Catholics sought to squeeze Bernadette's vision into existing traditions. The words 'I am the Immaculate Conception' struck them as so monumental in significance that they were unwittingly heedless of the visionary's statements on other matters. In acting thus they were neither wilful nor consciously manipulative. Instead they filtered Bernadette's words through the sieve of their religious imagination, filled with the iconographic traditions of childhood teachings. When faced with the choice between this authoritative heritage – recently reinforced by Catherine Labouré's visions – and the words of an ignorant and poverty-stricken girl, they chose to stay within the tradition they knew and venerated.

Bernadette's apparition was sensual and beautiful, but girlishly so, more a fairy-virgin than the *Mère immaculée* then sanctioned by official Catholicism. She had neither the prophetic doom of the Virgin at La Salette, nor the healing rays and rounder contours of the Immaculate Mother on the miraculous medal. What is striking is the absolute absence from her vision of any maternal references, a pre-pubescent guise that disturbed many believing Catholics unable to separate their notion of the Virgin from that of motherhood. In the descriptions that appeared after the apparitions, in the official statue placed in the niche, in imaginative representations in books and films, this girlish aspect is invariably lost. With it goes much of our ability to comprehend the world in which the visions took place, and the resonances that Bernadette's earliest public heard.

Bernadette's apparition convinced different audiences in different ways, and in this special capacity lay the essence of its success. Men like Peyramale, who never went to the Grotto to see for themselves, were convinced by interrogating Bernadette and by the message she relayed. Sceptics like Estrade were won over by the impact of first-hand impressions, as well as by the ability to see the events in a broader theological picture. The poor men and women of Lourdes, most of whom would probably have had little idea of what the Immaculate Conception meant, were converted by Bernadette's visionary ecstasy and their belief in the Virgin's special solicitude for them. And in the early days, at least, it was their belief that was of the greatest importance, because they first created the shrine and defended it against its many enemies with such stalwart devotion that the world beyond Lourdes soon heard of it.

3

After-visions: Cultists and Seers

After the naming of the apparition as the Immaculate Conception on 25 March, the poor began to make a chapel at the Grotto. This spontaneous and unauthorized nature-shrine, primarily decorated in April, both irritated the clergy and prompted rigorous official action to maintain public order, with Jacomet removing the gifts on 4 May and the administration building barriers to block entry on 15 June. The mixture of vacillation and high-handedness in this official response met with resistance from the Lourdais, who formed new spiritual and class alliances to defend their shrine. These early cultists are usually presented as the pious poor fighting for their convictions. But such a characterization oversimplifies the months of spiritual turmoil that followed Bernadette's visions. For between Bernadette's penultimate apparition on 7 April and Mgr Laurence's commitment to an investigation at the end of July, groups of the devout from the town and neighbouring villages began processions and erected home-made altars. Controversies arose and many individuals also claimed to have visions, with the children chasing after the Virgin in the fruit trees, local fountains, fields and farmsteads.

Although an increasing number believed Bernadette had seen the Virgin Mary, they were far from certain she was the only one to be so privileged, and had once more to assess evidence to distinguish between the divine, the diabolical and the dissembling. Even twenty years later some continued to believe that a few of the later visionaries were authentic. The clergy was still in the position of reacting rather than leading, sometimes giving tentative support to particular visionaries, more often seeking to suppress what they considered an outbreak of childish extravagance. What is certain is that there was no immediate insistence that Bernadette alone had had genuine visions, although as events progressed her particular qualities became almost a standard by which priests judged others.

Apparitions of the nineteenth and twentieth centuries frequently involved several children seeing the Virgin and generally tended to be a mutual and shared experience.[1] In the Lourdes story, however, the scattered nature of the later visions, their apparent derivation from Bernadette's experience, as well as their carnivalesque elements, raised concerns about a 'superstitious' or even demonic epidemic. In both the tale of the Grotto chapel and of the visionary wave that followed, the suppression of these 'superstitious' tendencies was crucial to the future of the shrine. With the chapel, resistance to authority never turned to violence, and clergy were able to channel unorthodox spirituality into more respectable outlets. As for the visionaries, while ultimately dismissed, they were characterized as neither possessed nor as hysterical, common enough diagnoses at this period in France. In the end, the peaceful resolution of conflicting claims was due to the positive attitude the Church took in assessing, and later supporting, Lourdes as a site of Marian apparitions.

The Grotto and the People

In the popular imagination the Grotto was now a place of magical attraction and spiritual potential, its shape, contours and cavities suggesting mystery and power. It had unconscious associations with femininity: the hard-headed imperial prosecutor Vital Dutour, a keen sceptic about the apparitions, noted the sinuosity and the special difficulty of penetrating the hidden cavities, which could be explored from an opening at the bottom right-hand side of the Grotto. These cavities were secret and mysterious, even more so than the niche where the Virgin appeared.

> The 'grotto' is like an immense, semicircular porch that narrows as it goes, at the back of which a circular cavern opens up. In the roof of this cavern, above an altar standing three metres above sea-level, you can see the opening of a long, narrow, twisting passage that runs north–south into the rock, getting gradually higher. To reach the opening you need a ladder; to go any further you have to climb into the passage like a lizard into its lair, and crawl along on your belly for four or five metres. Then comes a sort of vault where five or six people can stand, not abreast but following the shape of the rock. A bit above that, two people squatting on their knees could fit into niche-like hollows. It's not really possible to go any further, it gets too narrow.[2]

Underlying such imagery was the suggestion of an enclosed, dark and moist place, now subject to a kind of transgressive penetration. This kind of unconscious association was made by Dutour when he criticized the five women who borrowed a ladder from the nearby farm of Espélugues to get into the Grotto to explore its upper cavities. He accused them of a lack of modesty, 'an exploration that forced them to take up all sorts of positions that were scarcely decent',[3] and made insinuations against their morality, for they had needed to writhe into the opening in an unlady-like fashion.

The Pyrenean poor were preoccupied with the interior, for grottoes in the region were places that held fairies, demons or perhaps golden treasure; they were also a special haven for the Virgin and her family. The grotto at Campan in a nearby valley required a ladder to probe the vaulted octagonal room encrusted with 'crystals that reflected the light in their thousands of facets'. This natural miracle had bejewelled the grotto with diamond-like columns and made it resemble a Gothic church; and at the end of the gallery 'a carved sanctuary' held a naturally formed 'Virgin holding the infant Jesus in her arms'. The inhabitants of the mountains had been devoted to this natural statue that was always beyond the control of the Church, but the crystal image was destroyed by revolutionaries, and the grotto-cult there never fully recovered.[4]

Such traditions increased the fascination of the Lourdais with Massabieille. Its location on the border between civilization and the forest beyond, the deeper chthonic associations of the site conjuring up an almost womb-like place of entry and protection, all help explain not only its great success but also its subversive potential (see illus. 26). For when decorating the makeshift chapel there, they ignored

26. Justin Pibou, Notre-Dame de Lourdes, *nineteenth-century painting, Collège de Garaison.*
No representation captures the feminine symbolism more tellingly than this painting by a Catholic artist who later discovered his priestly vocation and became a Garaison Father

clerical and civil authority and entered a spiritual world of gift-giving that led them to break the law and bend the boundaries of orthodox worship.

Documents chronicle the wealth and multiplicity of objects deposited, and the special significance of the images installed to commemorate the apparitions. On 4 April, Easter Sunday, Jacomet described 'a plaster virgin on [nature's] flowered carpet',[5] while Adélaide Monlaur, in another newsy letter to her cousin, described the growing ambience of the site a few days later: 'People are taking fine pictures, small flags in blue and white, flowers, and so on. On Palm Sunday fifty-eight candles were lit.'[6] By 14 April Jacomet reported in exasperation that there were now *three* plaster virgins, one with a 'cross and gold heart of some expense around its neck'.[7] Eleven days later these statues were even more handsomely decorated: 'They are literally covered in fine crowns, bouquets of artificial flowers; around their necks are chains, medals, crosses in gold and silver.'[8] On 26 April a fourth statue was installed, with more jewellery and offerings.[9]

There was an intimacy in the process of decoration, as if each woman sought to make the statues both more comfortable and more beautiful, and to take credit for their installation. Dominiquette Cazenave said later that Bernadette herself had encouraged this reverence, and that the Virgin had looked warmly upon the tokens of devotion, 'above all the statue in the niche', an indication of the importance attached to making a perfect fit between the image and the landscape.[10] Justine Cassou then explained that it had been *her* family that had supplied 'the statue and the wire niche' of the Immaculate Virgin.[11] But the human embellishments only underscored the importance of the *local* setting. Their offerings were to the Lady of Lourdes, who engaged the spiritual loyalties of the poor, as well as their social identities as members of the community in which she had appeared.[12]

So many gifts were given that when Jacomet had to list them all he made known his annoyance that the poorest people in the community should 'waste' their money in such a fashion:

> The sick come, for the most part, from the countryside, the rest from the working classes. The biggest offerings come from these visitors, who are the poorest and the most unfortunate. In the basket for these offerings we have had only one gold piece. Do you want to know, M. Le Préfet, who gave it? Well, it was a poor tailor from Tarbes called Jacquet (I don't know his other name), who has been paralysed for twelve years. He is the father of a young and numerous family. He had himself been carried to Lourdes in a wagon,

then in a chair to the Grotto. He was the first to throw a ten franc gold piece into the Grotto.[13]

This gold piece was not the only generous gift. The community donated two old chandeliers from the church,[14] while individuals offered wedding bands and earrings, the most prized of women's possessions. One man gave the gold watch of his recently deceased wife, while everyone tried to leave candles and bouquets of flowers.[15] The poorest women left bits of handcrafted linen, the fabric associated with birth and death, and treasured articles of trousseaus, an expensive token in a world where cheap manufactured clothing was still uncommon. One woman from Asson in the Basses-Pyrénées gave five francs and a large cheese, the product again of personal labour, but perhaps also a common offering at shrines of the Virgin for those wanting to suckle their young.[16] When a man tried to give some of the money back to her, she reportedly cried out: 'It is all for the Virgin.'[17] Jacomet duly logged the money gathered in a basket and set it aside for charitable purposes. His scrupulousness reflected the sacred atmosphere, for there was no misbehaviour by either pilferers or adolescents, who were no doubt fearful of the divine punishment they might provoke.

By removing all these objects in early May, Jacomet set off a struggle that helped transform what might have become nothing more than another semi-clandestine site of pilgrimage into a titanic battle between the authorities and the community. The open breach was all the more shocking since Jacomet was well respected, even twenty years after the events. There were indeed those who accused him of being a 'skirt chaser', or gossiped maliciously that a priest who had lived in his house had been familiar with Jacomet's wife,[18] but in general he was credited with intelligence, generosity and humanity:

Jacomet was just, humane, great . . . before this business he was well thought of, even by the poorer sort. He was very indulgent towards them and knew his business well; we will never see his like again; he was conscientious. At the beginning the priests thought highly of him. He was a good lad, kind, charming, good-humoured; he wasn't proud. Cordial, friendly with everyone; he had two children, both died: that affected him deeply.[19]

There was no violence when he removed the objects on Prefect Massy's order, but even so the reaction was menacing: the daughter of a man who owned a wagon used to cart off the offerings remembered her terror at 'the women [who] gathered in front of the house, crying, "May the devil break your horse's neck . . . May it starve."'[20] Jean Vergès, the *garde champêtre*, recalled how he had not wanted to be the first to remove the objects and was dismayed when Jacomet threw candles into the river. He was shocked by the way one of the plaster virgins crumbled in Jacomet's hands, and noted that the police commissioner then dropped and broke his pipe, another sign of divine ill-will.[21] Jacomet was flustered by the dozen or so people screaming, 'It's bad luck to take that away', and the road-mender Léon Latapie described the growing ugliness of the scene:

On the road there were people everywhere, women and men, muttering as we went by. They said to us: 'You've done wrong. If we'd been there, horse and wagon would have finished up in the Gave.' . . . I wasn't afraid on the Pont-Vieux, but all the same I was afraid that the horse wouldn't get to Lourdes; there were around thirty quarrymen from the bridge on, shouting loudly. Jacomet was twenty metres in front of us, and he wasn't in uniform. He did well to go ahead to keep himself safe, and us and the horse.[22]

All who told this story were convinced that disturbing such sacred objects would bring divine punishment, and their convictions were strengthened when a sawyer who lent his hatchet to destroy the makeshift altar had his feet crushed by a falling beam the very next day.[23] The young woman whose family lent the wagon and horse recounted twenty years later how relieved she was that her family had not been cursed: 'Nothing bad happened to us; the horse was sold ten years later, and my father, my mother, we are all alive, except my sister.'[24] Jacomet also seemed well aware of the beliefs; when one of the men cutting away the rosaries pricked his skin on a thistle, he reportedly warned him: 'Hide your hand: if the public sees it, they'll say the Holy Virgin has punished you for removing the rosaries.'[25]

Stories of this kind abounded, and some of the most elaborate were told by the officials themselves. In a letter that mixed irritation with condescending amusement, Dutour recounted how he supposedly was woken by a terrible thunderstorm and was so frightened that he sprang from bed and took refuge with neighbours.[26] Another favourite featured Jacomet's punishment when he threatened Bernadette, and reduced the powerful official to a comic figure battling pathetically against divine vengeance:

The commissioner picked up his pen, but suddenly two tallow candles on the table were transformed into four great wax candles, the floor trembled to such a degree that the commissioner and the imperial prosecutor were dancing; the commissioner tightened his feet and his legs, and did his best to dip the pen in the inkpot. He could never quite manage it; his hat was jumping about on his head in a singular fashion; his hands and his body trembled.[27]

Women may have been prominent in decorating the chapel, but poor men also played an important role in these early stages. The largest workers' association, the quarrymen, felt themselves appointed by Bernadette's message to build the chapel, especially as one of their number, Louis Bouriette, was cured by the fountain before the end of March after years of partial blindness.[28] As early as April they enlarged the pathway to the Grotto, built a balustrade in front of the makeshift altar and constructed a basin to collect water from the spring.[29] The quarrymen also led the protests against the authorities, cancelling their patron's day festival to show their disapproval. Normally this raucous festivity was held on Ascension Day,[30] but, when Jacomet stopped the building work at the Grotto,[31] they went to mass instead and then processed to Massabieille, mixing local pride and self-interest with a growing piety. There was even talk of a petition to reopen the Grotto, but the mayor's refusal to sign the document undermined their campaign.

Unusual class alliances began to develop, with the poor helped in creating the shrine by more respectable women from the Children of Mary. Until recently headed by the saintly Elisa Latapie, whose 'good death' had so impressed Peyramale, their ranks were filled with the pious of good family, as well as any poor girl who could amass the savings to pay for the costume: 'I was poor but earned money enough to dress in white – a long white veil, white robe and belt.'[32] They prayed before the statue of the Immaculate Virgin in the hospice at Lourdes and, in these early days, their rosaries were specially blessed and worn on their wrists on days of consecration and of procession. After Bernadette's visions, everyone put on blue belts, which they usually wore on the day of the Immaculate Conception on 8 December.[33]

These rituals and clothes gave them as much a sense of collective identity as the quarrymen. On the evening of 11 May, in the month of Mary, some of them began a candlelit procession to the Grotto and sang litanies to the Virgin, the first in what was to become a ritual at the shrine.[34] Here was the tradition of honourable illegality once again, but executed with subtlety and flair. By leaving their candles there, they knowingly broke the law; although exasperated, Jacomet knew that to prosecute such pillars of the community would make him look ridiculous. Once the Grotto was sealed off on 15 June,[35] a contest began between the authorities and the people, but for the moment Jacomet was bested by the spectacle of rowdy men trooping off quietly to mass, and genteel women in white piously breaking the law.

The First Wave of Visionaries

Although not exquisitely beautiful like the grotto of Campan, the cave at Lourdes, once illuminated by candles, revealed a world of fantastical shapes that both frightened and beckoned. It was into this interior that the first wave of visionaries trespassed. Just a few days after Bernadette's penultimate apparition on 7 April, Marie Cazenave, the most devout and well reputed of the five women to enter – two were unnamed strangers – acknowledged a semi-conscious feeling of transgression. Nevertheless, she was pushed by a 'curiosity [she] could not describe' to follow Honorine Lacroix and Madeleine Cazaux inside. She encountered 'a stone at the far end of the Grotto . . . representing the form of a woman carrying a child'. Marie Cazenave felt certain that the Virgin had indeed been present and suggested to her hesitant companions – who seemed more inclined to flee back to safety – that they remain to say the rosary.

After the first decade of her rosary, she saw in the candlelight 'a white stone and, almost at the same moment, a bit to the right, a woman's shape, of average height, carrying an infant in her arm'. She also saw a smiling face, a head with long curling hair, then 'something white looking as if it were held up by a comb', and finally a white robe. Marie's excitement grew when her companions said they could see the same thing, and feelings heightened when Madeleine Cazaux pulled at her dress so hard they fell over. Only Honorine was initially left out, for the image disappeared as she came closer, but by placing the candle in the right place she too began to see the apparition. By the third decade Madeleine remarked on the beauty of the Virgin, whom she described as having joined hands, and Marie noted that the apparition changed as they prayed, covering her head with a veil during the Litanies and the recital of 'Remember O Most Gracious Virgin'. Honorine described the child in her arms as a four-year-old with blue eyes, blond hair and hands joined together. His cheekbones were 'plastered with red'.[36] They had no sense that their experience might be classed as some kind of contagious *folie* that had gripped them in the candlelit darkness, nor indeed did any local doctor put forward such a diagnosis.[37]

Who were these adventurers? By far the most important was the 22-year-old Marie Cazenave, universally noted for her ardent faith. By profession a seamstress, she seemed as good a candidate for divine visitation as Bernadette, if not better, so much so that Peyramale told his bishop that 'many things speak in favour of the girl; she wanted to join the Sisters of the Cross, and would already be a nun had her parents been willing to give their consent'.[38] Peyramale's letter showed that he at least did not instantly rule out the possibility of other visionaries, nor is there any sense that the exacting cleric saw Bernadette's poverty-stricken and marginalized position as counting in her favour; quite the contrary. The other women met with little approval, being socially less respectable: Dutour even accused Honorine Lacroix of being a 'shocking and abject prostitute',[39] whose testimony could be easily dismissed.[40]

Soon after this, another five entered the upper cavities of the Grotto, this time headed by an older servant woman, Suzette Lavantès. Once again the apparition occurred during the 'Remember O Most Gracious Virgin', although this time the figure was drawn more hazily: it was Suzette's height, but nothing more than a 'sort of vapour', like a veil trailing behind a long robe. The image seemed real enough for Suzette to cry out, clasp her hands together in prayer and then collapse in tears and tremblings.[41]

Finally, a third group climbed up: this included Joséphine Albario, a fifteen-year-old of respectable family, and Marie Courrech, the mayor's maid of all work. These two young women were to become the leading figures in the visionary wave, returning repeatedly to the Grotto and manifesting forms of ecstatic behaviour for others to witness and judge. On this occasion Joséphine become agitated and tearful, then declared she had seen the Immaculate Virgin holding a child, and a man with a beard standing beside them. This last group was also notable for being the only one that contained men, the mayor's secretary A. Joanas and the district road-mender L. Boyrie. Their experience was of some significance, for it was completely ignored. They aroused no interest in the authorities as potential frauds or in the populace as possible visionaries: only women and children, it seems, were considered likely candidates.

The images recounted by the later visionaries are striking for their divergencies. While they all saw something in white, none had the small stature of Bernadette's *pétito damizéla*, but rather took the form of a Virgin and child, a chubby, healthy infant with 'red cheeks' reminiscent of a polychrome statue or the coloured prints of images of piety. The reference to a man with a beard suggests Saint Joseph or possibly Saint Peter, since it was later claimed he was holding keys. When Suzette Laventès saw a misty woman in white with a dress and trailing robe, she offered a picture of virginal purity, or even a ghostly spirit, both embellished and romantic, and very different from the austere simplicity of Bernadette's vision. The primacy of her role was already established: while Bernadette was reticent about guessing the identity of her vision – hence the reference to *Aquéro* – these women immediately 'knew' they were encountering the Virgin because of her experience. Their preference, however, for a more maternal incarnation suggests how little they were concerned with the idea of 'immaculate conception'.

It is tempting to think that the differences explain why the later visions were ruled out, for, in contrast to Bernadette's dainty girl in white, these descriptions seem formulaic, even clichéd. As suggested, there was no consensus in the matter, as many sought to recast her vision into similar forms and insist she had seen a *dame*, a *Mère immaculée* of rounder contours and outstretched arms. More important for the clergy, perhaps, was that Bernadette's apparition constituted an entire mission on its own: twenty years later Abbé Pierre-Jean-Bertrand Pène, a young *vicaire* of Lourdes at the time and a passionate defender of the apparitions, suggested that Joséphine Albario's vision had been ruled out because it 'was silent, immobile and lifeless. No revelation was offered, no mission given.'[42] Such disparaging remarks reveal the later orthodoxy, however, rather than the impression of the moment.

In essence, it was not just the apparition that determined the verdict but, once again, the behaviour and piety of the seers. Joséphine Albario had witnessed Bernadette's experience, and she too remained insensible to the outside world for as long as three quarters of an hour during her visions in the second part of April. She showed the expected emotion, perhaps in slightly more intense form: 'she trembles – becomes agitated – cries – laughs'.[43] Repeatedly, locals emphasized beauty of expression, and the feeling that the visionary's face was somehow reflecting the divine by expressions of joy and sadness untainted by either human or diabolical grimaces. There were those honest enough to admit, even twenty years later, that they believed Joséphine's expression of sadness fitted into this special category. Estrade said that during Joséphine's first ecstasy at least a dozen people surrounded her, impressed by her expressions:

> Her face, without having the inspirational air of Bernadette, was still beautiful. Big tears fell from her eyes, her hands were placed together in an expression of pain. In her features as a whole, there was something that reflected the supernatural, ill-defined, no doubt, but quite outside the limits of ordinary expressiveness . . . Joséphine's beatific state also surprised me a great deal, so much so that for a moment I thought we were going to have a second genuine ecstatic.[44]

As important as these moments were others suggesting possible diabolical manipulation. Although at first Joséphine shared with the other seers a pure white vision of the Virgin, she later began to hint at doom and disaster. For example, she reportedly told Antoinette Tardhivail that the Virgin wore above her white dress a 'black helmet and veil', adding that the image was a prophecy of the end of the world.[45] These dark themes were repeated when she saw the scenes of the Passion and a black cross.[46] While her sadness was admired, the darkness of these later images was frightening and thought to be possibly evil. The local population expected beauty from the Virgin, and considered that such blackness might come from the devil, an assumption at odds with other apparition experiences in Europe that accepted the Virgin as bringing dark and apocalyptic messages.[47] Indeed, the gentleness of the messages of Notre-Dame de Lourdes may be another element in explaining the shrine's subsequent success. Even if in her earliest evocations she could be stringent in her punishments, the Virgin of Lourdes was notable for her mercy, a vision of love that the Church and the crowds at the Grotto eagerly embraced.

Even more disturbing was physical evidence that contrasted sharply with the first ecstasies. During her second visit to the Grotto, Joséphine had 'trembled convulsively' and needed help to walk away.[48] Eléonore Pérard claimed that her ecstasy was accompanied by 'cries, a sort of howling, contortions'[49] reminiscent of the possessed. In order to test Joséphine's authenticity she repeated the experiment conducted on Bernadette and jammed 'a long darning needle, the fattest and strongest I could get hold of' into the visionary's arm until it apparently touched bone. The result was exactly the same, and she said that the trial had been 'approved' by Abbé Pomian, Bernadette's confessor, suggesting that the clergy was also preoccupied with gathering as much evidence as possible.[50] This time, however, the conclusion was different, as she held that Joséphine's expression was so frightening she could not possibly be seeing the Virgin Mary. That the same experiment and the same result produced opposite conclusions is significant: the girl's insensibility indicated a supernatural phenomenon but did not indicate whether it was divine or diabolical.[51]

Joséphine Albario was soon dismissed from the ranks of the visionaries, the physical evidence telling against her.[52] Yet her story raises interesting questions about whether a biographical pattern can be discerned among the visionaries. At fifteen years she was a little older than Bernadette and, unlike her and Marie Courrech, came from a fairly prosperous milieu. However, her life story was pervaded by emotional rejection and family tension: she had lost her mother and was raised by an elder sister who credited neither her piety nor the reality of the apparitions. The sister was clearly furious when Joséphine chose a religious vocation, resented the twenty francs a month needed to support her at the convent, and was bitter when still more money was required to send her to a second religious institution in Toulouse when the first proved unsuitable. Joséphine shamed the family further by returning as a beggar, and was beaten and locked in her room for three days and nights. She finally escaped when her father died and left home to begin life as a pedlar of fabrics, a trade widely regarded as a means of disguising prostitution; even twenty years after the events her family still blushed at her name.[53]

The elder sister thought everyone would agree that Joséphine had been a bad lot, but this was not the case. An acquaintance called Antoinette Garros, seeing her in Barèges, recalled how Joséphine's family had exploited her, and how in 1858 she had been 'good, very well behaved, gentle'. Garros begged her to set aside her evil ways, to which Joséphine replied: 'Nobody likes me at home.'[54] Given her experiences, it is not surprising her apparitions were dark and foreboding, and that her face reflected the sadness and tears of the Virgin in distress. She would become in the public imagination the ultimate 'false' visionary, her later fate merely confirming her earlier 'deception'. Banished by her family and exiled from Lourdes, she was Bernadette's mirror opposite and, like the famous visionary, also learned the pain of permanent separation from Lourdes and the *pays*.

Bernadette's most important rival was Marie Courrech. Poor and oppressed, she was an orphan, separated from her four sisters and brothers and living in the household of the mayor, Anselme Lacadé. Another local woman, Dominiquette Cazenave, active in the Children of Mary, remembered the girl's hard life, her illiteracy and gentle piety:

> I went to work doing the ironing at M. Lacadé's house and she said to me: 'You can read, tell me a story . . .' She ran about the house all day because there was so much work; she was the only servant [and had to] look after the children, tidy the bedrooms, do the shopping, cook. 'How do you say your rosary?' 'A bit in the morning, a bit before going to bed, a bit after the first waking of the night to ask pardon for sins committed at night.'[55]

Marie came from the village of Tournous near Garaison and was steeped in the Marian piety of the locality. In some sense she was even more marginal than Bernadette, who at least remained in her own town, was part of a family, and had parents who oversaw her meagre education. Marie Courrech was so lowly she was generally called by her employer's name; Lacadé, in turn, felt strongly about her and sought to protect his household and its reputation by shaping her behaviour as a visionary.

She embellished Bernadette's performance by adding details to round out the narrative of Marian visitation, with visions between April and June, and others in late summer and winter. Like Bernadette, Marie was joyful and unaware of the outside world during her visions: 'I was happy, so gripped that I didn't know where I was; I was happy, and didn't even know I was at the Grotto.'[56] Although, at about sixteen, her apparition was a little older, she was in some ways a replication of Bernadette's: she was dressed in virtually the same garments – a long veil fell to the ground – but this time came with distinctively blonde hair, an aesthetic ideal among the Pyreneans. The apparition smiled often but spoke little, only once giving the message to pray for sinners and drink and wash at the fountain. Again, like Bernadette's apparition, this vision appeared according to the holy calendar. On the evening before the Assumption she came as the Queen of Heaven, so magnificent that Marie fainted when she beheld the brilliant crown, reflecting many colours, and her smile of heavenly sweetness.[57] On the day of the Immaculate Conception, she returned without the crown and asked Marie to tell the clergy to begin processions – mirroring, once again, the instructions to Bernadette. At this final encounter the Virgin 'rose up in a cloud' and disappeared suddenly; and, although nothing was said, Marie understood she would never see her again.[58]

It would be tempting to suggest that this experience was nothing more than a means for a young girl to transform her social marginalization and subservience into spiritual authority and ultimately personal freedom. Her behaviour suggests that she did temporarily step outside her normally subordinate role to defy superiors. For example, she admitted proudly twenty years later that she defied her employer and worked especially hard to find the precious moments to go to the Grotto:

M. Lacadé said he forbade me to go – that he'd lock me in – that he'd have to throw me out. Some people told him (some gentlemen, I don't know who) to throw me out but, when he said it, I wasn't upset; I simply said, 'I didn't mean to offend him and he wasn't offended.' 'As you wish, when you wish, monsieur.' M. Lacadé said (he was a good man, it was the others who were setting him against me): 'She does her duty; why I should throw her out I do not know.'[59]

Lacadé wanted her at home, but worried about thwarting divine will if she really was seeing the Virgin. His wife also exhorted him to let her go, and Marie went. One woman even suggested that Lacadé's scepticism was only broken by his servant's faith; without her, he might never have been convinced of the happening, a conclusion that implies the extent of the spiritual hold a poor woman of humble status could have on a local notable.[60]

Lacadé was not the only man in authority whom she disobeyed. When Peyramale visited the mayor's house, he also forbade her to go to the Grotto. She replied that her confessor – it seems that it was Abbé J.-M. Serres[61] – had told her that she had the right to go, thereby setting one authority figure against the other. She promised to ask permission first in future, but, when it was withheld, ignored the order and went anyway. Like many devout women at Lourdes, she climbed over the barrier to find her habitual spot of prayer, defying police authority as she did so. Her employer, her priest and the police were all thrust aside in her search for spiritual communion.

Marie tried to become a nun after her visions, but was disappointed when three convents turned her down, the first requiring a dowry of six thousand francs, the other two refusing her because she was a servant.[62] To see her actions as self-interested or manipulative, however, would be to misunderstand her spiritual experience and the comfort she gave others. Before and during the apparitions she took holy communion often, sometimes every day, but always at least two or three times a week, which, by the still relatively rigourist standard of the era, was considerable.[63] She was strongly religious, for she loved the Virgin, revelled in her life as a Child of Mary and took to heart what she learned at catechism. Her faith accompanied her throughout her life, and she always believed that she too had been privileged to see the Mother of God.

As much as Bernadette and Joséphine Albario, Marie was put under popular scrutiny. Undoubtedly Léonard Cros in his historical investigations guided witnesses with his questions years later, but nothing was more frequently compared than the physical demeanour of Bernadette and those of her competitors. Women were the keenest observers, watching for any untoward sign of evil; on the whole they were convinced, remarking, however, that Courrech was the more expansive: 'In her ecstasies she had the appearance of Bernadette, but more joy than her.'[64] Joyfulness was matched by a keen desire for union: 'She seemed to want to run to the Gave, as if to get to the Grotto.' During ecstasy she was like a palpitating creature whose whole physical being was centred on the apparition. 'While I held her, I felt her impulses strongly, her heart beat so strongly . . . like violent blows.'[65] Marie seemed to understand the elusiveness of the divine, playing with the apparition who seemed near but was still unattainable: 'I wanted to grab the Holy Virgin by the robe, but she always escaped me, and smiled to see I couldn't catch her.'[66] Such intensity – later to be contrasted with Bernadette's tranquillity – was not held against her; indeed, this witness went out of her way to underscore the similarities between the two by remarking that 'Her face was never confused, but calm . . . the same paleness as Bernadette . . . she often kissed the ground.'[67]

Marie felt her experience gave her special powers of prediction and understanding, and she did her best to fulfil the tradition of a *sainte fille*, a holy woman or girl who ministered to the community in an entirely lay capacity. For example, a *demoiselle*, the sole daughter of an unnamed family, asked her to attend their child in her death throes. But Marie was convinced the child would survive and believed in her gift despite her employers' scolding. 'I had the idea she wouldn't die. She was soon cured, and got better from that moment. At that period these notions came to me from time to time.' Twenty years later she did her best to subdue these thoughts and, when she failed, went to confess so as not to 'tempt the good Lord'. Her obedient attitude suggests the continuing importance of clerical direction in suppressing her claims.[68]

The genteel Antoinette Tardhivail also recounted how Marie came to her on Christmas Eve in 1859, when she was at death's door. Marie reassured the sick woman that she had heard the Virgin's voice and would ask for a cure through the intercession of the baby Jesus. After the *grande messe*, Marie returned to the Grotto and saw there the infant Jesus holding a little crucifix, a clear sign to both seer and friend that the latter would soon be cured. In fact, Antoinette recovered almost immediately, and went to the Grotto the next day in thanks. She later said the clergy had come to interview her and were impressed. They 'made me understand that there was some link between my cure and the deeds of Marie Lacadé',[69] an important indication that, even a year and a half later, Bernadette's position as the sole visionary was still undecided.

Marie's simplicity and faith made people seek her out in times of trouble. Laurentine Cazeau, the mother of three children, could not resign herself to death and was so despairing she threatened to come back as a revenant and hack her husband's new wife to pieces should he betray her by remarrying. So disturbed was Dominiquette Cazenave, one of the pious women of Lourdes, by this tale, that she asked Marie to pray before her little Virgin. That very night, it seems, the Virgin touched Laurentine's heart; she confessed, then begged her husband to remarry, to pray at her tomb, and even returned her ring, a gesture giving him his freedom. She then died happily, comforted in the end by Marie, who convinced her that she had a place in heaven. So moved was the husband by these signs of love and resignation that he never did remarry.[70]

Such tales illuminated the moral conscience of local society and suggested ways to bring spiritual harmony to a world marked by sickness and rage. Other stories demonstrate the savvy practicality of the poor and how they, in turn, saw the Virgin's power and Marie's role as intercessor. Dominiquette Cazenave told how her brother's pride and joy was his team of six horses, known locally as the 'chemin de fer', the keenest means of transport in the region. When they took the body of Jacomet's young son to be buried in Barèges, the animals fell ill with the glanders. Marie was called upon to pray for them, but the Mother of God reportedly replied: 'It's nothing to worry about.' None the less, the horses had to be put down: perhaps Jacomet's family had brought bad luck. Their owner was inconsolable, as he could not afford to replace them, but the Virgin's promise was fulfilled in a different way: he was saved from ruin by the generosity of peasants who sold him six new animals and deferred payment. He earned 6,000 francs that season: 'Never before, nor after, never a season like that.'[71] The moral economy in both the tale of the dying wife and the horses was similar: the Virgin took away, but did so in a way that moved human hearts to generous action. While in the former case she brought emotional solace, in the latter she engaged in the material dilemmas of the poor. In both instances the woman whose intercession counted was the poor, humble and illiterate seer, Marie Courrech, whose name virtually never figures in the history of the shrine.

No records explain how she was slowly eased off the stage. Peyramale believed that she might be genuine and, in a letter to the bishop on 8 May 1858, described her as a 'holy child if ever there was one'.[72] Her fate was decided by an Episcopal Commission of Inquiry set up at the end of July by Mgr Laurence to investigate the apparitions, the fountain and the claims of cure. Its eleven members were eminent local clergymen, most of whom came from Laurence's cathedral chapter. Peyramale was at first excluded from this distinguished panel, a hesitation perhaps due both to his passionate commitment to the apparitions and to protect him from accusations of self-interest. In the end, the commission could not do without him, and he was appointed as the twelfth 'apostle'; he also became a member of the roving subcommission that made journeys to interview witnesses and assess cases of cure. What happened to Marie during its deliberations is unclear: one witness said she was definitely interviewed, but no record of her testimony survives.[73] Only a few hints remain: a comment by Chanoine Ribes that on one occasion the commission spotted a discrepancy between Bernadette's and Marie's testimony, and decided in favour of Marie's version, suggests that she was being taken seriously. Noting that the Virgin's message to Bernadette mentioned only one procession, while Marie stated that any number were requested, he said: 'The Commission had been struck by the difference between the two accounts, but did not see any contradiction. It accepted the version of M. Lacadé's servant.'[74]

The seriousness with which Marie was treated at this stage was in marked contrast to the way she was later all but erased from the story. We cannot know why, in the end, her visions were rejected, for neither her bodily postures nor her messages were disturbing. She was also known for her piety and, unlike Bernadette, her devout nature was recognized even before her apparitions. But, although never condemned, Marie somehow came to know that her visions and premonitions were not gifts from God but dangerous temptations. Perhaps the commissioners rejected her because her visions added almost nothing to the corpus of messages already conveyed, and potentially weakened Bernadette's claims as well. What is certain is that they concluded there had been a unique gift of grace, all the more precious for its harmonious and singular quality. It did its job well, for it is hard to imagine Lourdes as a shrine of multiple visionaries and unseemly popular effervescence, so closely is it linked to the image of Bernadette Soubirous, the dispossessed shepherdess tending her flock in the Pyrenean countryside. But those who believed in Marie did not waver even twenty years after the events: 'I believe she saw the Holy Virgin.'[75]

The Children

While Marie Courrech, Joséphine Albario and the others were treated seriously, many saw nothing but an elaborate set of mischievous pranks among new tales of visions that came from groups of children. But for every dismissal there was another adult who was convinced, and for a few weeks between May and July the children seemed in charge. More than any of the others, they raised the prospect of diabolism, their frightening cries, prophecies and behaviour – which included mockeries of Christian rituals and, above all, of Bernadette's experience – leaving parents and priests at a loss, as they tried to assess the children's claims that they had seen the Virgin Mary, or other apparitions of a less friendly kind.

Surprisingly, historians have failed to make any connection between this outburst and the cyclical festivities of Saint John's Day, one of the many holidays associated with the Christian calendar that also celebrated the summer solstice on the night of 24 June. Saint John's Day was still an important aspect of communal life in the mountain world, despite Jansenist and Enlightenment attempts to repress and tame such explosions of popular sentiment. The period was known in the Pyrenees for its tolerated madness in the same way as Carnival and the festivities of May. The celebrations focused on water and sun, with pilgrims spending the night beside the nearby Lac de Lourdes, then bathing in it in the morning, 'to which they attributed great virtue'.[76] In honour of the Baptist, villagers rolled in the early morning dew and let their herds out to graze along paths of moist, scented herbs. People drank at healing fountains at midnight or before dawn, and those with particular ailments – goitre, infertility, eczema – went to the waters in search of help.

The bouquets of the season, traditionally made with seven yellow wildflowers, celebrated the sun, but above all Saint John's Day was a time to celebrate through fire. Large bonfires were burnt in the villages, and all that was evil was symbolically exorcized. Cats and snakes were flung into the blaze, the dead of the previous year were exorcized, and evil spirits and emanations burned; young women jumped over the fire to show their prowess, and courting took place. General licence, if not sexual misdemeanour, was integral to the festivities.[77] Like all the days of ritualized dissipation, Saint John's Day gave pride of place to youth.[78] Local youths noisily punished inappropriate sexual morality, their activities maintaining the proper balance between the human and divine orders. The rites of exorcism and expiation were linked to the annual hope for a bountiful harvest, and hence the general fertility of the community.[79]

Seen against this background, the behaviour of the child visionaries seems in keeping with the subversive activities of the time of year. When villagers from nearby Ségus and Ossen processed to Lourdes, they used the occasion for a classic display of village patriotism by insulting their hosts: 'There are good people in the Bastuguère valley, particularly at Ossen; at Lourdes there is only the rabble.'[80]

The children were not merely indulging in the traditional riotousness of the season, but also reacting to the specific events of the apparition. The occurrences began in May in Lourdes, then spread to the outlying villages of Ossen, Omex and Ségus. One of the most notable actors was Jeanne-Marie Poueyto, who claimed to see something white while making a bouquet for her grandfather in the week between Saint John's Day and Saint Peter's Day. Then she climbed a ladder and sat in the family's cherry tree for a quarter of an hour, coming down to tell her parents she had seen the Virgin, who had promised to return with some relics. Scolded the next day when she refused to say her prayers, Jeanne-Marie continued to insist her vision was real and presented her mother with a bit of wood that resembled a finger, saying it was the promised relic. The mother was disturbed enough to go to Peyramale, who told her to destroy the 'relic' and change the child's bed, a recommendation that suggests he saw only mischief at work, rather than any serious diabolical flirtation.[81]

Jeanne-Marie turned to more aggressive antics. She made a make-shift chapel of her cherry tree and climbed all over it in search of the elusive Virgin. She astonished her neighbour, Etienne Théas, by flinging holy water in his face, which he bore uncomplainingly when she explained that she had saved him from 'something not very nice'.[82] She reached the peak of her audacity when she ordered some fifty people watching her to kneel for a poppyseed communion, putting the seeds – classically associated with the pagan earth goddess Demeter – on the tongues of those willing to accept them. In later years she could honestly not remember what she had seen or why she had behaved as she had, noting only that she had been a constant visitor to the Grotto during Bernadette's apparitions and that in those old days 'the children were . . . more wild than today'.[83] Eventually the cherry tree was cut down.

As suggested, the Virgin was seen as having a special link with trees, especially the hawthorn and rose, but all trees and their fruits were thought to give protection against bad weather and ill-fortune. Chapels like Jeanne-Marie's were common throughout the region, and the *caperetos* – not dissimilar from the chapel in the Grotto of Massabieille – built near oratories, calvaries and road crossings often contained such offerings as bouquets and fruit trees. Laurel branches blessed on Palm Sunday protected the future harvest; crosses made from branches were used to ward off hail and frost, and were even planted in fields until the crops were in. Trees had a special relationship to children, used for play and shelter and also to chase away infantile ailments. When ill, children in the Pyrenees could be placed at the fork of a trunk where the revitalizing sap was thought to rise; after prayers a piece of the child's linen was left behind to signify the physical abandonment of the illness.[84]

With all these associations, it was not perhaps surprising that children made contact with the supernatural in trees. Jeanne-Marie Poueyto, however, caused further concern when she climbed on her knees up to the nearby caves of Espéluges, while her family and others walked behind her, praying and sprinkling holy water. Like Bernadette, she never failed or wavered, crossing the stones seemingly unaware of the pain. At the caves themselves she seemed frightened, and, as her mother sought to lift her out, the older woman fell two metres. She was unscratched: Jeanne-Marie said she had seen the Holy Virgin take her mother in her arms.[85] Twenty years after the event the mother hinted that some supernatural intervention had spared her from serious injury.

Another young visionary, Julien Cazenave, around seventeen at the time, brayed like an animal and made shocking grimaces, frightening, enraging and amusing all at once, as he tried to catch some invisible object:[86] his Virgin always seemed to be running away, as in a game of hide and seek. Despite his extravagant behaviour, there were many who believed in him: 'Almost everyone thought it was due to the Holy Virgin.'[87] Cazenave knew how to draw the crowds to the Grotto: 'Half the town was there, a crowd of people: you could see nothing but their heads. It was a Sunday.' He also knew how to make people do his bidding and, above all, seemed to enjoy making fun of Bernadette: 'He prayed, then gestured to them to kiss the earth, and the whole crowd went down on its knees to kiss the earth.'[88]

He crowned himself with laurels and went to the Grotto, where he dunked rosaries in the fountain (some said the Gave) and ordered the assembled to pray.[89] The ritual of the rosaries aroused considerable comment and suggested another kind of mockery: during the rogations, when people and animals processed to seek collective blessing in the church, they stopped at streams to bathe their branches in the water and to protect themselves, the fields and their livestock from disaster. He may also have been parodying the episode during the apparitions when Bernadette held out her rosary to the Virgin and the crowd followed suit, hoping for a generalized blessing.[90] More alarmingly, he told the crowd to recite the rosary and explained how God would do the same. As one scandalized woman said to those who believed him, 'Now here's the world turned upside-down: the good Lord praying to his mother.'[91]

While these children used the caves, streams, trees and fields, others stayed closer to home. Jean Labayle of Lourdes constructed a chapel at home around the time of Saint Peter's Day after he went to the Grotto. His mother encouraged his piety by giving him a small Christ and a Virgin, four blessed candles and another smaller one for the dead. She later said that as many as twenty to thirty people came to the house to pray of an evening. During one session a young girl saw the devil with horns, and Jean sprinkled the room with holy water and then fainted dead away. His body was implicated in the struggle with evil, his force momentarily undermined by the duel, a physical manifestation of momentary illness that was the first and only suggestion of the possibility of possession.[92]

He too accomplished some remarkable physical feats, one witness saying how he went down the stairs 'on all fours, kissing the steps of the staircase'.[93] He could also read people's thoughts – he knew for example when his mother sought to save money on candles – and could predict the future. Her husband had trouble with his nose and asked Jean to pray for its cure. Jean replied that the nose would be eaten away, but that his physical affliction did not matter because Jesus had died for our sins. In fact, his father's nose did disintegrate, and the progress of the painful illness was seen as evidence of Jean's prophetic powers. Nor did his visions stop entirely. As late as January 1859 he apparently told his godparents that he had seen the Three Magi.[94]

All the children involved in these happenings indulged their playfulness by making their elders take orders. Some parents were proud their youngsters were so blessed and seemed almost to encourage them, other adults laughed and refused, while still others saw them as part of the special happenings that had begun with Bernadette. At times a more personal message underlay the visionary's words. The young Marie Poujol claimed to see the Virgin at Lourdes and, with her new authority, was able to say things that would otherwise have remained unsaid: 'Daddy, you don't love Mummy: the Blessed Virgin told me you're making her suffer.' In fact, as Mme Poujol confirmed, she and her husband had not had conjugal relations for eight years, although the birth of a new baby some nine months later indicated that the daughter's comment had hit home.[95]

Lourdes and Morzine: An Aside

The flurry of visions, apparitions and strange happenings that spread over Lourdes and the surrounding area in the months following Bernadette's experience eventually died away; sharp words and sound advice from Peyramale quietened the children, and the Episcopal Commission later reduced the remaining serious candidates to Bernadette alone. In retrospect this has an air of inevitability about it, but it was far from certain that the situation would remain so calm; had the Church lost its grip, or responded in a less certain fashion, then events could well have turned out differently.

To demonstrate how differently, it is only necessary to look at a remarkably similar situation at almost the same moment on the other side of the country. The town of Morzine had many similarities to Lourdes: both were on the fringes of France and in mountains, Lourdes in the Pyrenees bordering Spain, Morzine in the Alps close to Switzerland. Both were desperately poor and depended on emigration for survival,[96] both had long traditions of magic in which divine and diabolical balanced each other.[97] Both had an outbreak of visions that began with reported sightings of the Virgin. The difference was that Lourdes became an established Marian shrine, while Morzine fell victim to a twenty-year epidemic of demonic possession.[98]

The difference between them lay both in the events themselves and, critically, in the way the inhabitants analysed the events, for while the Lourdais saw Bernadette's visions as divine and looked to their clerics for interpretation and guidance, the Morzinois believed that an angry priest had acted as a witch, cursing them and unleashing an epidemic of animal illness and possession. In Morzine no one questioned the reality of possession, except the physicians who pointed to a dangerous hysteria. Most of all the bodies of those possessed were convulsed, their words vile, sacrilegious and full of imprecations. They manifested the 'classic' symptoms of possession by trembling at the sight of the Eucharist, speaking in tongues and foaming at the mouth when exorcized.

The evidence at Lourdes was of an entirely different nature. None of the visionaries showed any of these extravagances. Bernadette herself remained sublimely tranquil both during and after her apparitions, and, although her body was transformed by her ecstasy, it showed no pathology. The apparitions had a momentary healing effect, and doctors called in by the authorities to examine her also concluded there might be nothing wrong beyond a passing hallucination. The women who succeeded her seemed to have a more tainted or banal imagination, but no one called them mad, only misguided or fraudulent; and, while their bodies and physiognomies were sometimes less pleasing, no one suggested exorcism or medical treatment. Joséphine Albario seems to have had disturbing tremors, but she never fell ill and never ascribed her sadness or pain to devilish influence. Peyramale seems to have had little difficulty in keeping the situation under control.

Because the Morzinois believed their priest had in some way instigated their troubles, this source of reassurance was lost to them, and as a result the afflicted women were forced on a long search to find their own cure, which took them to local shrines, healers and even magnetizers in Switzerland. More importantly, their interminable search and loss of confidence in their priests created a vacuum that was filled by the secular authorities: while Peyramale fought off attempts to send Bernadette to a hospital, the Morzinois had no such defence. As the clergy at Morzine were not able to control events, the new French administration sent in a noted alienist, Adolphe Constans, the chief inspector of lunatic asylums, to restore order. However, his ministrations – which involved sending the worst-afflicted women to hospitals, bringing in troops and opening up roads to connect the town with the rest of the country – succeeded only in pushing the malady underground; twenty years later some women were still suffering from their demons.

This comparison is instructive not least for the way it demonstrates the continued acceptance of religious authority in rural culture. For Parisian alienists and secular commentators, *both* Lourdes and Morzine were variations of the same overarching pathology. Diabolic or divine, visions, ecstasies, trances and tremblings were all manifestations of hysteria, and the reluctance to make much of a distinction between demonic possession and divine apparitions inevitably coarsened the medical response. Dismissive of the religious yearnings and torments of those they examined, they missed the careful reasoning of the rural poor for whom such evaluations were vital. For different assessments required different responses: laughter and firm discipline for the child visionaries of Lourdes, fear and a desperate search for remedy in Morzine.

Strengthened by their conviction that miraculous events had taken place among them, the Lourdais and many others were prepared to defy officials who dismissed what they knew to be true. Once the objects were removed from the Grotto on 4 May, the struggle between the early cultists and the authorities began to grow ever more serious. On 15 June a barrier was built, closing the Grotto and sealing off the now beloved site. Many of the exploits of the child visionaries occurred as tension between the authorities and the poor was on the rise. The prefect and commissioner argued that the chapel contravened both civil and religious authorities, and for that reason they closed it, hoping thereby to suppress 'superstitious' outbreaks. Their action offended the religious feelings of the poor and also their Pyrenean pride; as a result, a campaign began to break down the barriers and resist the law. The struggle between the two forces was finely balanced, and the outcome at the beginning was uncertain. But the outside world was starting to hear news of events in the town; and, when interested 'foreigners' came to see for themselves, the Lourdais' campaign began a process that irreversibly transformed the town into a centre for a national, then an international, pilgrimage movement.

4

The Bishop, the Nanny and the Journalist: Lourdes Emerges on to the National Scene

Without the intervention of two factors from the outside world – the polemical skill of the Catholic political activist Louis Veuillot, and the apparent support of the Empress Eugénie in the person of Amirale Bruat, her son's governess – the battle between the Lourdais and the authorities might have remained a purely local matter. In apparently serendipitous visits in the summer of 1858, both these outsiders came to the town, defied the authorities and crossed the barriers to pray at the Grotto. In so doing, they completely altered the local balance of power in favour of the bishop, the mayor and the conservative notability at the expense of the regional administration. More importantly, perhaps, their presence was the first sign of a nascent alliance between the poor of Lourdes and some of the Parisian elite, which foiled all attempts by the civil authorities to implement the directives that central government had ostensibly endorsed. Differences between the ministries of cults and of the interior over the Grotto between July

1858 and January 1859 further confused official policy, allowing the Lourdais to exploit divisions and unseat the prefect, Baron Oscar Massy.

Massy was a well-respected member of the prefectoral corps, a man of sincere religious convictions who had long been friends with Mgr Laurence. Until the apparitions the prefect and the bishop had lived in almost perfect harmony. For these reasons Massy seemed at first glance an unlikely persecutor, but he was convinced that firmness was needed to safeguard 'true' religion from the damaging onslaught of popular 'superstition' that Bernadette's claims threatened to unleash. He undoubtedly anticipated that Laurence would take the same line, and felt betrayed when the bishop, through the Episcopal Commission of Inquiry he set up, began to take the apparitions seriously. Their friendship never recovered, and, in the ensuing battle over how to react, Massy – supposedly the embodiment of imperial authority whose word could scarcely be challenged – was outmanoeuvred, disregarded and finally forced out, his reputation in tatters.

In essence, this remarkable defeat was the product of a coincidence of interest between the Lourdais themselves, a new Catholic constituency, and the way Louis Napoleon's immediate political needs translated into regional policy. These broad trends, however, can only be properly understood within the context of small events and local concerns. At no other points in the history of the shrine are networks of people and interest so tightly connected, an interlocking puzzle of power and influence that seems to imply that the shrine became nothing more than an instrument of politics. But Lourdes was not the cynical product of elites pursuing their own aims of creating a new, popular Catholicism. The alliance, at this juncture, was of equal partners, the peripheral world of the Pyrenees stamping for ever its imprint on the spiritual and political agendas of those far away. Lourdes became Lourdes above all because of the simple appeal of its story, encouraging a partnership between the local people and the Parisian world that helped to form the distinctive spirituality of nineteenth-century Catholicism.

The Affair of the 'False Reports'

The imperial regime of Louis Napoleon projected an image of itself as hierarchical, authoritarian, tightly centralized and repressive. Emerging after a period of social revolution that struck not only the capital but also a newly, if intermittently, radicalized peasantry, the *coup d'état* that inaugurated the regime in December 1851 unleashed a reign of terror in which thousands were imprisoned and killed.[1] In the Pyrenees, the Second Republic established in 1848 had brought a renewed struggle against the forest guards and the debt-collectors, the old battle recast in the revolutionary rhetoric of freedom and social justice.[2] Not unlike other regions across France, many Pyrenean notables ultimately acquiesced in, if not positively welcomed, the order promised by Louis Napoleon, whose grip on the population slackened only slowly once in power. The documents on Lourdes – especially the mountain of paper produced by Jacomet and Dutour – testify to his officials' desire to maintain order at all costs: Jacomet in particular spent the lion's share of his time in surveillance work, sending off reams of reports to Massy, who, strengthened by new powers, followed all disturbances with a watchful eye.[3]

Laurentin sees the stereotypical portrayal of Napoleonic repression and centralization, in many respects embodied in the figure of prefectoral power, as key to the Lourdes story and illustrates it with an idealized image of the workings of government (see illus. 27). At the top stands the emperor, the fount of all power; under him comes his minister of state, Achille Fould, who directed the three Parisian offices active in the affairs of the Grotto: the ministries of cults, the interior and justice. From these, the chain of command descends into the Pyrenees, to Tarbes and Pau, where the bishop, prefect and general prosecutor report to the higher echelons and direct the men underneath them – Abbé Peyramale, Mayor Lacadé, Police Commissioner Jacomet and, finally, Imperial Prosecutor Dutour. At the bottom of this pyramid stands the small and insignificant figure of Bernadette Soubirous, in Pyrenean costume, holding her rosary.

A brilliant representation of an idealized image of the imperial bureaucracy, the drawing encapsulates many assumptions about the

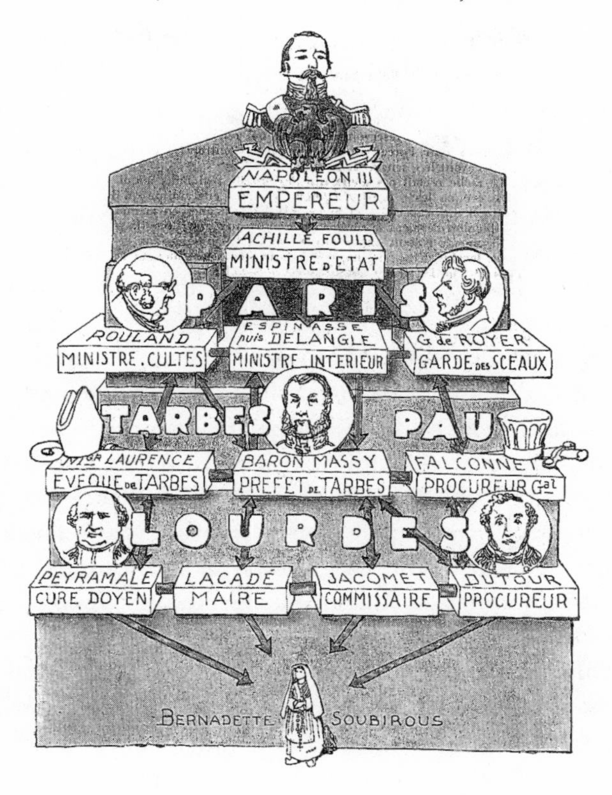

27. 'La Pyramide Administrative': France, from Napoleon III to Bernadette Soubirous, illustration from René Laurentin, Lourdes: Documents authentiques I, *1957*

relations between the Napoleonic state and the visionary. Although portrayed as a mere nothing, her fragile shoulders are made to bear the weight of this seemingly monolithic system. Such a picture suggests how miraculous her triumph was, for who could not be moved by the picture of the barely articulate representative of the devout poor triumphing so peacefully over all these powerful men? Yet, despite its appeal, the interpretation is wrong, for two important reasons.

First, Lourdes provides a remarkable example of how easily the administrative hierarchy, so integral to imperial self-perception and retrospective accounts of its power,[4] could be brushed aside by those claiming the direct authority of the emperor and the imperial court. For while the administration ran the country, the emperor and his wife sought to create a *personal* link with the French. The empress, Eugénie de Montijo, a languidly beautiful Spanish aristocrat of firm Catholic principles, hosted the new and glittering beau monde of the imperial elite at their chateau in Compiègne, bringing together the literati, the newly rich and the already established, forging a face-to-face connection based on a gracious, if formal hospitality.[5] But the Bonapartes were solicitous of more than the rich and famous only, paying particular attention to the rural population by making a series of well-publicized tours of the country in which the notability of the regions as well as the populace appeared to greet the emperor and his wife.[6] These elaborately choreographed affairs presented Napoleon as both distant head of state and man of the people, intimately acquainted and concerned with their welfare. Thus, during his triumphalist processions and displays of imperial grandeur – the voyage to the Midi and south-west in autumn 1852 passed through twenty-five towns and cities – he also received local deputations and established links with the population that bypassed the official channels of the administration.

This egalitarian and populist side of Bonapartism seems to have struck a chord among the peasant and artisanal population, for while the propertied classes looked to Louis Napoleon to fend off social revolution, the poor saw someone who could protect them from the machinations of the established political class.[7] Although the emperor suppressed the insurrection of the peasant left in the south-east after the coup,[8] the rural population in other regions supported him as a liberating messiah and defender of the poor. Nor was their allegiance of recent vintage; rather he drew on memories of a first Napoleon recast as the revolutionary emperor of the people.[9]

The strength of this tradition explains why the poor of Lourdes were able to believe in Louis Napoleon's special interest in their affairs. In particular, the story of the 'false reports', in which three women were taken to court for words thought dangerous to the security of the state, shows how nineteenth-century egalitarianism blended with older traditions of benevolent monarchism. Believing in the goodness of the ruler, subjects of absolute monarchs often convinced themselves that oppressive policies stemmed from self-serving or wicked advisers who misled otherwise well-intentioned kings.[10] The local officials' extreme reaction to what was essentially no more than idle gossip revivified this notion of purity at the top and corruption below, and thus unwittingly set the stage for the explosion of excitement that erupted when the imperial nanny arrived in the town.

The tale was banal enough, the result of local women's desire to find a solution to Bernadette's plight and their own wish to go to the Grotto. It seems that at least seven were involved, including Bernadette's mother and the sister of Abbé Pomian. The story first surfaced in the middle of May 1858, then became increasingly fantastical, its growth fuelled by the desire for powerful outsiders to break the impasse and defeat the increasingly hated prefect. Initially the story was that a Parisian journalist had arrived and spoken well of Bernadette, admiring her good fortune for having discovered the fountain. Before long this piece of news, retold at the communal bread oven, at the wash-house and then again on the common, grew until it was said that the minister of cults had sent a telegraph, then that the empress had sent Bernadette a present and asked her to pray for her. The final version was that the emperor himself had begged Bernadette to intercede for him with the Virgin and demanded that the prefect put back the objects Jacomet had removed.[11] At no point did anyone apparently consider that the emperor might be responsible for his local representative's actions.

The women charged for repeating these tales were the mainstay of the early struggles at the Grotto: Josèphe Barinque, a cobbler's wife; Cyprine Gesta, the *maîtresse* of the communal oven; and Anna Dupin, an impoverished housewife. Cyprine, the only woman not married and the mother of two children, knew the Soubirous family before the apparitions and helped Louise Soubirous with her children; she saw herself as one of the earliest patronesses of Bernadette and, after the second apparition, went every day to the Grotto.[12] When they spoke of deliverance by the emperor, their talk spread mistaken rumours that the Grotto was reopening.

Such irrepressible enthusiasm explains in large part an official response that, even twenty years later, dismayed the major participants. Dutour decided to take the matter to court, and warned Josèphe Barinque that she faced prison for spreading a 'false report'. Although Anna Dupin was frightened,[13] Josèphe merely laughed.[14] It turned out that Dutour was in effect bluffing, for the court appearance on 19

June resulted in nothing more than a fine of five francs plus costs.[15] Having overreacted once, however, the officials then made matters worse and, instead of letting the business drop, decided to take the case to appeal in Pau in the hope of getting a more severe punishment.

This fatal move conferred martyrdom on the three women involved, unified the opposition, and provoked some of the local notables to come to their defence. Already a new kind of alliance was forming *within* local society, crossing class boundaries in an extraordinary fashion. Thus, when Josèphe Barinque set off for Pau in an expensive rented carriage, she was accompanied by Dr Pierre-Romain Dozous – the local physician who chronicled the early miracles at the fountain – and had a letter from a Mlle Dauzat-Dembarrère, the sister of the local deputy, to give to the judge.[16] The women had free legal counsel (although it seemed that they later paid something for their defence) and arrived as virtual celebrities. Anna Dupin described how they stopped at the church of Bétharram on the way and there begged the Sisters of Igon to pray for them; all along the route the population came out to offer them good wishes and prayers.[17]

The case became acutely embarrassing for the administration, which was increasingly seen to be persecuting poor women with charges out of all proportion to their deeds. They were tried after a case of magic and extortion in which a Basque woman lost her fortune to a gypsy fortune-teller promising her love with a secret potion, and the contrast between the Spanish-speaking bohemians and these law-abiding women was made much of in the local press.[18] The defence attorney argued that what had occurred at Cyprine Gesta's oven was nothing more than gossip, a crime of which everyone's wife could be accused. His insistence that nothing they said had jeopardized the state's security convinced the judge, who, after making a speech against a too ready acceptance of miraculous healing, acquitted all three.

Twenty years later Josèphe and Cyprine were still aglow with triumph and considered the outbreak of a thunderstorm when the charge was read as proof of divine favour: Cyprine believed that the judges themselves had been afraid of this heavenly warning.[19] For others, the acquittal was evidence of Bernadette's prophetic powers: before they left for Pau, the visionary had remarked, 'Don't be afraid, it won't come to anything.'[20] The officials had not only made themselves look both cruel and ridiculous, they had also immeasurably strengthened the shrine's supporters. In a letter to the bishop, Peyramale could hardly disguise his glee:

There are great celebrations in the town. The women who had to go to Pau on Monday under accusation of spreading false information have been acquitted by the imperial court. Lawyers fought for the honour of defending them. Their accusers, the enemies of the Grotto, did not emerge spotless from this affair.[21]

Such local incidents built on the tradition of dissidence I have already described and added a matriarchal twist by the way poor women were seen as victimized and had to defend themselves in court. But while this resistance had a special piquancy because of the Grotto, it was not uncommon across communes in France during the Empire. The commune was the basic unit of administration and revealed the ambiguities of a regime that sought to contain all opposition and simultaneously offer an apprenticeship in democracy through the use of infrequent plebiscites based on universal male suffrage. It thus rested on a paradoxical mixture of repressive tutelage and the sovereignty of the people, in which universal suffrage lived side by side with strong centralized direction.[22]

This uneasy coexistence led increasingly in the 1860s to local struggles between the administration and population. These battles were largely divorced from the intellectual struggles of Paris and the great cities, which concentrated more on liberalism, anti-clericalism and supporting Italian nationalists against the Pope. Rather, disputes centred on the way the administration of the Church seemed to impose on the people. They were angered by the cost of building new churches, as well as by the upkeep and administration of presbyteries. Priestly power could be a cause of dispute, as when clerics withheld absolution at the confessional or overcharged for baptisms, marriages or funerals.[23] Historians have argued that out of such conflicts, small scale but endlessly repeated, emerged a rural republicanism in areas previously loyal to a Catholic social order.

This now conventional explanation supports a vision of nineteenth-century secularization and political development that led inevitably to the Third Republic, with its anti-clericalist and egalitarian ethos.

But the struggle over the Grotto shows dissidence against the state running in an entirely different direction. Instead of becoming a target for popular discontent, Peyramale led the movement against the prevailing secular authorities, a role not unknown in the Pyrenees, where clerics had, in the past, been important mediators between the state and local society.[24] Moreover, the mayor, Lacadé, despite moments of double-dealing, joined the clergy in urging the cause of the Grotto, rather than acting as the anti-clerical representative of the municipal council. Lourdes therefore overturned the opposition of cleric and mayor that is such a stereotype of this period in France.

At the same time there was nothing of the classic alliance between aristocrats and poor peasants that typified the 1793 counter-revolutionary reaction of the Vendée, for example.[25] Rather, in a fashion that defies the usual, even complacent categories of political left and right governing modern French history, the reaction of the Lourdais manifested piety and radical protest in equal measure. The struggle for the Grotto, far from alienating the populace from national currents, meant that the Lourdais became visible to the imperial court and involved in the fiercest and most significant Catholic polemics of the nineteenth century.

The Encounters

The trial and acquittal of the three women at Pau, while causing a stir, was nothing in comparison to the sensation aroused by the visits of two prominent outsiders. It is hard to know how much was choreographed and how much was coincidence in the almost simultaneous appearances of Louis Veuillot and the governess of the prince imperial, Amirale Bruat, in July. More than any other single event, their arrival transformed Lourdes and made it finally impossible for Massy and Jacomet to impose their authority. From then on the Lourdes story was no longer defined by local or even regional initiatives; it became part of a national movement, in which locals continued to play major parts, but now in alliance with powerful men and women from Paris.

When Veuillot (see illus. 28) arrived on the scene, he was the most powerful Catholic leader of his age, and his interest began the process

28. Louis Veuillot (1813–83)

that turned the Grotto into a focus for struggles between different visions of Catholicism.[26] The son of a master cooper and a woman from Boynes, not far from Orléans, his humble origins, which he enjoyed embellishing, were important for his populist credentials and for the contrast he drew between himself and the liberal elitism of his more intellectual opponents within the Church. He saw his family's irreligion as a dangerous legacy of the Revolution and bourgeois Voltaireanism and condemned both for producing the spiritual illiteracy of the poor that he considered the great crime of the century.

He rose to national and international fame through the law and journalism, his career taking off in the 1830s as the editor of the *Mémorial de la Dordogne* in Périgeux, a little-known regional newspaper quickly transformed by his peculiar brand of radical conservatism and literary virtuosity. Veuillot was an autodidact, learning both the French classics and later his theology through sheer wit and determination. His talent recognized, he moved in the highest circles of literary journalism, and was known for his extravagance, amorous entanglements and duels.

He was distinguished from other literary figures by his conversion, which took place when he went to Rome in 1838. There he had a private audience with the Pope, and later described his spiritual awakening in his books *Le Parfum de Rome* and then *Rome et La Lorette*. His move astounded his Parisian friends not simply because it happened, but because it was so extreme, embracing the religion of saints, miracles, stigmata and relics in an unquestioning faith totally at odds with his past scepticism.[27] He had not converted to ascend the ecclesiastical ladder, but instead sought to promote, as a layman, a faith explicitly opposed to the 'progress' of the modern world. True to his populist persuasions, he took over *L'Univers*, and began a collaboration with its editor, Melchior du Lac, an ultramontanist *émigré* – a term used to denote the aristocrats who had fled France during the Revolution – who shaped his Catholic education. By dismissing modern science and thought, the editors of *L'Univers* asserted their Christian faith and reassured the parish clergy that they need not be discomfited by their ignorance of new intellectual trends. All over France men like Peyramale read the newspaper, finding in it confirmation of their political views and often inadequate theological musings. It was a kind of ultramontanist forum with a militaristic stamp, with the priests who read it cast as soldiers in the papal cause.[28]

From the pages of *L'Univers* Veuillot advanced the cause of ultramontanism in France, a complex religious movement with political, social and liturgical dimensions. For in its origins, ultramontanism – literally, 'over-the-mountainism', referring specifically to Rome beyond the Alps – was a philosophical and political response to the disasters wrought by the Revolutionary and Napoleonic periods. In their wake, the conservative political thinker Joseph de Maistre sought to reinvigorate papal power in defence of the *droits de Dieu* against the secular, revolutionary appeal of the *droits de l'homme*. His *Du Pape* (1819) argued for papal infallibility and the Pope's central role as the guarantor of order and absolutism. Against the growing separation of Church and state and the privatization of religion, ultramontanists argued for a theocracy based on the necessary power of absolutism embodied in papal government, views popular among the political class during the Restoration.

In this incarnation, ultramontanism represented a conservative intervention, a call for the return of the political and spiritual culture of the Old Regime. But the movement took on a wholly different appeal in France during the 1820s and 1830s under the philosopher–priest Félicité Lamennais. His works reached an audience of young, intellectual Catholics who responded enthusiastically to the philosophical vitality of a believer who could compete with the *libres-penseurs*. Students, however, were only part of a movement that also touched many poor country priests and seminarians. For the reconstitution of the French Church in the wake of the Revolution and Empire had created a new constituency of discontented clerics. Under the auspices of the Concordat imposed by Napoleon in 1801, the Pope had reorganized the French dioceses, and the clergy had became employees of the state. The 'organic articles' invested the bishops with discretionary power over their subordinates, and ushered in a new and more fraught relationship with the lower clergy. These men resented their lack of security and the way bishops could summarily move them from one post to another. Often raw recruits drawn from the peasantry, they keenly felt their inferior education and status, and increasingly advocated an enhanced papacy to support them in their struggles against the bishops.[29]

Lamennais offered such people an appealing vision of a universal and egalitarian society under the Pope's beneficent direction, giving them a decisive role.[30] His ultramontanism, therefore, was decidedly anti-establishment, defying the episcopate, condemning the Jesuits, decrying the absolutist pretensions of many monarchists and denouncing the Cartesian rationalism that permeated the Sulpician establishment of Parisian educational training central to the formation of the Church's elite. When his targets in turn attacked him, he championed papal prerogatives and went so far as to advocate a Christian collectivity devoted to political and social justice, a programme increasingly inflected by a call to the masses: 'Religion, Catholicism, at the service of . . . the people!'[31] This attempted fusion of papal power with a prophetic vision of Catholic social solidarity, however, went too far for the papacy. Lamennais's political philosophy and his journal *L'Avenir* were condemned by the Pope in 1832; in 1834 he seems to have stopped practising his priestly functions and his bitter attack on the Church in the *Affaire de Rome* in 1836 confirmed the irretrievable breakdown between the idealistic theologian and the hierarchy.

Veuillot echoed Lamennais's anti-establishment tone while stripping it of his left-wing politics. He took up cudgels against the episcopate, which in France represented the Gallican strand of Catholicism. Gallicanism had sought to maintain the many prerogatives of the French Church against papal domination in the seventeenth century, to secure an independence in matters of appointment, patronage and liturgy. After the Revolution and Empire, the episcopacy no longer enjoyed royal protection, but retained its status through its training and higher social origins.[32] Within the Church, the bishops were wedded to maintaining their authority over those below them at the same time as they conserved their traditional independence from Rome in large areas of Church governance. It was these bishops who generally tended to support a more liberal view of Catholicism as a means of reconciling faith with nineteenth-century intellectual trends.

While the papacy ultimately rejected Lamennais's populist programme, there was sympathy with his assault on the Gallican ascendency, and the actions of Pius IX in mid century particularly demonstrated a desire to bring the bishops under tighter control. For example, by promulgating the dogma of the Immaculate Conception in 1854 virtually without consultation, he sought to show his power to decree on dogma without episcopal aid and support. The 1864 encyclical *Quanta cura* followed this path more openly still by denouncing everything associated with nineteenth-century political, social and scientific thought – rationalism, statism, socialism, political economy and naturalism – a blanket condemnation that blasted the hopes of bishops trying to develop an accommodation with secular government. Ultimately, ultramontanist doctrine culminated in the embrace of papal infallibility as a powerful means of bolstering the papacy and standing firm against modernism in all its forms.

The men behind the ultramontanist movement in France were the leading lights of Catholic intellectual culture. For example, a man like Charles de Montalembert, of aristocratic descent and English birth, whose father had fled in the wake of the Revolution, promoted the resurrection of the piety of the Middle Ages, advocating the re-enactment of some medieval 'purity' prior to the corruptions of

Gallicanism. Others, such as Jean-Baptiste Henri Lacordaire, concluded that the only hope for the French Church lay in the restoration of religious orders that would bypass the authority of the diocese; he became a Dominican in 1839 and opened a house in Nancy in 1843, but was ousted as the head of the French Dominicans for his moderate political views in 1850.[33] He in turn followed in the footsteps of Dom Prosper Guéranger, who had already refounded the Benedictines and begun re-creating plainchant at Solesmes,[34] an important move in the campaign to standardize the liturgy, eradicating variations that in France stretched back to the eighth century.

Veuillot stood on the shoulders of such men, sharing their ultramontanist convictions and attachment to the nineteenth-century cult of the medieval. But here the similarities end for, while they were the products of Catholic intellectualism, his uncompromising stance and mordant style required a populist mode of expression. Veuillot turned to the right during the insurrections of 1848, a move hastened by the death of the archbishop of Paris, Mgr Denis-Auguste Affre, killed while trying to mediate between the government and the insurgents.[35] Thereafter, his anti-socialist tirades, his exploitation of the cleavages between lower and higher churchmen, and his celebration of popular piety – what may have been seen as 'superstition' by many a bishop – were the elements that ensured his newspaper's widespread appeal.

By 1850 Veuillot's *L'Univers* was *the* mouthpiece of popular Catholic opinion, read by all religious men and women who resisted the secularism of the modern age. When he came to Lourdes, his words reverberated more forcefully within the Catholic community than those of any cleric. His influence, however, did not last that long. In the beginning Veuillot had seemed perfectly situated to defend the new order emerging under Prince Napoleon, who seemed to share his populist authoritarianism. But the moment the emperor began to threaten the temporal power of Pius IX, he reacted with vituperation: he accused Louis Napoleon of abandoning the Pope to Italian nationalists and was promptly shut down in 1860.[36]

Veuillot's initial contact with the Lourdais on 20 July appears fortuitous. In his mid forties and at the height of his political powers, he was in the region to take the waters, visit local Catholic dignitaries and see the mountains. Like many a tourist, he stopped at Lourdes to catch the stage-coach to Bagnères. One memoir recounts how he went into the local café, where he heard men pouring scorn on the Grotto. The pharmacist Clément-Dominique Pailhasson announced that he was ready to entertain the possibility that the apparitions were indeed supernatural. When he had finished, Veuillot shook his hand and discoursed at some length about miracles and the chance that one had indeed taken place at the Grotto. The intervention left his audience slightly dumbstruck, as it would appear that few of those present realized who he was.[37] Adélaïde Monlaur, who relayed all the gossip to her cousin, spoke only of an intriguing 'unknown gentleman who went into cafés, circles, and got involved in discussions about the Grotto'. But she soon picked up other details, which suggested that, whoever he was, the man was of singular importance: 'One day, just after the bishop of Soissons had said mass at Lourdes, he met this gentleman and immediately embraced him, telling M. Le Curé that he came from one of the most important families in the country.'[38]

This appearance of happenstance in Veuillot's arrival must be taken with a large pinch of salt, however. About three weeks before coming to the town, Veuillot had written to his brother that 'this Lourdes business may well become a second edition of La Salette',[39] a statement that perhaps indicates something of his thinking and intentions about the Grotto well in advance of his visit. While in Bagnères he met not only the local bishop, Laurence, but also his colleagues, Mgr Ignace-Armand de Garsignies, the bishop of Soissons, and the archbishop of Auch, Mgr Antoine de Salinis, an ultramontanist who was later a key figure in winning imperial favour for the Grotto.[40] This meeting took place only days before Laurence decided to appoint an ecclesiastical commission to investigate the apparitions and cures, and before Veuillot made his way to the Grotto illegally on 28 July. Jacomet noted with irritation the constant coming and going, and no doubt believed that they were planning to 'make' the miracles of Lourdes: it seems more than likely his suspicions were not exaggerated.[41]

Thus, on the 28th and with no apparent hint of his plans for the day, Veuillot wrote again to his brother and described the excitement the apparitions had caused. 'It's a miracle the administration doesn't want, in defiance of the people, who do',[42] a comment that sums up his populist and anti-establishment philosophy as well as his theology. In a letter to his sister, he described his burgeoning spiritual journey, beginning at Bétharram, where he had been greeted by Père Michel Garicoïts, a missionary of Basque origin famous in the region for his re-Christianization campaign.[43] This man, one of the most inspirational Catholics in the region, invited Veuillot to stay in the 'bishop's bedroom'.[44] So moved was he by the ambience that he spent the night of the 27th in prayer in the chapel, rose early and made his way up the famous stations of the cross, the crowning artistic glory of the region's nineteenth-century ecclesiastical renaissance (see illus. 29). From there he began the well-publicized advance on the Grotto.

29. The Calvary of the Stations of the Cross, Bétharram, which were reconstructed between 1840 and 1870

His journey was preceded, however, by that of Amirale Bruat, her three daughters and a nun. On one level, this woman seemed to be the soul of discretion, her comportment appropriate to a woman on pilgrimage to a holy spot. On another, the extent of her equipage and the nature of her attire alerted everyone to the arrival of a 'great lady', and, for those inclined towards political speculation, the intervention of the court and most probably the empress in the affairs of the Lourdais. Her trip to Lourdes seemed to answer the fantasy wishes expressed at the bread oven by the local women. Here was a clear example of someone within the emperor's domestic circle taking a special interest in 'their' Virgin, acknowledging the power of Notre-

Dame de Lourdes and also highlighting the scandal of the barriers. Abbé Pomian greeted her personally and believed in the providential nature of the visit. He also summoned Bernadette to be interviewed privately by the ladies, her narrative in patois translated by the tobacco warehouseman, whom they mistook for the schoolteacher.[45] Bernadette accompanied them in the afternoon to the Grotto but refused to cross the barrier, thereby demonstrating her obedience to authority and her unwillingness to be seen to be taking too active a role in events.

In the ensuing drama, the key local actor was the *garde champêtre* Pierre Callet. A member of the ragtail force of rural policemen under the authority of the mayor, Callet typified the demoralized and poorly paid functionary at the very bottom of the administrative hierarchy. Such figures guarded the fields against fire and vandalism, investigated forest violations, made arrests and composed *procès-verbaux*, or policemen's reports.[46] While keen to keep his job and hence obliged to toe the line in public, in private he was in favour of the Grotto; he liked Lacadé and sought to do his duty, but was disinclined to go against local opinion:

> I had a poodle: I met people on the road who were going down and they said, 'We're going to the Grotto.' I told them: 'I'm off to dinner . . . you've nothing to fear for a while.' So they went on down. When I came back, my poodle was following me. Before we got to the bridge, the dog started running, out of habit, up to the Grotto, as if the good Lord had given him a mind to go and have a look up at the Grotto and come back. When people saw the dog, they said, 'Callet's not far'; they climbed back up and laughed at me and I was laughing too. It was God's will that the dog played that trick; my dog was at the Grotto while I was still on the bridge over the Gave. He saved the others and he saved me from breaking the law; everyone was astonished – I called him 'sheep'.[47]

In the case of Amirale Bruat and her entourage, his position was more difficult. The entire town saw her passing through the streets, and Callet could hardly pretend to be unaware of her intentions: he had little alternative but to follow, fully uniformed and ready to impose his authority.[48]

He was extremely discomfited to find the great lady, her three daughters and the nun all praying, and was reduced to standing in a hiding place so as not to disturb them. At the same time that he was wondering what to do next, he was confronted with another, even more perturbing incident. Coming from the woodland path on the other side were priests surrounding an imposing figure in a white hat.[49] This stately figure was, of course, Veuillot, who had coincidentally, or purposefully, arrived only a few minutes later.

While the women were the picture of sumptuous supplication – all of them except for the nun resplendent in crinolines – the men were more active and even seemed inclined to provoke confrontation. Callet disappointed Veuillot by not putting up much resistance, sweating profusely instead and looking faintly ridiculous in his 'helmet with gold braid and eagle, and a guard's badge on his arm'.[50] Rather than arresting them all, he seemed to want them just to go away, pointing out the barrier and telling them that it was forbidden to enter. Veuillot dramatically replied, 'So they don't want anyone praying to the good Lord here!'[51] – a sentence that, one suspects, was more designed for the ears of sympathizers than for those of the policeman.

Perhaps more interesting was Callet's interaction with the women. In contrast to Veuillot, they seemed utterly unaware of the brouhaha caused by their piety and, when Callet asked for their names, appeared not to realize that they had broken the law. They willingly obliged, with one daughter politely inscribing her name in his notebook before returning to her prayers. Callet then made a show of doing his job, lowered himself into the Grotto and threw a few bouquets into the Gave. Far from being alarmed by the majesty of the law, the women treated him like a servant, asking him to fill their water container so they might offer it to an ailing friend in Paris; then they told him to cut some of the grass, a precious object that made Bruat visibly 'joyeuse'. Callet had now forgotten his duties so completely that he even picked flowers for them from the wild rose bush and was offered a tip for his pains.[52] This reminded him of his official capacity, and he refused the tip in horror; but Bruat was not to be put off from an act of charity she had determined upon, so she went to his house, found it empty and left 'a hundred sous' on top of the commode.[53] In this gesture Bruat imitated the charitable impulses of her patroness and superior, the empress herself, who was famous for such acts of generosity.[54] Callet, meanwhile, had run off to Lacadé to report the encounter and was sent back to their hotel:

> They stood up as though receiving a prince; they complimented me (without saying they'd left anything at my house), gave me a drink and clinked their glasses with me. I didn't dare [refuse]; with men I would have been more resolute, but I didn't want to spurn the honour they did me.[55]

After his appearance at the Grotto, Veuillot left Lourdes to visit the Cirque de Gavarnie, but he returned the next day with twelve ecclesiastics to the place Marcadal. This time he met local personalities and made an even greater impression, then went back to Paris, where he wrote an inflammatory piece in *L'Univers* describing the apparitions and championing the Grotto. This was a turning point in making Lourdes nationally known and a Catholic *cause célèbre*. Veuillot's reputation as a vituperative defender of the faith all but goaded opponents within the intellectual and political class of the Second Empire to respond in some way. The fierce polemic that ensued starkly contrasted his ultramontanist 'superstitions' with assertions of liberal and anti-clerical common sense. The debates were strident, and Veuillot did not necessarily carry the day, but this was of small importance. By the autumn of 1858 few literate French had *not* heard of Lourdes.[56]

Mgr Laurence and the Church in the Pyrenees

Veuillot came from outside the diocese, bringing with him the preoccupations of the capital and international Catholicism. Mgr Laurence, in contrast, was a man of the people, working to bring his diocese into the national mainstream (see illus. 30). His support for the Grotto was not simply another version of Veuillot's brand of ultramontanism, for his position on various institutional and religious matters revealed a flexibility and pragmatism that defied easy categorization. His training within, and then leadership of, the Pyrenean Church provides a microcosm of the hardships facing French Catholicism in the first half of the century. The lingering, embittered legacy of the Revolution, the

30. Mgr Bertrand-Sévère Laurence (1790–1870)

uphill struggle to find recruits and rebuild in the aftermath of the Concordat, all shaped his outlook and vision of the Grotto as both miracle and as sanctuary.[57] As a political bishop eager to work with the Empire, he saw the new order as both good for the Church and good for the region's development.[58] These themes appeared in his careful management of the apparitions, so that his diocese – distant, poor and relatively undistinguished – became one of the most famous in the world.

Although too young to have experienced the turbulence of the revolutionary years personally, Laurence's clerical career was in many respects an elaborate response to a period that divested the Church of much of its elite, its property and even its clergy.[59] He was born in Oroix, fifteen kilometres from Tarbes, and of substantial peasant stock. In his youth there was little inkling of his future vocation, or of his special contribution to rethinking the institution of the Church in the Pyrenees. The young Laurence began as an apprentice to an *officier de santé* and barber surgeon, which may have aided his later interest in the medical aspects of the cures at the Grotto.[60] Fear that he might be conscripted in 1809 led clerical patrons to place him in a seminary at the new institution of Saint-Pé, not far from Lourdes and close to Notre-Dame de Bétharram, where he later became a teacher and then director.[61] As in so many dioceses throughout France, the clergy of the Bigorre sought to educate new priests. Here the rudest of young peasants joined the ranks and, not unlike Julien Sorel in *The Red and the Black*, sought to travel one of the few avenues of social mobility.

Laurence was a typical product of this system and was permanently marked by his educational deficiencies, learning French as a second language and always retaining a strong Gascon accent and turn of phrase. But rather than hiding his origins, he sought to capitalize upon them: he was self-consciously Bigourdan, and enjoyed returning to his native village to joke with the peasant women and speak with local shepherds.[62] Laurence's Bigourdan dialect was in the same family as Bernadette's own patois; their shared language and Marian tradition[63] perhaps explain his instinctive veneration for an apparition that spoke in the tongue of the poor and illiterate.[64]

Long before Lourdes became his region's crowning glory, Laurence had restored Marian devotion in his diocese.[65] His pride and joy – indeed the centre of his bishopric – was Garaison, geographically at the intersection of three departments, the Hautes-Pyrénées, the Haute-Garonne and the Gers (see illus. 2). He saw Garaison as a centre of pilgrimage, missionary work and religious education, and drew from its past a vision of piety and militancy against the enemies of Christendom. From 1530 Garaison had attracted pilgrims, until it was ravaged in 1590 by Protestants seeking to destroy the statue of Notre-Dame de Piété that adorned, and still adorns, the altar. Restored between 1604 and 1635 by Pierre Geoffroy, who obtained the right to create a corps of twelve chaplains and to construct a new building, Garaison was ultimately consecrated by a papal bull of 1625.[66]

Laurence made the apposite parallels between his own era and that of the religious wars. The bones of the visionary Anglèze de Sagazan were saved by a pious woman in 1790,[67] but the buildings and land of the Garaison chapel were sold off as *biens nationaux* in 1797, suffering the same fate as other Church properties in the midst of the revolutionary turmoil. For forty-three years the chapel was closed, and then Laurence found the money to reopen it, thereby restoring to the Church what men like Laurence believed had been unwarranted dispossession. He installed there his diocesan missionaries, the Garaison Fathers, who later administered the shrine at Lourdes. This order was key to the region's re-Catholicization campaign, conducted in a manner that recalled the fervour of the Counter-Reformation. Its leader, Jean-Louis Peydessus, brought Anglèze's relics back from their hiding place in the village of Saint-Frajou, and villagers accompanied the return of the remains to the chapel, tapping deep memories of local piety: 'Such was the fidelity shown, over almost three centuries, to the memory of the apparitions!'[68] Forms of religious enthusiasm that might denote 'superstitions', such as processions, relics and miracles, despised by many eighteenth-century clerics with enlightened views, were reinvigorated by reinvented rituals with regional roots.[69] The new priests of the post-revolutionary generations often shared the same religious sensibilities as their parishioners;[70] once tamed by clerical direction, these popular devotions increasingly attracted the support of a hierarchy now peopled by men of humble origins such as Laurence.

This combination of regional Marian devotion and institutional re-Catholicization came together under the Second Empire, which Laurence saw as providential, enabling him to pursue his programme with the support of the Bonapartist bourgeoisie of Tarbes. The emperor made the south-west a priority in his provincial policy and spent summers at Biarritz, while the empress took a special interest in the region and patronized the hospital at Barèges, one of Laurence's pet projects.[71] Laurence gave his loyalty in return, delivering a celebratory discourse in June 1861 for the inauguration of the chapel of Saint-Sauveur, despite Louis Napoleon's perceived double-dealing on the Italian peninsula; if Louis Napoleon had decided to woo Catholics back into the fold, the bishop of Tarbes was willing to help, reminding listeners not only of his assistance in building the church, but also of his aid in opening up the region with the 89-metre Pont-Napoléon across the perilous mountain landscape.[72] For Laurence regarded himself as a modernizer. He saw religion not as a restraint on local mentalities, but as an essential cultural resource for mediating relations between the Pyrenees and the nation, an aim fully realized when Lourdes became such an important shrine.

Diocesan Power and the Imperial State

There is little evidence to suggest that at the beginning Laurence showed much interest in the apparitions, and he only paid serious attention when Peyramale sent him a report. As early as 11 April he delivered what was his considered view of events to the prefect, prefiguring the line of thought that led him to establish the Episcopal Commission of Inquiry at the end of July:

> The doctors rule out fraud; that's something; they allow that hallucination and ecstasy might follow from a cerebral lesion. It's possible – very possible; it's even very likely. For myself, I admit the value of their approach. I only want to add that I believe the supernatural is possible, although in the present case I await further proof of it.[73]

In arguing thus he distanced himself from his friend and ally Baron Massy, as well as from Dutour, Jacomet and others who saw such 'superstitious nonsense' as an affront to religion. Laurence held his ground against their scepticism and, perhaps, showed his better understanding of the faithful. However, he was also concerned to move such an important matter out of their hands, seeking – as he had with Marian shrines throughout the region – to channel belief in a manner that benefited the Church. For Laurence, the most moving aspect of Bernadette's description of the apparition was when she stated that the white vision was the Immaculate Conception, and he reportedly wept when the young girl placed her hands together in imitation.[74]

The Lourdes affair shows an important, if unusual increase of diocesan power at the expense of the prefect and, hence, of the secular arm of imperial administration. After considerable wrangling, Massy was forced out and transferred to another post,[75] an illustration of the way that religious authority, commonly deemed to be losing ground in temporal affairs in nineteenth-century France, could in the right circumstances show its still considerable mettle. At the end of

August the bishop's position was further strengthened by the growing number of seminarians, priests, nuns, bourgeois lay men and women, as well as people of aristocratic lineage who crossed the barriers and left their names for Callet to write down.[76] Although the interdiction was still nominally enforced, pilgrims visited every part of the site, and even climbed into the niche to pluck off a few branches from the wild rose bush. The poor were virtually absent from these lists, and indeed they seemed content to let their social superiors deal with the authorities, as the Grotto's fortunes began to enter a new stage.

By 9 September another tale developed in Lourdes to give form to the locals' belief in the emperor's personal interest in their affairs. The rumour stated that Louis Napoleon had sent 'an electric dispatch' to reopen the Grotto, and the telegram came to symbolize a means of cutting through levels of bureaucracy and obstruction. The story was widely assumed to have some substance, because of the arrival of Joseph-Gaspard Tasher de la Pagerie, a relative of the imperial family, who was personally interrogated by Jacomet until his identity was made known.[77]

Under the weight of this popular pressure, episcopal manoeuvring and outside interference, the local administration began to give way: on 18 September the Grotto briefly reopened, and Jacomet was obliged, once again, to begin logging the presents and objects deposited there by the faithful. Perhaps one of the most striking developments of August and early September was the way the Lourdais moved from centre stage, ceding place to eminent outsiders. Lacadé and Peyramale restrained themselves, and left the task of illicit entry to the more socially privileged. Thus when a bona fide clerical procession did take place, it was led not by Peyramale but by the somewhat unconventional 'Père Hermann', or Hermann Cohen, a priest of Jewish origins and passionate Catholic beliefs.[78]

The high point of Louis Napoleon's probable involvement at Lourdes came when Achille Fould, minister of state and one of the most powerful men in the country, arrived on 24 September 1858 to see for himself. Fould even expressed a desire to see Bernadette herself, a prospect a confident Peyramale viewed with equanimity.[79] The encounter never took place: Fould arrived late, rushed through the town and had not a moment to spare for the young shepherdess. The authenticity of Bernadette's experience seemed not to exercise him unduly; he seemed more concerned with the political implications, and the fracas caused by Veuillot's advocacy. The administration concluded that the Grotto posed no threat and it was allowed to reopen definitively on 5 October.

There was no obvious reason for Louis Napoleon to support the shrine, but timing and political events, perhaps, made it prudent, for the apparitions came during an uncertain period when his regime needed the support of the Church. The previous year had ended with elections that produced widespread abstentions and republican inroads in the big cities. This setback was followed by the Orsini assassination attempt, when the emperor and empress were nearly killed by a bomb. Aimed at hastening Italian unification by sparking turmoil in France, the attack resulted in a wave of repression against the leftists and an increased reliance on the political and religious right. The moment did not last long, however; in international politics Louis Napoleon soon swung back to a support for Italian unification, a switch that for ever lost him the trust of Catholics like Veuillot, who denounced what they considered his duplicity. Only in the south-west did such manoeuvrings have no impact. There, Louis Napoleon's frequent holidays in Biarritz and apparent support for Lourdes perpetuated his popularity among Catholics, when many in the rest of the country turned away from his regime.

The political background to the establishment of Lourdes shows the need for a revised interpretation of the way the Second Empire worked. Traditionally presented as adamantine in structure and chain of command, the Bonapartist administration, with its enlarged power for the prefects, was expressly designed to contain opposition and repress dissidence. In this scheme of things Massy should have been the most powerful man in the department, and the measures he took against the Grotto demonstrated at least his own unswerving belief in his authority. The ultimate fate of his decrees indicates that the distance between the theory of hierarchy and authority and its practice was considerable. Lourdes shows how the intervention of the imperial court – especially Eugénie's interest in religion – blended with popular belief to override its own administration. That a combination of Veuillot's populist piety and a group of interested bishops could sway the emperor himself shows how much flexibility Louis Napoleon allowed himself in the running of France.

The story of how Lourdes emerged on to the national stage blended old and new narratives of power, influence and patronage, revitalizing forceful myths and popular systems of belief in ways that promoted the shrine's fortunes. It did not matter that Louis Napoleon was a parvenu who took power through a violent *coup d'état*, for the Lourdais preferred to cast him in the role of the benevolent monarch unknowingly foiled by wicked advisers. Veuillot exemplified the militant and populist tendencies of the Second Empire, and the growing strength of journalistic opinion-makers; his arrival at Lourdes, however, was like that of a travelling grandee, a man of lordly patronage rather than the political activist he most certainly was. But it fitted the fairy-tale style of the story – his coming had even been prefigured in the gossip at the wash-house that landed some of the town's women in court. Petty officials like Callet – keen to retain their position at the same time that they sought to ingratiate themselves with neighbours and superiors – became representatives of the sturdy peasant class who stood by their religious convictions. Amirale Bruat was kindly and courtly, bestowing generous gifts and Christian charity; of the cast of characters, she seems to have played out her role with the least evidence of self-interest, although she too may well have served the Catholic lobby in the imperial court by unofficially representing the empress. The fact that the others did not play their parts as effectively did not matter. Achille Fould, for example, never interviewed the visionary, although one might have expected a moving scene between the monarch's emissary and the innocent seer. That such an encounter never took place, however, did not disturb the political calculations that moved the shrine into national prominence.

By the end of 1858 attempts to close the shrine had been tried and had failed. The Grotto was open to all who wished to visit it, and the development of Lourdes could proceed with little official hindrance. That did not mean that it would inevitably develop as it did. Essential to how events would unfold was Bernadette herself. What she wanted, how she would behave, whether she would fit in with the Church's plan for the shrine's future, were all as unknown as her own nature.

5

Bernadette

In the eight years after the apparitions Lourdes changed dramatically, and Bernadette grew into young womanhood. Neither process was straightforward, and a telling anecdote from May 1866 reveals the constant tension generated by the visionary's presence near the sanctuary. In that year the crypt was completed, the first structure to be finished since the beginning of massive building works four years earlier, a process that transformed the Grotto and created the domain of the sanctuary of Lourdes.[1] The festivities surrounding this inauguration were extravagant, lasting three days with ceremonies, processions and the first mass at the Grotto. Bernadette tried not to attract attention by hiding among the ranks of the Children of Mary;[2] she went so far as to resort to an innocent subterfuge to keep the curious at bay, giving the mother superior a beseeching look to make sure she was not pointed out.[3] She could not escape, however, for on the last day the courtyard of the hospice where she now lived filled with people greeting her appearances with excited ovations: 'Oh, the pretty saint . . . the pretty virgin . . . how happy she is.'[4] When she went to the Grotto, she only escaped being mobbed because the Sisters of Nevers formed a protective circle, fending off the groping hands trying to touch her or cut off bits of her veil. One man claimed that he would rather touch Bernadette's hand than have a thousand francs.[5] Later that night so many people climbed up on the walls and on to the columns of the hospice to see her that the mother superior had to ask soldiers convalescing inside for protection. In the end she directed Bernadette to promenade under the cloister, with the girl objecting: 'You're showing me off like a fattened cow.'[6]

The date of this story is significant, for within two months Bernadette had left Lourdes for ever to continue her noviciate in Nevers. More importantly, it symbolized the final moment of intersection between the visionary and the sanctuary she had called into being. From the moment the apparitions ended, Bernadette became marginal to events at Lourdes; indeed, Peyramale recognized this fact when he wrote in May 1860 that 'her mission is finished'.[7] None the less, he also realized that, for the moment, she was still essential: her Pyrenean simplicity, her rustic dress, her straightforward glance, her patois, were in themselves part of the message of Notre-Dame de Lourdes. In choosing her, the Virgin had singled out the ignorant, the poverty-stricken, the rural and the dispossessed. At the same time Bernadette was clearly a 'problem' as long as she stayed in Lourdes, with the behaviour of the crowds in May 1866 demonstrating the perpetual possibility that her presence would divert attention away from the sanctuary, the Grotto and the Virgin herself.

Lourdes is inconceivable without Bernadette, yet the shrine could not fully develop in the diocese's hands until she left. At Lourdes people visit her birthplace and early home, and see her statue and the image of her in the stained-glass windows of the basilica.[8] Otherwise, she remains omnipresent in the story but astonishingly absent from the place. In 1878, when she died in the convent in Nevers, suggestions that her body should be returned to her home town were firmly turned down,[9] with the result that her cult centres on the faraway town in central France where her body lies, waxed and sculpted, in a glass reliquary[10] (see illus. 31). This is not to say that she was bundled off to get her out of the way or that she became a nun under duress. On

31. The entombed body of Bernadette, lightly coated in wax after its third exhumation, presented in a reliquary after the beatification in 1925, Couvent de Saint-Gildard, Nevers

the contrary, shortly after the apparitions she expressed a hope for a religious life, and, as the visits and crowds became more onerous, she positively wished to be hidden from view.[11] Peyramale did not press her to make up her mind and was patient with her years of indecision about which order she should join. But he, more than anyone, understood the danger of her developing saintly pretensions and sought to ensure that her natural humility was reinforced at every opportunity. In the end, Bernadette's journey away from her birthplace would eliminate the shrine's vulnerability either to her weaknesses or to her charisma.

In the spring of 1860 Bernadette was sixteen and still living with her parents at the Lapaca Mill, the new business that Peyramale and the bishop had helped them set up. Poor, pious women like Antoinette Garros decided that this was not good enough: 'I heard she was running about with other children and said to M. Peyramale, "You're going to have to get her out of there; with parents like that, she's hardly surrounded by good examples."'[12] Lacadé, who was always concerned with the fate of the visionary and how it might effect the prestige and prosperity of his municipality, then gave money to move her to the Hospice–Ecole des Sœurs de Nevers, a charitable institution in Lourdes named after the town where these nuns had their motherhouse. Bernadette was received there as a 'malade indigente', although she was exempted from the regime of the sick. This administrative technicality enabled her to be educated for free, and she was taught how to read and write, and how to sew. She did not find this position humiliating or seek to exploit her status as a visionary; instead of entering the stream of the 'demoiselles en pension', the girls of good family who boarded, she went to school with the poorer day girls.

This process began a series of separations that culminated in her departure for Nevers. Her parents only permitted the move to the hospice on condition that they could see her whenever she wished, and she did continue to visit in the company of a nun, showing rare bouts of ill-temper when she was refused permission to go. At the same time she was adored and petted by the genteel and devout Tardhivail sisters, benefactresses of the Grotto and keen activists in its promotion. Yet the doting tutelage continued to separate her from the past,[13] only permitting her to visit the Grotto with a minder and with permission. In every way new restrictions and a new discipline were brought to bear on her life, and she reportedly told her companion Sœur Victorine Poux a few years before her death in Nevers, 'If I was a little bird, I'd go to the Grotto morning and night.'[14]

She was under constant surveillance and her slightest 'faults' were noted and criticized. Once she wanted to make a skirt look larger in order to give it an air of crinoline; on another occasion 'she put a busk in her corset, it was a piece of wood' in an effort to give some shapeliness to her slender figure.[15] Bernadette even had a secret vice: she hid a little white wine in her armoire, which the sisters allowed her to keep, knowing that it was a habit of her family and region.[16] For she treasured this wine as a medicine, and drank it on her family's instruction to give her strength from the bouts of paralysing asthma that suffocated her, a disordered digestion and the effects of general weakness and constant pain, like rheumatism, that never left her.[17] Otherwise, in every serious respect Bernadette's peasant wildness was domesticated, her image constructed, her 'essence' disseminated through photographs that still sought to capture a *soupçon* of that uncultivated quality by posing her in Pyrenean dress.

For all the 'construction' of her image, however, Bernadette was important to Lourdes because she was herself. Despite the many constraints, despite the emotions and spiritual qualities that visitors projected on to her, her few written words and interactions showed she would only go so far before she resisted. She did so quietly and persistently, revealing a quiet charisma, a sure gaze, a conviction of the truth of her story, a stalwart and dignified rejection of gifts and a simple generosity that stunned those who knew her poverty. Bernadette hides from us, as she was hidden from her contemporaries until the apparitions put her in the limelight. Her confessor and chaplain at the hospice, Abbé Pomian, testified that he did not even notice her when he taught her her catechism in 1858.[18] She had lived a life of humility when she tended her sheep in Bartrès or when she tried to master the rudiments of the catechism.[19] Apart from the apparitions, nothing before or after singled her out for special notice. There are only traces in the stories of her interactions and in a few letters indicating the strength of her personality and the particularity of her spirituality, but in these residues Bernadette begins to reveal herself to us.

The Popular Cult

For the poor, Bernadette was both miraculous and magical, and from the earliest days of the apparitions fabulous tales of her powers began to circulate. The second article on the happenings at the Grotto described how she

> was in the country, living with her wet-nurse's family, and working for them as a shepherdess. One day, the child was leading her lambs to a barren field, next to a fertile meadow. A peasant in the meadow saw them and said: 'Poor child, that moorland's no good and your flock is dying of hunger. Bring it into my meadow – if you can.' Now, this was mockery, because a deep stream separated the meadow from the moor, but Heaven wanted to teach the bad, rich man a lesson for having humiliated the poor child. He'd hardly finished speaking and turned away when the water stopped flowing, and the flock of sheep crossed into the meadow without even getting their feet wet.[20]

The story combined the pleasure of social inversion – the malicious rich man foiled by the innocence of pious poverty – with the majesty of the biblical tale: like Moses, Bernadette made the waters part and brought her flock safely on to the other side. This story was a typical mix of folk, biblical and magical tales. She was so light, people reported, that, like Saint Theresa of Avila, her ecstasies enabled her 'to rise above the ground and float in the air as if an invisible force wanted to carry her far from the gaze of mankind'.[21] And her physical prowess was matched by an exemplary courage, especially surprising in one so small, poor and ill. In her dealings with Jacomet she was said to show a cheerful heedlessness, with Jeanne-Marie Poueyto recounting how the crowds worried about her first interview: 'Poor Bernadette, they're going to put you in prison', to which she laughingly replied: 'Don't be afraid, if they put me in, then they will let me out.' The narrative conveys a sense of the police commissioner's looming authority next to Bernadette's diminutive fragility: 'He was big . . . Bernadette walked by his side . . . her parents followed and so did the crowd.'[22] But the overbearing, cajoling, even perhaps insulting attitude of Jacomet caused her no distress. In this early, popular guise – which fell away with time – Bernadette had a heroic dimension that derived from divine protection. When, for example, Jacomet and Dutour persecuted her, they in turn were persecuted. When they asked Bernadette to reveal her secrets and threatened her with arrest, Jacomet, according to the popular story already mentioned, began to tremble comically in her presence, so much so that he could no longer write or do his job.[23]

Bernadette's power also had a more serious side. An example of the popular belief in her ability to cure through touch occurred as early as 4 March 1858, when the faithful waited with frustrated anticipation for the miracle that did not happen. Determined to have a result, a story emerged instead of a miraculous encounter with Eugénie Troy, a girl from Barèges who had reportedly been so blind for ten years she could not even see the light of a lamp.[24] After the fifteenth apparition Bernadette briefly met her, and young Troy believed that the fleeting embrace they exchanged cured her sight.[25]

With the 'miracle' of Barèges, Bernadette's life was transformed. On 17 March Dutour noted with concern that she was now a saint with 'prerogatives', and hoped to arrest her if he discovered her profiting from her reputation.[26] He was disappointed: Bernadette described her meeting with Eugénie with such convincing innocence that he had to let her go.[27] According to her account, on returning to Lourdes along the chemin du Bois, she saw a young girl with a pretty red *capulet*, or hood, a long and striking headdress typical of the region's costume. It was a chance meeting of teasing, playful youth; they shook hands, kissed, broke into bursts of laughter, kissed again, and then went their separate ways. As Bernadette concluded, 'I don't think I cured anyone at all, nor did I do anything to bring it about.'[28]

The incident also brought home the torments of being a miracle worker. At home she was assailed by 'an immense crowd'. Bernadette hid in her bedroom on the instructions of her aunt, while her parents guarded the house from the bottom of the stairs:

> The people who came into the room came up to me, touched my hands, shook them, many kissed them; those with rosaries gave them to me so I could hold them in my hands and rub them against my own. The same day someone offered me money, which I refused, and a man offered me two oranges. Two women wanted to exchange their glittering rosaries for mine; I refused.[29]

Other stories of her healing powers began to circulate and she had to assure Jacomet of the innocence of an encounter with a crippled child of six or seven. Seated on a servant's lap, the child noticed that Bernadette had an apple and two chestnuts in her pocket. Since the child was unable to reach for them, Bernadette put them in her hand; they fell from her trembling fingers and were picked up by the servant. For Bernadette that was the end of the matter, but others had a different version.[30] Adélaïde Monlaur, for example, said the child walked over and picked up the apple herself, concluding: 'I don't know if they could swear to it on the Gospel, but everyone at Lourdes has heard about it.'[31] Another incident occurred during a visit to see a friend's sick brother at a farm on the way to Bartrès. While he seemed to improve with her visit, there was no quick transformation in his state. Bernadette 'didn't go as a miracle worker, but as a good friend',[32] playing the role of nurse that she later assumed at the convent in Nevers.

She and her family were also harassed by professional relic merchants who sought to profit from popular belief. A man named Houzelot from near Neuilly, who had already been to La Salette to buy Mélanie's dress and Maximin's tie and shepherd's crook, persisted with Louise Soubirous in February 1862 until she gave him the white *capulet* that Bernadette had sometimes worn during the apparitions, the cross of the rosary of her first communion and even an early letter to her parents wishing them a happy New Year.[33] Bernadette was revolted by such behaviour, and in later years, when accompanied by the Tardhivail sisters, a woman said, '"If only I could cut off a piece of her robe." She turned round and replied, "What idiots you are."'[34]

André Sayoux, the relation who had let the Soubirous family live in the *cachot* before the apparitions, recounted how people came at all times of the day and night to ask Bernadette for her help. It is clear that in many cases she, rather than the apparition site, was the first port of call, as pilgrims desperately sought physical contact with her to heal their sick. Although she sent people to the Grotto, her earliest remarks betray a slight ambiguity about her role that disappeared very quickly:

There were three of them . . . they arrived at two in the morning, and knocked on the door; Bernadette was in bed and asleep with my wife. They brought a child of fifteen or sixteen who'd been ill for a long time, and made Bernadette embrace her. They made the child kiss Bernadette, they touched her hand, and made her touch the sick child on the chest. Bernadette told them, 'I'm not sure of curing her. The water of the Grotto has value.'[35]

Sometimes she could not resist the hordes who encircled her even when she was living at the hospice in Lourdes. An outing with Sœur Victorine to a sister-house in nearby Pau turned into a nightmare:

Unfortunately someone recognized her by her *capulet*. In a moment the house was under siege . . . we had to call the police . . . a line of mothers with their children went into the courtyard of the convent; the officers kept order and she went round touching the children, even though it tired and wearied her . . . she was ill on the trip home, even before she arrived back – From Pau I took her to our sisters at Oloron: same thing again. She was already ill – I rushed to bring her back – she had a terrible sickness . . . they had realized she was there as quick as lightning.[36]

It seems that Bernadette's already fragile health was undermined both by the pressure to perform before the sisters and the harassments of the crowd. In this instance, at least, illness had the advantage of letting her withdraw.

An equally important and controversial aspect of the popular cult that surrounded Bernadette was the way she was asked to bless rosaries. During the twelfth apparition on 1 March she pulled out her rosary and raised it as if to show it to her white girl. The reaction was immediate: 'The spectators saw the visionary present this rosary to the apparition and thought the apparition herself was going to bless rosaries.' In response they presented their own rosaries, or readied themselves to submit them to her. This story disturbed many who believed that Bernadette was playing with her audience and assuming inappropriate powers, but she later told Abbé Pène that the cause of the uproar was a simple confusion, for on that day she had promised a woman to use her rosary while reciting prayers. Noticing the difference, the apparition asked her where her own was, and Bernadette immediately showed it. When Abbé Pène said she had no right to bless rosaries, she replied that 'as women have no right to wear the [priest's] stole . . . she had given no blessing'.[37]

Such evidence as exists suggests she herself was unclear of her role in this domain. For example, Marie-Madeleine Courrade testified: 'I once visited Bernadette . . . and we wanted to get her to touch rosaries: we asked her to touch them; she did, and then gave them back to us.'[38] Another time she was pressured by a Carmelite priest who should have known better, an example which shows clerical reaction could be as 'popular' as those of the illiterate faithful. As Antoinette and Marie Tardhivail recounted:

> I saw priests in the kitchen and a Carmelite (from Bagnères) who went down on his knees before her. Bernadette was washing her hands when he did this: 'Bless me, Bernadette.' – 'I don't know how.' – 'Say: "Holy Virgin, who appeared before me, bless this priest and this family." ' – A woman and two children and Bernadette repeated [the words]. They made her touch the rosary: she touched it, turned it in her hands, held it in one hand, and touched it with the other.[39]

From then on, they claimed, Pomian forbade her to touch the rosaries, and on future occasions she refused women and convalescing soldiers who came to her, saying that she was forbidden to do so. Although such events were thus successfully blocked, they none the less give a hint of how the poor believed that in some respects she was more powerful than, and indeed preferable to, the priests.

When she left home for a life supervised by the sisters, efforts were made to avoid such popular displays, except when she was recognized or 'let out' for public view as in May 1866. But while the popular cult was, in some sense, repressed and bubbled to the surface only on particular occasions, the Church sought to exploit Bernadette through photographs. The first saint to be photographed in her lifetime, she was presented in pious portraits or in the poses that she had supposedly held during the apparitions. In these images, taken first by priests and then by local photographers, Bernadette remains remarkably unchanged, even though careful, scholarly work has pointed out differences in dress and the thinning cheeks as she grew older and iller.[40] Taken from 1860 until her departure to Nevers, what unites the photographs is the preoccupation with her Pyrenean dress. When viewers responded to this imagery, they recognized a distinct, rural identity, but filtered through an urban, romantic prism. Garbed thus, she seemed almost a cipher for Pyrenean culture and the embodiment of an inarticulate tradition. Photographed first with the traditional white *capulet* of the Lourdes valley – the one item of clothing of ancient origin – or the headscarf of yellow and brown checks, the long dark apron, bordered shawl and faded calico dress, Bernadette and her poverty were idealized, these clothes already far superior to the woollen wrappings she had probably worn during the apparitions[41] (see illus. 32 and 33).

32. Bernadette in Pyrenean headdress, photograph by Billard-Perrin, Lourdes, October 1863
33. Bernadette in a check headscarf, photograph by Paul Dufour, Lourdes, February 1864

The portraits display the hallmarks of early Second Empire photography: the long poses for the sitters, the uncertainty of technique and, above all, the pride in artisanship. There is no sense of trying to capture the sitter naturally, but rather an attempt to follow the classical ideal of portrait painting. Photographers sought an easy means of grasping the characters of their models, using props and poses that would facilitate recognition.[42] Although the technique improved, the portraits became even more studied. By 1864 Bernadette posed in peasant garb in a studio, seated before a statue of the Immaculate Conception, on a prie-dieu, often with hands in lap, frequently with her treasured rosary. All the photographers hoped to catch her while in ecstasy, a position that Bernadette refused to duplicate for the camera, providing instead only stiff, awkward, even sullen profiles and front-views (see illus. 34). Perhaps most astonishing was Bernadette with fixed eyes posed in front of a backdrop of the local countryside, while around her played two little girls, also in costume, in the process of gathering wood (see illus. 35). These were not her sister Toinette and Jeanne Abadie, who had actually accompanied her during the first apparition, but young models acting their parts, later to be reproduced in lithographs in whatever imaginary scene was desired.

34. Bernadette looking sullen, photographed at Studio Annet by Paul Dufour, Tarbes, October 1864

35. Bernadette and two companions re-create the occasion of the first apparition, posed and photographed at Studio Annet by Paul Dufour, October 1864

This concentration on Bernadette's costume seemed intent on distilling some Pyrenean essence. The result showed her as virtually unchanging, a mystical childishness conveyed through clothes so thick that no sense of her emerging womanhood can be discerned. It was this very quality of timelessness that her admirers wanted. In his second and last encounter with her in October 1865, the Jesuit historian Cros remarked:

> Bernadette is twenty-one according to the register of births, but you have to believe in the infallibility of these lists to accept this: the eye that sees her declares that she remains a thirteen-year-old [*sic*] child. I don't think it would be possible to meet a thirteen-year-old [*sic*] with a younger-looking face than she has at twenty-one. It is impossible not to feel the supernatural charm of her youth. She herself is an apparition.[43]

This childishness supposedly embodied her innocence but also her peasant state. In nineteenth-century France it placed her within the growing cult for ruralism in art, which both acknowledged and idealized peasant poverty. The *Angélus* of Jean-François Millet showed their silent, intense piety, while his *Gleaners* evoked a romantic but austere vision of rural life; both won an enormous and enduring following (see illus. 36 and 37). Bernadette's portraits tapped into similar themes but also emphasized what was distinctive of the mountain world, an exotic Pyrenean flavour in the larger peasant bouillon. For the Romantic period saw the arrival in the distant borderlands of the cream of the literary generation: Vigny, Sand, Baudelaire, Flaubert, and with them their various visions of the Pyrenees. From other pens flowed an image of the generous mountain dweller who, untouched by urban vices, maintained a simple and direct virtue. Noble shepherds sleeping under starry nights, smugglers whose audacity made them generous, hermits who escaped civilization to live in the wilderness – these were all characters of the mountain people that enchanted and seduced; they acknowledged poverty but judged it as essential for the Pyreneans' special moral attributes.[44]

Travellers also sought to unveil a religious mentality untouched by civilized pretensions. For some, the peasants of the Pyrenees were 'devout as the sound of its waterfalls and the silence of its woods', their faith marked by a touching naïvety that evoked the period before

36. *Jean-François Millet,* The Angélus, *1858/9*
37. *Jean-François Millet,* The Gleaners, *1857*

the Middle Ages.[45] Despite their 'superstitions', these simple folk were 'true' believers, uncontaminated by too much dogma and doctrine. Such views were happily confirmed in Bernadette, whose communication with the Virgin came at the wild Grotto, and whose untutored religious psyche was the proper repository for the special mission she received. As one priest remarked on the special quality of mountain visionaries in a letter to Mgr Laurence:

> This is the way the Holy Virgin – who loves simple and artless hearts, and communicates with souls in solitude, far from the contagion of towns – wished once again to demonstrate this great truth in the mountains of the Pyrenees as in the Alps.[46]

These studied and artificial photographs disseminated Bernadette's image and transformed her popular cult out of all recognition. In the wider world she would be known not as a miracle worker who touched and healed, but as a virtuous yet ignorant peasant-child. These images rubbed any rough edges off her personality, while also hiding her physical degeneration, expunging from view the fleas, the life-threatening asthma and the creeping tuberculosis. Posed with symbols of orthodox practice – rosaries, statues of the Immaculate Conception and prie-dieu – these photographs neglected the wondrous tales of her powers and prowess, and hid away the tortured supplications of the poor and dying who ransacked her house for even the most paltry relics. Like the building works underway that transformed the area around the Grotto, Bernadette's wildness was also structured and reshaped. She almost began to resemble the Grotto she loved: enclosed behind an iron grille in 1864 to prevent pilgrims from plundering its rock, the Grotto's inner cavity was finally paved over in 1866 to make way for a more permanent altar.[47] Bernadette too, hidden more and more from public view, educated and protected, was increasingly packaged for pious popular consumption.[48] However, it seems that she, almost alone, remained detached from the process; when presented with the photographs and told that they would sell for ten centimes, she replied that it was more than she was worth.[49]

The Clerical Reaction and the Trials of Temptation

Separating clerical and popular reactions is often artificial, for there were many overlapping areas, especially in the perception of Bernadette's disinterestedness. But the clergy had particular concerns – the blessing of the rosaries was a case in point – and they were ever watchful of her behaviour. Her apparitions transformed the lives of the local clergy; from obscure priests, they became famous, and their own spiritual lives entered a new stage. Pomian was keen that Cros should note his key role in events, explaining how he was the 'first priest she confided in about the apparition'. Far from discouraging her or being sceptical, he maintained he had asked if he could convey her words to Peyramale, met her in the confessional or in his room on several occasions, and spoke of the events with his brother priests. After the girl in white named herself as the Immaculate Conception, Pomian sent her directly to his superior, an indication of how seriously he took her reports. In acting thus he showed the ambivalence of nineteenth-century clergymen, who were wary of impostors and frauds but also on the alert for a miracle to defy the scepticism of the age.[50]

Peyramale himself became integral to Bernadette and her family. He whisked her away to her new life in the hospice, supervised the taking of the photographs that gave her celebrity status and, at the same time, took charge of humbling her, constantly reminding her – especially in the company of celebrated visitors – that she was nothing. The intensity of their relationship was heightened by its mutual dependence and ambivalence. The stained-glass window in Peyramale's parish church, not finished till after his death, captured a vision of their relative positions: the priest is large and overwhelming, while Bernadette is an almost exaggeratedly tiny figure in traditional costume (see illus. 38). While it evoked the reality of her submission, it neglected the possibility that she might one day throw off his authority. Peyramale's enhanced status depended, perhaps not always comfortably, on belief in her veracity. He was all too aware that her experience had transformed religious life in Lourdes: 'Rightly or wrongly, what has happened at Lourdes has deeply affected the population. Never have there been so many people coming

38. Studio of J. P. Grant, Bernadette with Abbé Peyramale, *stained-glass window, 1921, Lourdes parish church*

to services during the week.' As a result he became a crucial mediator between the visionary, the believers and the curious, receiving letters from 'Paris, Rouen, all directions', which he laboured to answer.[51]

Peyramale's belief in Bernadette rested on many things: the astonishing message of the Immaculate Conception, the renewed piety of his flock, his belief that in the wake of the apparitions he was personally protected by divine providence.[52] He was much impressed by Bernadette and the way she refused gifts, relating, for example, how a wealthy foreign lady had tried with great persistence, to get her to take money. The child always refused with the feeling of offended dignity . . . it is one of the greatest phenomena to see this child of the people, poor to the point of not having enough to eat, refusing gifts with such dignity.[53]

In fact, it was the clergy who tempted her most frequently. The bishop of Montpellier, Mgr Charles-Thomas Thibault, came to Lourdes and interviewed Bernadette in patois, enabling him to better appreciate the nuances of her responses, which she ended always with a respectful 'M. Le Curé', not yet being able to discern the difference in rank between Peyramale and a bishop.[54] The questioning became more and more pointed, and in the words of Adélaïde Monlaur, he 'twisted the conversation in all directions, no doubt to test her, but the child was always steadfast'.

Monseigneur took Bernadette's hands in his and, while he held them in this way, made her touch his rosaries.

He said to M. Le Curé, 'This child is poor, is that not right, M. Le Curé?'

'Yes, sir. Very poor.'

'Oh, no. Bernadette, you are not poor. You are happy, yes, happy,' he said to her, gently stroking her hand.

M. Le Curé brought some food that he wanted the child to eat in front of Monseigneur. The child didn't want to accept anything and thanked M. Le Curé . . .

At the end [the bishop] wanted to give her his gold-mounted rosaries: but the child thanked him and refused. After this happened several times, he said, 'As you don't want my rosary free, let's do a swap: give me yours, and take mine.'

'No, no, Monseigneur, I prefer my own, thank you very much,' she said in patois.[55]

According to the testimony of Chanoine Baudassé, who accompanied the bishop, the rosary was special – 'coral mounted in gold and given an indulgence by the immortal Pius IX'[56] – and hence rich both in material and religious meaning, but nothing could make Bernadette relinquish her own rosary, worth no more than two sous.

Lay people too spoke of this characteristic. Anna Dupin, a poor woman who knew Bernadette's mother, told how she invited Bernadette home to talk with her neighbours, then offered her an apple: 'Apples were very scarce that year, and I had a fine one. I went to find it in the cupboard and offered it to her. She refused, even when I pleaded with her.'[57] When the Comte de Rességuier, a legitimist deputy and Pyrenean notable, came to interview her, 'he offered the girl a very beautiful and very attractive *Imitation of Christ*'. She refused it, and he tried again by asking her to say a decade of the rosary in exchange. She agreed to say the prayers but again refused the gift.[58]

Belief in her was not universal, however, and even within the Church there were many who remained sceptical. The superior at the hospice, Ursule Fardes, known for her intelligence and friendship with the visionary, was not convinced that Bernadette had seen the Virgin Mary; instead she chided Bernadette on her inability to learn her catechism, saying that she wished that the white lady had done more to teach her.[59] Frère Léobard, the schoolteacher, told Cros that, while Bernadette gave a first impression of simplicity, he was not certain 'if she wasn't more of an accomplished actress than a simple visionary'.[60] Chanoine Ribes, at the time director of the Grand Séminaire at Tarbes, was delighted by her simplicity but disturbed by the lifeless recitation of her story she gave in September 1858: 'Bernadette gave us her recital in patois for a whole hour in a monotone, without wavering, scarcely taking the time to take breath, just like a schoolgirl reciting a well-learned lesson.'[61] Both he and Frère Léobard were only convinced, they claimed, by the many cures.

Scepticism could occasionally turn into near hostility, as when a Jesuit, Père Nègre, sought to prove the white lady was in fact a devil by getting Bernadette to say she had cloven feet. In the interview, however, she replied with the resolute simplicity that always showed her in the best light. She insisted, as she had from the beginning, that the white lady had 'very pretty bare feet' and clearly visible hands. Not satisfied, 'he discoursed amply on the devil's deformities'. To her companion Antoinette Tardhivail, Bernadette remarked in patois, 'He doesn't want to believe, so let's go!', utterly unintimidated by the Jesuit's learning.[62] Such assaults did her reputation more good than harm – while she became a picture of uncomplicated candour, Nègre emerged from the encounter with a reputation for Jesuitical casuistry.

Even as late as 1879 and again in 1890, he was still having to defend himself, saying in letters that he had been misquoted and, in any case, had encountered the 'false' visionaries and cures in the aftermath of the apparitions and had been right to doubt.[63]

Bernadette shone in such circumstances; there were those who thought that her native wit showed only when she needed to defend herself. However, if these moments gave her satisfaction, she was never allowed to feel complacent. Peyramale was undeniably fond of her, but he hid his esteem and dutifully humiliated her in front of strangers. As early as September 1858 the curé of Estipou, Père Justin Nereci, went to visit Bernadette:

'Here's the little girl you've been asking for,' M. Le Curé said. 'The Holy Virgin has bestowed on her blessings she doesn't deserve, and many of her friends would have been more worthy.' M. Peyramale always treated her thus in front of strangers to test her humility. The poor girl blushed, lowered her head modestly and greeted us without a word. She sat on the chair that was presented to her with that endearing awkwardness that artisans have when they find themselves in well-bred company.[64]

Nor was Peyramale the only one to resort to these tactics. The mother superior who succeeded Ursule Fardes at the hospice was equally concerned to humble her, and in 1865 gave her a public dressing-down in front of another Jesuit, Père Jean Clavé, when she was already a young woman:

'Now . . . let me complete your education by telling you what the Holy Virgin has still not done for Bernadette: that is to convert her fully. And despite all these freely given favours, she is still on the road to purgatory, poor girl, and you would be charitable if you would pray for her to become better. Would you believe that Missy and I have recently had an argument? She wanted to throw some peel in the waste basket on the right rather than on the left . . . and I almost gave in to her.'

'My dear mother,' said the child with tears in her eyes, 'again I beg your pardon.'[65]

On this occasion Bernadette reacted with spirit, but as time passed she became more resigned. One of Veuillot's daughters recounted how, when she met Bernadette, Peyramale let her stay only ten minutes and then sent her away with the peremptory 'You may go now.' While they recognized his duty to humble her, they were shocked by his brusqueness and impressed by the way Bernadette 'always smiling, kissed us again and went after giving us a pretty bow'.[66]

Bernadette was under Peyramale's spiritual direction, but she was also a client in a system of patronage that affected not only herself but everyone she loved, a counterpoint to the obvious fact that, without her assistance, Peyramale's new eminence, the bishop's policies and the shrine itself would have all crumbled. Despite her obligation, she was indeed sometimes uncooperative. When Abbé Pierre-Marcel Montauzé arrived in September 1865, Bernadette was ill but none the less came down with Peyramale to meet him and a Spanish woman who kept on posing 'frivolous' questions about the Virgin's hair style. Bernadette refused to answer, and Peyramale expressed their mutual irritation: 'Her hair was covered in a veil, madame. You women seem greatly preoccupied with hair.' The Spaniard effectively silenced, Abbé Montauzé turned the discussion to more 'serious' matters, asking Bernadette to show him how the Virgin had crossed herself. When she again resisted, he explained how important it was for him to see this gesture, so he could teach it to others. Even though he noted her exhaustion, he kept on pressing her:

> Bernadette stayed still and made no reply.
>
> I was astonished.
>
> The Curé of Lourdes then said: 'Bernadette, make the sign of the cross that M. L'Abbé has requested.'
>
> She soon obeyed and made the sign.

Montauzé was only reassured when the mother superior told him later that Bernadette reacted thus because 'she had such an elevated notion of the piety and perfection with which the Holy Virgin made the sign of the Cross that she didn't dare try to depict what she had seen'.[67] The full flavour of the narrative offers a different story – one of physical exhaustion and spiritual demoralization, a dislike of being asked to act out an endless and repetitive role, and a priest who was both harsh and unrelenting. Like the photographs that tried to capture her during the apparitions, Bernadette obeyed, but seemed to leave her heart somewhere else.

Bernadette's Charisma

From as early as the beginning of April 1858 men and women came to see Bernadette, and, as with the clergy, she could show her visitors a wit that charmed and disarmed. When asked whether she would disobey Abbé Peyramale if the apparition told her to come to the Grotto, she replied that she would go to the priest and ask his permission and go anyway if he refused;[68] when asked whether she wanted to be a seamstress or a nun, she replied that she preferred the latter but would do what her parents wanted.[69] In both these instances she demonstrated a sense of self, combined with the virtue of obedience and a considerable degree of tact. Although different from clerics with their probing questions and authority, lay visitors also tried to test her. While the clergy questioned to be convinced, others interrogated to be converted or to expose her. For example, the Comte de Broussard was, by his own reckoning, a debauched atheist who decided to talk to Bernadette in July 1858 purely 'to catch the little one in a blatant lie'. His first glance told him she was 'common enough', but her simplicity and self-assurance soon disturbed him. After hearing the story of the apparitions, he asked Bernadette to show him how the 'belle dame' smiled.

> 'Oh, monsieur, you'd have to be from heaven to imitate that smile.'
>
> 'Can't you do it for me? I'm a non-believer, and don't hold with apparitions.'
>
> The child's countenance darkened, and her expression became severe. 'Then, sir, you think I am a liar?'
>
> I was completely disarmed. No, Bernadette was not a liar, and I was on the point of going down on my knees to ask her forgiveness.
>
> 'Since you are a sinner,' she went on, 'I will show you the Virgin's smile.'
>
> Since then . . . I have lost my wife and my two daughters, but it seems to me that I am far from being alone in the world. I live with the Virgin's smile.[70]

This conversion of a sinner was matched by an equally famous tale of the way Bernadette transformed the life of an English Protestant, Mme Joseph, by bringing her to the 'true' faith. A late and ardent convert to the Grotto, Elfrida Lacrampe described how she and Mme Joseph came to Bernadette when the visionary could barely speak. The Protestant woman reportedly fell to her knees, head in hand, and began to sob. Bernadette insisted that the woman rise and said:

> 'I want to give something to this lady, what can I possibly give her?' She took off her medallions from her neck so she could choose. 'Mme Joseph, Bernadette wants you to choose a souvenir.' She rose, then went back down on her knees. 'No, I want nothing, I'm not worthy.' (This woman was very calm, sensible, intelligent, above her condition, and without a trace of exaltation; you could see she was searching for the truth: the soul of goodwill; the effect of grace was clearly visible.) Then I said to Bernadette, 'You choose what you want to give to this lady.' I cut the string and returned the objects to her. She took a cross and a medal and gave them to her. 'Take them, madam; the cross is for you, and the medal so that you think of me.'[71]

Her willingness to give and her request for Mme Joseph's prayers in return revealed a straightforward but exacting spirituality that touched and transformed; here it was Bernadette herself, not the story of the apparitions, that made the difference.

As a result, people perceived in Bernadette not only someone who could respond with alacrity to doubters, but increasingly a model of piety and spiritual contentment, regardless of physical suffering. She was able to remain gentle and unembarrassed even when women asked her advice on intimate matters: 'They talked to her about very delicate matters, consulted her . . . asked for her prayers. She remained impassive. She answered that she would pray for them.'[72] In this respect she had become not too different from the 'sainte fille', Marie Courrech, who had also had visions of the Virgin and had tried, through her prayers, to tend to the needs of the sick and the distressed. She remained eternally modest on the subject of the apparitions, responding to questions but never raising the matter herself. This lack of *amour propre* impressed the local population and the sisters at the hospice, and was as important a quality as her generosity and refusal to accept gifts.

When people spoke of Bernadette, they concentrated on her simplicity, poverty and ignorance, qualities born from the daily knowledge of hardship, loss and illness. For of the family of nine children only four survived, the last dying without a birth certificate. Bernadette was accustomed to submission: childish transgressions were punished with beatings, harshness tempered by her mother's struggle to keep her alive through a few special morsels of food. When removed from home, she dutifully submitted to the new regime, learning to read, write and take dictation, tackling spelling and wrestling with the exigencies of French grammar, conventions she absorbed only haltingly and superficially. She sought to master letter-writing, and was taught to compose letters in response to hypothetical situations dreamed up by her teachers to gain practice. But it was never a skill that became second nature to her; even today scholars have difficulty in deciding which of her surviving letters are genuine and which written only for practice.[73]

'Finding' Bernadette through such texts is thus extremely difficult, for her writings are unembellished and graceless to the point of brusqueness. In them, she is as hidden from view as she was as a member of the poorest family in the town. Her written recitals of the apparitions are short and to the point, with a distorted chronology that none the less shows an impeccable spiritual reliability. She stood firm on all points to do with her mission – the message she was to relay to the priests – and the example she provided through prayer, penitence and drinking from the fountain.[74]

She took the same tone in her writings to the many who sought her prayers. Under constant pressure to respond to appeals, Bernadette did so straightforwardly, promising her aid and asking for the prayers of others in return. What might seem formulaic from the hand of other writers, seems in her absolutely sincere. The words were abrupt and few, first because they were difficult for her to compose, but also because she so clearly saw no need to say more. When she had to refuse a lock of hair from a correspondent, she did so sadly, explaining how she was forbidden to receive such gifts. Were she able to perform another service, she wrote, she would gladly do so.[75]

A special spirituality emerges from letters to those who were more intimate. During these years before her departure she was frequently ill and occasionally mentioned the fact. Although resigned to sickness and death, Bernadette preferred health, and her discretion about her illnesses contrasts sharply with the way suffering became almost celebrated at the shrine. Nor was Bernadette always of a sanguine frame of mind. When she asked for others' prayers, she meant it, for she not infrequently alluded to unspecified psychological and spiritual pain. To Ursule Fardes she wrote:

[My happiness] would be all the greater if the good Lord would give me the grace of seeing you for a moment. My poor heart has so many things to tell you. All I can tell you on paper is that it would be charitable of you to pray for me, for I greatly need it.[76]

Nor was Bernadette without her spiritual fantasies. In a rare and enlightening exchange of letters with a Père Bouin, she expressed an unadulterated pleasure in hearing from a young man who confessed to a desire to become a hermit in the Grotto. Bouin sent his letters via her family in the hope that they would not be read by the sisters, an innocent intrigue that, in the circumstances of supervision and surveillance, was delightfully mutinous. Bernadette was overjoyed to receive his portrait, and in a moment of rare coquettishness admitted to having looked at it several times. The letters betray a warm, mischievous, even rebellious side to her temperament, as she stepped outside the constraints imposed upon her.[77] In Bouin she found a man who shared her devotion to the Grotto, to the Immaculate Conception and to Lourdes. His desire to become a hermit appealed instantly to her own wish to be hidden, and she confessed that she was weary of the multitude of visitors. She hoped for a different life and, although she could never retreat into the darkness of the Grotto, her first choice of vocation was to become a Carmelite. She dreamed of strict enclosure behind the grill, and only gave up this desire when her ill-health made it impossible to observe the rule.

This correspondence was the closest she ever came to a 'spiritual friendship'; it was entirely unlike such famous spiritual collaborations of the Counter-Reformation as the letters between Saint Jeanne de Chantal and Saint François de Sales, which resulted in the growth of the Visitandines and the mission to help the sick and poor, or that of Louise de Marillac and Saint Vincent de Paul, which affected the direction of the Sisters of Charity in their aim to minister to the sick.[78]

Nor would it resemble the wordy and often tortured exchanges between the men and women of the Assumption, which, as will be seen, was to be so important to the emergence of the pilgrimage movement at Lourdes itself.[79] In this correspondence there was no theological meditation, no yearning to make spiritual conquests. Instead, Bernadette revealed the side of her that radiated strength and joy. Perhaps her status as an *héritière* filtered through in this exchange, explaining the force that supported her during the endless questionings about the apparitions.

But even the correspondence with Bouin produced only two letters, making Bernadette an inconvenient person from the historian's point of view to have at the centre of the Lourdes story. She is not susceptible to the standard techniques of analysis, for she left behind few words to study. Her spirituality provides a striking contrast to that of Thérèse de Lisieux, the other late-nineteenth-century saint who was to become France's *princesse de Dieu*, the favourite of soldiers in the trenches and Edith Piaf's beloved intercessor. Thérèse entered a Carmelite nunnery with a special dispensation at fifteen after a personal visit to the Pope. The youngest of five daughters, she came from a tightly woven, tormented family in which a self-conscious, sometimes morbid religious belief permeated every aspect of life. Both her parents had hoped, in vain, for religious vocations; when married, they had decided to live as brother and sister, a vow broken only under the pressure of priestly direction. Her mother, Zélie Martin, ran a prosperous embroidery business in Alençon, and her father was a beloved, if ineffectual man, adored by his bevy of daughters. Of right-wing, legitimist convictions, the parents taught the children to accept without question the perceived conspiratorial links between Freemasonry, Jews and the devil. Politics, however, was of no great concern to Thérèse: she saw something like France's imperial expansion purely in terms of the opportunities it offered to convert the heathen.

Thérèse's spirituality emerged from her family's aspirations and was recorded in a multi-volume correspondence that has invited retrospective psychoanalysis.[80] In addition there was her autobiography, *Histoire d'une âme* (1898), which was continually edited and reshaped by a family in which all the daughters became nuns and who actively constructed a religious image of their youngest sister in a way that sustained their family mythology. This extraordinary bestseller insisted on the special spiritual capacities of the theologically untutored to experience Jesus Christ with child-like innocence,[81] a view summed up in the notion that she was nothing more than God's plaything. At the same time she sought to emulate Christ by becoming a mother to sinners, and even saw herself as a mother to the baby Jesus, making herself utterly available to his infant needs. Her mysticism exalted suffering not in the name of redemption, but rather as a kind of childbirth, a creative experience that saw God as mother, not as judge.

In contrast to Bernadette's taciturnity, Thérèse provided a world of words, which have produced more words in the form of commentary and analysis. In these words lay her fame and importance, but to assess Bernadette by the same criteria would be to miss the point. Her appeal was non-verbal and non-literate, not unlike the apparitions themselves, in which her bodily comportment was more important than language, except for the brief messages conveyed to the priests. Her spirituality was invested in a mission accomplished, in which she was hidden behind the enormity of her encounter. Nothing typifies Bernadette's reserve better than her virtual silence over the three 'secrets'. When asked if she would tell the Pope, as Mélanie and Maximin, the visionaries of La Salette, had done, she replied, 'The Virgin forbade me to tell any person, and the Pope is a person.'[82]

Thérèse and Bernadette represented two divergent aspects of nineteenth-century Catholicism. Thérèse seemed to embody bourgeois sentimentality in her preoccupation with childishness as a desirable spiritual state (see illus. 39). Bernadette too was the product of her times, invested with the associations of *pyrénéisme* in particular and the cult of folklore and rustic simplicity more generally. But, despite their radical differences, they united this Catholic culture by incarnating childish innocence for the faithful. For Thérèse, this was a spiritual imperative, an innovative means of transposing a nineteenth-century vision of maternal–child relations on to the vision of God and believer. In contrast, Bernadette did not talk about the spirituality of childishness, for her childhood was hard, poor, riddled with illness and had nothing of the sentimental about it. But in presentation, she *was* the eternal child – inarticulate, simple, naïve, occasionally mischievous. She was thirty-five when she died in 1879,

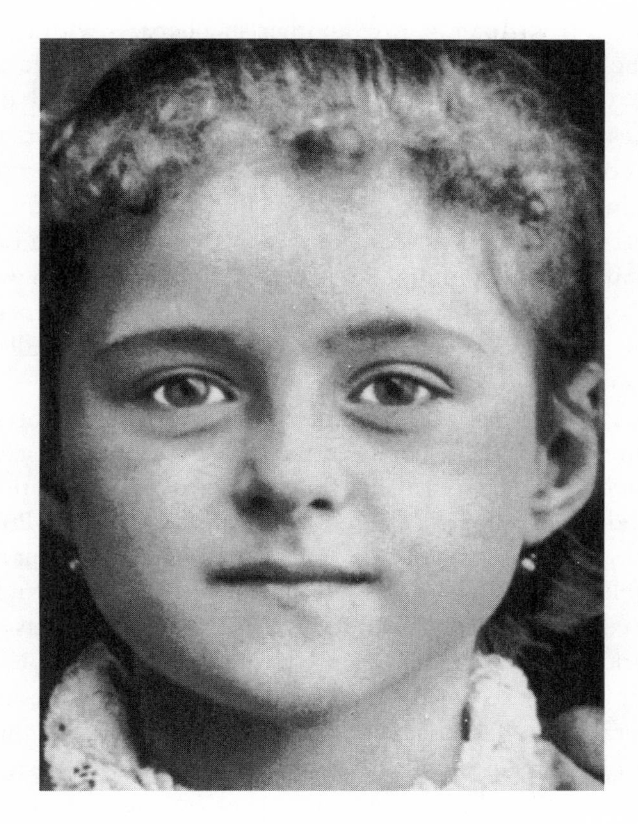

39. Thérèse de Lisieux, aged eight, 1881

but she was still perceived of as a fourteen-year-old, kneeling in peasant clothes in the Grotto.

During the apparitions the Virgin told Bernadette she should never expect to be happy in this world. The Church made sure that this would be the case. Despite the kindness of the sisters and the attentions of the Tardhivail sisters, Bernadette was watched, questioned and disciplined, all at a time when she was subject to frequent illness. Her suffering was, however, artless. She was not the heroic early Christian martyr resisting paganism through the dismemberment of her body,[83] nor was she like Catherine of Siena and other female medieval saints who gave to posterity a powerful vision of female spirituality. She also differed from Joan of Arc, another shepherdess with deep rural roots, who became a leader of men, and from the respectable widow–saints of the Counter-Reformation, doggedly pious and devoting themselves to charity. Except for the apparitions, there were no later moments of spiritual ecstasy, nor writings that expressed a spiritual position in a tradition that ran from Hildegard of Bingen through Saint Theresa and her near contemporary Saint Thérèse de Lisieux.[84] She was humble and poor like some others, but her heroism was quiet endurance, a quality that only grew as her illnesses worsened in the convent where she was enclosed, the only nun there never allowed to leave.

Bernadette presents a portrait of quiet strength out of keeping with many of her saintly predecessors. The way others sometimes constructed her suggested their need to project on to her their own desires and needs. The tale of Bernadette's conversion of the Protestant woman brought along by Elfrida Lacrampe found the visionary virtually unable to speak, and yet somehow still able to bring about the desired spiritual transformation. Abbé Montauzé was near to exasperation when Bernadette refused to perform, insisting, it seemed, on a dumb show to satisfy *his* vision of the sign of the cross. In these interactions, Bernadette seemed almost on show, not unlike the hysterics of the medical clinics, obliged to perform the gestures and commands suggested to them by medical operators and audience alike.[85] What separated her from these women was a sense of self that obeyed but did not bend. By keeping herself always slightly hidden, Bernadette protected her visions and her integrity, able to resist the pressure of photographers, priests and pilgrims alike.

When she entered the convent in Nevers a new stage in her life began. There she was apparently 'persecuted' by Mère Marie Thérèse Vazou, who kept Bernadette a novice for ten years.[86] It is at this juncture that her personal destiny and that of the shrine diverged. Bernadette was not forgotten at Lourdes, but the direction of her life mattered not at all to the development of the shrine. Unlike Mélanie and Maximin, who embarrassed by their psychological disequilibrium, Bernadette stayed closely within the fold, hidden behind the convent's walls, acting as a nurse in the infirmary when her deteriorating health permitted her this rare joy of service. All devotees of the shrine hoped for her beatification and sanctification, and no doubt found confirmation in their beliefs when her body remained 'miraculously' intact after three exhumations. Such disputations and investigations were, however, of the twentieth century, when the shrine she called into being was already an international institution.

Part Two

The Lourdes of Pilgrimage

Prologue

Bernadette's departure for Nevers in 1866 marks a decisive break in the history of the shrine, but the transformation of Lourdes and the Grotto was well under way before she left. The Episcopal Commission of Inquiry, set up in 1858 as news of the visions was spreading across France, came out in support of the apparitions only in 1862. In the intervening four years Lourdes became a place of local pilgrimage, despite the lack of the bishop's official approval. Laurence himself was not prepared to wait for the results of his commission. Instead he showed his confidence in both Bernadette and the shrine's future by buying Massabieille and the Grotto from the commune in 1861. Both he and Peyramale interpreted the apparition's message personally; they saw themselves as the priests mentioned by the Virgin who were meant to build the chapel and organize the processions, and both envisaged grandiose projects virtually from the start.

The central importance of the Grotto led to a preservation process that in fact proved to be quite destructive of its original appearance. On the one hand, clerics recognized that its natural quality was an essential part of the message of Notre-Dame de Lourdes; on the other, they sought to remake this wild and even unprepossessing site into something more picturesque and convenient. Peyramale was devoted to making the Grotto look impressive, for it appeared undistinguished in a landscape famous for its magnificent caves. He thought the interior needed to be excavated and the rubble used to extend the embankment for crowds to gather, with a dry stone wall to border the river. The early building works thus concentrated on 'beautifying' the Grotto and making it easier of access through a tree-lined promenade along the Gave and a curving descent from the forest. The installation of the grill in 1864, after the wild rose bush had already been destroyed, was indicative of the desire to contain the depredations of pilgrims (see illus. 40). What was left was a vision of the picturesque that accorded well with pious and respectable sensibilities: like Bernadette, photographed in her faded calico showing a Pyrenean allure that was not quite authentic, the Grotto became a carefully presented stereotype that covered over its wild, unhealthy and decidedly unkempt original state.

40. This French postcard of 1905 shows how the grill erected in 1864 separated pilgrims from the Grotto

If the 'natural' state of the Grotto in some sense remained, the 'chapel' the apparition demanded was from the outset envisaged as a monument. The project went to an architect of regional extraction – Hippolyte Duran, a recent convert whose spiritual director was Abbé Dasque, an important cleric working at the seminary of Saint-Pé, where Mgr Laurence had begun his career. For Duran and the local clergy, the building of the chapel was a unique and highly coveted opportunity to express Mary's magnificence through earthly forms. Duran was a student of Viollet-le-Duc, the most famous restorer and remaker of medieval buildings in nineteenth-century France, and a favourite of both the emperor and his court. Whether it was the re-creation of the Romanesque cathedral of Vézelay, the restoration of the Gothic Notre-Dame de Paris, or the reconstruction of the medieval fortress town of Carcassonne, Viollet-le-Duc imprinted his vision on the past so totally that he all but rebuilt the buildings he was working on. His taste exemplified the century's preoccupation with the society of the Middle Ages, another strand of the medieval 'mood' that played so strong a part in nineteenth-century Catholicism generally and the pilgrimage movement to Lourdes more particularly.

Duran, however, was no Viollet-le-Duc and had neither the talent nor the practical abilities of his teacher. At first he favoured a Romano-Byzantine design, one quickly abandoned in favour of the cathedral architecture of the thirteenth century. Apparently this style appealed more to clerics like Laurence, who saw the Gothic model as essentially French, the cathedrals to Notre-Dame exemplifying the high-water mark of medieval piety. The execution of the project, however, at first proved a disaster. Rather than accord and mutual endeavour, the various foremen and building entrepreneurs fought among themselves, and work stalled for almost two years; Duran stayed in Bayonne and visited only infrequently, costs spun out of control, and in September 1863 part of the building for the new residence of the Garaison Fathers collapsed. Duran was exonerated, much to the exasperation of Peyramale, whose concern at this stage stemmed from his hope that the chapel would be a dependence of his own parish church.[1] At this juncture pilgrims often began their journey to the Grotto from his church, a habit he wished to sustain with a more worthy building. Like those he criticized, however, Peyramale also failed to stay within budget and died with his new church unfinished; even worse, his own vision for the shrine slowly faded as control transferred to the diocese and the role of the parish diminished.

Work began again on the chapel in 1864, and only then were the problems of the site fully appreciated. For the decision to leave the Grotto 'untouched' meant that Duran's construction was placed on the hill of Espélugues twenty-four metres above the Gave, and one side had to be levelled to create a plateau big enough to accommodate the structure. Massive engineering works were also necessary to provide a stable foundation for the crypt, which was completed in 1866, and the chapel, finished only in 1872 and declared the Basilica of the Immaculate Conception in 1874. Despite the paving and clearing, the Grotto never entirely lost the many animistic associations that the fountain, rocks and green plants offered as a vision of fertility and femininity. But by placing the massive basilica on top of it, the Church ensured the symbolic imposition of orthodoxy. The tall spire that soars to the heavens is the most prominent feature of the valley; what one sees from afar is not the Grotto but the basilica that dominates it (see illus. 41). With this building, the shrine was subsumed by the Church, the magical and legendary aspects of the apparition story shorn from the conventionalized tale that the local clergy and the hierarchy preferred as they rooted it more securely in orthodoxy.

41. A bird's eye view of Lourdes in 1877, chromolithograph by Erhard & Müller, from Henri Lasserre, Notre-Dame de Lourdes, *1878*
This shows the extent of the transformation of the town with the Basilica of the Immaculate Conception towering over the Grotto and dominating the valley, the tree-lined avenues along the Gave and the beginnings of the sanctuary complex

For example, the main altar has a carving in which the cycle of Annunciation, Visitation, Assumption and Coronation of the Virgin is completed by the apparitions at Lourdes; the great stained-glass windows of the basilica record the Mystery of the Immaculate Conception through to the dogmatic definition made by Pius IX and the apparitions at Massabieille.[2] In this way Bernadette's visions were firmly embedded in the long history of what was now one of the Church's central dogmas. Equally, the stained-glass in the side chapels pairs events in Church history with episodes during the apparitions – for example, one of Saint Marguerite-Marie Alacoque, the visionary of the Sacred Heart in the late seventeenth century, was just above another of Bernadette standing before the Episcopal Commission. Finally, the basilica became a repository of contemporary struggles. Filled with the banners, flags and medallions of the national pilgrimage of 1872, the basilica housed the standards of the first pilgrimage of penance to come to Lourdes after the Franco-Prussian War and the civil war.[3]

From the moment of this 'pilgrimage of the banners' in 1872, the diocesan authorities began to envisage the third and final addition to the structure, the lower Basilica of the Rosary, begun in 1883. Like the basilica of Sacré-Cœur in Montmartre and Notre-Dame de Fourvière in Lyon, the officials chose an Eastern, Romano-Byzantine style decorated with mosaics (see illus. 42). Again the project was complex, as it involved extensive dynamiting, demolishing the temporary residence of the Garaison Fathers, and running the great ramps up and around the structure with massive concrete foundations (see illus. 43). Completing the sanctuary was the esplanade, which accommodated the hundreds of thousands of pilgrims of the latter part of the century, and the Asile Notre-Dame, built near by when Lourdes took on its character as the shrine for the sick.

By the end of the 1880s the sanctuary had created a whole new world at Lourdes, a world of the established Church that typified the aesthetic and spiritual style of an era. The mix was eclectic, the result heavy, imposing, almost industrial in aspect, despite the attempt to adhere to forms of architecture that conjured up the artistic harmonies of earlier Christian centuries. For the novelist and Catholic convert Joris-Karl Huysmans, it was the epitome of ugliness, bringing up the worst associations of mass culture and commercialism:

At Lourdes there is such a plethora of vulgarity, such a haemorrhage of bad taste, that the notion of some intervention by the Prince of Depravity inevitably springs to mind . . . One cannot help wondering what style it derives from, for it comprises a smattering of everything. There is Byzantine and Romanesque, the style of the hippodrome and that of the casino; but

42. *The Basilica of the Rosary, Lourdes*
43. *The ramps of the basilica,* Le Pèlerin, *2 September 1894*

mainly, when one looks closely, there is the style of the machine depot, the roundhouse engine-shed . . . As to art, which is, after sanctity, the only clean thing on earth, you shall not merely be deprived of it, but, as I describe things, you will be relentlessly insulted by the persistent blasphemy of Ugliness.[4]

As an aesthete, Huysmans loathed the place; none the less, he realized that the crowds scarcely noticed what he considered the most appalling bad taste.

It was not only the shrine that transformed the rustic *bourg* beyond all recognition. While all its neighbours except for the spa towns experienced an emigration of unprecedented proportions, Lourdes in the 1860s both grew and underwent the process of urbanization that was in full flood in Paris and many another French city in the period. Connected to the outside world by a railway line from 1866, the town grew closer to Bordeaux, and through Bordeaux it became closer to Paris. Telegraph access rented from the rail depot made it a city of progress, making full use of the magic of electricity. Few complained about the influx of visitors that brought hotels, inns and conveniences to the town, but the new wealth and expectations also sowed discord. Plans to enlarge access to the Grotto brought court cases, as old buildings in Lourdes were condemned to make way for wider roads. An entire section of the old town was destroyed to make way for the Boulevard de la Grotte. This main thoroughfare, begun in 1879 after four years of wrangling, created bad feeling between the town's inhabitants and the sanctuary's officials. Thus, the exigencies of 'progress' wiped out the older patterns of living; by the time the great national pilgrimages took on definitive shape in the late 1870s, Lourdes was changed almost beyond recognition.[5]

The second half of this book takes place in this transformed, newly prospering city, now the Lourdes of pilgrimage rather than the Lourdes of the apparitions, a town of hotels, restaurants and railway lines rather than the poor market town of the first half of the century. The Grotto of Massabieille was no longer in the wild, nor did pigs roam there; the arrival of strangers was an everyday occurrence, not something to be remarked upon. Those who had witnessed the apparitions were still important personages in the community, but, with their deaths, new, largely clerical organizations would take the lead. This was a different world from the early part of the Lourdes drama, but even more tempestuous in the debates it inspired and extraordinary in the events it witnessed.

6

The Battle of the Books

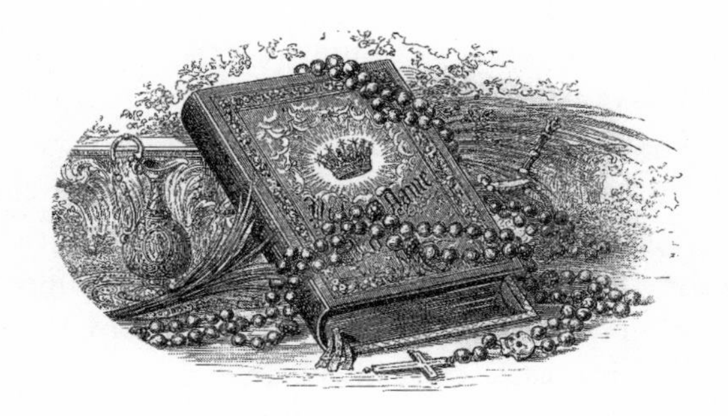

At the same time that the sanctuary was being constructed, another struggle focused on building the history of Lourdes, a battle over whose version of events constituted the 'truth' about the apparitions and their aftermath. Although distant from the scaffolding on the site, this intellectual and spiritual debate none the less paralleled the construction projects. Both were concerned with which traditions and images of events would be commemorated, both were major features of the shrine for the rest of the century, and both were critical for the reputation that Lourdes attained in the outside world.

Lourdes became Lourdes because of Henri Lasserre, a journalist and polemicist of rare rhetorical power. Millions read his *Notre-Dame de Lourdes*, which captivated the entire Catholic world after its publication in 1869, but this monumental success brought great bitterness and rancour in its train. By claiming audaciously that his was the only true history and by seeking to repress all competitors, Lasserre was almost immediately beset by dispute, enmity and scandal. As he attacked the Garaison Fathers, Laurence's missionaries at the shrine and authors of their own version, and they in turn attacked him, a Jesuit historian named Léonard Cros pledged to write *the* definitive account and demolish Lasserre's edifice. He too encountered little but trouble for his temerity.

The struggle was more than a titanic fight of personalities, although this was an important element in generating much of the ill-humour; more, it depended on a contest between different visions of the shrine that derived from conflicting tendencies within nineteenth-century Catholicism. The resulting debate showed how historical narrative mattered to the living practice of Lourdes and the pilgrimage movement that grew up around it. Just as the linkage of Veuillot's ultramontanism, the empress's clericalism and charity, and Laurence's ambitions for his diocese propelled Lourdes into public attention in the first place, so different forces shaped its legendary status and institutionalization in succeeding decades. This time, however, they were as often in conflict as they were in alliance.

Lasserre and His Book

Born in the Périgord in 1828, Henri Lasserre was the son of a naval physician and a devout mother, a journalist who worked at three newspapers before his history *Notre-Dame de Lourdes* catapulted him to fame and controversy (see illus. 44). He had long been an ardent Catholic, personally engaged with the new ultramontanist currents of nineteenth-century France, encountering at Solesmes the revitalized ambience of plainchant that pervaded the abbey and writing verses to the Virgin infused with the flavour of nineteenth-century Marianism.

He first became widely known in 1863 when he penned a successful and vitriolic attack on Ernest Renan's *Vie de Jésus* (1863), which had caused outrage in Catholic circles by denying Christ's divinity and subjecting the historical Jesus to German techniques of biblical exegesis and new theories of folklore. Renan argued that Christ was the product of race, milieu and historical moment, and concentrated on the context of tribal Judaism, the Galilee and the impact of Roman

44. Henri Lasserre (1828–1900)

oppression, concluding that the divine Jesus was a poetic legend based on the collective reconstruction of a human existence. Using comparative philology, he looked at the Gospels and highlighted faulty chronologies and transitions, demonstrating how oral tradition was affixed to the crucifixion story. Far from condemning the legends, however, his literary, even novelistic biography praised their power and significance, for he held that they induced poetic wonder and hence had the extraordinary capacity to convert and bring about moral transformation. In this, rather than in any divinity, lay Jesus' uniqueness and historical significance.[1]

Renan's work was important to Lourdes because his critical spirit stung all Catholic intellectuals and brought the subject of biblical revelation to the forefront of lay debate. It also provoked men like Lasserre to respond, first in his pamphlet, *L'Evangile selon Renan*, and then in less direct ways. Lasserre's critique was one among a multitude and far from the most rigorous contribution,[2] but was important insofar as it revealed his own view of miracles. In his opinion Renan had sought to separate 'the Christ of Jesus, the history of God from the history of man', negating a transcendence that was essential to Catholic thinking.[3] He assaulted Renan for what he called his 'retreat into hypothesis' when faced with the miraculous – an obscurantist theorizing that ignored or dismissed everything it could not understand. *Notre-Dame de Lourdes* was another, if indirect response, with the miraculous paraded and celebrated on almost every page. For the faithful, his history became the 'Evangile de Lourdes', a gospel in its way as revelatory as the Bible itself.

Lasserre seemed almost predestined to write such a work, and was already known in Lourdes both for his attack on Renan *and* for a miraculous cure to his eyes that took place in the same year of 1863.[4] Peyramale singled him out as the best man for the job, and urged Laurence to authorize the project, a recommendation that showed the early and fast connection between the two men and their shared vision of Catholicism in combat.[5]

Published as a single volume in 1869, Lasserre's history was probably the greatest bestseller of the nineteenth century, going into 142 French editions in its first seven years,[6] translated into at least eighty languages by 1900 and apparently selling over a million copies.[7] The pace and beauty of the narrative was matched by the physical magnificence of the large edition, which had copious colour plates in the sentimental Saint Sulpician style and a text presented like an illuminated manuscript, encased in recurring neo-Gothic motifs and stylized representations of the town (see illus. 45 and 46). In this way the holy worlds of contemporary Lourdes and that of the medieval Church were visually bound together.

The once-upon-a-time narration began with a romantic description of Lourdes in the foothills of the Pyrenean piedmont, and a song of praise for the 'races montagnardes' who lived, unchanging, in a world of custom and piety passed on from the Middle Ages.[8] Lasserre acknowledged that the Lourdais knew of modern ways, but maintained that they proudly preferred their own traditions. The setting and anthropology of his work romanticized 'the people' from the outset, and they remained one of the leading aspects in his story, as idealized in his vision of Catholic populism as they were in the anti-clerical, republican account of the Revolution made famous by the ideologue and historian Jules Michelet.[9]

PRÉFACE

DE LA PREMIÈRE ÉDITION (1869)

A la suite d'une grâce signalée dont le récit
trouvera place dans le cours de ce livre, je
promis, il y a quelques années, d'écrire l'histoire des événements extraordinaires qui ont donné

45. Clerget & Huyot, 'La Basilique et la Grotte actuelle', engraving from Henri Lasserre, Notre-Dame de Lourdes, *1878*

46. Laugée & Jehenne, 'Bernadette bergère', chromolithograph, from Henri Lasserre, Notre-Dame de Lourdes, *1878*

Even more striking was the Manichaean portrayal of good and bad he laid out. His vision suggested a Holy Trinity of Bernadette, Peyramale and 'the people', a conception that landed him in trouble because of its implication of a struggle between diocesan authority and the parish. Bernadette is not quite a Cinderella, but her gentleness and stoic virtue are all qualities that predestine her to greatness. Against her are ranged the villains of the piece, portrayed in suitably melodramatic terms: Jacomet is intelligent and capable but dissatisfied with his lowly position, equal to the task of undoing criminals and cheats yet unable to understand the motivations of honest people. Like a night bird who can see in the dark, or an old Pyrenean horse who can make his way through tortuous mountain paths, he has a twisted mind that sees evil rather than good. Massy, although a devout Christian, believes only in the miracles of the Gospels, and holds that the days of wonder are past. The prefect is a desiccated official who thinks that 'everything out of the ordinary is an assault on eternal law. He confused method with order, and mistook bureaucracy for law.'[10]

Lasserre thus depicted a struggle between Bernadette's 'childish weakness, defenceless apart from her simplicity', and the machinations of the imperial state.[11] His tale of strife mixed nineteenth-century melodrama with the eternal qualities of the fairy-tale. The men of order threatened Bernadette with prison or hospitalization, blocked off the Grotto from worshippers, tried to prosecute trespassers and took away the offerings given by the poor. But they were continually frustrated in their efforts. Bernadette was examined by three physicians, but was deemed healthy of mind; defiant marauders tore away police barriers; and outsiders coming to the Grotto were too important to prosecute. Although the sometimes sinister, sometimes comic vision of officialdom was largely denied by the people of Lourdes, who acknowledged Massy's integrity and Jacomet's acumen, they still approved of Lasserre's account. It was as if they acknowledged its essential verity, accepting that even if the characterizations lacked nuance, a deeper 'truth' was to be found in the book's penetrating outlines.[12]

The hardy poor folk, the second main element in the drama, built on their native virtues and were transformed by their belief in the supernatural presence. Despite their poverty they showed acts of selflessness, as when the workers enlarged the perilous path to the Grotto for free. Criminality ended, and quiet protests of prayer and procession rather than violence irritated the authorities. At no time did the crowds disturb the peace, despite what Lasserre saw as unjust provocation. He quickly skates over the episode of the false visionaries and hints that they were encouraged by the conspiratorial tactics of officials to divert attention from Bernadette and to force Laurence to denounce *all* the events.[13]

The third hero, Peyramale, is praised for his early caution and decision not to attend the apparitions, thereby avoiding the risk of accusations of clerical direction.[14] He is providentially situated at Lourdes, ready to take up the special burdens that the crisis created. His early doubts and brusque attitude were part of his capacity both to test the visionary and then to accept her as genuine: 'This man, so strong, felt himself beaten by an all-powerful weakness.'[15] He was a triumphant defender of Bernadette, enraged when she was examined by the physicians in an attempt to detain her as insane, but a peacemaker when Jacomet's removal of the objects from the Grotto made him fearful of an ugly protest among the poor. While the bishop was suspicious if not hostile to popular faith,[16] Peyramale lived and breathed the faith of his parishioners, his adherence preserving a special place for him in posterity.[17]

Here was Lasserre exacerbating the institutional cleavages between higher and lower clergy, making Laurence and Peyramale represent two opposing visions of Catholic belief. That Laurence shared many of the same ultramontanist tendencies as his subordinate mattered little; Lasserre wished to amplify what he considered the differences between the hierarchy and its authority on the one hand, and the impulses of a parish priest close to the 'people' on the other. Laurence becomes little more than a channel for the populist torrent. In the nineteenth century 'the universal faith began with the little and the humble, such that, as in the Kingdom of Heaven itself, the last were the first, and the first the last'.[18] He even feared that the Church's delay in approving the apparitions might potentially stimulate anti-clerical feelings. Above all, Lasserre condoned a belief in miracles as part of contemporary Catholic evangelism, a position that had no patience for the conservatism of the hierarchy, or its attempt to determine on the miraculous without lay meddling.

However, these qualities alone did not make the book such a tremendous success. Lasserre was a rhetorical genius, and he gave his melodramatic oppositions greater resonances by mixing biblical imagery with contemporary events. There are moments when Jesus and other characters of the ancient Judean world walk across the page with an almost breathtaking immediacy. When, Lasserre maintained, God wished to come to earth, he chose the dwellings of his ministers and particular friends: 'And this is why he habitually chose the houses of the poor and the insignificant.'[19] The Lourdes story was seen as an echo of the Acts of the Apostles, in which the poor were raised up and the powerful confounded. He also used biblical parallels to enhance his tale: when Bernadette went to gather wood with her sister and friend before the first apparition, she was not simply a poor Pyrenean maid, but like Ruth or Naomi gleaning in Boaz's fields.[20] He saw a multitude of coincidences between the apparitions and the liturgical calendar of Lent, the period of the cycle of visions.[21] When, for example, Bernadette discovered the fountain on 26 February, the diocese of Lourdes were celebrating the festival of the Lance and Nails. For Lasserre

> the spring we are talking about, whose memory is glorified by special services in the diocese, was that great and divine spring that the spear of the Roman centurion, piercing the right side of the lifeless Christ, caused to gush forth like a river of life to regenerate the earth and save mankind.[22]

The Bible pervaded his history, and Lasserre and his supporters eventually came to regard his work like scripture, and to consider those who disagreed with him as heretics. He set out to enchant and catered to the 'miraculous mood' encouraged by the likes of Veuillot. The book indeed met all of Renan's criteria of the legendary, with its chronological vagaries, mixing of reality and magic, and literary wonder. But Lasserre was too much a man of his era not to defend his history on empirical, positivist grounds in much the same way that Renan defended his own work. In his Preface Lasserre stressed his objectivity, identifying the official documents and witnesses' statements he had used. He claimed a further expertise by relying on interviews with the historical actors, maintaining that he had voyaged across France to test their various accounts. Finally, he asserted that he was the disciple of Adolphe Thiers, the politician who wrote learnedly on the Consulat and First Empire, thereby identifying himself with the documentary strand of romantic history.[23]

At the same time Lasserre was straightforward enough to acknowledge his personal engagement with the subject through an almost post-modernist insertion of the authorial 'self' into the narrative. The penultimate chapter – the point of Lourdes's triumph over officialdom and before the hasty description of the building of the sanctuary – deals with his own 'miraculous' cure by Lourdes water after a terrifying period of unexplained blindness. As a journalist and intellectual, this period had brought increased isolation, so much so that he had to rely on a secretary and was preparing to retire to his native Dordogne. Lasserre recounts his suffering, as well as his resistance to spiritual surrender, and the consequent obligations that a miraculous cure would impose upon him. Urged along by his Protestant friends, including the future republican premier Charles Freycinet, who was concerned for his friend's fate but also interested in the experiment, Lasserre bathed his eyes and forehead in Lourdes water.

> I took out the cork, poured the water into a cup and took a cloth from the chest of drawers. I made these banal preparations with meticulous care, and I still remember that they were endowed with a secret solemnity that struck me even then, as I went to and fro in my bedroom. I was not alone there; it was clear that God was present. The Holy Virgin, whom I had invoked, was no doubt also there.[24]

When Lasserre later argued that his history should be the *only* story of the shrine, he cited the congratulatory papal brief of Pius IX:

> You have taken great pains to prove . . . the recent Apparition of the most merciful Mother of God; and done so in such a way that precisely the struggle of human malice against divine mercy makes the luminous self-evidence of the facts stand out with greater force and clarity.

The Pope was utterly convinced of the truth of the work on all levels and saw in it many morals for the tumultuous nineteenth century. Lourdes was an example of how the poor benefited from Roman Catholicism, how religion maintained order peacefully in the face of adversity, and how 'the mischievous' were always overpowered by 'the divine counsels of providence'.[25] Such an endorsement, given in 1869 virtually on the eve of the First Vatican Council, which saw the promulgation of the dogma of infallibility, showed how Lasserre's work combined the different dimensions of nineteenth-century ultramontanism to perfection. The book linked the aspirations of the pious poor and the parish clergy to those of the Pope himself through Marian piety and the Immaculate Conception, Pius IX's almost personal dogma.

Such a ringing endorsement made it all the more embarrassing for Laurence to refuse his official imprimatur, especially after he had authorized the project in the first place. His hesitation arose from Lasserre's hostility to the work of his two leading missionaries at the sanctuary, Pierre-Rémi Sempé and Jean-Marie Duboë, the leaders of the Garaison Fathers, who had written their own *Petite histoire de Notre-Dame de Lourdes*. Advertised in the prospectus of the *Annales de Notre-Dame de Lourdes* in 1868, they hoped to bring a wide readership to the journal by retelling the tale in serial form. In contrast to Lasserre's volume, theirs was little more than another pious memoir in which Bernadette became somewhat prim and the bishop crucial in recognizing the apparitions.[26] Although it also drew on local testimony, the result was edifying rather than entrancing, and in this crucial difference lay the reason for their relative successes.

The Garaison Fathers were Laurence's representatives at the Grotto. They oversaw the sanctuary from 1866 until their dissolution in 1903 when, as a result of anti-clerical legislation two years earlier, the sanctuary's property was expropriated and the fathers exiled from the Grotto's domain.[27] Under Sempé's leadership, the fathers inaugurated many of the early liturgical traditions at the shrine, and in the early years recorded the numerous claims of miracles[28] (see illus. 47). Their role, however, was hotly challenged by the most prominent member of the local clergy, Peyramale, concerned by the transfer of control from the parish to the diocese. In some sense the struggle typified the enduring strife between bishop and lower clergy that so permeated ecclesiastical relations in nineteenth-century France and in this instance was further complicated by the quarrel between Lasserre and the bishop's camp. The result was to make Peyramale and Lasserre inseparable allies.

47. Père Rémi Sempé (1818–89)

Lasserre believed that his book, and his book alone, should be the official history, and defended himself fervently against criticism from the bishop's supporters, who were wary of the 'novelistic' style of his work, its many factual errors and severe characterization of the officials.[29] In response to Sempé, he wrote:

As for charity, I agree with you in principle but perhaps not in form. The Lord of Lords, in his charity, did not hesitate to call Herod a fox. Strip charity of this rigorous element and you render it insipid; instead of wine from the true stock, nothing is left but a sickly syrup. From a literary point of view, I think the suppression of this element would have a similar effect. In my opinion this is one of the greatest defects of many good books, which harp on a single string and are consequently as tedious as they are well intentioned.[30]

Speaking of the documents he had consulted and the research trips he had undertaken (later criticized in turn by Cros), Lasserre denied his work was too much like fiction and instead levelled the same accusation at his rivals. Sempé and Duboë, he wrote, had produced a work 'based on one or two sources picked up at the wash-house or mill, like Alexandre Dumas or Eugène Sue'. Later he likened their *Petite histoire* to trying to write a history of the Empire by chatting to three or four 'brave soldiers of Napoleon's army'.[31]

This escalating enmity came to a head with an argument about the sale of his book. Lasserre wanted the bishop to sell the work near the Grotto to pilgrims, and offered half of the profits to the sanctuary in exchange.[32] The bishop was unwilling, so Lasserre tried again, offering to write a more popular edition and hand over the receipts, but only on condition that the work of Abbé Fourcade, who had written an account of the apparitions in 1862, be suppressed.[33] The conflict escalated further when Lasserre vented his anger against the missionary fathers by taking his case to Rome. In this, he followed in the footsteps of other laymen such as Veuillot, and demonstrated the growing willingness of both Catholic opinion-makers and ultramontane lower clergy to circumvent the episcopate by a direct appeal. Addressing the Congrégation du Saint-Office Romain, as well as all the bishops of the Catholic world gathered for the 1870 Vatican Council, Lasserre published an open letter to Laurence, who in fact had just died. In this polemic – designed to show the scandal and corruption of the Garaison Fathers – he portrayed himself as a 'simple and humble layman' – yet laid implicit claim to authority because of the providential success of his work:

> The good that it [his book] has done, and the conversions it has already effected; the innumerable pilgrims and donations it has attracted to the Grotto; letters of praise from more than sixty bishops; the brief from our most Holy Father saying his Holiness believes that, along with the miracles, such a book is part of the Mother of God's plans; all this has helped to convince me that, despite my unworthiness and perhaps even because of it, the noble Virgin who appeared to Bernadette deigned to choose me to tell this sublime story, and make it heard by mankind.[34]

The polemic juxtaposed excerpts from the Garaison Fathers' *Petite histoire* with declarations by Bernadette, declarations that were as much a part of the dispute as the works themselves. For Lasserre had gained permission from the local bishop, Mgr Forcade, to go to Nevers to see the visionary, and used the resulting interview to attack the Garaison Fathers.[35] It was not long before they also took the road to Saint-Gildard and in turn tried to blacken Lasserre as a man who was not to be trusted, and who had badgered Bernadette and twisted her words until they supported his own account. They claimed that, far from supporting Lasserre, she had confirmed *their* version, and added that she had forgotten much, thereby suggesting that what she could not confirm was a product of loss of memory.[36]

Nor did this end the matter, for in due course Cros also arrived to see Bernadette, to find that the door was now soundly barred. Cros held Lasserre responsible for this refusal, and he was only able to submit written questions to her after he obtained a papal brief in 1878.[37] This subsidiary struggle over access to Bernadette shows how she too became embroiled in these disputes, yet lacked the authority to control her own story, for interviewers noted enthusiastically when she confirmed their opinions, but claimed she was too tired, or too forgetful, to remember when she contradicted them. Although they all saw themselves as devotees of her simplicity, they also seemed to believe that this very quality made her inadequate for the task of historical reconstruction: she needed to be helped to express the truth by people wiser than herself. Their attitude was not dissimilar to the way commentators had altered the age of the white lady, her words and gestures.[38]

Although Lasserre's rhetoric was the more effective, there was as much invention and inaccuracy in his *Notre-Dame de Lourdes* as there was in the *Petite histoire*; nor was there that much difference between the two over interpretation, for the disputes centred more on details of acts and gestures. The bitterness derived from the overall proximity of the narratives rather than from their divergences. Like Freud's narcissism of marginal difference, the closeness increased the enmity: there was never the same sustained polemic against anti-clerical authors who scorned every aspect of the apparitions tale, except, perhaps, for the fury triggered by Emile Zola's novel about the shrine.[39] None the less, Lasserre was determined on the total obliteration of his rivals: the first part of his open letter ended by providing, word for word, what Laurence should say to disavow the *Petite histoire*, arguing for its publication to be stopped in the *Annales de Notre-Dame de Lourdes*.

The second part began with what was perhaps the more serious charge, and one that did considerable damage to the shrine's reputation. In essence, he charged the Garaison Fathers with outright venality, accusing them of doing business at the sanctuary, of prospering like the merchants in the Temple, debasing the shrine by the profusion of 'petit commerce' and portraying himself in contrast as the humble layman trying to stop abuses. He argued, with some justification, that the missionaries should have left this 'petit commerce' to the poorest families of Lourdes, who were, as in Boaz's fields again, entitled to the gleanings. What he did not reveal were his own attempts to have his book sold exclusively by the men he was now accusing.

Instead, he charged that trafficking was unsupervised, with all manner of people selling 'rosaries, candles, photographs, medallions'.[40] Even worse was his allegation that the missionaries were making an unfair profit on the Lourdes water they sold at home and abroad, demanding the same price from rich and poor alike. He also criticized the diocese for its rapid acquisition of property and massive building works, 'as if the Most Holy Virgin, instead of asking for a temple, had asked for land, property'.[41] With such statements Lasserre trod a well-worn anti-clerical path, bearing the standard, once again, of popular Catholicism against the ecclesiastical hierarchy and what he saw as their aggrandizing tendencies.

Sempé responded by producing another declaration from Bernadette that confirmed the fathers' account and maintained, with the help of Pomian, that their portrait was 'a perfect photograph'.[42] Tables of statistics sought to show that they made nothing, or virtually nothing, from the bottles of water, explaining how 'the storage costs, the labour of those who wash, fill and sell the bottles, the numerous breakages'[43] made it difficult to make a profit. They defended their sale of 'that which is the legitimate and legal property of the sanctuary, such as photographs, images, statues, medallions'[44] as common practice throughout the Catholic world.

While they fought back – claiming that the acquisition of property had come from diocesan monies and from the labours of the missionaries themselves rather than from the sanctuary's funds – Lasserre's criticism none the less stung. The rapid expansion of the shrine, the destruction of the wilderness around Massabieille, and the sale of pious objects and photographs had indeed commercialized the Grotto; if his specific accusations were excessive and unjust, the general thrust seemed fair enough. Nor did he keep silent even when his campaign in Rome failed and he was ordered to abandon his criticisms.

Lasserre's legacy at Lourdes was intensely ambivalent; having brought the shrine untold fame, he spent much of his remaining years tearing into any deviation from his personal vision. In the process he caused great damage, for his attacks on the supposed wealth of the Garaison Fathers caused donations to fall so much that work had to be stopped on essential projects.[45] Like a gadfly, he jumped from one 'scandal' to the next, championing always the populist and localist perspective that had infused his original narrative. For example, in another campaign against the missionaries, in the newspaper *L'Echo des Pèlerins*, he accused them of conspiring with the administration to build the Boulevard de la Grotte and divide the Grotto from the town, a view also held by some Lourdais;[46] he railed against the embellishments and transformations near and around the shrine, once again arguing that they were ruining the wildness of the place:

think . . . you are turning Lourdes into a pleasure garden . . . preserving the focal point of the divine event but destroying the surroundings . . . you are levelling the ledges, breaking up the rocks, diverting the stream, canalizing the Gave . . . you are making grassy slopes . . . you dare erect rock gardens . . . caves of Calypso. You are substituting your works for God's . . . When you destroy these places, you destroy the physical proofs of the apparition.[47]

Even worse for the missionaries was the way he allied with Peyramale to oppose the spirit and practice of their undertaking. Well known because of his early support for the Grotto, Peyramale was a doughty adversary, and his vision was also radically different from that of the missionaries. Peyramale wanted a new parish church in the town, with pilgrimage processions going from there to the Grotto. Like so many clergy across France, Peyramale was a mason–priest, with grand building schemes designed to strengthen a vision of the parish as the centre of a Christian collectivity in which the faithful travelled beyond its boundaries to the chapel of the wild.[48] His desires, however, were utterly frustrated when the arrival of the Garaison Fathers effectively meant the shrine was taken over by the diocese. The Grotto was increasingly split apart from the parish; the church he built was an organizational and financial nightmare completed only years after his death, and processions from one to the other never attained the significance he had desired.[49]

Lasserre claimed Peyramale's death in 1878 had been hastened by disappointment and implied he had been the victim of 'a secret persecution' by the diocese.[50] Here again was the ultramontanist slant that showed a lowly servant of God being destroyed by the magisterial power of the bishop. Lasserre amplified the campaign in *L'Echo des Pèlerins* by working for the priest's beatification, discussing the miracles that were apparently occurring at his tomb.

In fact, through M. Lasserre's efforts, the tomb has been turned into a proper chapel with the bier at the centre. On top is a sculpted head of Mgr Peyramale, with a lamp burning above it and large candles all around – all a clear violation of Urban VIII's decrees on the canonization of saints. Prie-dieu facing the sepulchre are ready for the pilgrims.[51]

Rebelling against the diocesan authorities himself, it seemed Lasserre also encouraged others to do the same by organizing people to go to the train station in search of pilgrimage leaders who would then bring hundreds to Peyramale's tomb.[52] In the leaflet describing this monument, Lasserre suggested that the Virgin herself had suggested the route:

It was through the person of this priest that Notre-Dame de Lourdes was brought to men's attention; it is through the sepulchre of this priest that men now pass to go to Notre-Dame de Lourdes. One might say the Virgin herself laid out this route; the people climb the path down which Mary came.[53]

The battle between the two sides never seemed to conclude and, at the very end of December 1877, Mgr César-Victor Jourdan, Laurence's successor, sent every bishop of France an expanded version of a confidential memoir to gather their support. But even though the episcopate was beginning to close ranks, Lasserre still had formidable moral power. He asked how the bishops of Tarbes and Lourdes had let his book stand without any public condemnation for almost ten years, having profited from the work in order to enhance the image and popularity of the shrine.[54] It was clear that no authority was going to silence him. In the end the hierarchy decided that the best way of countering his challenge would be to undermine the edifice that gave him his authority. They needed a new history written by someone with the stature to take on Lasserre's book, and for this task they chose the Jesuit Léonard Cros. In so doing they unwittingly unleashed an even more bitter episode in the story of the shrine's official history.

The Jesuit Intervention

Père Cros had met Bernadette for the first time in 1864, and it is no exaggeration to say that he was marked by the encounter for the remaining half-century of his life (see illus. 48). For Cros was utterly convinced of the verity of her experience, and the events of Lourdes coincided perfectly with the intellectual issues that preoccupied him as a scholar. For the modern reader of his work, the result was an extraordinary combination of faith and scepticism that makes both him and his books difficult to classify; for Cros himself, the eventual result of the encounter was decades of labour, frustration and bitterness to produce a book that was only ever partially published.

Cros's *personal* commitment to Bernadette cannot be overemphasized, for however much his project was due to the needs of the shrine, the requirements of the diocese and the desires of the Pope, none of these could demand belief: it was Bernadette herself who swept away the doubts of a man highly cautious about miracle tales. The impact the visionary had on the Jesuit belies any suggestion that she was in some way bland or a cipher: certainly, Cros was more impressed by meeting her than the other way round.

When he first came to Lourdes and saw Bernadette, Cros was so overwhelmed he wrote to his brother, 'I've seen a photograph of her, but it is a very bad resemblance. If one comes to hand, don't think you have seen Bernadette.'[55] A second visit, in 1865, reinforced his

48. Père Léonard Cros (1831–1913)

initial impressions: Bernadette now had a 'supernatural charm';[56] she possessed 'a celestial simplicity! . . . *complete simplicity and guilelessness*, but dignified, above all simple in a way that earthly *nature* could never imitate'.[57] At the end of this second meeting 'I begged Bernadette to dictate to me the words in patois of the Very Holy Virgin . . . I seemed to hear the Very Holy Virgin herself, and truly I have never felt such intimate, celestial joy in my poor life.'[58] Cros's encounter with Bernadette brought him as close as he ever came to the divine.

His personal commitment to writing the history of Lourdes thus long preceded any desire to challenge the work of Lasserre, although this latter factor was crucial in turning the project into a defence of the Church against the onslaughts of what he considered fatuous legend-making. The defensive stance of the diocesan authorities in the face of Lasserre's unrelenting attacks increasingly predisposed them to Cros's desire to begin work. Laurence gave his blessing as early as 1865, or so Cros claimed, although other projects interfered;[59] by 1870 Sempé was also urging him to take on Lasserre, but it was only in 1877 that Sempé and Cros's Jesuit superior in Toulouse came to agreement.

The research began auspiciously the following year with a blessing by the new bishop, Mgr Jourdan, and a papal brief from Leo XIII. This sign of approval signified something of a reorientation of policy, for, while Lasserre's work had suited the spiritual proclivities of Pius IX, fighting the revolutionary and liberal tide that engulfed him in Italy, Leo XIII was engaged in other battles – modernizing the Church and providing room for a more avowedly 'social' dimension to Catholicism. By 1879 the ecclesiastical authorities were united in their opposition to Lasserre and wanted a work that would embarrass him for his errors and unbalanced interpretation. The papal brief maintained that Lasserre's book was not definitive, that the errors found in it arose from a lack of official documents, and that they could now be corrected.[60] From then until 1884 Cros remained 'chosen by Our Lady, by the bishop of Tarbes, by the Garaison Fathers'.[61] It was only after this date that he too would have barriers placed before him.

The choice of Cros was not just a happy coincidence of his desire to write such a history and the authorities' wish to possess one; the fact that he was a Jesuit was also crucial at this particular juncture. By 1879 moderate republicans were outmanoeuvred by radicals who, in pressing for the dissolution of unauthorized congregations, caused the dispersal of the Society of Jesus in France.[62] This was one of several anti-clerical laws that punctuated Lourdes's development during the history of the early Third Republic. Although the Jesuits had many detractors within the Church, the propaganda that portrayed them as casuistical fanatics, servile to the Pope, was now aimed at all clerics; in defending the Jesuits, the Church was also defending itself.

In tone, style and content, nothing could be further from Lasserre's account than the history that resulted, for Cros produced a scholarly and compendious work that revolutionized the study of the apparitions. However, for a series of political, religious and personal reasons, the new work was also subject to assault, this time before it was even published. The struggle became so rancorous that the work did not fully see the light of day until 1927, fourteen years after Cros's death, and then only in abridged form.[63] It was in 1957, to mark the centenary of the apparitions, that the first three volumes were finally published in complete form, as was an edited version of his witnesses' statements.[64]

In his disdain for Lasserre and his work, Cros was often unbalanced, some might say unhinged, so much so that he devoted the unpublished fourth volume of his *Histoire de Notre-Dame de Lourdes* to a blow-by-blow account of the troubles he faced in fighting against his great enemy. In his unpublished manuscript entitled 'M. Henri Lasserre et son livre' Cros shows how the refutation of Lasserre was as important to him as the recording of the events of the apparitions, and incidentally demonstrated the extent to which control over the historical record was crucial in the evolution of the shrine's reputation. Unlike later generations who have never even heard of Henri Lasserre, Cros knew that the author had 'made' Lourdes with his *magnum opus*. None the less, he was horrified by its romantic and literary qualities, and set out both to overturn his general theses and to correct his many factual errors.

Cros's letters and journals written during the project show a fanatical devotion that brought quick and important results, but then alienated potential supporters and friends. To his opponents, he came to seem a caricature of Jesuit fanaticism. He appeared to be trying to dominate through his intellectual superiority and methodological rigour, a tactic not designed to win friends among the practical Garaison Fathers, whose intellectual attainments were meagre in comparison. Their disenchantment shows the perennial struggle between various orders within the Church, and the resentment that the highly educated Jesuits in particular could generate.

The cooling of Cros's relations with the Garaison Fathers was nothing in comparison to the feud that erupted between Cros and Lasserre. The latter saw Cros's labours both as an attempt to undermine his own work, and as a profoundly dangerous assault on the shrine itself. A record exists of one meeting between the two men on 11 September 1879 in Pau. Cros claimed to have received the great man as a friend, to have spoken to him gaily, affectionately and with kindness. None the less, Cros asserted, Lasserre was hostile, angry the Jesuit was not using his work as a touchstone for his own researches:

Lasserre: I'm told you haven't read my book?
Cros: I heard some pages read at the college at Bazas.
A moment later he called his book 'this monument'.

Lasserre: You haven't read my Bernadette and the items in the appendix?
Cros: I haven't read any of it.

But while these early questions show Lasserre's preoccupations with his own work and Cros's perhaps disingenuous replies, the interview revealed how much more was at stake for both men than their literary and scholarly egos:

Lasserre: You'll ruin the work of Notre-Dame through the scandal your labours will cause!
Cros: The dear Lord and Our Lady will take care of that. The truth never ruined anything.
Lasserre: You'll kill the work, if you publish variants of Bernadette's words!
Cros: The four evangelists published variants of the words of Jesus Christ without killing Christianity.
Lasserre: You'll ruin the work if you reveal the errors of the commission, of M. Fourcade's book, of Mgr Laurence's decree!
Cros: The truth ruins nothing.
Lasserre: I support that decree!
Cros: You should support only the truth in the decree. I've read some of your letters in which you threaten to make public the errors of the commission, of M. Fourcade and of the decree.
Lasserre: Reveal fraud so late?
Cros: You know perfectly well that to reveal errors, and even fraud, you have to be able to provide proof.
Lasserre: Starting to do that, after pocketing millions of francs!
Cros: No priest has embezzled millions of francs.[65]

Cros portrayed himself as a searcher after truth, and may have exaggerated Lasserre's replies to show the man in the worst possible light. In contrast, Lasserre identified so strongly with the apparitions that he believed undermining his work was tantamount to undermining the Grotto. In this interview, he apparently conceded he might have made mistakes, but insisted that any deception now needed to be maintained. How, Lasserre asked, could the Church acknowledge after more than twenty years that the events at the Grotto had not occurred as he and the authorities had claimed? He feared being discredited, and clearly felt uncomfortable about the vast amount of money donated to the shrine over the years because of the popularity of his book.

Cros saw his work as part of the Church's spiritual edifice and dedicated himself to accumulating more evidence than any previous historian. He was such a singular success in this respect that even today his endeavours in seeking out witnesses and recording their impressions of events astonishes. Cros's technique merged the long-standing Catholic tradition of gathering statements on miracles and apparitions with the latest techniques of scientific history that depended on the systematic use of official documents; the interweaving of the two traditions produced a work that relied as much on the poor and illiterate as it did on the rich and educated. Paradoxically, although Lasserre professed himself to be the champion of the 'people' against officialdom, he conducted no systematic inquiry among them, while Cros, who had a low opinion of what he considered popular superstition, took enormous pains to record their opinions.

For Cros was concerned to separate the 'real' supernatural – the apparitions of the Virgin – from what he disparagingly called the 'marvellous', the superstitious beliefs and aberrations that he maintained were the work of the devil. As much as Lasserre, he saw the divine will as an omnipresent and potent intervener in human affairs; less powerful but equally important was Satan, who busied himself by obscuring the 'real' miracles through the many irregular manifestations of false visions and social indiscipline that Cros so deplored. While Lasserre virtually ignored the unorthodox after-visions in order to idealize the 'people' and congratulated them on their willingness to protest against authority, Cros took a diametrically opposed view. He no doubt applauded the growing authority of the papacy within the Church, but *his* brand of ultramontanism, in line with his status within an elite order, was more sceptical of the populist contribution.

Throughout the book the echo of Renan reverberates, for, in deploying all the techniques of critical and analytical history, Cros was engaged in a project to establish a sure place for the miraculous. Whereas Renan denied the existence of miracles, and Lasserre ignored all the currents of nineteenth-century scepticism, Cros sought to distinguish between superstition and supernatural intervention, intending his work to secure an inviolable, if reduced realm for the holy. Most striking to the twentieth-century reader is the way he combined an almost Rankean rigidity in his research techniques – he is, above all, a document hound, and even sometimes ignores Bernadette's statements in favour of official accounts – with a providential interpretation of events. His tone was very much of the nineteenth century, his desire to unite positivism and providentialism showing how much the work was rooted in the era. It demonstrates the way churchmen, and especially a Jesuit like himself, sought to meet the challenges of the age and were themselves integral to such intellectual debates.

Cros's book was structured by a Manichaean opposition between God and the devil, in the same way that Lasserre built his narrative around the confrontation between the official world and the people. While the supernatural guides his story, the majority of his work is given over to human activities and testimonies, an area in which he is immeasurably superior to Lasserre. For Cros was above all things meticulous, a trait symbolized by the tiny handwriting that laboriously filled up box after box of notebooks. Even he, however, had his sensitivities and felt a need to censor: the notebooks reveal ribald, gossipy excesses and often inelegance in the language of the poor, and these Cros smoothed over by sometimes deleting or slightly altering the cadences of their speech in favour of 'proper' French.[66]

Remarkably, such bowdlerizing did not strip the testimonies of all their revelatory power. Even today his depiction of the religious mystique of the poor demonstrates how often it was opposed to orthodox teaching. By putting together the documents of 1858 with the retrospective accounts of the participants twenty years later, Cros provides a narrative in which event and memory are tightly intertwined, a perspective curiously in line with modern historiographical trends. Although the later documents clearly carry within them the self-aggrandizing tendencies of witnesses seeking to justify their actions and exaggerate their importance or faith, they still provide a picture that official texts only touch upon. While the documents of 1858 show how Jacomet, Massy and the local magistrature sought to repress, contain and watch, the interviews of 1878 reveal how people subverted, mocked, and gave voice and physical expression to their religious imagination – or how they remembered doing so. The interviews go into such questions as people's motivation, bringing out the variety of views and demonstrating the extent to which the interpretation of events was still not finalized. Cros's work proves – ironically considering his wish to write *the* definitive account – how the history of Lourdes was yet in the making.

As suggested, his first and overriding preoccupation was to distinguish between the 'marvellous' and the supernatural. In this task he dissected specific aspects of the accounts written by men such as the tax inspector, Estrade, a highly regarded witness of passionate convictions but poor historical sense who had influenced Lasserre. Thus, he dismissed the widely held belief that during the seventeenth apparition, on 7 April, Bernadette had accidentally put her arm in a burning candle and had been utterly unharmed. A story propagated initially by the local physician, Dozous, who saw it at first hand,[67] recounted in fulsome terms by Estrade[68] and then immortalized by Lasserre,[69] Cros spent an entire chapter debunking this 'myth of the marvellous', examining the depositions, describing the events as circumstantially impossible, and demolishing the testimony of the witnesses.[70] Throughout, he was concerned to demystify Bernadette's experience and contrast her human ordinariness with the remarkable nature of divine encounter. In this instance Cros's determination to rid the history of Lourdes of 'superstition' meant that he may well have misquoted witnesses to strengthen his case.[71]

Even such a small attack on orthodoxy would have caused dismay, but Cros also launched an assault on Bernadette's family, her father's drunkenness and the general disorder of the household. For him, the miracle was the contrast between this deplorable milieu and the divine innocence of the visionary.[72] Other sacred cows were also slaughtered without mercy: interviews with local men confirmed that the fountain was already known to those who frequented the wilds of Massabieille, and Cros argued instead that the miracle was not the source itself, but the way the Virgin had directed Bernadette to consecrate it.[73] Even more audacious was the analysis that showed how the official description of the apparition had very little to do with Bernadette's vision, once again implicitly charging Lasserre with error for having put the Virgin's age at twenty years old.[74]

While for Lasserre 'the people' were the heroes and heroines of the struggle against the official world, for Cros they were the impressionable mass who become the marionnettes of the devil's designs. He spent pages first on the 'saintes filles' and followed with vivid descriptions of the religious turmoil among the children of Lourdes and surrounding villages. Despite his evident repugnance for the events he described, he none the less saw this process as part of a divine plan, in which disharmony and scandal set off, by contrast, the purity of Bernadette's experience. Far from being the fount of a wise and pious simplicity, 'the people' in Cros's hands become instead the instrument of chaos. He seemed to revel in demonstrating how many of the early miracles were nothing more than passing delusions.[75] Those who overturned the barriers were no more than vandals, while the women who decorated the makeshift chapel in the Grotto were trespassers who went against both episcopal and civil authority.[76]

Given this view, it is not surprising that Jacomet and Massy, Lasserre's villains, become Cros's heroes. Perhaps no other interpretation so assaulted the convictions of the faithful, nor so completely ensured that Cros's work would fail to make much of an impact on the popular imagination. For by doing away with the simple dichotomies that Lasserre had created, Cros also removed the understandable stereotypes of good and evil and, thus, much of the story's melodramatic appeal. In his view it was natural that they repressed Bernadette with the other impostors. How, he asked, were they to have distinguished between the wheat and the chaff? He spilt much ink demonstrating how their incredulity was matched by that of others in the local community. Their caution, rather than being condemned, should be applauded – Jacomet, Dutour and Massy failed, but they did so honourably; their opposition made them the true but unknowing champions of the miracle: 'It will be the work of God, and the glory of it will come to Him alone, but the civil authorities will unwittingly do no less, indeed more, than the people and the clergy.'[77] This last remark, critical also of the clergy, suggested that the local men of God were too keen to accept the veracity of the apparitions.[78] For Cros, Bernadette and her apparitions were only truly confirmed when all the administration's repressive measures failed and when few in the local population continued to adhere to the claims of the other visionaries. When this period passed, Bernadette's experience shone through like a beacon of light, incomparable, unique and blinding in its truth.

Cros wanted to rehabilitate these good Catholic officials whose reputations had been destroyed by Lasserre and, in the interview mentioned earlier, tried to shame him for the harm he had done.

Lasserre defended himself by saying that their silence on the matter was an admission of guilt. Cros, however, pointed out that Jacomet had turned down the offer of a vast sum of money for his documents from Renan himself, as he did not want to be defended by an 'enemy of Religion'.[79] Similarly, Dutour had failed to pursue Lasserre because he felt he could not win against a professional writer: 'A magistrate risk his reputation with a man of letters?'[80] Finally, Massy died before the publication of Lasserre's book but left behind a widow and children whose reputations were seriously compromised. She corresponded with Cros, and in one letter, which Lasserre apparently read, she wrote:

> Frankly, our patience is exhausted. Remember, father, that we have been the victims of bad faith for twenty-two years . . . you can imagine how indignant we feel . . .
>
> Oh! May Our Lady hear our prayer and do justice to a cherished memory . . .
>
> If I have some ambition, it is only for my children: isn't it natural to want to see them married, and well married at that?[81]

These sentiments, and Cros's advocacy of Massy, did not, however, prevent a rupture with the family, which ended in Cros never being able to secure the prefect's papers because he refused to let them vet what he planned to say.[82]

The Long Road to Publication

Cros was an inveterate chronicler. In addition to the unpublished manuscript on Lasserre, he wrote another unpublished work, 'Notre histoire de l'événement de Lourdes', detailing his own struggles from April 1864 onwards. This manuscript demonstrates yet again how the writing of any history of the apparitions was fraught with danger, for, although brought in by the authorities to contest Lasserre, he ended up fighting just as bitterly with the bishop, the missionaries and even his own order because of demands for revisions and corrections on which he stubbornly refused to compromise. In the end their squabbling left the field wide open for Lasserre's version of events to triumph.

During the years of debate and interminable correspondence that delayed Cros's publication, six issues repeatedly appeared. He was criticized for his (1) depiction of the Soubirous family (2) conviction that the spring had been known prior to the apparitions (3) debunking of the 'miracle of the candle' (4) criticism of the early miracles (5) less than complimentary vision of the clergy, whom he saw as often not sceptical enough, and (6) heroic portrayal of the civil authorities. Interestingly, few were disturbed by his dualistic portrayal of God and the devil, or by the way he linked this struggle to the epidemic of false visionaries, although concerns were raised about the amount of time he spent investigating the 'diabolical' in the aftermath of Bernadette's apparitions. Nor did they seem concerned by his depiction of the Immaculate Conception as a very young girl. It is almost as if these complicated arguments of interpretation and technical assessment passed them by in the larger battle of accusing or acquitting the human actors in the drama.

The story of Cros's work demonstrates the difficulty of remaking the Lourdes story. By casting his net so widely and interviewing so many witnesses, Cros certainly showed the methodological inadequacies of his predecessors; unfortunately, this included the little narrative prepared by the Garaison Fathers as well as that of Lasserre. Accordingly, an increasingly worried Sempé began to see the need for greater control over Cros, and wanted the text vetted by his collaborator Duboë, and subject to other judgements from Garaison. Minor criticisms focused on the excess of documents that the fathers believed (undoubtedly correctly) would weary lay readers; more important concerns surfaced over the way Cros had given too much of the 'beau rôle' to the civil authorities and not enough to the clergy.[83]

Sempé wanted the book examined and revised by clerical commissioners, but, rather than seeing this process as an independent review, Cros believed that 'this revision and approval, rather than giving authority to the work, would paralyse it'.[84] In April 1883 he questioned the objectivity of the assessors, coming as they did from the Sempé camp, and was particularly fearful that they might use his documents to write their own history before his could be published. He was blunt in the unmasking of his former allies, showing glaringly their prejudiced investment in a history that would flatter them.

The Fathers of Lourdes, and particularly Father Sempé and Father Duboë, have invested too much in the matter of the history of Lourdes to be appropriate to write [about it], because they cannot write truthfully without at every moment demolishing the edifice they built together fifteen years ago.

At the same time, through ignorance, they also took on board most of M. Lasserre's errors.[85]

In May 1884, harping on the same point, Cros stressed Sempé's dangerous need to defend the Grotto and its evolution: '[the history] concerns him as the originator of, or inspiration for, all the Grotto's monuments. Because of this, he cannot want the history to reveal errors now embodied in wood, marble, silver and gold. Besides, consciences must not be troubled.'[86] In a letter apparently designed to soothe, Sempé conceded that Cros could make his arguments but only if he did so less forcefully. Cros was outraged: 'The real aim of Father Sempé is revealed: he wants to change the true story so much that most of the public won't notice that his *Petite histoire* contains about 254 mistakes in 75 pages, so that falsehoods can live on in perpetuity in books, monuments and traditions.'[87] Cros feared that the entire sanctuary was built on illusions, promoted first by Lasserre and then by the priests ostensibly devoted to the truth of Notre-Dame de Lourdes.

As each revision process began, Cros became more and more disillusioned with those who wanted him to compromise. At an ecclesiastical inquiry in May 1884, for example, the first volume of his work was criticized for the points raised above, especially the condemnatory picture of the Soubirous family. Sempé hoped to retain Lasserre's vision of the spring as completely undiscovered, while Duboë hoped that the miracle of the candle would not be portrayed as 'contemptible'.[88] But Cros would not budge and ultimately won the day – the first volume of his work was unanimously endorsed by the inquiry – only to find that Sempé had been lobbying against publication in its present form.[89] Those who argued with Sempé, such as the Jesuit Père de Blacas, pointed out that the failure to mention Bernadette's father's time in prison for theft, for example, could easily be shown up by reference to papers in the hands of the court of Lourdes, in which Soubirous's name was plainly written on the 'register of crooks'.[90]

Cros, and in this instance his defender, believed that the only way to fend off accusations of dissimulation was to deal with the incident frankly and openly first. Such arguments demonstrate Cros's conviction that the only real weapon against Lasserre was historical truth, and that his conception of the history embodied that truth. In sometimes moving passages in his journal and letters, he said that Sempé wished to impose ideas on him that would sanitize the truth, diminishing the value of his work without accomplishing the aim of undermining Lasserre.[91]

Winning the argument, if not yet the battle for publication, did not reassure Cros that all would soon be well, and for a while he even worried that his own order was conspiring against him. Thus, when his superiors demanded that he hand over some of his work to the Garaison Fathers, Cros was convinced that Sempé intended to use the material himself under the cover of another author.[92] This author was Estrade, who had been sceptical about events at the Grotto until, at his sister's urging, he became one of the few bourgeois men to witness the apparitions and was convinced. Encouraged in 1888 by the missionary fathers and by Mgr Benoît-Marie Langénieux, archbishop of Reims and devotee of Lourdes, Estrade ultimately wrote his own first-hand account. Tremulous in tone, it was first published as a very limited edition in 1889 and, in some measure, was viewed as the sanctuary's approved publication from 1899 onwards.[93]

Although full of factual errors – particularly in chronology – its status as an eyewitness account lent it special weight. Its respectful and gentle tone fitted well with the aims of the Garaison Fathers, for not only were the civil authorities no longer accused of dastardly deeds, the clergy were also portrayed in positive terms. In fearing this history, Cros was not entirely paranoid, for much of what *was* factually correct did indeed come from his investigations. Nor was this the only time he feared for the misuse of his labour, and, when he learned that Sempé was intent on publishing his own history, Cros insulted the Garaison Father, accusing him of exploiting the manuscripts and notebooks through deceit. Exasperated, Sempé replied, 'Of all the rascals, you are the most rascally . . . you will be another Lasserre.'[94]

Like Lasserre before him, who lost his friends at the sanctuary and became the bane of the authorities, Cros seemed determined to make enemies, and even alienated his own superior. Each author seemed to believe that he alone possessed the truth, but, while Lasserre managed to publish his histories, Cros's path was perpetually blocked. By early 1885 he had had comments from thirteen known official revisers and a further eight anonymous commentators. These gave him contradictory criticisms, making it impossible, he claimed, to satisfy them all. One reviser showed the extent to which good Catholics believed in the veracity of Lasserre's depiction of the authorities, and how scandalous was Cros's attempt to overturn it; few, in effect, could judge Cros's work without the feeling that he had transgressed an edifying, if not holy text:

> M. Lasserre wrote the history as it should be written . . . He was particularly strong on portraits; those of the laymen are admirably brought off: Massy and Jacomet . . . are painted from life. M. Lasserre has even toned down a little . . . sides of them that are said, at times, to have been repellent. Massy is proud and obstinate . . . The bureaucrats displayed immense stupidity, and odious bad faith . . . Throughout this affair, the imperial functionaries committed abominable abuses of power. M. Lasserre was remarkably indulgent.[95]

It is easy to sympathize with Cros's frustration with such comments. For even if they argued with his interpretation, few, after reading the documents, could have discerned the evil and machiavellian officials that Lasserre had devised. The more Cros received such remarks, the less yielding he became, for underlying his justifiable view that it was virtually impossible to satisfy all the objections lay a growing refusal to satisfy any of them. His superior emphasized what he saw as Cros's 'mission to justify the role of the authorities in the affair of Lourdes' and predicted that this approach would ensure the work would not be published.

By this stage Cros seems more detached from the passion of earlier years and more willing to accept that his work might never see the light of day. And the more he realized this, the less he felt any need to compromise at all, instead busying himself with endless revisions and the collection of yet more manuscripts. Between 1900 and 1907 bits and pieces of his work appeared, but the definitive three-volume history was yet to be published.[96] Until 1905–6 the failure of the book to appear may well have come from a desire to placate the devotees of Lasserre, Estrade and the Garaison Fathers, as well as Abbé Georges Bertrin, whose later apologetic and highly popular volume once again transformed the historical landscape.[97] After then, however, the delays were due to Cros himself. By 1912 all paths to publication were open, but Cros now wanted the last volume, on Lasserre, to be published as well, and this insistence was enough to stop production once more.[98]

Behind these final delays no doubt lay Cros's own ambivalence about publication. He visibly liked the role of sufferer for the truth that his history had given him; he saw himself as the champion of Notre-Dame de Lourdes against the knavery of those both within and outside the Church. At the same time he may very well have feared publication; although by now accustomed to criticism, the prospect of the torrent of abuse that probably would have erupted may have worried him. Having tested the waters through the numerous revision processes, Cros knew in some sense that the Catholic world was *not* ready for his account: 'publication did not worry me much; in a hundred years' time we'd see if it was right to write about these events in this way; there have been many books not published until many years later'.[99] There was a prophetic air to these remarks: though abridged, the version of 1925–7 was still too early for the Catholic public to appreciate fully his scholarly acumen, and it received a series of bad reviews from sanctuary publications.[100] Only with the complete publication of the version of the first three volumes in 1957, to mark the centenary of the apparitions, were his labours finally recognized.

For all his effort, dedication and suffering in producing a work of genuine scholarship and extraordinary ambition, Cros's volumes must none the less be judged a failure. By allowing what had begun as a personal fascination with Bernadette to be transformed into a crusade against Lasserre, he almost seemed to court disputes that ultimately prevented it from appearing in complete form for more than half a century. Moreover, its highly intellectual, methodical tone was ill suited for countering the appeal of the Lasserre version among believers, nor did his attempt to carve out a niche for the miraculous carry any conviction for those who continued to find belief in the supernatural absurd. Ultimately, the battle against Lasserre was conducted more effectively by the Garaison Fathers, for it was they who preserved the magical account while at the same time marginalizing the man who had produced it. Lasserre's version, perfectly attuned to a populist Catholicism in a way that Cros could never have emulated even had he so desired, lived on; his book was in print until the 1960s, and its echo can still be heard in works on Bernadette today. But the official world of Catholicism fell silent on the subject of a man who had caused so much trouble, so much so that the author of the most successful publishing phenomenon of the nineteenth century, who shaped the Lourdes story and gave the shrine an all but ineradicable international fame, does not even have an entry in the Vatican compendium, *Enciclopedia Cattolica*.

7

The Assumption and the Foundations of Pilgrimage

The publication of Lasserre's text in 1869 brought an image of Lourdes into national and international consciousness that was almost impossible to change. No amount of 'scientific' history, however considered, thoughtful or faithful to fact, could undermine the beatific vision of contact with the divine, or nuance the melodramatic oppositions that he so brilliantly constructed. But the rituals of pilgrimage that are now commonly associated with Lourdes – the trains, the stretchers, the crippled and dying escorted to the Grotto by nuns and lay helpers, the massive Eucharistic processions – were still to be established. Narratives of healing filled the pages of Lasserre's and other volumes, but there is still no sense of the extraordinary diffusion of such miraculous tales that would make Lourdes *the* shrine of miracles.[1]

The idea of a *national* pilgrimage to Lourdes – the great annual staging of piety and penance – took shape in the aftermath of French defeat and civil war as part of an attempt to encapsulate and channel a mood of national soul-searching. In 1870, after a series of diplomatic squabbles, the long-anticipated war between France and the newly unifying Germany took place, and ended in cataclysm: Bismarck's armies launched a lightning campaign, defeated the emperor at Sedan and besieged Paris. In a matter of weeks Louis Napoleon's Second Empire collapsed, France lost Continental hegemony to the new German Reich and had to pay their enemy to go away. If this humiliation were not enough, the Commune erupted in Paris. Working-class artisans seized power, and the new government organized by Adolphe Thiers dispatched what remained of the army to deal with the uprising; 25,000 workers were massacred before it was suppressed.

Large-scale pilgrimage to Lourdes emerged in response to these shattering events and was shaped by the Paris-based Assumptionist Order as part of an overall campaign aimed at nothing less than restoring the Bourbon monarchy,[2] releasing the Pope from his 'Vatican prison'[3] and re-establishing the alliance between throne and altar. All three aspirations were seen by the charismatic Père Emmanuel d'Alzon, the order's founder, as vital for securing a harmonious and Christian society destroyed by decades of secularism, revolution, defeat and civil war. The first implied a return to the legitimate monarchy of the Bourbons that reigned before the Revolution of 1789 and again between 1815 and 1830. D'Alzon saw the regimes that ruled France thereafter as an indication of divine misfavour and reserved a special hatred for Louis Napoleon. He regarded Bonapartism, born out of the disorder and violence of the revolution of 1848, as illegitimate, meretricious, philistine and opportunistic. He detested it so much that he celebrated its demise, believing that the horrors of national defeat and the Commune were necessary punishments for French iniquity. The defence of the Pope following the loss of temporal power in 1870 grew out of the same moral, political and theological principles.[4] D'Alzon was one of the Pope's great defenders and linked the return of his temporal authority to the restoration of the Bourbons and the spiritual influence of the French Catholic Church.

D'Alzon's programme was based on belief in hierarchy and theocracy, and the development of the pilgrimage movement was driven by an almost inseparable bond between the spiritual aspirations and political visions of its supporters. The energy that powered the movement's organization, furthermore, was generated by personal relationships, especially those that grew in and around the Assumptionist Order during the process of spiritual direction. This chapter deals not with pilgrimage itself, but with this turbulent psychological background; it is a search to understand the personal motivations of a cause in which idealism, spiritual turmoil and political preoccupations all merged. Such encounters created a generation of activists, often women, and gave them a means of exploring their strengths and of realizing their ambitions in practical terms. At the same time they reveal a disturbing world of pain, frailty and religious doubt. It was precisely this mixture of the intimate and the political, the fervent and the calculated, which gave the pilgrimage movement such force.

Three different kinds of relationship were most significant. The master–disciple relations between Père d'Alzon and the Assumptionist priests show the way men of diverse social backgrounds and different spiritual temperaments 'grew up' under d'Alzon's tutelage, taking up his torch and leading the order into new and sometimes daring areas of political activism, the media and pilgrimage. They in turn often had profound impact on the women of Notre-Dame de Salut, a lay charitable organization that raised the funds to transport the sick to the Grotto. We must follow these women of aristocratic lineage and their priestly directors as they discovered their shared vocation to serve the sick in the uncertain political climate of the early 1870s. They were joined in this devoted service by the Petites-Sœurs de l'Assomption, the nuns who nursed the sick with the society ladies of Notre-Dame de Salut, and who celebrated an ethos of selfless sacrifice and sisterly piety that would make them famous throughout Catholic France.

The wide range of psychological, spiritual and political impulses animating the movement are part of what in recent years historians of the nineteenth century have called the 'feminization of religion'. Although indispensable for understanding pilgrimage and its origins, this notion has pejorative overtones that misrepresent the emotions involved. The idea of 'feminization' was developed to account for the massive influx of women into the religious orders and the so-called devotional 'revolution' of the nineteenth century.[5] This element of the argument is supported by incontrovertible statistics: by 1880 women comprised three fifths of Church personnel in France and supplied an army of welfare and educational workers,[6] continuing a long-term trend that flowered during the seventeenth century.[7]

A further aspect of the 'feminization' thesis, however, dwells on the renewed popularity of Baroque styles of worship and seeks once more to link these with the increasing numbers of women in the Church. The explosion of the cult of the Virgin, growth in such emotive practices as the cult of the Sacred Heart, the adoration of the infant Jesus and the lure of pilgrimage are cited as evidence of a self-conscious 'return' to apparently seventeenth-century practices and a desire to bring the spiritual passion of the Counter-Reformation to bear in the nineteenth-century struggle against scepticism and rationalism.

This aspect is more controversial, as it implies that the shifting devotional patterns were largely negative, an anachronistic response to the turmoil of the Revolution and the growing influence of secular thought. The Church, rather than continuing to fight against 'superstition', as in the eighteenth century,[8] now seemed to embrace a tamed and clerically directed version of it in order to retain a diminishing number of adherents. In its retreat from rationalism, it is argued, the Church fell back on the support of a multitude of ill-educated, 'anti-modern' women who opposed progress and thus gave new emphasis to the 'sentimentalized', 'meretricious' and 'irrational' aspects of devotion that they most appreciated.[9]

It was a classic republican cliché of the era to link women's rejection of the Revolution and republican principles to their apparent submission to priests,[10] a view best expressed in Jules Michelet's *Le Prêtre, la femme et la famille*, first published in 1845. Michelet was France's most famous mid-century historian, a zealous republican and chair of history at the Collège de France until removed during the Second Empire. An indefatigable researcher, he opened up a new world of historical sources at the same time that he revealed an imaginative, even poetic vision of whatever subject he was exploring, be it the history of the Revolution, witchcraft or various topics in natural history. *Le Prêtre, la femme et la famille* was one of his most influential works and painted a phantasmagoric picture of the relations between priests and women, in which clerics destroyed conjugal intimacy and alienated women from the republic.[11] In this view, women were manipulated, their spiritual concerns and political aspirations condemned as outmoded relics of a defunct religion. So important was this vision of women outside the control of husbands and masculine, republican rationality that it remained – and in some sense still remains – a central, if unspoken, feature of anti-clerical ideology.

Michelet's vision impinges directly on the story of pilgrimage to Lourdes precisely because it has an element of truth, even though it misses the larger story. Women *did* dominate the movement numerically and *did*, with militant priests, promote forms of devotion that confirm the stereotype. The female leadership *was* determinedly anti-republican and some of the activists had intense relationships with their priestly directors. But pilgrimage was more than this, and the women involved more than marionettes. For Lourdes was an enterprise jointly imagined by priests and women, and its distinguishing feature – the care of the sick and dying – was the brainchild of the female participants. Lourdes is unique because of this special mission and because of the women who shaped it. The world created by the needs of the sick vividly illustrated the society they wished to create, and the emotional, psychological and physical bonds they hoped to forge. Their actions during pilgrimage revealed their idealized view of a Christian collectivity as organic, intensely physical and often ecstatic in its spirituality. This perhaps deserves the label of a 'feminized religion'; but the emotional content of this experience cannot be easily reduced to such derogatory adjectives as 'meretricious' or 'sentimental'.

The Master and His Disciples: Père d'Alzon and His Legacy

Père Emmanuel d'Alzon, the founder of the Assumptionists, was a nobleman, educated at the Collège Stanislas in Paris. He later abandoned the study of law as he considered it too worldly. He was shaped by his upbringing in the southern Gard, the area around Nîmes in south-eastern France, whose history was tied to the bitter struggle for supremacy between Protestants and Catholics in the seventeenth and early eighteenth centuries. D'Alzon fought against the romantic image of the Camisards, the Protestant peasantry of the Cévennes, the rugged mountains of southern France, who organized a guerrilla resistance in the first years of the eighteenth century after the revocation of the Edict of Nantes. Later commemorated as a struggle for religious toleration against absolutism, the Camisard revolt was for d'Alzon nothing more than an early version of all the dangerous modern tendencies he abhorred. For him, the Camisards were dangerous rebels fighting against the integrity of Catholic values, and he readily linked the first enemy of his youth, Protestantism, to the other evils of revolution and materialism that he saw as following in its wake.[12]

D'Alzon's religious and political background are important because the Midi remained the spiritual base of the Assumptionist movement, despite his ultimate decision to move his disciples to the eighth arrondissement of Paris, where he rightly believed their influence would be greater. When he died in 1880, the shift to the capital became ever more complete; but the *provincial* dimension of the movement – with deep roots in the soil of religious turmoil – continued to shape the

49. Père Emmanuel d'Alzon (1810–80), with pupil

Assumptionists' desire to make their ideas accessible to Catholics in other regions. For d'Alzon was an educator, a maker of men and a shaper of clerical destinies: his college in Nîmes attracted the region's elite, whom he clothed in military uniforms like those of the Zouaves, the volunteers who defended the Pope[13] (see illus. 49). His spirituality was rigorous and explicitly militant, a 'virile' Catholicism manifested in the revitalized pilgrimage to Notre-Dame de Rochefort from Nîmes in 1873[14]: d'Alzon accompanied 5,000 men to this shrine thirty kilometres from his headquarters in a style worthy of the Midi's reputation for processional flamboyance.[15]

Of special importance in his work was the creation of a cadre of dynamic young priests, men such as François Picard and Vincent de Paul Bailly, who later played a critical role in the Lourdes pilgrimage. Picard, a native of the Gard, was also anti-Protestant,[16] but had intelligence, diligence and ambition, all qualities that d'Alzon knew how to channel. After practical and educational training in Nîmes and Rome, Picard went to Paris and began the slow process of building the Assumption in the rue François Ier. These headquarters became the hub of a network of publications and charitable activities of every sort, especially Notre-Dame de Salut. Like his *maître*, Picard had a strong impact on the women whom he gathered around him, as they sought to fulfil both his practical and spiritual directives. Under his control, the rue François Ier ultimately became highly influential in Catholic circles and a source of concern for successive republican regimes. When the Assumptionists were accused during the Dreyfus Affair of plotting to destabilize the regime,[17] it was Picard, looking like an orthodox patriarch with his flowing beard and intense demeanour – carried into the courtroom by his brother priests because of an injured leg – who made the eloquent but unsuccessful plea to avoid dissolution[18] (see illus. 50).

National pilgrimage was Picard's special enterprise; as will be seen, he made the first troubled and ill-fortuned sally to La Salette in 1872, followed by the more successful venture to Lourdes the following year. In 1882 he organized, in conjunction with the professional pilgrim and biblical scholar Abbé Tardif de Moidrey, the first national pilgrimage to Jerusalem, a voyage explicitly compared to the crusades.[19] This model, so important a part of the medieval mystique, was also central to the Lourdes adventure. He later masterminded the

50. Père François Picard (1831–1903)

'pious audacities' of the Eucharistic procession – today the moment when miracles are most likely to occur at Lourdes – and initiated the procession of *miraculés* for the Jubilee year in 1897, when those cured returned to demonstrate their good health.

In contrast to Picard, Vincent de Paul Bailly came from the Catholic elite (see illus. 51). His uncle was one of the Lazarists who transferred the relics of Saint Vincent de Paul in 1829 from a remote village in Picardy to the capital, an undertaking aided by Bailly's mother, Marie-Sidonie Vrayet de Surcy. Such translations typified the Restoration cult for saints, as believers sought to recover relics that had been hidden or dispersed during the Revolution. Bailly's father was seen as something of a lay saint, working as part of the developing movement around Antoine-Frédéric Ozanam, the founder of the charitable Society of Saint Vincent de Paul and an inspiration for many nine-

51. Père Vincent de Paul Bailly (1832–1912)

teenth-century French Catholics. Bailly met d'Alzon through these interlocking networks when he was stationed in Nîmes, for he only found his vocation late in life after a career in the Postes et Télégraphes distinguished for his decoding of diplomatic messages. During a visit to Notre-Dame de la Garde a voice murmured to him, saying, 'Come, come', and soon he saw the tall figure of d'Alzon framed by the familiar view of Nîmes.[20] The anecdote resonates with biblical images of Christ calling his disciples, but reveals more about the spiritual culture of the Assumptionists than about their strong identification with the Gospels: their conversions tended to be dramatic experiences, rather than gentle incorporations, and once again stressed the centrality of d'Alzon himself.

Bailly become famous, perhaps even notorious, as the head of the Assumptionist press, his early training making him the ideal person to adapt the tools of modernity to the order's use. He transformed *Le Pèlerin* into a bestselling weekly by giving it extraordinary illustrations, biting satire and increasingly venomous anti-Semitic and anti-republican assaults. He was editor of *La Croix*, the leading Catholic daily at the end of the nineteenth century and the organ that, along with the militant, right-wing Action française, led the campaign against Dreyfus, the Jewish army captain wrongfully imprisoned on Devil's Island in 1895 for selling military secrets to the Germans.[21] The Assumptionists may have been inspired by the piety and Christian hierarchy of the Middle Ages, but they were very much men of the nineteenth century, willing to use every tool of the modern age to accomplish their religious and social vision. Under d'Alzon's inspirational direction in the pioneering days of the 1870s, they sought to unite past models with contemporary needs, and compared their fight to that of the Jesuits in the Counter-Reformation: 'The Assumption took the same stance against the Revolution that the Jesuits took, three centuries earlier, against the Reformation.'[22] Pilgrimage was one of the greatest weapons in their re-Christianizing arsenal.

D'Alzon's personal allure was always matched by his spiritual and political message. He showed tremendous confidence in Picard's future, their paternal–filial relations generally untroubled by emotional discord, and offered him the chance of upward social mobility, the possibility of an active, even militant career that would allow him to replace d'Alzon at his death. Bailly also benefited from this same paternal attention, but his vocation was of a different kind. Already of a well-known Catholic family, Bailly found in the Assumptionists an outlet for his particular talents in the press empire he created and the polemics he promoted. In the case of both men, their veneration of d'Alzon, as well as their obvious desire to please him, were central to their dynamism. Although the bonds linking the two generations of men were strong, they showed less of the intense ambivalence that would mark Picard's and Bailly's relations with the women under their direction.

If d'Alzon attracted disciples by his personality, the Assumptionists attracted a mass following by finding a practical means of implementing and popularizing his religious programme. D'Alzon deliberately sought to inflame Protestants and rationalists by promoting the idea of the Immaculate Conception precisely because it defied nineteenth-century science. Central to the order's appeal was the Marian fervour epitomized by its commitment to the Assumption of the Virgin.[23] He believed, for example, that the impressive crop of miracles at the national pilgrimage of 1877 was a special sign for *his* order:

> I ask myself why so many miracles in the octave of the Assumption, on a pilgrimage directed by Assumptionists, why among the cures at Lourdes there is a Petite-Sœur de l'Assomption and, at Nîmes, an Oblate of the Assumption. Could it be that the Holy Virgin is beginning to set out the first markers for a definition for the dogma of the Assumption?[24]

From the 1840s his observance turned increasingly towards the frequent taking of the Eucharist, the second plank of his spirituality. Rigourist and Jansenist teaching of the seventeenth and eighteenth centuries condemned moral laxity in the confessional, demanding full and complete repentence before the giving of absolution.[25] Such stringency meant that many took communion only infrequently: 'There are those who believe that they should exempt themselves from communion because of their weakness, but they are much to blame, since they acknowledge their impotence, but refuse to take refuge in the might of Jesus. Why should they allow themselves to be halted by absurd scruples, and question whether they are ready for communion?'[26] D'Alzon and many other priests no longer insisted on such scrupulousness, a theological approach that inspired Picard when he promoted the Eucharistic processions at the sanctuary.

Despite what might be considered a softer line over communion, however, d'Alzon was a hard taskmaster, trying to subdue the passions in the search for spiritual perfection. When directing women, for example, he exhorted them to remember Christ's suffering and to devote themselves to spiritual pain and physical mortification. His 'dolourist' conception of religion would become important to the Lourdes enterprise, as the idea that redemption came through pain and suffering permeated the ambience of national pilgrimage.[27]

His spirituality was inseparable from his politics. Like many intelligent Catholics coming of age in the 1820s and 1830s, d'Alzon could not escape the influence of Lamennais. He appreciated the Catholic intellectual's belief in the beneficent leadership of the Pope and shared his anti-establishment populism.[28] But the revolutions of 1848 swept away any vestiges of the political progressivism that d'Alzon might have entertained in his youth. Instead, he directed all his attention to the Pope's position as victim of the Italian nationalists, aided in their perfidy by the Second Empire. The plight of Pius IX was one of d'Alzon's abiding preoccupations in the 1860s and 1870s, the themes of exile, persecution and martyrdom all essential to his vision. He was in Rome during the Vatican Council of 1869 and 1870, and joined the majority in supporting the promulgation of papal infallibility. D'Alzon saw this controversial doctrine, which defined all papal *ex cathedra* declarations as dogma and represented the Pope as an absolute monarch in both the spiritual and temporal domains, as one of the prerequisites of the Catholic renewal.[29] When France was defeated by Germany, then torn apart by civil war in 1870–71, he saw this 'martyrdom' of his country as a mirror of the 'martyrdom' of the Pope. D'Alzon interpreted the disasters as a sign of God's wrath and argued that all good Catholics should separate themselves from atheistic states. He hence applauded the Pope's unwillingness to come to terms with the new Italian regime, a move that encapsulated his more generally intransigent attitude to changing political circumstances in much of Europe.[30]

D'Alzon's ultramontanism was matched by his legitimism, his belief in the need for a restoration of the Bourbon monarchy. Like other Catholic aristocrats, he envisaged a hierarchical society based on tradition, in which social ties were strengthened by mutual obligations and duties. He none the less prided himself on his populist style. His charismatic personality, aristocratic lineage and manly allure – repeatedly mentioned by contemporaries – enabled him to attract young men, *jeunes filles* and respectable ladies, as well as the poor of his region, who appreciated the trouble he took to speak in their native patois. He tirelessly promoted charitable activities designed to ensure Catholic solidarity and to lure the workers away from the 'false' blandishments of socialism.

In this way he intended to set the *droits de Dieu* against the *droits de l'homme*,[31] and urged the faithful to fight against liberalism and socialism to build a moral order humanized by a belief in the equality of all before God. This aspect gained full expression in the national pilgrimage to Lourdes, where, for one fervent and frenzied week, pilgrims expressed their vision of Catholic social solidarity. Pilgrimage became a public, even a theatrical manifestation of Catholic piety in the face of godlessness. While left-wing opponents sought to establish their political and cultural legitimacy in the public domain through a range of symbols and rituals – from Marianne to Bastille Day – d'Alzon and the Assumptionists used similar methods but focused instead on prayer, procession and Marianism.[32] They were just as concerned as the republicans with the mobilization of crowds in the public arena and sought to conquer that domain through the mass media, the train lines and the public square.[33] The capacity to assemble such crowds, among whom women predominated, was precisely what worried anti-clerical commentators like Emile Zola, who saw them as a seedbed for the growth of dangerous hysterical tendencies.

The Assumptionists feared, above all, the relegation of religion to the 'private sphere' and its removal from the central rituals of power and authority – hence their struggle to help the Pope maintain his temporal kingdom. Their efforts, moreover, encapsulated their hatred of the 'Voltairean' bourgeoisie, who wished to leave religion to the individual conscience, a matter as private as the details of domestic life. Pilgrimage was a way of proclaiming Christian values in public[34] and this often self-conscious attempt to return to the religious pageantry of the Middle Ages was one of the defining features of the movement. Finally, it created a national – and ultimately international – view of Catholicism: travelling from far-flung parishes, pilgrims from all corners of France gained a vivid sense of the enormity of their country, while Lourdes assured them of the deep similarity of religious feeling that united them all as Catholics.

Their rejection of the secularizing tendencies both of government and of society none the less left d'Alzon and the Assumptionists with a central paradox. They wanted massive public manifestations of piety, but wanted to maintain a safe distance from the contaminating effects of a secularizing world. How, in effect, were they to transform society from afar? Many questions of strategy and religious priority were tied up with this issue. Was it sufficient to build a parallel Christian culture that would serve as an example, or were there more potent apostolic means? On the one hand, the pilgrimage became a kind of counter-culture in which the values of Christian solidarity and piety were displayed for all to see every year; on the other, the journey to Lourdes was an *exceptional* interval in the yearly calendar.

Pilgrimage was essential to promoting the *droits de Dieu*, but not enough in itself. None the less, the Assumptionists in some sense became defined by their visible success in this area, and hence continued to invest in pilgrimage as the best means of propagating the faith in miracles and the inadequacies of the secular worldview.

The Disciples, the Franco-Prussian War and the Commune

The outbreak of the Franco-Prussian War transformed the lives of the disciples irrevocably. While d'Alzon remained in Nîmes, frantic with worry, his young priests lived in an atmosphere of excitement and high tension, and both witnessed and participated in events that changed their view of Catholic action for ever. Letters – Picard's routinely floating away by balloon during the siege – to each other and especially to d'Alzon in Nîmes, expressed their astonishment at the sad turn of events for, like all patriotic Frenchmen, they had expected victory against the Prussians.[35] When increasingly bad news showed how misplaced their optimism was, Picard remarked, 'A blush comes to my brow every time I think of the shame that our poor country has deserved and is now incurring. Lies have combined with incompetence to humiliate us.'[36]

But, as is so often the case in France, the defeat of one regime signalled political opportunities for dissidents, and the Assumptionists found hope in the destruction of Napoleonic *grandeur* and its crass materialism. Above all, they thought it was a punishment for deserting the Pope, for when the war began French troops garrisoned in Italy departed, leaving him to face Victor Emmanuel's forces alone. In fact, d'Alzon summed up the tone of their correspondence when he mused: 'At the moment we can say nothing about what will happen to France, caught between the Prussians and the revolutionaries . . . Prussia should crush us, but God may come to our aid.'[37]

For Bailly, the national catastrophe brought a rare adventure. With Père Pernet, another priest who will figure in the pilgrimage tale, he followed the French army to Metz in the early part of November 1870, and from there learned of its defeat at Sedan. Imprisoned, then released, but separated from their charges, they found their way to the cathedral town of Mainz, putting themselves under the patronage of its bishop, Wilhelm Emmanuel von Ketteler, who allowed them to tend their French flock.[38] This German bishop was the learned advocate of social Catholicism and one of the intellectual inspirations of *Rerum novarum*, the 1891 encyclical seeking a Christian middle way between godless capitalism and socialism. Von Ketteler fascinated the young Frenchmen, who were impressed by his zeal, warmth and personal willingness to reach out to the lowliest of the faithful. In spite of fundamental disagreement – Ketteler opposed papal infallibility – Bailly admired his generous, open-hearted Catholicism. Despite the increasing intransigence of the Assumptionists' views in the decades after the 1870s, many of their charitable and pilgrimage activities sought to recapture both the warmth and populism of Mainz, as well as the heroic role they saw themselves playing alongside the imprisoned French troops.

This encounter with the German 'enemy' contrasted with their depiction of the 'real' enemy at home. Early spring found Bailly back in Paris with Picard, as they lived through the Commune and its anti-clerical fury. They were forced to flee, making their way to the safety of Versailles, afraid of meeting the same fate as the sixty-two priestly hostages massacred on the rue Haxo on 5 March 1871.[39] The worst and most shocking misfortune for the Catholic clergy was the execution of Georges Darboy, archbishop of Paris. In taking hostage the effective leader of the Church in France and doing away with him, the Communards threatened all clergy with a return to the dark days of the Revolution. Picard was deeply grieved by the need to get rid of his vestments so as not to be captured by the Communards: 'You will see ridiculous costumes; I refused them until now, but we shall have to reconcile ourselves to fancy dress in April.'[40] Bailly equally was dismayed by a friend who arrived in Paris at Easter 'heavily disguised, moustache, dressed up', precautions that none the less failed to prevent his capture.[41] He also described jeering children who shouted to priests 'à la guillotine', thirsty, it seemed, for the blood of priests.[42] They were finally subjected to a battalion of the National Guard, who surrounded the Convent of the Assumption, one of their sister orders in the district of Auteuil outside Paris, and searched it minutely, accusing the nuns of conspiring with the troops from Versailles, sending signals to the enemy and hiding arms and men. These were desperate days as, tracked and hounded, they went underground, suffering a loss of dignity and identity that they never forgot.

The experience of the Commune also made them focus on the people whom they felt were especially responsible for the violence. Although the National Guard threatened them with capture, more venom seemed to be reserved for the working women of Paris, who were portrayed as ferocious harpies. 'At the seminary of Saint-Sulpice, three days ago, they pillaged everything, defiled the church with the women's nocturnal orgies, drank from the holy vessels that had survived till now, performed sacrilegious processions, broke everything.'[43] In the behaviour of these women Bailly saw the moral collapse of society, which led to the 'hideous heroines of murder and arson'. He was shocked to see the 'groups of prisoners where there were as many women and children as men'.[44] Confronted with this drama, Bailly prayed for a programme of moralization for those susceptible to improvement, and exile for the rest.

What is important for the tale of pilgrimage and religious rejuvenation is the way this fantastic image of feminine danger was contrasted with an equally idealized portrait of 'good', 'Christian' womanhood who would save the nation from turpitude. Bailly believed that there was a constituency of women from what he called 'le populaire' who were both deeply Christian and instinctively patriotic. He maintained that, like him, these women condemned revolutionary materialism on the one hand and the 'cowardice' of the emerging republican regime of Adolphe Thiers on the other.[45] The Assumptionists, in fact, believed as much in the 'people' as their leftist counterparts, and were convinced that they would lead them to a new and better society once the destruction was over. Their hatred of the Commune was such that they seemed relieved when the city lay in ruins. Picard saw the burning monuments as a kind of punishment: 'Paris is ablaze, the Tuileries, the Louvre, the Palais-Royal, the rue Royale, the Ministry of War, etc. . . . are consumed. Babel perishes. Word this morning is of a massacre in the prisons, the archbishops and all the priests are said to have been killed last night.'[46] He was convinced the most severe punishment was necessary in order for a new society to rise from the ashes, comparing France to an ostentatious woman who needed to be stripped. Such showy wealth was evil: 'The devil is much more cunning than the children of God. Everything is to be feared in this

Babylon, which is rediscovering its finery and life. France is still too rich, and must be ruined.'[47]

Picard's and Bailly's vivid characterization of the Commune as a reincarnation of the Terror was hardly unique. Hippolyte Taine's influential history of the Revolution, for example, made the same explicit parallels, while their concentration on the heinous acts of women was little different from other mainstream histories. Like many others, the Assumptionists focused on the *pétroleuses*, revolutionary women accused of setting the capital alight and transformed by fantasy and fear into special symbols of ruthlessness.[48] Their rhetoric differed from that of secular commentators only in its explicit reference to religious themes and metaphors of Satanism, requiring a purification so extreme that fire alone would suffice. In their emerging eschatology, women increasingly came to be seen as the moral litmus test of society, with two kinds of women struggling for two different visions of society. Picard made the juxtaposition explicitly to the women of high society whom he hoped to enrol in his Catholic army, envisaging a white army of purity against the other 'scarlet' women with 'red' politics:

> Under the Commune [secret societies] let the *pétroleuses* loose on Paris . . . [Now] women well placed through position, fortune, rank and sometimes by their name or birth [want] to form a league of truly Catholic women to affirm their faith through prayer and good works, and by boldly raising the banner of the supernatural.[49]

Stalwart, pious but feminine, the leading organization would be Notre-Dame de Salut, in which women would defend the *droits de Dieu* in the public arena.

Women, Priests and Notre-Dame de Salut

The aftermath of the Commune galvanized the Assumptionists, with d'Alzon committing his entire social network to the launch of Notre-Dame de Salut. For this project he depended on his close collaborator and friend, Mère Marie-Eugénie Milleret, who had formed the thriving Sœurs de l'Assomption in the Parisian suburb of Auteuil. Their friendship stretched over more than forty years, produced 2,000 letters on both sides, and created a spiritual intimacy that reads like a religious love story. They came from very different backgrounds and different parts of France, she from Metz in the east and from a father with Voltairean sentiments, he from Nîmes in the south-east and aristocratic lineage. They shared the ultramontanist vision of a revitalized France in which the moralization of the poor and a special love for the Virgin and charity were central.[50]

As a woman of the elite, Mère Marie-Eugénie had access to women of the best society. As early as January 1872 a group including Bailly and Picard met at Auteuil under her auspices; out of that meeting was born Notre-Dame de Salut, a lay organization of women specializing in charity and prayer that received papal approbation soon after its creation. With organizations in other dioceses across France, Notre-Dame de Salut was led from the rue François Ier and named after a famous Madonna sculpture of reputedly medieval provenance that inspired their religious activities.

Picard's enthusiasm for these female associates emerged from the campaigns for prayer and penitence that immediately followed defeat and civil war: 'Notre-Dame de Salut is growing rapidly. We have already received twelve episcopal approvals. The women are enthused by the signing of the petition in favour of Sunday [observance], for the spreading of the mass for Deliverance, for the establishment of decades [of the rosary].[51] They believed that campaigns for prayer and pilgrimage were necessary preludes to monarchical restoration and Catholic revival.

Notre-Dame de Salut was about more than prayer and pilgrimage, however. In its original conception the Assumptionists wanted a charity specializing in the moralization and evangelization of the workers. All members were to watch over their servants, workers and salaried personnel, to set a Christian example and to demand, in turn, the fulfilment of Christian obligations from those beneath them in the social scale. Female sponsors sent money to help evangelize the capital's 'red' suburbs, and activists stoutly made their way into Belleville and La Villette to convert those who had 'succumbed' to socialism. In line with many right-wing Catholics of the era, they hoped to re-Christianize workers through social solidarity, through the 'circles' that would bring employers and workers together in

Catholic fraternity; hence Notre-Dame de Salut's intention to establish 'support for apprentices, industrial schools, military charities, workers' associations, employers' groups'.[52] In this, the highest and most cherished aim of the association, Notre-Dame de Salut was to make only indifferent progress, falling behind the more famous devotees to the cause such as Albert de Mun, the legitimist Catholic politician.[53] Thus, at the outset there was absolutely no sense that the major activity of the organization would become a form of charity that helped the sick poor make the expensive journey to the Grotto. In fact, its growing concentration on Lourdes would later disturb d'Alzon, who feared the way it drained energies away from his other beloved charitable works.[54] Picard had no such doubts; when he took over the Assumption on d'Alzon's death in 1880, Notre-Dame de Salut became ever more focused on the national pilgrimage.

At its inception Notre-Dame de Salut was presided over by the venerable Mme de la Rochefoucauld, Duchesse d'Estissac, née Ségur, a woman of illustrious name and tremendous fortune. An accomplished Catholic, whose condescension was highly prized by the less elevated women who did the work, Mme de la Rochefoucauld lent an air of unquestionable grandeur to the enterprise. She tended the sick herself at the Hôpital Saint-Joseph and was known affectionately as 'la bonne Duchesse' by the small army of 'clients' – workers, orphans, the sick and the poor – whom she aided with her purse and sometimes with her attention. Her influence was particularly felt in the diocese of Orléans, where her chateau, Combreux, was situated. So great would be her love for the Grotto at Lourdes that she had a rather large facsimile re-created in the park, and once a year opened her residence so the locals could come on pilgrimage.[55]

D'Alzon, Picard and Bailly depended on women like the duchess, and others of less elevated aristocratic and *bien pensants* backgrounds, for the realization of their goals. But they were more than just self-interested. The movement was pervaded by the special pleasure of mutual idealism and shared sense of endeavour, the utter conviction that they worked selflessly for 'the cause'. Notre-Dame de Salut was predicated on a neat division of gender roles. As d'Alzon said, 'The women will get together to procure the funds needed for the work of the men.'[56] Women would do more than collect money, however, although he correctly spotted their special aptitude as fundraisers, emulating the activities of the Jesuits, who harnessed women's charitable impulses during the Counter-Reformation.[57] Bailly developed this vision at the organization's first meeting, when he mentioned the Gospel story of the wedding of Cana, where Mary notices that more wine is needed for the celebrations; Jesus obliges his mother (although preceding his act of generosity with a rather brusque remark) and produces his first miracle, the lesson being 'that which women want, God wants'.[58] This biblical inspiration was reiterated at succeeding gatherings, with Bailly seeking to define the limits of Notre-Dame de Salut's feminine mission and to contrast it with the Comité Catholique des hommes, which united legitimists – especially deputies – against republicans and thereby stressed the overtly *political* nature of their masculine calling.[59]

In their work the women were meant to follow Mary's example: 'In effect, the Association will serve in the same way that the Holy Virgin served the infant Jesus.'[60] Women were to extend their role as nurturing mothers, especially to the young workers and apprentices who, like Jesus, required help. An explicit contrast was made with the military metaphors that Bailly reserved for the male activists, who looked instead to the heroic models of the Counter-Reformation, be they the Jesuits, the Capuchins or the Lazarists. Men were to be the dynamic leaders, women the essential logistical support:

> The ladies of Notre-Dame de Salut also perform a social and religious function, but one appropriate to their God-given role. Men are destined to be soldiers and missionaries; they march at the head of charitable works, but it does happen that generals, when leading their armies to war, forget about those supplies without which the army will perish faster than from enemy fire.[61]

The activists of Notre-Dame de Salut sometimes bridled when these strictures interfered with their work. For women inspired by the message of ultramontanism, legitimism and the moralization of the poor, no such easy divisions could be maintained.

Several of the women had a business-like, if pious relationship with Picard and Bailly, volunteering their services or responding to the individual demands of the priests. But some of the correspondence comes from women whose interaction with these charismatic Assumptionists was of a different, and more intense, emotional kind, and they were often the ones who were most active. The biographical details of these women are very sketchy, although their personalities emerge vividly through their letters to the priests. Mme Laforest, the organization's secretary, came from Boulogne-sur-Mer, and seems to have been of modest circumstances. Her status was alluded to by Picard, who suggested that her train fare to Lourdes be paid, a concession made in recognition of her work, but hardly an honour in a world where many went first class.[62] He was the mainstay of her spiritual life, encouraging her in her labours of self-sacrifice. She worked for the regeneration of France and sought to convince Picard that she understood the difference between this elevated mission and a bureau for charitable subscriptions. She was an assiduous secretary and went on the first national pilgrimage to Lourdes in 1873, thereafter remaining its faithful advocate. Like so many, she experienced her time at the Grotto as moving and momentous, and described with terror how she inadvertently fell at the Virgin's feet, fearful that her tumble meant that Mary wished to punish her for her sins.[63] She was also an avid collector of money; her colleagues were often irritated by the way she dropped the names of aristocrats to persuade people to contribute, seeing the technique as a vulgar habit out of keeping with Notre-Dame de Salut's elevated image. She was not without courage, making her way into the schools in the rougher working-class suburbs, trying to establish a regime of prayer among the poor.[64]

Another activist was Mme Dumont, who corresponded with her spiritual director, Bailly. Even more than Mme Laforest, she understood the political consequences of the organization's strategies. For example, she fully grasped the tension between the archbishop of Paris and the Assumptionists, the former fearing their growing support among the rich and influential in the capital and their resistance to episcopal authority. She was actively engaged in the administrative work designed to bring all of Catholic France into the orbit of Notre-Dame de Salut. She was a constructive critic who disagreed strongly with Bailly over the direction of *Le Pèlerin*: 'I believe *Le Pèlerin* is on the wrong course for a serious paper . . . To spend time stoking up people's extravagant imaginations and sanctioning superstitions, this, I believe, is nonsense and unworthy of your apostolic time, and I tell you so now.'[65]

Finally, like d'Alzon, she was a tireless champion of the evangelization of the poor. When she felt Notre-Dame de Salut was *too* engaged in contemporary struggles and propaganda, she said so, and repeatedly returned to the long-term project of the cause. She saw the special role of women in the struggle and felt no compunction in reminding Bailly of their importance: 'I love powerful, burning words, and without mentioning our retreat, those of Mme Dulong on the apostolate of women in good works in the world and in the family produced an extraordinary emotion in me . . . In my opinion, evangelization is the finest thing. This path, this love of workers' charities, is God-given!'[66]

Such exclamations of pleasure indicate the pioneering enthusiasm of both priests and women for their shared political and spiritual goals. But alongside their exciting, even liberating endeavours, the correspondence between these two women and their directors also demonstrates less pleasing emotions of thwarted passion, ambivalence and rank pettiness, as they competed for attention. The priests felt little responsibility for the disarray that occasionally marred working relationships in their absence, and Picard's attempts in one instance to 'put things right' showed how he played one woman off against another, a technique justified in the name of consideration: 'Here is a note for Mme Dumont, deliver it to her without letting her comrade see it; women easily become jealous, we have to avoid hurting people who are so devoted to the cause.'[67] The remark, however, indicates his half-conscious realization of the importance of his letters in the women's lives. In trying to settle a dispute over the management of correspondence, Picard colluded with Bailly to get the women to do their bidding. For Mme Laforest he counselled severity; for the more equable Mme Gossin he recommended an appeal to her selfless devotion to the cause. The men faked a fight between themselves, which was meant to have the effect of reassuring the women, demonstrating both a masculine complicity and their unwitting contempt for those who worked so devotedly for them.[68]

Using consciously or not the religious language and emotional style of seventeenth-century Catholicism, Picard's and Bailly's spiritual direction of Mme Laforest and Mme Dumont followed in d'Alzon's footsteps, who spent years corresponding with elite women, directing and admonishing them to perfect themselves through exercises of moral and spiritual mortification.[69] D'Alzon focused on the need to exert willpower in the face of spiritual lassitude and sensual desire. The female correspondents appreciated rather than resented his obsessive moralism and overweaning paternalism, and hungered for his special time and attention. Such epistolary intercourse was also emotionally charged for the priests. D'Alzon, for example, in one of many such letters, wrote to an unmarried female charge, Mlle Chaudordy, after her pilgrimage to Lourdes:

> Your little note gave me great joy, my dear Valentine, short though it was. I have many things to tell you, and it seems a good idea to write to you about them on your return from Lourdes. Our Lord wants you more for himself every day. There are delicate things in your soul that he wishes to penetrate completely. You have to open up wide to him and, when you are open, open yourself to him still further, because the divine Master has an insatiable need for your love and intimate sacrifices.[70]

D'Alzon had no monopoly over the expression of divine love in eroticized terms, an area of mystical writing in which medieval and early-modern women specialized.[71] What is jarring here is his use of this language to a young woman whose 'penetration' must come through his spiritual direction. This process is couched in terms that saw love and sacrifice as almost inescapably painful. The letter reveals more than the flowery language of epistolary romanticism; it seems to conjure up his own unacknowledged sexual fantasies.

Mlle Chaudordy was not a member of Notre-Dame de Salut, and so we do not have her response and hence cannot gauge her reaction. But the women of Notre-Dame de Salut do indicate the deep emotional significance of their correspondence and how it infused their spiritual and working lives. Clearly, writing to Picard and Bailly gave them the chance to open their hearts, to reveal feelings perhaps too shameful to confide in others. For example, Mme Laforest almost never spoke of her husband, and when she did she suggested that at the heart of her relationship with Picard was his knowledge of her conjugal difficulties.[72] Mme Dumont wrote rambling and intense letters describing her emotional life and its difficulties, and at one moment even acknowledged thoughts of suicide as a means of escape.[73] These letters are windows on lives of love and commitment, but also on feelings of deep unhappiness.

Mme Laforest had a sense of emotional self-discovery when she found her faith and vocation simultaneously through Picard's influence. She seems hopelessly in love: 'Why do I avoid the theatre and visits as much as possible (too much)? It is because you have changed everything.'[74] She laboured hard to transform herself, but was angered that the demands placed upon her at Notre-Dame de Salut often made it impossible for her to 'sleep and eat'.[75] She did all this work for him: 'Every time you leave, father, I seem to lose everything . . . Father, would you really say you are pleased with me? . . . And also what displeases you? Father, I intended to write as a "secretary" and not as a *child*, but with you it is so difficult to be sensible.'[76] In such words she played with the double meaning of 'father', revealing her vulnerability to his special emotional appeal. She was also jealous, showing her envy of a Mme de Damas in Dijon who was to take care of him during a convalescence. Desperately concerned about his health, she lectured him on his duty to France, which depended on his special role in the Assumption. She went so far as to suggest that people might be more devoted to him than to the service of God: 'Certainly one has to serve Our Lord but, for holy souls, don't you admit that this devotion to the service of God can be doubled by the trust one has in his minister?'[77]

Her passion for Picard was intimately tied up with the beginnings of a new piety. She admitted she found it hard to say her rosary in public, and expressed doubts about the hypocrisy of devout women who hid their gossiping and malice behind a religious veil.[78] There were moments, however, when she proudly recounted to him her spiritual conversion, her 'courage moral', and willingness to confess and embrace suffering.[79] At the end of 1874 she remarked on his moral force: 'I have to admit . . . that to overcome me you didn't shrink from extreme measures, you almost killed me.'[80]

If Mme Laforest's relationship to Picard was characterized by adoration, in which she was the patronized 'child' of an older and wiser male director, Mme Dumont had in contrast a greater sense of her rights and expectations in her correspondence with Bailly. She frequently hectored him, acting more like a disgruntled wife with a neglectful husband. Repeatedly she asked him to ask her counsel: 'When you have a question about the cause that worries you, talk it over with me, as I don't think anyone can offer a more lucid judgement on any situation than I can.'[81] While her desire for a true collaboration was genuine, her vision of their emotional and spiritual connection was more ambivalent. She perhaps gave herself away when she spoke of her own direction of those whom she jokingly called her penitents, contrasting Bailly's careless approach to her. She explained how she claimed an 'absolute authority' over these 'very religious but too lukewarm men', how it pleased her 'to chain them hand and foot to the chariot of my imaginary sanctity'.[82] Did she too wish to 'enslave' Bailly, or did this vivid language unconsciously express the wish of his greater and more powerful focus on her? In any case the imagery she used showed once again a sexualized fantasy of desire only half hidden by religious language.

Mme Dumont undermined her position with her extreme outbursts against Mme Laforest, outraged that as secretary her rival controlled the distribution of correspondence and sometimes delayed giving her letters. She accused her rival of other kinds of petty outrages: 'My dear enemy, Mme Laf., who shows me the most personal letters and ones in which she complains about me, my husband and everything else as well.'[83] Her exasperation was such that she even thought about poisoning Mme Laforest with a grain of hellebore. Here was the ultimate fantasy, the murder of a competitor: in psychological terms the struggle suggested an imaginary triangle of intense sibling rivalry or a legitimate wife fending off the advances of an unworthy opponent in the battle for an elusive husband.

Such relationships seem to confirm Michelet's phantasmagoric fears: women confided in priests and demeaned themselves with 'unseemly' emotions that, in the case of Mme Dumont, even brought murder momentarily into her mind. But while the correspondence reveals flagrant feeling, it was far more emotionally productive than the historian could ever allow. In such interactions Michelet would have seen nothing more than the corruption of marriage vows, a dangerous, despicable means of spoiling the intimacy between husband and wife. He suggested that such relationships impassioned women to such a degree that they were incapable of emancipating themselves from Catholic obscurantism. How, he asked, could these women ever take on responsible positions within a republican polity if their vision was distorted by charismatic priests and their energies channelled into defending the Church? However, to reduce the feelings between priests and women to some kind of sexual perversion is to misunderstand

1. Altarpiece showing the apparition, c. 1620, Notre-Dame de Bétharram (see also page 40)
2. *La Procession du village* (detail), arthex painting, 1699, Notre-Dame de Garaison (see also page 62)

3. & 4. Painted wooden reliefs, ghteenth century, Notre-Dame de Sarrance (see also page 37)

5. The apparition of Notre-Dame de Garaison, painted wooden relief, seventeenth century, Notre-Dame de Garaison (see also page 41)

6. The first apparition of the Virgin to Anglèze de Sagazan, nineteenth-century painting, Notre-Dame de Garaison (see also page 42)

7. Jean-Marie Soubirous, *Bernadette Soubirous*, undated, Couvent de Saint-Gildard, Nevers (see also page 43)
8. Laugée & Jehenne, 'Bernadette bergère', chromolithograph, from Henri Lasserre, *Notre-Dame de Lourdes*, 1878 (see also page 182)
9. Justin Pibou, *Notre-Dame de Lourdes*, nineteenth-century painting, Collège de Garaison (see also page 86)

10. 'Those Who Do Not Want to See'. Satan: 'Do you see the miracle? ... Peuh! ... Let's say rather magnetism ... suggestion ... mineral water.' Emile Zola: 'Yes ... the healing breath of the crowds!' Cartoon by Clérac showing Zola in league with the devil, mocking Lourdes with reference to the scientific theories of the day. *Le Pelèrin*, 1923

11. 'Lourdes: "There will no longer be a temple, nor any outward form of worship; for the temple is in thine heart." ' Citing Revelation **21:22**, I Corinthians **3:16–17**, this anti-clerical jibe by Bellery-Desfontaines shows a priest pawing a pile of money near signs promoting the sanctuary's miraculous attributes, such as the only brand of candles officially approved by the Virgin Mary. *L'Assiette au beurre*, 10 September 1904

12. A group of invalid pilgrims lie awaiting the passage of the Holy Sacrament outside the basilica. Photograph, *c.* 1900, from Gustave Boissarie, *Les Grandes Guérisons de Lourdes*, 1900

13. The Grotto of Massabieille, *c.* 1905. This French postcard shows the statue of Notre-Dame in the niche, the grill that sectioned off the Grotto, and the discarded crutches of the pilgrims (see also p. 170)

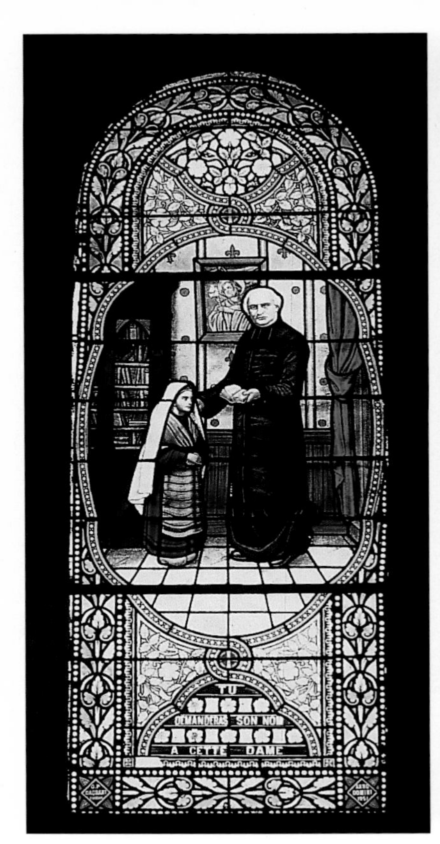

14. & **15.** Studio of J. P. Grant, stained-glass windows, 1921, new parish church, Lourdes. *Left*: Abbé Peyramale, the priest of Lourdes, insists that Bernadette determine the identity of the apparition. 'Tu demanderas son nom à cette Dame' ('Ask the Lady her name'). (See also page 152.) *Right*: The moment when the apparition proclaims her identity. 'Je suis l'Immaculée Conception' ('I am the Immaculate Conception')

16. Interior of the Basilica of the Rosary, Lourdes (see also page 174)

17. Crutches abandoned by those miraculously cured at the Grotto, photograph, *c.* 1930s

18. Entombed, waxed body of Bernadette, presented in a reliquary after the beatification in 1925, Couvent de Saint-Gildard, Nevers (see also page 138)

19. Pilgrims in the 1990s

Photographic Acknowledgements for Colour Section

Author: 1, 19. Archives de la Congrégation des Sœurs de la Charité et de l'Instruction Chrétienne, Nevers: 7, 18. Monique Claude-Hermant: 2, 5. Mary Evans Picture Library, London: 10, 11, 12, 13. Iain Pears: 3, 4, 6, 9. Pascal Piskiewicz, Toulouse: 14, 15, 16. The Wellcome Institute Library, London: 17.

the benefits women gained from such encounters. Spiritual direction gave them a unique opportunity to talk about religious preoccupations and to confront issues of identity and selfhood, to share with intelligent, educated men problems close to their hearts. In a pre-Freudian world, these encounters enabled them unselfconsciously to act out and play with many imaginary roles. Mme Laforest became a needy child, Mme Dumont a querulous wife or combative sibling, fighting for precious psychological territory. In other relationships, not directly impinging on the history of Notre-Dame de Salut and pilgrimage, Picard counselled high-society patronesses to resign themselves to the lowest state of spiritual abnegation.[84] Nor were these relations static. The early letters of Mme Laforest show an explicit desire to be loved as a child, and with a child's naked adoration, with her basking in the security that Picard steadily offered. A later letter of 1885, telling him of her imminent move to a new home with her husband, however, reveals her as calm and mature, still very concerned with his good opinion and their joint charitable enterprises, but in search of a new father confessor closer to home.[85]

I believe that no sexual contact occurred in these cases; on the contrary, the passion displayed was so intense precisely because the women felt 'safe' to express what was inexpressible elsewhere. The relations between the priests and women were far more ambivalent than those between d'Alzon and his male disciples, but the apparent excess of feeling also liberated remarkable energy. The women embarked on an adventure in which they blended spiritual direction, a worthy institutional endeavour, and a kind of frustrated but all-embracing love in a bubbling cauldron of emotion. Surrounded by an aura of voluntary labour and godly inspiration, an intensity of feeling otherwise dangerous was here appropriate and even encouraged. In just the way Michelet feared, women worked for the Church and against the republican vision of society through charitable and educational activities. Rather than victims, however, they were willing agents who deserted the republic for warmly felt reasons, taking up opportunities that the secular regime denied them. As much as their male counterparts, they worked to regenerate France through Christian solidarity. It is difficult to think of any sphere in the parallel universe of the republic where women had such constant, institutionalized influence. Although clearly the subordinate partner, they were still powerful, their authority deriving from the moral stature that came from the secondary, servicing role they played, a role that was central to the organization, ethos and spirituality of the national pilgrimage to Lourdes.

The Petites-Sœurs de l'Assomption

While the charismatic Assumptionists would lead the pilgrimage movement to political conflict and national notoriety, equally present and more universally admired were the Petites-Sœurs de l'Assomption, who came, year after year, to tend the sick on the arduous train journeys to Lourdes, in the hospitals and at the Grotto. Set up in 1865, the Petites-Sœurs were built on different psychological and social foundations from either the lay women of Notre-Dame de Salut or the Assumptionist priests. Yet the experiences of the order's co-founders, Père Etienne Pernet and Mère Marie de Jésus, were similar in that their vocations grew out of personal dramas of spiritual direction.

Pernet came from near poverty in the Franche-Comté and left his adored, adoring and deeply Catholic mother at an early age to study for the priesthood, parting from a family sunk in poverty and illness[86] (see illus. 52). Accounts emphasize the impact of this experience on his vocation and conviction that the Church must tackle the spiritual misery of the poor through the family and practical help. But such clearly defined and articulated preoccupations were still far in the future, as Pernet limped, both spiritually and physically, towards a late ordination.[87] After years of vacillation and self-torment, he found himself at Nîmes in the spellbinding presence of d'Alzon, who nurtured him on a steady diet of paternal love and cajoling; for Pernet was tortured by doubts and a timidity that d'Alzon sought to vanquish: 'You have no idea of all the miracles that God performs for those incapable of goodwill. As to being frightened, it is a waste of time; set humbly about being joyful. Be docile and rejoice in the uses the Lord seeks to make of you.'[88] During the late 1850s Pernet had suffered bouts of nervous and stomach trouble, evidence of a profound uncertainty that only years of spiritual direction could assuage. The bond between them was intense; Pernet comes across as an orphan

52. Père Etienne Pernet (1824–99)

in search of a father, an often weak and debilitated man who even wore down the impulsive and strong d'Alzon. 'Let me tell you, dear friend, how troubled I am by the tendency of your soul, which is so easily discouraged. How can you sustain others, if you are so little able to sustain yourself?'[89]

Ultimately, Pernet would plough a different furrow from the more famous Picard and Bailly as the 'father of the poor and consoler of the afflicted'.[90] Nor was his path disdained by the more vocal and impressive leaders of the Assumption, for they constantly reiterated the importance of charitable works and the bridges such initiatives built to the poor. Pernet put this theory into practice when he met his collaborator, Mlle Fage, and urged her to become the mother superior of his new order.

If Pernet knew hardship and poverty, Antoinette Fage was an even greater expert in adversity. Brought up in a broken home when her father deserted her mother, the future Mère Marie de Jésus survived on the meagre earnings of her seamstress mother in a benighted quarter in Paris's fifteenth arrondissement. Destitution was made worse by a terrible fall that seriously injured her spine, and Fage grew to be twisted and stunted, with one shoulder higher than the other (see illus. 53). These handicaps left her often ill and weakened, her health

53. Mère Marie de Jésus (Mlle Antoinette Fage) (1824–83)

a serious preoccupation both for Pernet and for the sisters who sought to prolong her life and make her comfortable. She received her meagre education from the Catholic sisters in the quarter, and was perhaps influenced by preachers in the 1840s who began to talk sympathetically of the 'social question'. Her growing commitment was exemplified by participation in charity work and her connection – like so many young and enthusiastic Catholics – with the fervour associated with the Archiconfrérie of Notre-Dame des Victoires, an organization established in 1838 to re-Christianize a parish in central Paris through a devotion to the Sacred Heart.[91] Her special love for the Virgin led to increasing work among the poor, whom she visited with food and offerings of money from her savings. She became so well known in the quarter that the aristocratic Mesdames de Mesnard, who needed someone to direct a new orphanage for young adolescents, asked her to become its new head.[92]

Antoinette Fage's story gives a perfect illustration of the 'feminization of religion' in the nineteenth century, in which a particular spirituality underpinned the charitable activities of elite and poor women in alliance. But despite the heady hopes behind the orphanage, personal antagonisms hampered its development. By the time she met and began to receive spiritual direction from Père Pernet in 1864, Fage was in the midst of a personal and professional crisis, not knowing whether to leave or to remain.

The tone and nature of their exchange differed from that of Mme Dumont and Mme Laforest. There is the same excruciating longing for love and devotion, in Fage's case intensified by the loss of both parents in her youth: 'Despite myself, I am devoured by my need for affection; I need to feel helped, sustained and encouraged, I need never to feel alone and abandoned in my hours of weakness and discouragement and to find the protection and affection of a father in the devoted zeal of a director.'[93] However, what distinguishes her from these other women is her self-perception. Fage articulated exactly what she wanted and needed from a spiritual director, and in these short phrases conveyed an almost overwhelming need. What is astonishing is the degree to which Pernet responded, and seemed to do for her what d'Alzon had done for him.

Pernet was all gentleness. Nor was his task an easy one, for she tested him and his devotion at every opportunity. She believed she sensed his every change in mood, and revealed a debilitating sensibility where he was concerned: 'I think I noticed a certain constraint in you yesterday that I cannot account for and that made a strong impression on me.'[94] Nor was she able to take his advice for inner tranquillity: 'The calmer I appear on the outside, the stronger the tempest within.'[95] She was destabilized by his absences: 'I must have seemed very surly yesterday, but it's your fault [because] you paralysed me when you arrived by saying, "I'm here but have to go back immediately." '[96] She recognized that she was in love, and was afraid lest she poorly or inappropriately express the nature of her feelings:

> The excessive attachment I feel for my father is by no means the source of my suffering, which persists only in fears that this attachment (which I cannot help expressing in word and deed) may be misunderstood or misinterpreted – in a word, be deemed harmful or offensive to the father who inspires it. Indeed, this is inevitable; he knows my past, he knows to what extremes the fatal inclinations of my nature and weaknesses of my heart have led me.[97]

In the face of this passion, Pernet was loyal, filled with words that focused on her uniqueness: 'Because you are *yourself*, you will probably soon have a visit from me.'[98] He believed that her vulnerability was a potential source of strength and reassured her that 'when I am weak, it is then that I am strong.'[99] Throughout, he urged her towards a closer union with God, and in this he pointed the direction to 'the external works through which you can search for Jesus'.[100] He recognized and expressed to her the importance of their relationship for him, with her accepting his authority but knowing that their collaboration was an essential part of his spiritual universe as well. In 1866, when the foundation of their work was assured, he wrote:

> Your soul is as dear to me as my own
> I ignore the past and it does not bear on my considerations
> I wish to live with you in Our Lord

Such devotion, with time, reassured her, and ultimately their discussions moved slowly but surely to their mutual work in its minutest detail.[101]

As they grew closer, he criticized her. Her fidgeting fingers came in for reproof, as did the way she betrayed her sentiments on her face, or talked about her own past.[102] He made her realize that she must bear in mind the possibility that her 'daughters' might criticize her during their communications to *him*.[103] He insisted that she bear this as part of the responsibility of being the head of a new order. But with the growing severity came a matching insistence that she accept her new authority: 'Continue as you are doing. Your daughters are very content; they already think of you as a good mother, and you *must* let them call you by this name.'[104] He demanded that she accept this title; it was an indication of a rite of passage as well as a new spiritual condition, for now it was her turn to become a spiritual director and mentor, accepting the pleasures and pains of this special new role.

Out of the relationship came an extraordinary working partnership and a vision of the work for the 'gardes-malades', the sisters who cared for the sick. The women involved in the initiative were called the 'little coal-women' because of their early costume of sombre black bonnets and sober *pèlerines*. Their mission was not to catechize but to convert through example, and to this end the Petites-Sœurs, especially in the early years, lived from alms, giving away any surplus. They tended the sick at home, and through their presence hoped to help them recover and take up once again their place in the world or to die in Christian dignity (see illus. 54). Although neither Pernet nor

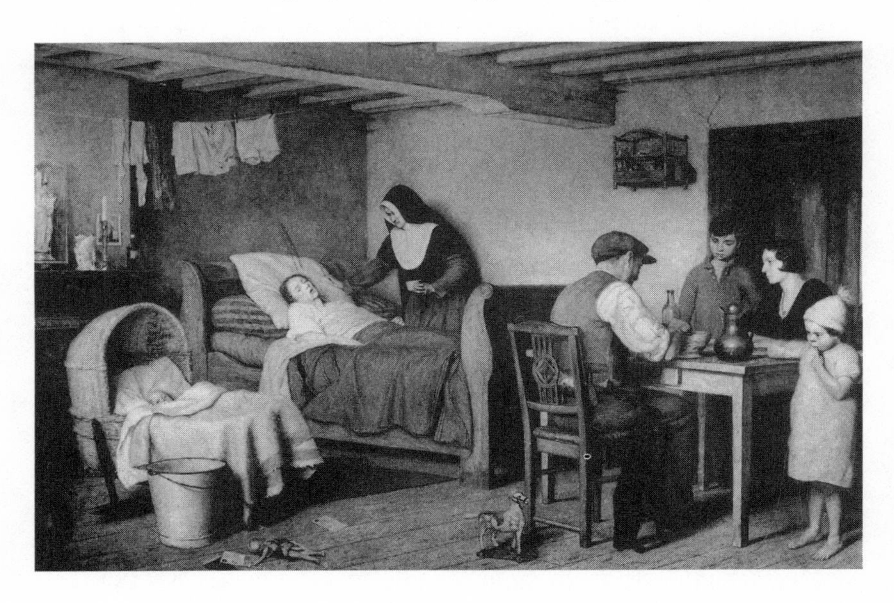

54. *Paul Wante,* The Mission of the Sisters, *1934.*
This twentieth-century painting seeks to capture the special mission of the Petites-Sœurs de l'Assomption, who sought to share the lives of the poor and evangelize through example

Fage urged a campaign of social justice, they began a social analysis of poverty. As early as 1868, only three years after the order's foundation, the word 'milieu' appeared in a report of their activities. While this ubiquitous term was filling the social inquiries of secular investigators throughout France, it had a novel ring in such a religious context. The concentration on family and neighbourhood demonstrated the importance placed not on individual fault, but on wider social and structural circumstances often beyond the individual's immediate control.

The actual work that they did in their daily lives was readily transferred to Lourdes, where their special vocation for tending the sick was widely acknowledged. Lourdes represented a profound rupture with daily routine for the priests and helpers whose lives were transformed by the yearly outing, but the Petites-Sœurs simply did what they always did, only this time on trains or in the mountain town rather than in Parisian garrets.

Antoinette Fage became a powerful personage through spiritual direction. She maintained always that Pernet was the inspiration, she only the instrument of his vision, but within twelve years of the foundation of the Petites-Sœurs there were twelve communities in France and abroad. She had a special charisma, reinforced by the feelings that her gentle countenance and physical vulnerability aroused. She signed her letters to her charges as 'your puny mother', and did not seem to mind when people called her 'the little hunchback'. She was 'frail in appearance, physically unfortunate, deformed and sickly, her face ravaged by a type of eczema', a fragility that belied a strength of purpose and an invincible belief in God. Like Thérèse de Lisieux, she saw herself as nothing more than 'God's poor, dear little plaything', an image that focused on her capacity as an instrument, but also released her powerful spirituality and drive.[105]

This vision of the self as a toy in the hands of the divine implied a maternal relationship to humanity: children in God's hands, they were mothers to God's children.[106] For the vocation of the Petites-Sœurs was to act like Mary, to show maternal concern for the sick and dispossessed who were most like Christ. By imitating Mary they were suffering mothers who took in the pain of others, a powerful vision of femininity that saw suffering as productive.[107] Mère Marie de Jésus seemed to exemplify this theme in her own physical form. Sickly, deformed, she was the 'puny mother' who could not help but arouse maternal sentiments in Pernet, and among her daughters, who sought to perform any service that might make her more comfortable. But this apparent dolourism, so typical of Lourdes in the nineteenth century, veiled the other side of her spirituality. Ill and frail she certainly was, but her special cachet was her capacity for psychological strength and spiritual wholeness. Compared to the tortured, self-doubting creature of the 1860s, the Mère Marie de Jésus of the early 1880s was liberated and serene, directing her dynamic movement from a position of strength.

In directing the Petites-Sœurs, she was the 'good' mother. She counselled Sœur Marie de la Croix, for example, when dealing with her charges: 'Be severe with yourself, indulgent with others', advice that she no doubt imposed on herself. She continued, 'Be gentle and charitable, careful to help in all ways, whatever repugnance and aversion you may feel for some of them.'[108] She was understanding of their spiritual anguish and counselled rest when they overworked. To one who could not accept obedience she remarked gently, and with comprehension, 'Alas, dear child, it is not a virtue one acquires in a day.'[109] When discouraged, she reminded another nun, Sœur Stéphanie, how unwilling people were to sacrifice for God, while wasting their energies on the material things of this world.[110] With words of this kind she won an extraordinary loyalty, and a group of devoted sisters whose capacity for cheerful work by the bedsides of the dying in poverty and on pilgrimage astonished all who observed them.

From the spring of 1876 the sisters had reached out to the *dames servantes*, 'all those who, without prejudice to their private and social duties, could take the time each week . . . enrolled in this holy army that allowed them to engage more closely with those who suffer'.[111] Some came to be near Mère Marie de Jésus, hoping that her spirituality and piety might act as a prayer in soliciting God's favour in their own lives. One older woman who had not attended a meeting because of a cold admitted that she did little for their mutual work but found in Mère Marie de Jésus 'courage, tranquillity and edification'.[112] The rich and powerful aided with money and their time, some even appearing at the new chapel at the rue Violet to express their solidarity. One explained how she had found a sample of black cashmere for six and a half francs, offering to send more of the material if it would help

Mère Marie de Jésus in her work. What is extraordinary is the difference in tone between these gentle and everyday missives and those addressed by the lay women of Notre-Dame de Salut to their spiritual directors. The nature of this maternal bond – based on a vision of sisterly and daughterly piety – produced a very different climate, one transferred to Lourdes, where Petites-Sœurs and lay women worked together for the alleviation of the suffering of the sick.

Bringing these stories of devotion and loyalty, exploitation and manipulation, love and even hate into the light gives a sense of the individual and personal inspirations of the pilgrimage movement. The stories show the inadequacy of the Michelet thesis to illuminate the complex motivations of women who chose the Church as the outlet for their energies. Michelet's portrait of repressed eroticism also misjudges the nature of the intimate relations between priests and women by undervaluing the equal significance of shared idealism and endeavour. The erotic feeling on display in the letters of Mme Laforest and Mme Dumont is so flagrant that it almost embarrasses readers today. But our discomfiture does not necessarily mean that the women involved did not find considerable benefit from these encounters. Their more troubled interactions must be compared to the example of Père Pernet and Mère Marie de Jésus, whose connection brought psychological liberation. For both concerned, their spiritual 'love affair' was possibly the greatest human relationship of their lives, involving them in work that made them feel closer to God. Indeed, in these relations they seemed to be reliving the passionate and productive encounters that typified the 'spiritual friendships' of the seventeenth century. In style, tone and inspiration they shared an ardour that led them from personal torment and despair to active and creative lives.[113]

The spiritual ambience of Lourdes owed much to these different kinds of intimate connections. D'Alzon conveyed to his disciples the vital need for a dynamic, masculine leadership, which for him meant a constant recognition of the relationship between religion, politics and a certain vision of a re-Christianized society. Picard organized and inspired the crowds, his letters showing a hatred of a world that diminished the status of priests and undermined the belief in the miraculous. Bailly brought the press, and with it anti-Semitism, biting satire and a taste for populist politics. All detested the republic and fraternized with those who opposed it or even sought its downfall. They successfully targeted women of the upper ranks, and through them found workers willing to donate their money, time and energy.

Lourdes, then, contained all the elements of embittered opposition politics, much of which was incorporated into the rituals of national pilgrimage. But the movement also expressed a willingness to serve, a passionate commitment to the sick and a belief in the bonds uniting people of different ranks. It was in this area that the urgings of the women workers dominated. The various impulses of the movement were best expressed by diverging responses to the sick and wounded during the civil war. For d'Alzon, writing in 1877, but no doubt referring to 1871, the Communards were nothing more than the *canaille*, the revolutionary rabble that the Petites-Sœurs should love only in order 'to make them blush for being so hateful'.[114] Mère Marie de Jésus did not think in these terms and treated her 'enemies' in the same manner in which she treated her friends. At Lourdes too an ethos of exclusiveness existed side by side with an ethos of inclusiveness. Participants walked a spiritual and moral tightrope, as we must in any historical assessment of their motivations and actions.

8

The Past, the Present and the Rituals of Modern Pilgrimage

During the 1897 Jubilee pilgrimage to Lourdes, after a long day full of exertions, Père Picard asked for a drink. Rather than drawing some water afresh, he asked a stretcher-bearer to fill his glass from an infected pool, filled with the pus, blood and scabs of the sick pilgrims. 'When the father had received [the water], he made the sign of the cross and drank slowly, right to the end. Then, he gave back the glass and concluded with a smile: "The water of the good Mother of Heaven is always delicious." '[1] With this gesture, Picard drew dramatically on a largely female tradition of medieval sanctity. He was showing how he, like Catherine of Siena or Angela of Foligno, could eat the scabs of lepers and suck the pus of the dying.[2] For such women, the holy food of physical suffering had been transformed into delicious fare and, like the Eucharist itself, embodied the pain of redemption. Picard both enacted a nineteenth-century vision of medieval fervour and underlined his belief in the power of faith over science at the height of the Pasteurian 'revolution'.[3] The action enlisted the past as an arm in the contemporary struggle, helping to merge age-old spiritual concerns with the modern political battle against republican secularism.

The traditionalist, hierarchical message of the national pilgrimage to Lourdes was always cast in a modernist, populist idiom, and it was the potent, if uneasy marriage of the two that explains the fantastic success of the movement. National pilgrimage was made possible by mass circulation press, train links and the managerial techniques of hospital administration; it cannot, therefore, be dismissed as the final appearance of anachronistic superstition. Over 400,000 pilgrims came in some form of organized pilgrimage in 1908, the fiftieth anniversary of the apparitions, while over a million visited if one includes those on unorganized journeys.[4] The labour movement could only rarely mobilize such crowds, and no republican institution even conceived of bringing so many women out into the public arena.

The national pilgrimage achieved these results because its organizers self-consciously evoked the past when constructing new rituals. In some ways the movement was a perfect example of the 'invention of tradition', in which nineteenth-century elites sought to remake and reinvigorate dying customs reminiscent of a 'pre-industrial', 'pre-modern' age. Whether it was through the wearing of Scottish kilts or the pageantry of royal ceremonials, such rituals associated themselves with a vision of timeless continuity, in order to construct a world free of what participants saw as the divisive social conflicts of contemporary societies.[5] The pilgrimage movement, with its Eucharistic processions and aristocratic cavaliers, offered a contemporary version of medieval fervour and chivalry as well as a vision of an organic, hierarchical social order in which the rich served the poor. The men and women who organized the national pilgrimage had an alternative image of France that they sought to promote, one that bound spirituality to politics, and France to the ancient traditions of rural, aristocratic Catholicism.

With the Assumptionists in charge, the movement became a means of competing with republican ceremonies and symbols in the age of mass politics. For their opponents in the 1870s and 1880s also strove to establish their legitimacy with new rituals and ceremonies, from the singing of the 'Marseillaise' to making Bastille Day a national holiday. For every Marianne, the symbol of the French revolutionary tradition, there was a newly crowned Virgin, for every statue of a republican notable, there was a panoply of Catholic saints, for every Eiffel Tower, a Sacré-Cœur.[6] But while the idea of the 'invention of tradition' explains something of how the movement was orchestrated, it does not explore the popular beliefs and practices that animated and sustained it. The pilgrimages were not created solely through the efforts of activist clerics like the Assumptionists and the women of Notre-Dame de Salut. Rather, these elite men and women drew their inspiration from the examples of local community worship and solidarity that they so admired.

The pilgrimage movement evolved in response to events, for the pilgrims of the early 1870s came to do penance for the nation in response to the shock of defeat and civil war. This programme was associated with the attempt to restore the Bourbon monarchy, a plan undertaken in 1871, when the Comte de Chambord returned briefly to his chateau on the Loire and declared his wish to become Henri V. His chances seemed more than good when Thiers fell in May 1873, and the French premier, the Duc de Broglie, and the president, Patrice de MacMahon, respectively supported or remained benevolently neutral to the legitimist cause. But just as a restoration seemed imminent, the Comte announced he would not accept the tricolour flag and so rejected the legacy of the Revolution. His insistence on the white flag and fleur-de-lis of Bourbonism was not based only on a sense of personal honour, however. Rather, the flag represented the principle of legitimacy that the nation must freely accept if the Restoration was to succeed. Nor did his resistance to the tricolour denote a desire to return to the old regime. Instead, he envisaged decentralized communities in which there existed a solidarity between rich and poor, expressed through patronage and Christian charity.[7]

Chambord's symbolic stance on the flag none the less fatally undermined the royalist cause; in 1875 a republic was adopted as the new form of government and any residual hopes of Restoration were finally ground to the dust in 1876 when elections showed the population's preference for a moderate republicanism. But it was in these crucial years of growing political disappointment that the special mission of tending the sick at Lourdes emerged. Only then did the numbers of sick pilgrims begin to rise, requiring the organization of special trains, the aid of the Petites-Sœurs and the institutionalization of the Hospitalités, the lay organizations designed to transport the sick from train to Grotto, tend them in the hospitals and bathe them in the pools.

In this enterprise the sick came to take centre stage, almost as if the organizers wished to display their bodies and exhibit their deformities. Whereas today pilgrimage seeks to break down the distinction between sick and healthy, in the nineteenth century it highlighted the division between the two. The sick were consciously patronized as 'nos chers malades', those whom science had failed, and their presence promoted a vision of suffering humanity and the need for God's miraculous assistance. The rituals established at the shrine over the years came to emphasize the physical – the touch between helpers and sick, the carrying of inert bodies, the immersion of those unable to bathe themselves. Lourdes highlighted Eucharistic processions, accentuating the parallels between Christ's passion and resurrection, and the pain and potential cure of the sick. Pilgrims yearned for Mary's merciful intervention and maternal embrace, finding in the water of the fountain both a bracing physical test and the possibility of ultimate solace.

These rituals created a community of extraordinary solidarity in which the poor and weak were serviced by the rich and strong. But this vision of an ideal Christian collectivity was perennially marked by the political hatreds that infused the movement from the end of the Franco-Prussian War to the celebrations of twenty-five years of national pilgrimage in 1897. The pressures of Third Republican politics and the leadership's hatred of anti-clerics, Freemasons and especially Jews continued to influence the ambience surrounding the movement. The Dreyfus Affair at the end of the century showed how the likes of Vincent de Paul Bailly sought to tie a positive spirituality to an anti-Semitic race hatred and a vision of France purged of contaminating 'traitors'. In this, as in so many other areas, Bailly 'reinvented' and revivified an old tradition.

The Origins of the Early Pilgrimage

The last chapter showed how the Commune of 1871 was crucial for forming the political and spiritual aspirations of the Assumptionist Order. The pilgrimage movement also emerged from the same circumstances of national disaster, with a flood of vows, prophecies, supernatural signs and apparitions signalling both warning and consolation. In January 1871, in the shadow of occupation and before the Commune, Catholic notables took the vow to build Sacré-Cœur at the top of the Mount of Martyrs, a site higher and more majestic than that of the secular classical temple of the republican Panthéon.[8] In Lyon a similar vow led to the construction of Notre-Dame de Fourvière to thank the Virgin for her timely intervention in sparing the city in 1871.[9] In Pontmain in the Mayenne, a village that trembled in January 1871 before the thunder of the advancing Prussian guns, a group of children saw an apparition of the Virgin, dressed in vaguely Byzantine style, at the moment of the *aurora borealis* in a brilliantly starry but moonless night. Ultimately her message was spelled out in the sky, 'But pray, my children. God will soon grant your prayer', and the halting of the Prussian advance was accordingly attributed to her intervention.[10] Nor was this appearance unique: in several villages in Alsace a wave of apparitions of the Virgin with sword in hand took place.[11] She also made her images move in mutilated Lorraine: in an old convent in Nancy a humble statue of the Immaculate Conception blinked when implored to 'Sauve, sauve la France' at the moment when Strasbourg lay in ruins and Metz was shamefully capitulating.[12]

The Assumptionists wanted to know the meaning of these events and were touched themselves by the signs of divine providence. Bailly, for example, described the appearance of the Virgin to two schoolchildren in the working-class district of the Butte Montmartre, a 'part of the city steeped in blood by the first murders of the Commune in Paris'. The first occurred to an Alsatian boy in a lay school, which he later had to leave because of the mockeries of his fellows, the other to a young seminarian who also saw a majestic lady in white. Both had debilitating and dangerous illnesses, and enjoyed complete recoveries afterwards.[13] The Assumptionists propagated the news of such divine appearances and prophecies, publishing accounts in the newly established *Le Pèlerin* from its beginnings in July 1873; six months later Picard wrote

> The supernatural and the marvellous have pervaded society and today engage the thoughts of those most refractory to notions of faith. From the more or less clear-cut prophecies that circulated in France throughout the Prussian War to the more or less veridical apparitions that are even now causing astonishment in Germany and Alsace, everything reveals a new state of society, everything shows a veritable effervescence of prodigies and miracles.[14]

Their commitment to tell these tales was risky, for all priests knew of the need for caution and due episcopal procedure to verify claims of supernatural occurrence. They persisted because they believed in the immediacy – both political and religious – of salvation. Aware of the prophecies of the priest Torné-Chavigny from the diocese of La Rochelle, who predicted the imminent restoration of the Comte de Chambord as Henri V, they believed that divine intervention would come in this moment of confusion and despair, even if they did not give credence to his particular utterances. Their willingness to countenance the miraculous – thereby risking the criticism of catering to superstition and credulity – was also a way of bringing back faith into the lives of the 'people'. Following a line developed most cogently by Veuillot, they were less fearful of publicizing the 'false prophecies' of the pious than of submitting to the *real* 'falsities' of revolutionary doctrine.[15]

The first national pilgrimage organized by the Assumptionists in 1872 was made not to Lourdes but to La Salette in the French Alps, in the midst of this climate of awe, fear and repentance. The Pyrenean shrine, therefore, had no predestined role. However, the venture to the Alps served as a testing ground for the future, and a comprehension of its drawbacks proved crucial for the later success of Lourdes. The ambiguous outcome was perhaps partly due to the fact that the idea came not from the Assumptionists at the rue François Ier, but from the obscure Abbé Thédenat, vicar of the parish of Saints Gervais-et-Protais in Paris. Although the order was enthusiastic when first approached, its leaders realized later that they had taken on a hefty institutional burden for which they were not entirely prepared.

The sanctuary of La Salette, seventy-three kilometres from Grenoble and at an altitude of 1,200 metres, seemed a most appropriate site for expressing the mood of contrition. There in 1847 two little shepherds had encountered a weeping Virgin whose prophecies of disaster seemed all too apposite to the later generation living the reality of catastrophe. The apparition's language suited the tone of the national pilgrimage; however, other problems marred the enterprise. First, La Salette was surrounded by an unseemly display of clerical factionalism, with the bishop of Grenoble unable to control priests who condemned the apparitions as frauds. More worrying were the visionaries themselves: Mélanie had tried the religious life but seemed emotionally unstable and ultimately acted as a self-made prophetess in France and Italy, predicting the 'misfortune of the times'. Her contemporary Maximin fared little better: he had also begun religious training, then served in the Pope's volunteer army, but when back in La Salette gave his name to an entrepreneur who manufactured a liqueur called 'Salettine'. Maximin was a drunk, and by 1872 was selling souvenirs to pilgrims and retelling the story of the apparitions to all comers.[16]

Both were an embarrassment and left the Church vulnerable to anti-clerical attack. In contrast, Bernadette was exemplary and her removal to Nevers shut off any possibility of similar criticism. Picard expressed his disappointment that the Grotto had not been chosen in the first place,[17] perhaps echoing d'Alzon's uneasiness with the Alpine shrine and the controversy it had generated. As early as 1868 d'Alzon had contrasted the two sites: 'La Salette left me, I don't know why, incredulous or at least hard and dry, Lourdes brought me I know not what perfume of peace, confidence and hope that I shall one day convert.'[18] Nor was the region particularly welcoming: Grenoble had not only supported Napoleon in the Hundred Days, but had also had its own Commune. In contrast, the relative conservatism of the south-west made the region around Lourdes a much more auspicious environment. Finally, the site in the Alps discouraged pilgrims who required both wagons and mules to reach it from Grenoble. Once again Lourdes, with its train link in place since 1866, was more commodious, especially for the thousands who would soon come on stretchers.

This first venture to La Salette was both worse and better than the Assumptionists had hoped. It was worse, insofar as the organization was a nightmare, involving negotiations with the rail companies and extra work for the order.[19] Also, they feared that the pilgrimage might become *too* political, a venue for legitimist speeches rather than a site for prayer; instead of the predicted 50,000 pilgrims, only 1,400 arrived at Grenoble, and, of these, a hundred were legitimist deputies from the National Assembly. On top of that, they were heckled by soldiers, artisans and labourers: 'They are royalists who are going off to plot and carouse at La Salette. They should be put away. To [the lunatic asylum of] Charenton! To Saint-Robert with the black gang [of clerics]!'[20]

None the less, the venture was not a total disaster, and the difficulty of the conditions was turned into a positive feature by the bishop of Grenoble: 'Most of them spent several nights sleeping on the bare ground, and not a single complaint was heard of.'[21] The layman Vicomte de Damas, president of the General Council of Pilgrimages, also wrote with feeling to Père Picard: 'The pilgrims who came with us suffered, you know; however, despite all the insults, the stone-throwing, the privations of every kind, they are ready to start again.'[22] In these trying circumstances Picard cut an impressive figure, meeting a deputation from Grenoble who apologized for the poor behaviour of their fellow townsmen. News of the pilgrimage made its way to Paris and the National Assembly, where the difficulties of the expedition were quickly mythologized.

Just as La Salette was absorbing the Assumptionists in 1872, a rival *manifestation de la foi* took place in Lourdes, which was well organized and a success, albeit a unique occasion. It demonstrated the powerful nostalgic fantasies of its organizers, visions that the Assumption would also learn to exploit. In October 1871 Abbé Chocarne of Beaune went to Lourdes to pray at the Grotto and was struck by

> One of those country processions from Bigorre, such as strangers adore for the simplicity and éclat, the pious gravity and grace that are the essence of their charm, [which] had come to Lourdes for the ceremony of the Rosary. Now on the heights of the rock, under the chapel vaults, now along the

pathways, now on the banks of the Gave, the religious peasants filled every hour of this great day with prayers and hymns.[23]

He was impressed by the Children of Mary in white, the young girls crowned with flowers and carrying lilies or roses in their arms. He believed he had participated in some rural idyll of piety untainted both by recent events and by the sins of urban living, and hoped to tap into some age-old continuity, to absorb some of the 'gravité pieuse' of the peasants.

Chocarne thought he was drinking in some undistilled Pyrenean essence, but no such pure liquid existed, for the expressions of devotion he beheld had already been transformed by the changes at the shrine. As early as 1864 20,000 people – villagers in ranks, Children of Mary, clergymen and Mgr Laurence – had made their way from the parish church to the Grotto to inaugurate the statue in the niche[24] (see illus. 55). This robust public display was no less authentic for its choreographed quality, but was already a far cry from the parish processions of the eighteenth century and before. The celebrations of

55. Paul Dufour, 'The Procession to the Grotto, 4 April 1864', lithograph from René Laurentin and Bernard Billet, Lourdes: Documents authentiques VII, *1966*

1866, in which Bernadette had almost been mobbed, showed the processional extravaganza that the Pyreneans produced in honour of the inauguration of the crypt.

In Chocarne's plan, delegates were to come from all the major sanctuaries of France to pay homage to the Virgin of the Rosary, who 'preserved . . . for the Christian nations their independence and faith'. The event took place on 6 October, with representatives from all parts of the country and its colonies; the banners they brought were left in the basilica to commemorate the occasion, representing a religious map of France, a world of parishes and dioceses that little heeded the borders of revolutionary departments. Although not repeated, the pilgrimage epitomized the historical, spiritual and aesthetic proclivities of the movement as a whole, recalling an age of medieval splendour and pageantry. *Le Pèlerin*, founded in 1873 by the Assumptionists, also evoked the Middle Ages and hoped to revive 'the France of Clovis, of Charlemagne and of Saint Louis',[25] the great Christian kings of France: 'Never, since the time of the Crusades and Saint Joan of Arc, has such a manifestation been seen.'[26] This message was to be communicated all the more effectively through modern technology. 'Christians have seized upon modern inventions and created more numerous and rapid channels for their devotion.'[27]

Le Pèlerin was launched with specific aims in mind. Notre-Dame de Salut and the organizing committee hoped for a month of pilgrimage between 22 July and 22 August in 1873, with a two-pronged attack that was to be both national *and* local, incorporating the most famous sanctuaries and regional centres. The national sites were to be La Salette and Lourdes, where massive crowds could proclaim the *droits de Dieu*, show their repentance, and rededicate France to Mary as the 'eldest Daughter of the Church'. Their ardour to save the nation was matched by support for the Pope, who in turn encouraged the movement by allowing his special sign, 'a small cross in red wool', to be worn on the pilgrims' clothes.[28] Militaristic metaphors against godlessness and revolution pervaded the movement, with the Assumptionists calling themselves the 'uhlans de Dieu', willing to act even like Prussian cavalry in the service of ultramontanism and France's re-Christianization.

The month of pilgrimage was part of a larger programme that extended beyond the narrow confines of the thirty-day period. In May

20,000 people led by fifty deputies went to Notre-Dame de Chartres, the nation's most venerated Gothic monument. Important politicians thus demonstrated their piety and strengthened the links between the movement and monarchist politics. Paray-le-Monial, shrine of the Sacred Heart and symbol of Bourbon legitimacy, also attracted a crowd moved by the appearance of the defeated papal Zouaves; another went to Notre-Dame d'Issoudun on the festival of the Nativity of the Virgin. Finally, in a venture in which tourism and social snobbery mixed with genuine spirituality, pilgrims massed at Mont-Saint-Michel in September and October, showing the strength of a revitalized confraternity whose 40,000 members included many prominent aristocratic families.[29]

This movement went hand in hand with the revitalization of local pilgrimage, a trend that shows how the 'invention of tradition' was not imposed by elites but rather depended as much on poorer parishes and the enthusiasms of local clergy, who sought to restore links only recently lost and perhaps still in living memory.[30] The project was exemplified by the small and little-known pilgrimage of the parish of Loubajac to Lourdes in April 1864, almost a decade before the national pilgrimage itself. Six kilometres from the Grotto, Loubajac expressed its communal devotion at Lourdes by seeking to re-enact some ancient processional discipline from Notre-Dame de Garaison:

> ... the men, arranged in two rows, formed the vanguard; we priests ... occupied the centre; behind us came two parallel columns of men, plunged in thought and telling their rosaries. At regular intervals, from one end to the other of the centre of this handsome procession, were the many litters, on which stood magnificent artificial niches, each of them holding a statuette of the Immaculate Conception.[31]

While the men guarded the images of Mary – carrying facsimiles to the apparition site – the women mainly supplicated on their knees. Fêted by a group of musicians, the procession made its way into the *bourg*, to be greeted at the hospice by Bernadette herself. Bells rang, observers came running, female penitents came to be blessed on bended knee, rituals that recalled the enthusiasm shown for Anglèze de Sagazan on her visits to Garaison after her removal to a convent in Fabas at some unknown time after her apparitions in 1520. The pilgrims of Loubajac felt they were enacting rituals 'whose origins are lost in the mists of time', finding justification for their current devotions in their vision of the past.[32]

The Assumptionists learned from such popular piety with their call to pilgrimage in 1873, and the first national pilgrimage to Lourdes was also suffused by the appeal of the past. The pilgrims stopped first at Tours and paid homage to Saint Martin, a fourth-century soldier turned bishop famous for his mass conversions, humility and work among the poor. Then they went on to the village of Pouy, the birthplace of Saint Vincent de Paul, who, with the help of aristocratic women, had founded the Sisters of Charity in the seventeenth century. The similarity between this partnership and that of the Assumptionists with the women of Notre-Dame de Salut and the Petites-Sœurs was obvious, as so much of the nineteenth-century social vision of the French Church took its inspiration from this source.

The train journey that took the pilgrims to these shrines, then on to Lourdes, met with mixed responses, the mockery and sarcasm of non-believers matched by the warmth of rural France, of women and children 'tending their flock' who 'knelt down in the middle of the fields, crossing themselves'.[33] Compared to La Salette, the enterprise went off without a hitch, with the sober crowd of pilgrims spending most of their time in prayer. There were no riotous crowds, no unseemly clerical disputes, and, above all, there was the Grotto at journey's end and a sense of reaching an uncontested spiritual sanctuary. Despite this success there was still no sense that the trip to Lourdes would become *the* annual national event of the Catholic community.

Those involved from the beginning recalled this early venture nostalgically, when Lourdes was yet a small town and Bernadette's friends and companions remained to tell visitors of the great events. Even in early 1873 the history of the apparitions still belonged, in some sense, to the Lourdais; as one anonymous pilgrim recalled:

> These first pilgrimages . . . had a particular charm. Lourdes was not yet the large town it is now, with these vast hotels and the wide boulevard. We put up in the old houses of the place Marcadal or the market. But how exciting it was to meet the brothers and sisters of Bernadette Soubirous in the narrow alleys! We actually went into the houses of Jeanne Abadie or Antoinette

Peyret, or some other companion of the Visionary. And there, people told you about the apparitions, as if they had happened the day before.[34]

Whether all liked the rough-and-ready conditions, or felt the same proximity to the supernatural, is not clear. In any case, the participants returned to Paris with no idea of the tradition that they had initiated. The sick and dying had played no special role in this first demonstration.

The Sick and the Evolution of Pilgrimage

The first noticeable contingent of around fifty *malades* joined the pilgrimage in 1875; in 1877 they counted for 366 out of a total 1,200. Every year thereafter the total increased, with 441 out of 1,460 coming in 1878, and 555 out of 4,000 appearing in 1879. In 1880 seven trains left Paris alone with 4,500 pilgrims and 700 *malades*. Picard's report in 1879 typifies this period, showing the spiritual, physical and psychological atmosphere of a movement in creative flux but already establishing a solid grounding for the future.

On this occasion participants came from the north and east first, so that when the train stopped at Orléans they were greeted by the sight of the sick and dying waiting for them at the platform. The management of the sick would set the tone for the kind of Christian solidarity that was to identify the national pilgrimage. Picard wrote:

> The charity of the pilgrims intensified their devotion and tact. At the porters' cry of 'Make way for the sick', the most zealous gave way with fervent respect. Lay persons worked with priests to alleviate the suffering of the sick, society hostesses carried stretchers like the merest working women, railway employees of every status and rank joined with the directors of the Charity to prepare the railway, transport the poor invalids and place them in the carriages.[35]

The train then continued to pick up other pilgrims in Poitiers, a diocese famous for the tutelage of Mgr Pie, a legitimist bishop who had waged war against Louis Napoleon and defended papal prerogatives. The name 'Poitou' 'evoked the entire mythology of royalist

France' with its Romanesque churches and chateaux dotting the countryside.[36] After 1871 Mgr Pie supported the Comte de Chambord's bid to become Henri V, and, although this campaign had met defeat by 1879, local aristocrats turned out to meet trains arriving from Etampes, Gien, Vendôme, Châteaudun, Chartres, Blois and Tours. The 'grandes dames' demonstrated 'the traditions of chivalric devotion' by organizing the welcome, and physicians and priests tended the physical and spiritual needs of the pilgrims.

Picard recognized the arduousness of the journey and revelled in it, even though he acknowledged that such exertions for the sick contradicted good sense: 'Faith alone can brave such anguish and penetrate such rashness.'[37] This assault on rationalism, which appalled anti-clerical critics, remained a distinguishing feature of the movement: it took three long and trying hours to transport the *malades* to the basilica of Saint Radegonde near Poitiers, a patron saint of France famous for maintaining her faith in the face of pagan intimidation, where the assembled watched a procession of her relics. The suffering continued with the sick pilgrims having to endure the horrible August heat when back on the train: 'The heat was overpowering. Almost all the carriages contained patients who lay unconscious, while around them prayed their fellow travellers, who had become their relatives and friends. Everyone suffered'[38] (see illus. 56). But prayer, Picard maintained, turned the emotional tide: 'For the first time, perhaps, the prayers of the Church resounded under these crystal vaults, which till now had echoed only to the strident whistling of locomotives.'[39] Ave Marias rang out for a dying person, and a mute woman from the Pas-de-Calais regained her voice. On the train to Lourdes pilgrims showed their belief in the continuing relevance of prayer (see illus. 57).

In this context death was not frightening, and medical treatment was useless; when the train passed Bordeaux, one woman received extreme unction: ' "We must get there quickly." "Listen, doctor," said the father, "everything is for the best, we are praying. No remedies." '[40] Others lay unconscious in the train and had yet to endure the gruelling four and a half hours that it took to get from the station to the Grotto: 'To the gravely ill fell the places of honour, the mattresses that had been prepared; there were more than 200 of them, stretched out beneath the gaze of their mother. Behind them were those who could

56. Pilgrims in the heat, c. *1900*
57. Une messe dans le train des malades, c. *1900*

Although of the turn of the century, these photographs show the difficulty of the conditions and the way the train became the church of the pilgrims sit; then the lame, the blind, etc. Finally, the able-bodied pilgrims, standing or kneeling, always ready to bring aid to their brothers.'[41] Mass then began, with priests going from stretcher to stretcher to give the Eucharist, which for some was the only solid food they had taken in weeks. At this moment

> a poor dying woman raised her eyes; she cast upon Mary a look full of tears, then stood up and advanced, radiant, towards the Grotto. She was cured . . . What a spectacle! In less than an hour fourteen of the sick were standing. Before my very eyes they stood up, prayed, thanked Mary and took refuge in the Grotto to avoid the enthusiasm of the crowd. One woman had received the last sacrament at Poitiers, another had, at Bordeaux, given us the greatest anxiety; a third had not set foot on the ground for twenty-eight years; three others had received absolution *in extremis* between Poitiers and Lourdes. These are veritable resurrections.[42]

Pilgrims were willing to risk death, and saw their audacity as a test that might hasten the 'resurrections' they sought. The belief in the miraculous was encouraged by the Assumptionists, who chronicled the cures with the Garaison Fathers until the Medical Bureau took over in 1883 to bring greater rigour to the process of assessment.[43] During the 1879 pilgrimage Picard wrote with pride of the seventy 'written records of complete cures and considerable improvements',[44] an extraordinary percentage of the 555 who had gone on the journey. Lourdes had now become the 'pilgrimage of miracles' and continued as such thereafter. In 1880 they claimed as many as 150 cures and ameliorations, not to speak of spiritual graces.

In order to achieve these results, devotion became physically intense. Bailly wrote to his brother priest Galabert: 'At Lourdes one wears oneself out; little sleep, scarcely anything to eat, one prays a great deal, leads prayers and sees great things.'[45] Within Christian tradition of pilgrimage, such self-sacrifice and supplication were hardly novel; indeed, in imposing this ascetic regime with its ecstatic inflection, the Assumptionists once again harked back to their own imaginative vision of medieval piety. There is no denying that hunger, tiredness and the emotional pain of tending the sick – who often cried out in agony or simply fainted in distress – acted upon the psychological climate. During the week of national pilgrimage both helpers and the sick lived a reality different from ordinary life; the atmosphere of constant prayer, death and the possibility of resurrection urging those present on to ever greater feats of self-denial.

Bodily sacrifice was admired above all else, with the sick on stretchers using their last bit of strength to imitate the Passion by putting themselves in the position of Christ on the cross. Throughout the pilgrimage, the esplanade before the Grotto resembled a mixture of a battlefield hospital – with the sick and dying on the ground in their stretchers tended to by the nuns who accompanied them – and an open-air church. Physical abasement was crucial to the pilgrimage experience and, less overtly, to a programme of political resistance, for individual sins were linked to those of the fallen nation. 'There supplications and prayer chants never ceased, by day or night. People often prayed with their arms held wide, like the Saviour on the Cross or the orants of the early Church . . . Only Christian France is capable of such devotion; for her great love, she shall be pardoned many things.'[46]

In a stylized engraving of the pilgrimage of 1880 produced for *Le Pèlerin*, the first impression is of the multitude kneeling before the Grotto (see illus. 58). In the far distance is the statue of the Immaculate Conception in her niche, with a glowing cluster of candles beneath her. Closest to the viewer is a series of priests: the one on the left is a Carmelite or a Benedictine, in the middle a secular priest, and in the far right-hand corner, with outstretched arms, an Assumptionist with his distinctive robe. The priests in the foreground emphasized both the distinctive role of the clergy at the pilgrimage and Lourdes as a place of union for its officers and its flock. All pray together, most on their knees; ladies in their finery genuflect, and one even lies prostrate on the floor. A poorer man in a plain white coat holds his rosary, rather dramatically, in the position of the cross, with many others joining him with raised arms. Closer to the Grotto are the vague figures of the sick on stretchers, here held by women, or prayed over by the nuns in attendance.

Anti-clerics were terrified and repelled by these 'excessive' displays, and alarmed by the Grotto's capacity to generate such crowds. For these critics Lourdes produced an unhealthy, if not dangerous, ambience of abandonment, which might lead to crowd hysteria.[47] The intensely physical nature of the devotions – which meant that even

58. 'Aspect de la Grotte de Lourdes pendant les Grandes Prières du 20 au 23 août', Le Pèlerin, *4 September 1880*

the most elegant ladies might find themselves praying face-down in the dirt – showed how extreme were the emotions generated. The emphasis on the crucifixion was particularly provocative in 1880, the moment when the anti-clerical prefect of Paris, Jules Ferry, was removing crucifixes from the capital's schoolrooms. This move was only one aspect of his anti-clerical legislation, which more importantly removed Catholic teaching orders from primary education, and thereby attacked the very foundation of Church influence.[48] The crowds who came to Lourdes in this period, therefore, were living through the trauma of republican assault; while anti-clerics were disturbed by the public display of so much suffering and death, the pilgrims themselves took comfort in exhibitions of physical and spiritual humility demonstrating that only in supernatural intervention could redemption be found.

For the Assumption, pilgrimage always blended politics with institutional needs and spiritual preoccupations. D'Alzon, for example, believed that the miracles of Lourdes were a special sign for his order and prayed to Notre-Dame de Lourdes when taking specific decisions about its future.[49] But, despite this great loyalty, he was still concerned lest the enormous annual enterprise bleed the Assumptionists dry.[50] Picard, in contrast, had no doubts whatsoever, and, when d'Alzon died in 1880, he indulged his passion to the hilt. The crowds on their knees, the *malades* on their stretchers, the fear that the sick would die on the trains – these were all aspects of the drama that he welcomed as part of a saintly mission. He revelled in the difficulties, the sarcasm of the anti-clerical press, and particularly the opposition of anti-clerical physicians,[51] supported throughout by the conviction that the growing success of the movement was the surest indication of divine favour:

> But . . . it is God's will; God had sent the thought and the money. God has created attendants, the nuns and monks, gentlemen and ladies, who will all, for a whole week, be Brothers of Saint John of God and Sisters of Charity. God wills it, the steam train carries away all these infirmities, all these wounds and all this suffering. The world is astounded and admires; the railway employees take off their hats . . . and become attendants themselves.[52]

The women and men who organized the national pilgrimage looked to past models to build a movement with a distinctively gendered division of labour. Notre-Dame de Salut itself took its name from a legendary statue of the Virgin in Paris, supposedly sculpted for the crypt of the Sainte-Chapelle and the greatest of medieval Catholic monarchs, Saint Louis. The legend recounted how John Duns Scotus, before submitting his defence of the Immaculate Conception at the Sorbonne in 1302, saw this Madonna lean towards him and smile, a gesture for ever imprinted on the stone (see illus. 59). The women of the organization venerated this image (which is, in fact, of uncertain provenance), not least for the link it provided to the piety of Saint Louis and the Bourbon ascendancy as well as the medieval champions of the Immaculate Conception. As it escaped destruction during the Commune, it was seen as especially powerful in fighting the godless enemies of the present.

This attachment to symbols of past glory and devotion accompanied

59. Notre-Dame de Salut, *possibly late thirteenth/early fourteenth century, Chapelle des Pères Assomptionnistes, Paris*

a very practical capacity to raise funds. In 1875, when the first significant numbers of *malades* – over fifty – went on pilgrimage, Notre-Dame de Salut raised 10,644 francs and kitted out the first 'wagon ambulance' to take them to the Grotto. By 1879 it could boast: 'In two months she throws at the feet of Notre-Dame de Salut the huge sum of 46,122.75 francs; 590 invalids, who are completely without means, will be able to see Lourdes and take part in the wonders that Mary Immaculate is pleased to lavish upon this place of prayer and benediction.'[53] The organization was able to generate funds more successfully for this enterprise than it could for its workers' charities, an indication of the special appeal, public visibility and symbolism of the Lourdes pilgrimage for French Catholics.

While the women of Notre-Dame de Salut found the funds, they worked with the Petites-Sœurs in tending the sick. Père Pernet again looked to the past for inspiration, seeking women who combined 'the active and the contemplative life', 'the heart of a missionary and the soul of a Carmelite',[54] and who could withstand the moral and physical misery they encountered every day. The reference to the sixteenth-century Carmelites was important, for they were enclosed, devoted to prayer and famous for their mysticism, a new ideal of the Counter-Reformation designed to keep women from an active life and its temptations.[55] The Petites-Sœurs were somehow supposed to blend this model of spiritual purity with the work of penetrating such quarters as the Communard stronghold of Belleville, and earning respect in contemporary society.

The Petites-Sœurs were devoted to helping the most impoverished and benighted, to serving selflessly and to taking nothing in return: 'Think of the poor man suffering on his wretched litter as Jesus Christ, the divine leper.' Dressed in a 'wide black robe, coif and white wimple and, for professed sisters, a black veil similar in shape to Bernadette's hood',[56] they became a familiar sight on pilgrimage. Mère Marie de Jésus came to Lourdes every year from 1876 to her death in 1883, and her eighty nuns continued the work thereafter.[57] Despite their efforts, however, the arrangements in these early years were often makeshift, with pilgrims lodged at the temporary Chalet Saint-Joseph in 1874, then going to the newly constructed Hôpital des Sept Douleurs after 1881.[58] But the growing numbers meant many had to stay in the Hospice–Ecole des Sœurs de Nevers where Bernadette had been educated, as well as the Abri des pèlerins, later the Hôpital de Notre-Dame de Salut. As late as 1881 the lack of beds meant some had to stay in private homes.[59]

Mère Marie proudly described their devotion to the sick, and the exhaustion and hunger of her 'daughters',[60] who showed their mettle when moving the *malades* through the rain and mud using whatever transport was available:

> [The *malades* were] carried in wheelbarrows or on the backs of the fathers, in railway trolleys or little hand carts; very exceptionally, for some, in horse-drawn carriages . . . Until 1883 one saw veritable caravans of pitiful stretchers, requiring arduous efforts on the part of the generous porters; only in 1883 did more comfortable hand carts come into use.[61]

Amidst all the bustle, the letters occasionally reveal the intimacy of caring for the sick. One Petite-Sœur, for example, unconsciously evoked an image of the Virgin holding Jesus in her arms when speaking about a sister's attitude with a moribund pilgrim: 'The return took place without great difficulty, the gravest cases having been cured or relieved. Only Brother Simon gave cause for real alarm. For three hours Sister Marie des Anges held him in her arms. We thought his last hour had come.'[62]

In these early years the Petites-Sœurs took care of all the jobs that later became the tasks of specialized groups: 'Some stay at the hospital during the day, the others remain at the pool to bathe the sick. For my part, I stay at the Grotto to take care of those who may be forgotten at the Grotto and who, since they cannot walk, would get nothing to eat.'[63] Like Notre-Dame de Pitié, the Petites-Sœurs saw themselves as maternal presences tending to the bodies of Christ, and in this way followed Père Pernet's injunction to care for the 'divine leper'.

But the special place of the Petites-Sœurs did not last long, nor could the skeletal administrative system survive without cracking. Letters in the early years between Mme Laforest, Père Picard and the Garaison Fathers at Lourdes – essentially Père Burosse – reveal the problems of establishing a working relationship between the capital and the sanctuary. At each juncture they fretted over the erection of the huts and tents designed to shelter the sick,[64] or discussed the organization and manning of the *piscines*, or pools in which the sick were bathed.[65] Relations between Notre-Dame de Salut and the sanctuary were none the less amiable. Laforest, for example, thanked Burosse for making available a house in which the Assumptionist fathers could stay and live in community during the pilgrimage.[66] Picard wrote warmly and honestly to his brother priests at Lourdes, counting on their aid in the venture but hardly taking a commanding tone.

This easy atmosphere, as well as the organization, changed dramatically with the foundation in 1880 of the Hospitalité de Notre-Dame de Salut. Distinct from the Association de Notre-Dame de Salut but with overlapping personnel, the Hospitalité took over many of the tasks previously performed by the Petites-Sœurs. The idea for its establishment apparently came from the aristocratic activists, M. de

Combettes de Luc and M. de l'Epinois, and in his inimitable journalistic fashion, Bailly's 1887 report raised the tale of its creation almost to the level of legend:

> One day when the thousands of sick of the Association of Notre-Dame de Salut, several of whom were dying, were crying out in loud voices at Lourdes station for willing hands to carry them quickly to the Grotto, like the paralytic at the pool of Jerusalem, two sons of crusaders, who had come partly out of curiosity and partly as pilgrims, were moved; they went and found the director and asked him:
>
> 'Do you want to make use of us?'
>
> 'Yes, be the servants of the poor.'
>
> Vested with this new dignity, for three days they received the baptism of fire of servants of charity. And at the end of the pilgrimage, to judge by their expressions, it had taken hold in them.
>
> 'If you wish,' they said to the director, 'we shall be an army, we shall be what the hospitallers of Saint John were to the sick pilgrims of Jerusalem. Are you willing to bless our recruitment and welcome us as the Brothers of the Association of Notre-Dame de Salut?'
>
> 'Are you willing to obey?'
>
> 'With all our hearts.'
>
> 'Well, then, receive the blessing and let us work together.'[67]

Many of the favoured themes of the Assumption appear in this account, with Picard calling these disciples to him, as d'Alzon had once called him and Bailly. These aristocratic gentlemen were to be latter-day versions of the hospitallers of Saint John, who had helped the sick on the way to Jerusalem, once again uniting the masculine qualities of chivalry, prowess and manly faith. A military style pervaded the organization: as one stretcher-bearer remembered his experience of 1891: 'We marched in military fashion with a rather severe discipline on the part of the leaders. It was necessary for the training of the young men who would one day be required to command in their turn.'[68] Bailly recognized the shift in emphasis: from now on men were to have an important and recognized role in the tending of the sick, a chore hitherto left largely to women. A few months later the Hospitalité de Notre-Dame de Salut was founded in Toulouse, with the organization's members appearing for service at Lourdes in 1881.

These *hommes du monde* were to be the *brancardiers*, 'stretcher-bearers to the poor', and the vision of the new balance was encapsulated in an engraving that appeared in *Le Pèlerin* that same year (see illus. 60). On the left was a courtly, mature aristocrat in top hat and

60. 'Foi, Espérance, Charité', Le Pèlerin, *13 August 1881*

elegant coat, holding a chair in which sat an inert *malade* clutching her rosary. On the other side was a Petite-Sœur recognizable by her distinctive garb. The three figures are in partnership, with the leadership of the man evidenced by his forthright gaze. The sick woman casts her eyes heavenward in a searching look of supplication and/or pain, while the Petite-Sœur has eyes only for her charge, her face virtually invisible to us. Above the three figures are the three theological virtues, faith, hope and charity, each associated with the person they embody. Masculine faith is joined to the hope of cure and redemption, and in turn held by the charitable embrace of the nursing sister.

However, away from the idealizations of *Le Pèlerin*, the archives reveal the turmoil the appearance of this organization caused. Rather than earning gratitude, the behaviour of the *hospitaliers* in the summer of 1882 caused outrage. 'What is this band of laymen, who . . . shout, insult and shove the pilgrims, prevent access to the Grotto, and chase from this blessed place priests, monks and nuns?'[69] This protester feared the way such arrogant men were outside clerical direction, imposing their will on a centre of prayer and spirituality. Far from being Christian gentlemen, they were accused of insensitivity, authoritarianism, even brutality, with one critic complaining that the *hospitaliers* were asking for money before they bathed the sick.[70]

As late as 1884 a letter from the head of the Burgundian pilgrimage, long established and with its own traditions, complained bitterly of the interference; while recognizing the Hospitalité's utility during the great national event, the Burgundians wanted none of it for their own endeavour. They complained especially about the *dames hospitalières*, the female branch of the new organization, and their dominance of the *piscines*, accusing them too of insensitive unwillingness to take into account 'the desires and observations made known to them by the ill or by the persons who accompanied the ill'. Their worst offence was locking up and going off to mass at the moment when several *malades*, 'with tears in their eyes', were waiting to be bathed.[71]

The desire for order and discipline, therefore, brought new tensions. In a letter to Picard, Burosse expressed his concern and his deep mistrust of Combettes de Luc, whom he thought too independent, and insisted on a split between the Hospitalité de Notre-Dame de Salut and the Hospitalité de Notre-Dame de Lourdes, the latter under his own authority and more likely, he thought, to run the pools in a fitting manner.[72] Combettes de Luc fought the idea. In a long letter to Burosse, he used a mollifying tone that could not veil his irritation and clear conviction that the abilities and resources of his organization were simply superior.[73] Ultimately, Burosse carried the day, but in a compromise the two Hospitalités divided the labour, with the Salut concentrating on the national pilgrimage, and Burosse's Notre-Dame de Lourdes focusing on the diocesan pilgrimages that came at various times of the year.

The dispute showed the long way the pilgrimage movement had travelled. The Petites-Sœurs may have been unable to cope with the growing task of transporting the sick to the Grotto, but they produced no controversy and certainly no complaints of insensitivity. Mme Laforest, Picard and the Garaison Fathers offered minimal administration to deal with the arrival of the sick, but this meagre organization left local pilgrimages to their traditions, for which many, like the Burgundian president, were deeply grateful. But the pilgrimage movement was now too massive for such free-and-easy methods; or so the leadership of the Hospitalité de Notre-Dame de Salut believed.

As the pilgrimage movement matured, the division of labour became more evident. The ethos underpinning Notre-Dame de Salut was transposed on to the working relations of both Hospitalités, with the pilgrimage idealizing gender relationships and a certain vision of the Christian family. While men carried and organized, the women took the more polluting jobs dealing with the waste products of the sick. There were some important exceptions to this general rule, however, as the emphasis on masculine chivalry brought with it the obligation to care as well as to labour. Most of the praise and attention in this domain went largely to upper-class women, who dirtied their hands with work normally performed by servants:[74]

And there they are, hard at it from morning till evening, seeking out among the sick the weakest, the most sorely tried, the most unfortunate, and the most repulsive, and not one of them gave the slightest sign of repugnance or disgust! And yet these Hospitalières have by no means been brought up to perform tasks of this kind.[75]

Images of the Petites-Sœurs in the trains also show the crowded and difficult conditions of the work, although photographers often preferred the 'picturesque' sight of the nursing sisters in the so-called *fourgon*, or wagon-van, their black robes highlighted against the whiteness of the linen, bottles and shining metal equipment that surrounded them (see illus. 61). Such images evoked a world of order and cleanliness, a vision more idealized still by *Le Pèlerin* in 1900, which showed the Petites-Sœurs joined by the *grandes dames* to hand out food and remedies (see illus. 62). However, such sanitized representations should not blot out the reality of what the week of

61. Sœur Marie de l'Enfant Jésus in the fourgon, *1901*

pilgrimage involved, for service was no mere token gesture. While Lourdes today specializes in non-infectious neurological ailments – especially multiple sclerosis – the nineteenth-century pilgrimages brought many with infectious diseases, tubercular conditions and especially deforming lupus. Purulent abscesses were common in an age before antibiotics and steroids, and all who came to Lourdes were distressed by the often pustulant, decaying bodies they saw there.

The domain *par excellence* of the women was in the pools and in the hospitals, where the Dames Infirmières of Notre-Dame de Salut worked with the Petites-Sœurs, Sœurs de Nevers and the Sœurs de l'hôpital des Sept Douleurs to feed and tend the sick. The women were divided into different categories with varying responsibilities: there were clearly those with some managerial authority on the wards – the *dames hospitalières* who were also members of Notre-Dame de

Salut – and those underneath, women who had the former title but not the honour of membership. There were, moreover, the *dames auxiliaires*, whose role was to make themselves useful at the behest of women with more experience or status.

These ladies were to show their penitence by their bearing, to be 'dressed as simply and as inconspicuously as possible, and were not to wear jewellery that could be seen'. The work was hard, the hours long, the demand for punctuality strict. The scenes of sickness were distressing enough that 'young women – under twenty-five – are not admitted to the rows [of beds] where the sick are laid' unless supervised by their mothers. For the sake of hygiene and humility, the *jeunes filles* were not allowed to wear their hair loose over their shoulders.[76] Instead, they helped with the food, organized the refectories, and kept the sick and the helpers fed, a seemly training ground for the later challenges awaiting them. Again, discipline, hierarchy and obedience, the keystones of the military organization, were prominent throughout.

62. *'Le Train Blanc': The Petites-Sœurs de l'Assomption and the* hospitalières *of Notre-Dame de Salut distributing food and medicine,* Le Pèlerin, *19 August 1900*

The Mature Pilgrimage

The growth of the Hospitalités and the evolution of the pilgrimage movement cannot be divorced from the wider currents within the Church and in politics, for just as its origins lay in the chaotic aftermath of the Franco-Prussian War, so its later development was profoundly touched by shifts both within France and outside it. The 'pilgrimage of the sick' in particular gained strength as the Vatican was revising its attitude towards the poor and the 'social question', and rethinking its approach to the secular world. In 1891 Leo XIII broke with the intransigence of his predecessor Pius IX and promulgated *Rerum novarum*, which enjoined Catholics to find a means of regulating the excesses of capitalism through Christian activism.[77] The encyclical was open to a variety of interpretations, some radical enough to form the basis for Catholic initiatives in trade unionism in France.[78] At Lourdes, however, this renewed commitment to the poor was considered a recognition of the programme of solidarity that the pilgrimage movement had encouraged from the start.[79] In 1883, for example, Combettes de Luc had written: 'Its overall goal is prayer and the bringing together of ruling and working classes through bonds of sympathy, which cannot fail to arise amid the community of care given and received in sickness, and from the boon of spiritual consolation.'[80] The intransigent Catholicism that he and the Hospitalité de Notre-Dame de Salut once typified evolved in the 1890s into varieties of social Catholicism under the auspices of *Rerum novarum*. All of the preoccupations of the 1870s were still there, even though the legitimist cause had been abandoned. If anything, their dissident stance was more extreme in its anti-socialism and anti-Semitism, and was tempered only by their growing activism in the field of social welfare.[81]

But, while the leaders of the pilgrimage movement were able to absorb and even champion *Rerum novarum* according to their likes, no such easy acceptance greeted the softening stance towards secular political regimes that Leo began from his accession in 1878. *Immortale Dei* in 1885 and *Libertas* in 1888 were major moves towards an accommodation with liberalism. More important for France was the second encyclical of 1891, *Au milieu des sollicitudes*, which instructed French Catholics to engage with the republic and participate fully in politics, rather than abstaining as Pius IX had commanded. In France this movement, called the *ralliement*, won less than wholehearted approval even before the Dreyfus Affair, which began in earnest in 1895, and Leo's death in 1903 reduced the initiative to ruins.[82] Still fiercely anti-republican and often legitimist, elite Catholics, particularly the Assumptionists and the right-wing aristocrats of the Hospitalités, were unenthusiastic about the *ralliement* and its call for compromise.[83] Having battled the republic for more than a generation, such people did not find it easy to change direction, and the Dreyfus Affair gave them a perfect reason not to do so.

From the outset, the activities of the Assumptionists showed the connections they saw between religious revival and the nation's broader political future. The rituals of pilgrimage at Lourdes were the expression of a social faith that also encompassed a political vision, one that had changed with the political climate of the *fin de siècle*. By this time the Assumptionists had become an important influence in national politics through *La Croix* and *Le Pèlerin*, publications that reached over a half million readers weekly in the 1890s. Through editorials that spouted an irrepressible hatred of the republic, Jews, Freemasons and financiers, *La Croix* had become the favoured newspaper of the Catholic faithful, outstripping the meagre readership of *L'Univers*, which, although the Pope's official organ in France, attracted only 20,000 subscribers.[84] The Assumptionists at first tried to obey papal directions to join the *ralliement*, but ultimately rejected the lacklustre right-wing alliance that awaited them and opted instead for ever greater, and riskier, militancy. Bailly even briefly cast around in 1898 for a suitable general to mount a *coup d'état*;[85] two years later the Assumptionists were punished for such treasonous flirtations and expelled from France. The Dreyfus Affair, which provided the backdrop for both events, thus marked the high-water mark of their ambitions and their ultimate collapse.

The details of the affair are well enough known. The Jewish army officer, Alfred Dreyfus, was falsely imprisoned for allegedly giving military secrets to the Germans, setting off a campaign to release him that included Emile Zola's article, *J'Accuse*, of 1897. This polemic accused the army of a cover-up, a charge that landed Zola in court for defamation and ultimately led to his self-imposed exile.[86] The affair divided France, and indeed transformed political allegiances for decades to come.[87] For while it became increasingly clear that Dreyfus was not guilty, there were many – including the Assumptionists in the Catholic camp, but also many republican extremists – willing to prolong the battle to flush out their enemies, and draw ever stronger distinctions between the 'true France' and those who wished it ill. Dreyfus himself became the occasion for this titanic political battle, giving him a symbolic value that delayed his pardon until 1905.

The reaction of the Assumptionist press shows how the longing for a strong Christian collectivity, which gained an outlet through pilgrimage, was shadowed by an equally strong ethos of exclusionism, an 'us and them' mentality that made the order among the most vehement attackers of both Dreyfus and his supporters. Thus, alongside *Le Pèlerin*'s illustrations of miraculous cures, gentle nuns and chivalric gentlemen, there were routine caricatures of Jews, Freemasons and republicans, all of whom were outside the spiritual circle

63. 'He dishonoured the French uniform': an attack on Dreyfus, Le Pèlerin, *30 December 1894*

64. 'You'll admit that it's a bit much! . . . Here it is starting again, despite the masterpiece I wrote': an attack on Zola, Le Pèlerin, *30 August 1896*

of pilgrimage. Dreyfus himself was a regular target (see illus. 63), and Zola, who had defended Dreyfus but attacked Lourdes, was depicted as the peevish Freemason, angered that his 1893 novel, *Lourdes*, had not undermined the shrine's success (see illus. 64).

While some of these images could conceivably be classed as political cartoons and might have appeared in many magazines of the period, other pictures went much further, peddling a hateful, racial anti-Semitism increasingly more extreme in its violence. *Le Pèlerin* produced contemporary caricatures of deceitful, greedy and treacherous Jews (see illus. 65), as well as old German engravings illustrating the

65. In a German accent, father asks son, 'When you're big, my little Jacob, what will you sell?', in front of paintings that show Judas selling Jesus, Joseph sold by his brothers and Dreyfus selling France. Le Pèlerin, *27 September 1896*

ritual murder by Jews of Christians (see illus. 66), accompanying them with texts maintaining that such atrocities were still occurring in Corfu, Alexandria and Hungary. These tales tapped into medieval beliefs, in which Jews were supposed to have used the blood of Christian children to make matzos for Passover. Paralleling such

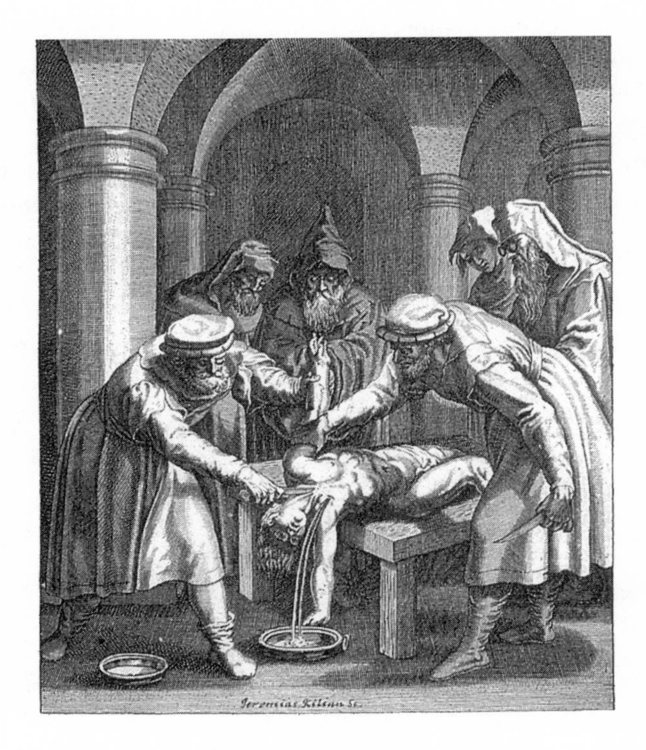

66. Jeremias Kilian, 'The Blessed Henry, bled and then stabbed seventy times by the Jews of Munich in 1345': seventeenth-century German engraving used to illustrate an attack on Jews, Le Pèlerin, *17 June 1892*

visions was an alternative image of the Virgin as comforter, willing to extend her compassion even to Jews in an effort to convert them.[88] Old Marian traditions of conversion were still current in the nineteenth century; in fact, the most famous Jewish convert of the period was Alphonse Ratisbonne, an Alsatian who came into the Catholic fold after a vision of the Virgin in 1842 in Rome.[89]

In this way of thinking, for every Jew willing to convert, there was a host of others who resisted and ostensibly wished to undermine Christian society from within. This religious anti-Semitism blended readily with the ambient racialism of the nineteenth century that saw Jews as contaminating the purity of the race. In a period in which France was feared to be 'degenerate', losing strength in comparison to its German rival, the Jews easily became 'enemies within', with little loyalty to the *patrie*.[90] As the Christian version employed the symbolism of Jews bleeding Christian children to death, so scientific racism expressed itself in metaphors of their 'bleeding' the nation of its vitality.

For the leadership of the Assumption and many in the Hospitalités in this period, anti-Semitism was an integral part of their piety, the dark side of their veneration for the Virgin and the Eucharist. That this was the case should not, however, lead on to the conclusion that pilgrimage was an anti-Semitic campaign rather than a journey of devotion in aid of the sick. In the enclosed world of pilgrimage, devoid of republicans, Freemasons and other 'enemies', the venom and rancour of life under a distasteful regime faded, and the positive aspects of the Catholic programme came once again to the fore. Priests might mention the republic's persecution, and indeed the movement's origins and growth show the indissoluble relationship between spirituality and politics, but the week in Lourdes sought more to focus the religious imagination on to the sick, to give spiritual comfort to participants and pray for the alleviation of suffering.

Central to this programme was the establishment of the Eucharistic procession as the high point of the pilgrimage's rituals.[91] The idea of 'holy applause for the Holy Sacrament when it is carried from the basilica to the Grotto for evening benediction' belonged originally to Abbé Lagardère, who came annually with a group from Quercy,[92] and it was picked up by Picard in 1888 as a form of 'holy audacity'. This preoccupation ultimately derived from d'Alzon's wonder at a divine paradox: 'Jesus Christ, wholly present in the Eucharist, is there present in the most profound abasement. What could be more abased than a God made man, hidden under the appearance of a little bread and a few drops of wine?'[93] Jesus was 'la Victime par excellence',[94] an identification with pain and suffering that resonated powerfully among the sick and dying at the shrine. His stress on the miraculous underpinnings of Eucharistic devotion made it an ideal symbol of opposition to the modern age:

> The century that witnessed the foundation of my religious family is a century of revolt; it makes a god of man, and denies the rights of God. This is why the Church has made this the century of Mary and of the Holy Sacrament . . . Proclaiming the rights of God, the rights of Jesus Christ at the heart of

these Eucharistic abasements, restoring the cult of the Holy Sacrament . . . processions; in a word, all the acts by which man affirms the rights and triumphs of Christ in his Eucharist: such is my mission.[95]

Following d'Alzon, Picard saw the Eucharist as the means for a 'fervent communion' and as a consolation.[96] At the same time he highlighted it as a form of *public* devotion that could be realized through re-establishing the processions of the 'fêtes-Dieu': 'His feast days are the feast days of rich and poor alike. He is the God of the humble and the lowly. By hiding him in the tabernacle and forbidding his processions, you attack the worker, you deprive the child and the poor man's wife of these purest of joys.'[97] Spectacle, he suggested, was for the poor, who would find solace in a revitalized nineteenth-century vision of medieval pageantry.

Lourdes provided an ideal vehicle for these ideas, and the Assumptionists promoted a kind of frenzy during which the crippled and sick got up, discarded their crutches and followed the Eucharist in prayer and thankfulness (see illus. 67). The emotional climax occurred when

67. Eucharistic procession, Le Pèlerin, *2 September 1894*

the cortège passed the Grotto and the pools; people fell on their knees, their arms outstretched, asking for a cure: 'Lord, if thou wilt, thou canst cure me.' The procession contributed to the 'miraculous mood' at the same time that it focused attention on transubstantiation and the central Catholic belief in the possibility of breaking down the boundaries between the physical and the spiritual.[98] The Eucharist was 'heaven made human and humanity made divine'.[99] Lourdes, so populated by broken bodies and physical torment, was a profoundly evocative place for the performance of this primary religious act. As the body of Christ was broken to take away the sins of the world and to cleanse sinful bodies, so a few pilgrims received the ultimate grace and were cured, in turn becoming whole once again. The procession implicitly linked the Eucharist to the 'passions' and 'resurrections' among the sick and dying, and for this reason was anticipated with an expectant fervour still palpable on pilgrimage even today.

Picard continued his campaign against secularism with other forms of procession, perhaps the most famous of which was the 1897 commemoration of the *miraculés* and twenty-five years of national pilgrimage. Notre-Dame de Salut had lost track of some of the cured, their poverty making it impossible to find the homeless; the official report also acknowledged the death and renewed illness of others. But these disappointments did not diminish the triumphs. Eighteen trains left Paris and other regional cities, with over 30,000 pilgrims, almost a thousand of whom were *malades*. As usual, they arrived in the white trains, but another, painted the papal colours of white and yellow, was reserved for over 300 *miraculés*, whose presence altered the psychological climate of the pilgrimage.

All the choreographed and ritualized aspects of the pilgrimage season were there in force. The 325 *miraculés* paraded with the men of the Hospitalité – 'the chivalry of nineteenth-century France'[100] – the ladies of Notre-Dame de Salut, eighty Petites-Sœurs, and clergymen, many of whom held colourful banners (see illus. 68). The procession caused great emotion among the crowd, as it moved among the sick and dying in front of the Basilica of the Rosary. Despite the splendour of the proceedings, Père Picard wanted more:

Well! My dear invalids, the procession is finished; we have fulfilled our duties, we have glorified Our Lord, the Blessed Virgin, the Pope; it is for you to do the

68. 'Procession of the miraculés', *from Anon.,* Pèlerinage national du jubilé de 1897, *1897*

rest. I have been asked to suggest invocations; I do not tell you to cry aloud. I ask you to listen to the voice that you hear within you, and faithfully to obey the supernatural impulses that you feel. Look at these, who have been cured; see the examples that you have before you; these are your models; believe as they do; like them you will be cured! Now, invalids, if you have faith, arise![101]

At this remarkable command a few of the dying began to get off their stretchers and to walk away from the nurses. Spontaneously, the crowd began to sing the *Magnificat*, and the emotion reached unprecedented heights. Before long, there were more than forty *malades* walking towards Picard, with the priests doing their best to organize a path so this procession of the newly risen could evade the groping hands of onlookers. Picard's charisma was such that some even credited him with miraculous power, a power that he believed came from the Holy Spirit.[102]

The introduction of the Eucharistic procession consummated a campaign to sacramentalize the shrine. Early cultists at the Grotto often prayed at the site without clerical sanction and the pilgrimages of the poor were notable for their *lack* of sacramental trappings.[103] From the outset the fountain's location in a grotto in the near wilderness, with a Virgin of fairy-like proportions, were aspects of the Lourdes cult that explains its great success but also its subversive potential. For these 'folkloric' associations touched unconscious chords of memory and feeling that brought the faithful in droves, but also opened up the possibility of dangerous deviations that clerics might not always be able to control. Just as the construction works 'tamed' the Grotto with pavements and grills, and the basilica above superimposed a physical symbol of orthodoxy, so the Eucharistic processions reasserted the centrality of doctrine in the spiritual realm.

Their great success also hints that a Christocentricism was successfully asserted over the excesses of Marian piety in much the same way that the gendered division of labour within the pilgrimage movement rigidified with time. But such a parallel – in which the masculine directed the feminine – is far too neat and reductive in both cases. As I have suggested, women in pilgrimage seemed to accept and live out their subordinate role with enthusiasm, but it was precisely this position that strengthened their moral authority. Similarly, the devotion to the body of Christ that the Eucharistic procession represented was perfectly compatible with an intensification of Marianism. The focus on the human Jesus deepened in the nineteenth century through the cult of the infant Jesus and the Sacred Heart, both of which concentrated on Jesus' vulnerability as helpless child and sufferer for the sins of humanity. And yet, despite their growing popularity, pilgrims still yearned after Mary, as Christ remained for some the remote judge, at the centre of an ascetic and juristic system of salvation. The appearance of Mary on earth to direct and console made her a more immediate and often compassionate presence.

Much of this veneration was channelled into orthodox directions. The hymn of the national pilgrimage, *Ave maris stella*, extolled Mary's powers and beneficent qualities. She would break the chains of the guilty, lighten the eyes of the blind, deliver sinners from their faults, but all within a context that recognized that 'praise be to God the Father, Glory to Christ the King and to the Holy Ghost!' Marian devotion reached new and hitherto inconceivable heights in the nineteenth century, encouraged by both Pius IX and Leo XIII, despite the very different political and social tone of their papacies. They encouraged the coronation of statues to emphasize Mary's role as Queen of Heaven and avidly accorded plenary indulgences to pilgrimages, thereby promoting devotions like Lourdes as an important means of assembling the faithful.

Within the Church, Mary had many different titles and attributes. For example, she was easily politicized, and in her immaculate guise could be seen crushing the sins of a materialistic and godless nation. As Queen of Heaven she easily became Queen of France:[104] the Assumptionists, moreover, sought in 1885 to counter Bastille Day by making 15 August, the day of Mary's Assumption, France's national holiday, arguing that the nation was consecrated not by revolutionary violence but when Louis XIII put his person and his kingdom under the Virgin's protection.[105]

But such political messages were muted when the faithful implored her to intervene on behalf of sinners,[106] to cure the sick and injured, aspects that predominated in the *piscines* when the naked and vulnerable sought her aid. As will be seen, while the Eucharistic procession produced miracles, the bathing pools filled with water from her fountain generated just as many. At Lourdes, Mary was the Immaculate Conception, a designation of stainless and pure perfection that contrasted markedly with the damaged and diseased bodies of those who invoked her. But while this purity and perfection gave her power, it also distanced her, and the comforting humanity of the Mary who suckled Jesus gave way to an image more like alabaster.[107] She became like the woman on a pedestal, powerful as an ideal but cold to the touch. Alongside this image of perfection, however, there was another strand that perpetuated Mary as a gentle *jeune fille*, more like the ministering angel of domestic ideology, active in her concern for suffering humanity.

In this last guise and as practical nurse, manager, patroness and psychological intercessor, Mary's attributes were remarkably similar to those that the women and daughters of Notre-Dame de Salut and the Hospitalité were meant to assume. Mary's special powers were enunciated in a way that recalled the role of women towards the sick, society and the nation:

> It is these women who brought the multitude of the sick, they who paid for them to travel, bandaged their ulcers, kept vigil by their pallets, they who shared their suffering.

Mothers, wives, young women, they are the balm that alleviates the wounds of our society; they are the joy and ornament of the private hearth, they are France's great resource against selfishness and disbelief.[108]

The image of the Virgin in the nineteenth century was remarkably similar in some ways to the idealized woman of bourgeois nineteenth-century Europe. This parallel is of more than incidental interest; it recasts the long-standing interpretation of the dogma of the Immaculate Conception. Long seen as a reactionary response to the challenges of secularism, an insistence on faith as the assault of rationalism reached a peak, it was in fact fully in step with larger ideological preoccupations about the moral and domestic role of women in society. Like the women who tended the sick at Lourdes and the ideal woman of bourgeois ideology, Mary was mother, wife, ministering young woman, all attributes fundamentally rooted in her moral purity.

The Virgin's ubiquity in the religious psyche of the period meant that often Mary, not Christ, was seen as *the* intermediary between God and his suffering people. The clergy were not always able to control the impulses of the pilgrims who seemed to worship Mary as a deity in her own right, and some priests even seemed to countenance such deviations in an effort to galvanize popular piety and, perhaps, to give expression to their own intense feeling. This tendency was manifested most clearly in an 1895 image in *Le Pèlerin* (see illus. 69), which showed an impoverished and moribund woman releasing her crutches into the stylized picture of death, a skeleton waiting with a shroud. But rather than falling into Jesus' arms, she is shown coming to greet the youthful embrace of *Mère immaculée*. In this instance the Virgin is not the intercessor, but the worker of miracles herself, a vision of divine intervention rather at odds with Catholic teaching. We will see how such feelings of Mary's presence manifested themselves in the next chapter when the recipients of cure, largely women, met the Virgin and felt her grace.

Much has been made by social anthropologists of the strangely liminal quality of pilgrimage, of which Lourdes would seem to be a perfect illustration.[109] Betwixt and between, pilgrims make their way from home to the destination, losing all affiliations of class and status en route. Not only did individuals undergo initiatory religious experi-

69. 'Death was already preparing a shroud, but Notre-Dame de Lourdes restores life', Le Pèlerin, *1 September 1895*

ences, they also lived intense feelings of solidarity reinforced by the focus on the sick and the need to leave other petty considerations aside. The ideal was somewhat marred by the persistence of first-class carriages in the pilgrimage trains, and the occasional group of *révoltés* who escaped the pious atmosphere and human misery to picnic in the mountain countryside when the trains stopped.

On the whole, however, the pain of the *malades* did turn the world upside-down, albeit very temporarily. But pilgrimage was not Carnival. Carnival is about bodily excess and loss of inhibition,[110] whereas the rituals of Lourdes wrapped the body's miseries in layers of spiritual clothing. The sick and dying, usually relegated to the unseen margins of society, took centre stage. The attentions of the *grandes dames* astonished precisely because such people were normally protected from contamination. Women competed to show their heroism in the harrowing atmosphere of the trains, hospitals and pools, while men toiled to move bodies on stretchers. The sick and the *hospitaliers* bonded through touch, consolation and care, and, although women had a much higher proportion of *malades* to bathe than did the men, all the helpers in the *piscines* shared this experience.[111] By immersing sick men in the pools, men also came into close proximity with physical pain and distress. We should not underestimate the psychological impact of such experiences.

Lourdes made the disgusting elevating and brought the hidden into the open. The rich acted like servants, and servants were tended by the rich, a temporary inversion that paradoxically reinforced social hierarchies at the journey's end. Women in particular heightened their moral and spiritual authority by revelling in an exaggerated subordination, which in turn became the source of even greater admiration: Lourdes was unique in demonstrating publicly the strength of this model of feminine power.

The week of national pilgrimage, therefore, provides a window on to a world that sought to counter the blandishments of the republic. Pilgrims envisaged secular society as atomistic and hubristic, and were determined to create an opposite ideal of Christian social solidarity that would show up all its failings. The pilgrimage to Lourdes reveals how deep the vision of Christian collectivity went for both priests and lay pilgrims – especially the women. Charity went beyond good works or the giving of money, and was invested instead in touching and consoling the most vulnerable. Faith was expressed through the body: how the sufferers conducted themselves, how others in turn treated and cared for them, was the most perfect expression of the spirituality they sought.

9

The Cures

The transformation of Lourdes into the shrine of the sick gave it the character for which it is best known today; the hope of cure, however remote, draws millions every year and makes it reviled by the incredulous and loved by the faithful. Cures are so much a part of its reputation that it is again easy to forget how unforeseen this evolution actually was. For there was nothing in the Virgin's message suggesting such a possibility – the injunction to build a chapel, come in procession, pray for sinners and bathe and drink at the Grotto held no promises of miracles. Lourdes as a site for the sick grew out of the fountain, and the possibilities the Lourdais saw in it. The first cures took place among the many of the local inhabitants who flocked to the Grotto to wash in its waters, but another two decades would pass before the national pilgrimage made miracles the focal point of its mission.

The tales of cures that attended the formation of the shrine's reputation in the nineteenth century reveal an extraordinary mingling of themes and flavours, of peasant practices and middle-class reverence, feminine piety and organized ritual. They also highlight the ambivalent relationship of both the devout and the Church to medicine, for, while these narratives celebrated the miraculous, they also contained an uneasy accommodation with medical findings. Lourdes was unique as a sanctuary because it so vividly contrasted faith and science, reasserting the importance and even the existence of the miraculous at precisely the moment when science attained an apparently unquestionable authority. Because of the power of these scientific claims, the miracles were seen as a special sign to the modern world.

So important are the cures for understanding Lourdes that the two final chapters of this book concentrate on them. The first focuses on healing narratives, bodily experiences and the recurring theme of communion with the divine, the second on the polemics surrounding science and religion. The separation between them is artificial, justified only insofar as it provides structure for so much that is unwieldy and diverse. The account will not rehearse the most famous miracles, nor simply examine those that the Church has confirmed.[1] For both medical and clerical authorities sought to limit too closely the experience of cure, placing 'objective' criteria on a polymorphous and often intensely subjective experience that was best validated not by 'experts' but rather by individuals, their families and communities. The character of the healing experiences changed over time, an evolution partly explained by the new constituency as well as by a changed devotional culture. Even more important was the way pilgrims from mid century and those of the *fin de siècle* found different ways of describing the body in pain, and the joy associated with the release of cure. Such a change revealed a transformation in Catholic culture more generally and in the relationship to the divine more specifically; the narratives may even show how new notions of selfhood were forged in the crucible of life-destroying illness.

Healing Fountains and the Pyrenees

Early pilgrimages in the days after the apparitions in 1858 gave no indication that the Grotto would become anything more than a local centre of worship and penance, mirroring the development of other semi-orthodox healing fountains across the Pyrenean chain, and fitting into a venerable tradition of reverence for 'gushing waters' central to the spiritual heritage of rural France. Occurring most frequently in the Limousin and in Burgundy, such fountains were also important in the piedmont regions of Béarn and Bigorre.[2] This tradition differed completely from the fashion for taking the waters, which developed in France in the seventeenth century from a conviction that mountain spring water had special mineral properties. Such visits to the spas, the most important industry in the Pyrenean region in the nineteenth century, had no religious associations at all; both types of waters sought to allay physical maladies, but while sacred fountains sought spiritual transformation, towns like Cauterets and Bagnères-de-Bigorre near Lourdes tried to divert their adherents through tourism.[3]

We get a sense of the spirit in which the initial pilgrims approached the Grotto by examining traditions of belief collected by local historians and ethnologists. Sufferers who came to the fountains sought solace and cure, knowing that they entered a magical arena, where even fairies may have lived. The Pyrenean word for fountain, *hount*, means eye, the transparent window between human existence and the nether reaches of the underworld: when a spring dried up, it was often said that the eye of the fairy had closed. Christian, magical and animistic beliefs mingled, reinforced by the wildness of these sites and by the spiritual and physical distance from Church and sacraments.[4] These fountains were part of the inhabitants' close relationship to the rocky, wild and watered landscape of the mountains, with the spring at the Grotto, for example, apparently known to the pig herder, the sawyer, fishermen and nearby farmers long before Bernadette's epiphany.[5]

Like so many other pilgrim sites, the Grotto mixed the elements, with pilgrims adding candle flame to its stone and water. When stone did not occur naturally – as it did at Massabieille – it was brought to the site in the form of statues, tombs, decorated altars and crosses.[6] Pilgrims desired direct contact because the saint's miraculous power was thought to be transferred to the physical location;[7] they sought to touch the primordial, with eczema sufferers, for example, roiling up the water of the fountain at Ozenx in the Pyrenees to benefit from the mud. Echoing thermal therapies of today, such gestures also revealed a preoccupation with 'improving' the water by mixing it with the earth from which it sprang.[8]

Most fountains specialized in particular ailments, and show the way in which the local imagination associated certain saints with certain illnesses. In the Pyrenees, Saint Auzit helped the deaf recover their hearing (from the Latin *audire*), Saint Claire or Saint Luce (from the Latin, *lux*, or light) aided eye conditions, Saint Christau healed *les cristailles*, or skin conditions,[9] and Saint Rose cured *le mal d'arroses*, or a kind of eczema of the scalp.[10] They also linked the landscape's physical form to human body parts. Nursing mothers washed at Saint Poupette's waters at Madrian, with the aim of filling up their breasts. This apocryphal saint took her name from the Occitanian word *poup*, the feminine chest, and, in the grotto that housed her fountain, 'she turns herself to stone representing the teats of different kinds of animal among which there are even women's'.[11] Although Massabieille had few specific associations – indeed it was distinguished by its universality – the descriptions of poor and notables alike hint at the way its sinuous openings and weird stalactite forms suggested both elemental femininity *and* religious images of the Virgin and the Holy Family.[12]

Pilgrimages to healing fountains were enveloped in a system of prescriptions and prohibitions that emphasized their magical dimensions.[13] Pilgrims felt themselves 'stained', and the object of the journey was to remove the dirty patch on their bodies and souls, a physical image of contamination requiring purification. Appeasing the saint's animosity or exciting his mercy required giving themselves entirely (*se vouer*) to the process, best accomplished through unquestioning belief, fasting and silence. Once begun, there could be no stopping, turning back or accepting of gifts *en route*. Pilgrims sought to create a magic circle to ward off evil, and emulated the poverty-stricken wanderer through practices of abnegation, such as arriving on bare feet. Women frequently walked through the night with babes in arms, an inversion of the normal habits of staying at home, tending domestic routine.[14] As one ethnologist has suggested, 'What is enacted here is the idea that you must leave behind a part of your past at the threshold of the home if you wish to leave your illness behind on the pilgrimage.'[15]

Consultation of divining women to discover which saint was angry and required propitiation demonstrated how willing the faithful were to turn from priests to 'parallel', often feminine authorities they considered more effective in the battle against disaster, illness and bad luck.[16] At Lourdes the early pilgrims had no need of such a figure, since the apparition herself, and then Bernadette's example, had already shown them the way. They too, however, turned away from the priests, bypassing the hierarchy in favour of personal, and unauthorized, supplication. As has been seen, their vision of the Virgin mixed a frightened respect for an awesome, sometimes mercurial power with a belief in gentle intercession and forgiveness, a combination that suggests prayer, penance and propitiation were all dimensions in their worship. There are also other familiar aspects, for they too bathed and drank the water and ended their pilgrimage – particularly if a cure occurred – with a celebratory meal, elements that would reappear in an almost formulaic guise even in later healing narratives.

As with other shrines, leaving gifts was integral to the spiritual journey, and tampering with them led to the possibly dangerous 'transfer' of illness and bad luck; hence the anger that greeted Jacomet's removal of such objects. One Pyrenean legend spoke of a poor man near Pau who stole seven sous from a healing fountain and found he had inherited the fever of the man who had left the money.[17] Commonly, pilgrims left behind linen and garments belonging to the sick. The Fontaine de Humas, for example, a dried-up source near Cieutat in Bigorre, once treated the rheumatism of the inhabitants of Bagnères, who left their linen as an offering and to symbolize – in a material way – the abandonment of the illness.[18] In leaving behind linen, the nappies of a child or a piece of clothing associated with the disease, pilgrims believed the illness was also left behind in a process that entailed neither violence nor pain. Similarly, the Grotto's water was applied to infected or diseased parts of the body when the poor washed in the small makeshift basin that the early cultists constructed. The process of abandonment was perceived as peaceful and potentially restorative, in striking contrast to later narratives that focused on the tearing and painfully expulsive qualities of healing.

Fear of chills, belief in the indecency of personal hygiene and the association of water with rites of passage – especially birth and death – combined to increase the awesome quality of healing rituals.[19] Rather than seeing a necessary relationship between water, cleanliness and health, the rural poor tended instead to see dirt as a protective envelope against the environment. Only small children were immersed bodily; such desperate measures were intended to force a cure and 'are of enhanced effectiveness with the total fusion brought about by immersion'.[20] They regarded water as both a threat and a boon, suggestive of fertility and possible cure as well as precarious transitions from one stage of life to another. When on pilgrimage, therefore, they accepted neither the latest hygienic thinking on cleanliness nor the logic of spa bathers, who, in contrast to penitents, showered, bathed and drank mineral water to absorb its beneficent properties and purge themselves of illness.

Rural pilgrims seemed not to distinguish between *santé* (physical health) and *salut* (spiritual well-being), and in their rites sought to break down the boundaries between the material and the spiritual.[21] For example, at the fountain of Crastes at Asté, the inhabitants of the valley of Campan brought their goitrous children and put a fish from the stream on their tongue, hoping the act would enable them to speak. A functionalist assessment suggests that parents were hazily aware of the physiological relationship between iodine deficiency and the ravages of this chronic illness. But there is also a religious mystery attached to the rite, which seems to have resonances of the Eucharist.[22] In this instance spiritual conversion and physical transformation were thus entwined.

The Early Cures

The Episcopal Commission appointed by Mgr Laurence spent much of its time investigating the cures, a process that was not completed until the early part of 1860. They were led in this undertaking by a member of the subcommission, Canon Germain Baradère, who waded through the substantial documentation that came into his hands. The churchmen deliberated and, like the clerics of the medieval and early-modern period, consulted physicians only when they deemed it necessary.[23] For example, they assessed the reports of Dozous, the enthusiastic local doctor who regained his faith after witnessing the miracle of the candle. He had been the only physician to attend to the sick at the Grotto, to witness their healing and keep a record of all the cases that he observed. But, despite his diligence in the Grotto's cause, Dozous was of a mercurial temperament and had already lost friends because of various professional scandals.[24] Because of these failings, the clerics excluded him from the commission and instead relied on letters from brother clergymen to reach their decisions, a pattern that the Garaison Fathers continued. The commissioners diligently sifted through the documents and concluded that twenty-nine cases from fourteen communes were worthy of investigation. Between November and March of the following year, their peregrinations brought far-flung parishes into the view of the bishop and his officials, with the commissioners interrogating both healed individuals and witnesses.[25] The collective narrative of transformation was almost as important as the healing itself. For example, Sophie Latour was cured of a pustulant eruption on her body, but the 'miracle' could not be investigated because she had never told her closest friends or relatives.[26] As will be seen, the *social* dimension of the miracle would remain a central feature of most narratives of cure.

The poor and ailing went to the fountain not least because it was one of the few therapeutic options available to them. Lacking medical personnel, even the lower grade of *officiers de santé*, who were less qualified than physicians, the poor relied instead on the remedies of healers, sorcerers, blacksmiths and shepherds. Tales are legion of incantations to stave off toothache, bulbs of garlic worn against rabies and vermin, and a pharmacopoeia still influenced by Hippocratic principles. Local physicians raged against the peculiarly repugnant and, in their view, ineffective remedies that the poor inflicted on themselves: 'poultices of frog spawn against inflammation, poultices of human blood against old ulcers, spider oil to reduce fever'.[27] Indignation could not hide their own therapeutic inadequacy, however, which, until well after mid century, meant that their methods of disease control produced scarcely better results. Their general unwillingness to treat the poor, except in rare instances, exacerbated the local population's already low opinion of them.

Even the accounts of romantic travellers sometimes attested to the plight of the Pyrenean poor, commenting on the misery of their households, the penury of their food and the illnesses that afflicted them.[28] The reports of priests, notables and especially Dozous confirmed this picture of local ill-health.[29] In this context, perhaps, the instant appeal of the Grotto becomes far more comprehensible; Jacomet did not exaggerate when he remarked on 11 April 1858: 'People visit the Grotto and come from afar; night and day, a continuous pilgrimage. Endlessly, the sick of every age and sex, whom they bring to the miraculous fountain to rub and wash.'[30]

Pilgrimage itself was a kind of penance, as ill-health often made the journey a difficult and precarious business. Before the works that levelled the site and cleared paths, men and women came in rickety carts, hobbled with sticks and even slid down when they could not walk.[31] If they could not come themselves, they sent relatives[32] and, rather than adopting a uniform strategy, used the water in different ways. While some parents carried children on their backs or in their arms to the fountain[33] and plunged them into the makeshift basin,[34] one woman, deaf for twenty years, syringed the water into her ears until she could hear the church bells again.[35] Most people placed the water on the afflicted area. Only Mme Lanu-Domenge, instead of placing it on her tired legs, employed it like holy oil, a source of physical blessing rather than as the medium of cure itself.[36]

For most of the early pilgrims, water and proximity to the site were ingredients essential to healing. For the clergy, however, such emphasis on the physical intermediaries potentially undermined the spiritual power of the Virgin. Priests continually sought to make the distinction between the beneficence of Notre-Dame de Lourdes and the water, even if the faithful were not always able to apprehend such theological niceties.[37] By the 1870s the Church would highlight those cases in which prayer to Notre-Dame de Lourdes sufficed, thereby seeking to break the links between the water and healing.[38]

Supplicants also took various approaches towards prayer and spirituality at the site, running from a seeming insouciance to the most solemn and elaborate piety.[39] This range suggests the personal nature of such pilgrimages, as well as the layered religious culture of the Pyrenean world. Early narratives of the healing of children glorified the shrine and moved hearers; early engravings expressed the drama of child cures with the sensationalism of news items in the penny press. This genre of religious story-telling may in fact have been a descendant of early-modern tales of Marian fountains, which were credited with reviving dying babies long enough for them to be baptized, so permitting these innocent souls a just release from the miseries of purgatory.[40] However, despite the similarities, the Lourdes tales focused more frequently on children with a fatal listlessness, an inability to walk or an incapacity for speech – developmental problems, in other words, not infant death.

For example, in the earliest days Dominique Lasbareilles, a boy of nearly seven from the village of Ger, was able to take a few steps after baths at the fountain. Both Peyramale and Jacomet were, at different times, called to watch this extraordinary feat, only to be disappointed by the child's halting and exhausted gait. Jacomet raged against the temptations used to lure the child to his feet: 'the mother stroked him, calling her to him, offering him another piece of bread' and was further shocked when the child was bribed to get up with the promise of a new goat. All these cajolings were, in Jacomet's view, in vain: 'in six minutes . . . his whole body trembling [he managed] with great difficulty to place one foot in front of the other just three times'.[41] For the Lasbareilles family, however, the change was still miraculous: their son continued to walk, although he was sick and weak for the rest of his short life.

These kinds of 'cure' fed the flames of scepticism, but, while such examples were numerous, there were also others in which the Virgin's grace seemed limitless. The most famous story concerned two-year-old Justin Bouhorts, the enfeebled son of Croisine Duconte and her day-labourer husband. The family was both poor and ugly: 'Croisine [was] very ugly and her son uglier still, not to mention her husband, who was no better . . . The mother's faith was as strong as she was ugly. It was a godly family.'[42] In other words, no worldly favours shone on this devout family, which, perhaps, made the divine grace they received all the more remarkable.

The mother claimed to have taken the child to the Grotto on 28 February 1858, only three days after Bernadette had 'found' the fountain, deciding on this extreme course in mid winter because he was hardly breathing and had such 'terrible thinness and a cadaverous complexion' that she was already looking for linen for a shroud. As she plunged the child into the water, the other women present accused her of murder. Without even wiping him dry – still a custom at the pools today – she carried him home in her apron and placed him in his crib. He slept peacefully and woke hungry; the next day he crawled out of his crib for the first time and walked, and from that day forward enjoyed good health. Although the details of the drama may not add up – Laurentin gives a plausible explanation for how Croisine probably misremembered the dates and bathed the baby in July rather than in the winter cold[43] – for the Lourdais such details were of little account. Even in the hottest of summers the water was glacial, and the transformation in the grey and ugly Justin Bouhorts remarkable.

While the release of suffering children caused amazement, the behaviour of adult pilgrims was often more mundane. Some seemed not to accompany the bathing of the afflicted body part with prayer of any kind, or did not see fit to mention their private observances to the sub-commission. Marcel Peyrègne of Agos, a forty-year-old man with a wen the size of a hazelnut, dipped his hand in the fountain when in Lourdes on business, and returned eight days later to do the same again because of the good results.[44] Jeanne Germa de Pontac also decided to go to the Grotto to heal a big wart, bathed her hand in the waters, took some of the liquid home and, after a month, saw the wart dissolve. In neither case was there mention of worship of any kind at the Grotto's edge, although de Pontac was convinced of the Virgin's grace.[45] Even those with more severe afflictions did not necessarily bring an elaborate piety to their curing rituals. Louis Bouriette, a quarryman whose eye had deteriorated rapidly after an accident twenty years before, described the way he bathed his eye and began to see light and distinguish objects. He never mentioned any act of contrition when describing his cure to the commissioners, and seemed more concerned to impress them with the reality of his physical renewal, reading with one eye and then the other, now miraculously returned to health. But while his piety may not have been exemplary, Bouriette readily attributed his cure to the power of the Virgin and made the proper distinctions: 'It is to this powerful protection that the waters of the Grotto of Massavielle [*sic*] owe their curative properties.'[46]

These narratives, all taken from the poorer classes, can be contrasted with those in which priestly and family piety seemed to play a much stronger role. For example, young Henri Busquet of Nay, a thirteen-year-old, had a recurring tumour in the glands of his neck and on his chest. Time and again doctors opened it up to drain the infected matter away, but to no avail. The first to report on his case was the local priest, Abbé Jean-Pierre Batcave, who recounted how the adolescent boy made the sign of the cross, recited the 'Remember O Most Gracious Virgin' and drank Lourdes water with 'faith and confidence'.[47] He then poured some on the dirty dressing of his infected wound, defying the physician who had forbidden him 'cette lotion'. As in so many miracle tales, Henri Busquet preferred the Virgin's grace to worldly knowledge and was rewarded for his faith. He stupefied (and convinced) his physician by returning several days later completely cured. 'He has on him only the very clear marks of an ulcer that appeared incurable.'[48] Such a tale was above all significant for its effect on others – Busquet's family, friends and the medical man in attendance.

Busquet's experience stood midway between the simple supplications of the poor and those of a more elevated position whose cures were not just social events but edifying communal dramas. The Widow Rizan of Nay had been ill for almost twenty-five years with an unspecified malady that attacked her whole system and left her weak and virtually unable to eat. She acquired Lourdes water from a friend, drank, bathed and, within an hour, 'under the eyes of the astounded Sisters of the Cross, dressed, leaped out of bed, and ran to prostrate herself at the feet of the statue of the Virgin, giving thanks to her with fervent emotion'. She became a source of local wonder and her case showed how an entire community could be touched: 'On Sunday and Monday it was a real procession, there were so many people who wanted to see and touch [Mme Rizan].'[49] Often the community sought physical signs of improvement. In all miracle narratives – from the poorest to the most high – individuals with wasting diseases needed to prove a return of appetite, and Mme Rizan passed this test by eating a rich sausage. She further impressed her neighbours by making a tiring journey to the shrine of Bétharram, where she sat through two masses and then retired, to eat once again with gusto.[50] What is remarkable here is that she did not go to the Grotto and brave the treacherous journey to the fountain in the wild. True to her background, she went to an established chapel to pray to a Virgin who conformed better to orthodoxy.

These early tales imparted a sense of renewal and rejuvenation unaccompanied by narratives of pain, a pattern entirely different from that of tales later in the century.[51] In these early days the poor went to the Grotto in the same spirit as those who sought the waters at religious sites throughout the region. As suggested, these journeys frequently lacked the imprimatur of the priest, but they were not improvisations. Even those who went on business to Lourdes and dipped their hands in the water came prepared to pay special homage. In their devotions the poor mixed an intense Marian piety with a strong animism, seeking both the Virgin's aid *and* the power of the water and the Grotto. For them, the supernatural was a mixture of qualities and powers, not an easily distilled orthodox essence. There were, however, those who brought the entire array of pious practices. Interestingly, neither Busquet nor Mme Rizan went to the Grotto, and, although the water was an important element, the central focus of their recitation was on the nature of prayer and faith. Priests and nursing sisters pervade these stories, lending an entirely different, and more orthodox, tone to the proceedings.

Perhaps no case better illustrates the shift away from the style of the early pilgrimages of the poor and illiterate to that of the bourgeois and *bien pensant* urban world than that of Mlle Moreau, the last to be studied by the commission. An adolescent of good family, she was afflicted by failing sight and had to leave the convent that was educating her.[52] After physicians and spas both failed to help, her family read about the miracle cure of Mme Rizan in their local *Messager catholique*, and decided on a novena, a nine-day discipline of prayer. When it was over, the young girl placed a headband impregnated with Lourdes water around her eyes, and the next day found herself cured. The family's prayers were joined to a vow to voyage to Lourdes, where the parents dedicated their daughter to Notre-Dame de Lourdes by wearing blue and white clothes for a year. She was greeted by the inhabitants of the *bourg* with an outpouring of joy, and was to become one of the most famous of early *miraculés*; Peyramale said she had 'the most beautiful eyes in the world'.[53]

Mlle Moreau's cure caused rejoicing because she was young, innocent and beautiful, and also because she symbolized how the shrine's reach was extending beyond the Pyrenees. She came to know of the Grotto through the Catholic press, demonstrating the growing renown of the fountain. More importantly, she epitomized the high piety of the nineteenth century that in many respects sought to model itself on Counter-Reformation orthodoxy. The novenas, the vow of consecration, the change of costume – a custom with peasant origins but widely practised among the richer classes – were all rites that a seventeenth-century pilgrim would have well understood. Such behaviour encapsulated a 'Baroque piety' that the organizers of the national pilgrimage built on later.[54] Finally, her cure was also a means of bringing Lourdes to the regional capital of Bordeaux, and Bordeaux to Lourdes. The two worlds of Catholic piety intermingled, neither entirely imposing its rituals on the other, but showing, once again, the accretion of another layer of Catholic civilization on to the Grotto.

The Making of Curing Narratives

Laurence's first Episcopal Commission confirmed the initial wave of miracles in 1862 and there were no moves to confirm any more until the beginning of the twentieth century in the midst of the great struggles to separate Church and state.[55] This is not to suggest Lourdes was no longer considered the centre of the miraculous; rather, the official imprimatur of the bishops was not a priority, so strong was belief in the cure among the faithful, until political forces made the need to confront the sceptical world outside a necessity.

In Lourdes, between 1867 and 1877, 'Every Sunday, at the two o'clock service, the requests for prayers that [the Garaison Fathers] had received and the cases of divine grace were read out.'[56] Scores of narratives – including some of the most famous of the era – were sent to the Fathers, either by the *miraculés* themselves or by their priests and other interested lay people. Not all had been pilgrims to the Grotto, although *all* had received aid through Notre-Dame de Lourdes, often through the medium of the bottled water. Others were printed in the *Annales de Notre-Dame de Lourdes*, which recounted at least a dozen and sometimes as many as forty cures per year between 1873 and 1883.[57] In both, medical description and clinical analyses were virtually absent until the mid 1870s. Instead the stories were often highly crafted moral tales that commented on society and religion just as much as on the illness and ultimate cure of the protagonist. The nature of the reading during religious services demonstrates the devotional quality of such an exercise.

For example, the first volume of the *Annales* told the tale of Françoise Pailhès, beginning with a description of the small village of Maquens near Carcassonne. The narrator lamented the loss of religion there, due, it seemed, to the moral disarray brought about by the 'great cotton mills and cloth factories'.[58] From being formerly a devout village, Maquens had given itself over to dances and desecration.[59] A new priest arrived in this den of iniquity, and managed to establish a Congregation of the Children of Mary. Girls who had sought money and luxury learned instead a life of sacrifice and devotion, with Françoise giving her beautiful earrings to the Virgin in order to remain in the congregation. Her illness was a 'rheumatism confined to the membranes of the heart', a disorder contracted from her work in the sheet factory. In her illness Françoise turned increasingly to the Virgin for support, was visited by Sisters of Charity from Carcassonne, and was finally cured by Lourdes water at the moment when white clothes were being prepared for her burial. An unnamed physician was rude and sceptical about her claims,[60] but, despite his incredulity, Françoise recovered, people converted, and her brothers renounced their normal pleasures in the name of the Virgin. Ultimately Françoise saved enough money to go on pilgrimage to the Grotto.

Medical confirmation was insignificant in such a tale, which sought instead to propagate the faith through details of spiritual trials amid a crisis of industrialization, here described as the 'resurrection of a parish'. Given this nature, it is not surprising that physicians appear almost as stereotypes of dismissive freethinking. In 1868–9 the narratives are notable for their militant tone, and the condemnation of medical intervention was one of their strongest characteristics.[61]

With time, however, the tales become less straightforward in their attitude to science; by 1873–4 the stress is still on the insufficiencies of medicine, but greater weight is none the less given to 'scientific' information. Although critical of the physicians, for example, M. Frances showed his grasp of medical jargon in recounting his cure: 'according to the medical report, all the varieties of fever assailed me: typhoid-form prostrating fever, tabetic or malignant fever, etc., etc.', a listing that shows at least some respect for the knowledge of the men who could not heal him.[62]

It is only in 1878, a decade after Françoise Pailhès's case, that claims of cure begin to be accompanied by a certified diagnosis of illness, starting with the case of Mlle Marie-Catherine Papalini, who suffered from a traumatic paraplegia.[63] The subsequent cure was also confirmed medically, this time by Dr Vergez, who, as will be seen, was the only physician to review the clerical commissioners' work and was instrumental in establishing a medical presence at the sanctuary.[64] This was the period when the growth of the national pilgrimage and the intervention of the Assumptionists ensured that publicity surrounding cures reached new levels, with the sick becoming the centre of the mission at Lourdes.[65] It is perhaps more than coincidental that it was also the moment that the Garaison Fathers published new directives in the *Annales*, asking correspondents reporting cures to provide specific details and adhere to a preferred order in their accounts. Not only was the civil status of the ill person requested, but also some indication of his or her character, conduct and piety. More information about the illness was also requested, and writers were asked to supply medical certificates, if possible. If not, they were at least 'to report their words, their opinions on the seriousness of the illness, the remedies used, how effective or ineffective they were'.

Equally important was the spiritual state of the *malade*: 'to know the spiritual means used to obtain it: prayers, masses, novenae, Grotto water, the attitudes of the ill person, their trust or fear, what they felt at the moment of the cure'. They now wanted the testimony of 'some serious person', especially a priest or the confessor, who knew the development of the illness and its spiritual impact. By this time both doctors and clergymen were seen as worthy attendants of the sick, but the insistence on 'a reliable witness' demonstrated a continued preference for fellow clergymen and the belief that such figures were needed to support statements from the mainly female patients. They sought evidence that piety counted, that a life of devotion and prayer would be rewarded. Last, they wanted to know the impact of the cure 'on the soul of the privileged person, their family and parish, the public', for it was not only the recipient of cure who benefited. Cures were miraculous interventions in society that could have a profound effect on those around the *miraculé*, and they avidly sought tales of spiritual conversion among unbelievers and sceptics.[66]

Witnesses, local consensus and impact on family, neighbours and friends were, therefore, often considered as important for validating a cure as a medical affidavit. An engraving in *Le Pèlerin* in 1895 showed the return of a *miraculée* to a humble household, meeting the embrace of a devout mother (the central figure in the composition), father and siblings, with one brother carrying a crutch as a trophy of cure (see illus. 70). Surrounding this family group were nuns in habits

70. 'Le retour d'une miraculée', Le Pèlerin, *8 September 1895*

and an awestruck monk, the central theme of the family ringed by a clerical periphery. In this context medical debate meant little; what was important was the subjective faith in the miracle more than any empirical verification.

This social aspect of the miracle drama was in keeping with the earliest tales of 1858–9, but otherwise the Fathers' request for ordered tales reveals an attempt to narrow the narrative possibilities and with them the diversity of healing cultures. No longer was an unceremonious immersion of the hand in the Grotto's water a seemly approach, although undoubtedly such journeys among the locals continued despite the growing clerical dominance of the shrine. By the 1880s the Garaison Fathers had succeeded remarkably; in the *Annales* medical certificates appeared in greater numbers and medical detail increased, even if doctors were still the butt of criticism.[67] At the same time the passages concerning the individual's piety, spiritual and devotional exercises became even more elaborate.

The Vision of the 'Self'

From the 1870s the discussion of the cures became increasingly embroiled in the politics of the Third Republic, as clerics and anti-clericals battled over events at the shrine, a debate that intensified with the publication in 1893 of Emile Zola's *Lourdes*. This work, to be discussed in the next chapter, thrust the sanctuary into turmoil, in particular infuriating those who had welcomed the author and sought to show him their truth. Instead of providing a positive portrait in response to the openness with which he was received, however, Zola responded by portraying the *miraculés* as hysterics, the cures as ephemeral, and divine mercy as the power of suggestion.

Zola's fictional heroine, Marie de Guersaint, a young virginal hysteric, is cured during the Eucharistic procession in a passage that reads like an orgasmic sexual encounter, a description that abused the holiest rite of pilgrimage by transforming spiritual encounter into pulsating physicality. He also described the relapse of the tubercular Marie Lebranchu, alias La Grivotte, turning her cure into an example of faith disappointed and abused. The account of Marie Lemarchand – called Elise Rouquet in the novel – was also transformed, with the hideous tubercular lupus that ravaged her face becoming nothing more than an hysterical ulcer, washed away by the combination of Lourdes water and suggestion.

Zola's novel hit so hard and hurt so much for two reasons. First, his reworking of the case of Marie Lebranchu was palpably untrue: she never did relapse and remained the living embodiment for Catholics of his bad faith. More important, however, was the novel's underlying analysis, which did not deny the possibility of cure, but rather used contemporary science to undermine the belief in supernatural intervention. Replacing divine mercy was suggestion, a powerful tool that acted upon the 'nervous' or 'functional' disorders of pious women and young girls; underneath, he implied, lurked hysteria, so that the devout were stigmatized with the taint of nervous disorder as well as naïve credulity.

Even though Zola's vision has been refined and made more sophisticated than the rude polemical version presented in the novel, it is still close to the interpretation of 'charismatic' or 'miraculous' healing employed by many psychiatrists and anthropologists today. The unspecified notion of suggestion pervades the analysis of clinical situations between physicians and patients, the assessment of the abilities of charismatic healers and shamans, and the understanding of the role of communities in dissolving tensions between individuals and in healing sickness. At the heart of all these studies, suggestion operates as a vague, undefined, biocultural mechanism that explains everything and at the same time nothing.[68] Moreover, while anthropologists tend more than psychiatrists to grapple with the cultural meaning of such experiences, many of the studies continue to emphasize the importance of the 'placebo effect', a notion that implies the importance of manipulation and imposition in bringing about cure.

Even if divine intervention is rejected as a possibility, reducing such occurrences to the pejorative notion of suggestion is to misconceive the process of healing, and to stay within the analytical trap that Zola and his fellow *fin de siècle* protagonists created. Understanding what took place requires an imaginative sympathy for the psychic and physical world that pilgrimage generated, for the way intense prayer, unabating pain and extreme humility were bolstered by the support of helpers and believers convinced of the ubiquity of miracles at Lourdes. Sufferers recounted how they were remade, reborn or resuscitated, how they were redefined by coming close to infinite power and grace. In essence, they described what twentieth-century philosophers would call an existential encounter with an infinite Other. The extraordinary changes involved suggest individuals' capacity to transform themselves, to live through new unconscious processes and bodily habits.

In contrast, the notion of suggestion implies both an explanation and a mechanism. Even if it truly provides neither, to challenge the idea seems to require alternatives of a similar order. I can pretend to no such completion, but will instead advance new ways of thinking about the problem of cure. For example, sometimes sufferers seem to have been at the 'margins of disability': arthritics were able to unfurl their hands and tuberculars breathed effortlessly again, but these were clinical transformations that may not have been confirmed by pathological findings. Those with crippling and painful myelitis were suddenly able to walk again, but did they still have the microbes that infected them? It is impossible to know. Cures of cancer and heart disease are more extraordinary; none the less, pathbreaking psychoanalytical work has shown how even life-threatening illness *may* have a psychogenetic component – those whose fathers die of heart attacks at forty, for example, sometimes find they have a near-fatal heart attack at the same age, emerging from a struggle with death believing that simple coincidence cannot explain their trial.[69] They are forced to confront the painful and unacknowledged aspects of the body's and psyche's destructive impulses; if we accept that such near-death experiences exist, then it seems reasonable to suppose that radical cure might contain such elements as well.

Some sense of what took place may perhaps be gleaned from the memoirs of those wishing to participate in the 1897 procession of *miraculés* planned by the Assumptionists for the twenty-fifth national pilgrimage.[70] Of these 127 records, only 10 were by men, and only 30 of the women were married. The largest age cohort – between 20 and 40 – had 51 women, most of whom were single. These 127 are a special group, for they were willing to show themselves in public and proclaim their belief to the world. They included cures from as early as 1873, although *miraculés* of the early and mid 1890s occupied a larger place, suggesting that some of the healings had not stood the test of time. They came from all parts of France, although the largest contingents were from secular Paris, the devout north and the Loire, all areas where the national pilgrimage seemed to be well promoted. Many seemed to have learned the narrative structures that the Garaison Fathers aimed to promote, and yet, like all stories that are told within a genre, such tales none the less reveal individuals, their subjective particularity shining through the conventionalized language.

Women were the main workers in the pilgrimage movement and also the primary recipients of cure, a fact that supports the broader picture of a 'feminized Catholicism' in the nineteenth century. Among their ranks were humble seamstresses who were Children of Mary and Tertiaries of Saint Francis,[71] employees of Catholic charities,[72] nuns, as well as girls and women dependent on relations. When deciding to come to Lourdes, they received help from priests, Sisters of Charity, Children of Mary and workmates with similar religious beliefs. The process of going to Lourdes and receiving the grace of cure certainly enabled some to validate the strength of this emotional network;[73] for others it was a means, at least in the short term, of breaking the shackles of trying social and psychological obligations. Far from undermining their past lives, the proof of grace validated their piety. Such women are interesting precisely *because* they confirmed all the stereotypes so dear to anti-clericals. Catholic apologists indeed went out of their way to stress their pious and deserving nature, creating an image that in turn encouraged opponents to depict them as almost caricatures of devout spinsterhood. For if female activists found in pilgrimage a means of expressing their political and spiritual visions of France, often through the guidance of a priestly director, then *miraculées* found in it the surest way of achieving a direct connection to the divine which bypassed all human intermediaries.

To understand their recitations, it is necessary to remember that they came at a unique historical moment in the history of the shrine. As will be seen, by establishing the Medical Bureau in 1883 the Church accepted both the need for scientific verification and for many of the epistemological criteria of modern medicine. Even the Catholic doctors at the shrine increasingly adhered to *fin de siècle* notions of 'nervous' illnesses as functional disorders, with Dr Gustave Boissarie, the head of the bureau from 1892, distinguishing ruthlessly between such illnesses and the 'organic' maladies alleviated at Lourdes. But while the Church increasingly depended on medical opinion, the perception of the faithful remained tied to popular traditions generally heedless of doctors. This tension was never resolved, and many cured individuals simply refused to undergo the gruelling process of medical investigation and the subsequent episcopal investigation, preferring instead their subjective certainty and the empirical verification of families and local communities. The sample from 1897 is full of women of this kind, and only one or two of them ever received the Church's imprimatur. Accordingly, it is their own vision of sickness and healing that is important.

Women often made little distinction between the psychological and physical manifestations of illness. Elisa Fichelle acknowledged her illness as hysteria, and recognized its dangerous impact on her disintegrating digestive system and wasting body; by her own account, her nervous crises were so extreme 'several men were needed to hold me'.[74] Léonide Calmels described how she had lost her voice after exhausting herself by shouting at her young charges as the directrice of a workshop for young orphans. Mme Hugot did not know why for nine years she could not speak in an audible voice, but was convinced that her cure would bring about the conversion of her husband.[75] In a case that reads like an entry in Breuer's and Freud's *Studies of Hysteria* (1895), Mlle Bedogni explained how she sat for sixty-two nights by the bedside of her dying father to nurse him, contracted a fever that lasted a year and then broke her ankle. She claimed that the long months in bed left her with an incurable myelitis that the passage of the Holy Sacrament and an immersion in the pool cured.[76]

Anti-clerical physicians may very well have pointed to this series of conditions to 'prove' the reality of suggestion in both bringing about their cure and causing them in the first place. The women, however, saw their ailments more holistically, alluding eloquently, if unselfconsciously, to the impact of work, marital tension and grief. Significantly, they applied similar reasoning to illnesses that were *not* nervous, seeing links between traumatic psychological episodes and seemingly unrelated physical maladies. Pulmonary conditions, choloroanaemia, paralysed or shortened limbs, arthritic conditions, stomach disorders and especially neurological failure were all among the cases described. Zulma Ranson, diagnosed with cancer of the stomach, claimed psychological trauma and its physiological aftereffects as the starting point for her 'organic' complaint. She described how, at fifteen, she went boating on the Somme, fell in and thereafter stopped menstruating. After this crisis of puberty, she contracted jaundice, a bloated belly and ultimately the tumour in her stomach.[77]

Often, women describe their illnesses as having a protean nature, a view of the disease process quite detached from the logic and causality accepted by contemporary medicine. Such was the case of Léontine Aubain, whose illness began with the inflammation of her fingernails, developed into an abscess in the envelope of her spinal cord and left her with an inert leg and hip.[78] She seemed to view her symptoms as a part of an underlying invasion, a view of illness that was central to these women's conception of cure as release through wholesale and crushing ejection. Both Aubain and Ranson provide narratives that *could* conceivably be reconciled with the physiological descriptions of nineteenth-century medicine, but their language and reasoning reveal a parallel world of mind–body relations heedless of contemporary medical theory.

Many of the women described lengthy physical and emotional trials before deciding to go to the shrine, and continued a tradition of Catholic scepticism by referring to medical inadequacy and even torture at the hands of science. Eugénie Hanceaux described the 'ignipunctures (1,200), the injections of Dr Brown-Sequart, the electric cells, the lotions of cold water, the wet clothes, the belladonna poultices' for her painful and debilitating myelitis, none of which made any difference.[79] Such descriptions became increasingly frequent, as more pilgrims turned first to medicine and its growing therapeutic repertoire. Their often intense feelings of communion with both the Virgin and Christ revealed a search for a caring presence that physicians administering such treatments seemed to lack.

They frequently did not see their transformations just in terms of their own cure, but as part of the Virgin's plans for mankind, a belief that echoed the way Christ's miracles were interpreted through the Gospels. Thus Mme Hugot, who had seen fourteen physicians before coming to Lourdes, believed that her malady had widespread benefits, for her atheistic husband fell to his knees in thanks to the Virgin when she was cured, and on her return to her native town of Bellême half the inhabitants turned out to welcome her.[80] The care that the Virgin manifested in such cases was presented as firm, even authoritarian, as often as gentle and kind. Significantly, it was the maternal incarnation that predominated, not the young girl of Bernadette's initial inspiration. The memoirs reveal a sternness at odds with the sentimentalism often associated with the Virgin of the late nineteenth century, for, while the faithful were released from the rigourist exercises of the past, many still believed that suffering was expiation and essential to healing.

For example, Mlle Crosmier, who had an astigmatism in both eyes, described how she had an excruciating malfunction in her whole body right before her cure: 'So far from being afraid, I consoled myself with the thought that the Blessed Virgin wished to make me purchase my cure by suffering and that this suffering was, moreover, the harbinger of the cure.'[81] This combination of strength and gentleness was also felt by Jeanne Delasalle, who came with 'so unshakeable a trust as to brave everything to come and implore her [aid] in the sanctuary';[82] she visited Lourdes twice, in 1893 and the following year, but saw only slight improvement in her tubercular arthritis. When she was preparing a 'novena of novenas' with her family for the festival of the Immaculate Conception, she fell awkwardly on the stairs and hurt herself. Despite it all, she continued to have faith, and, after some time, she claimed, she regained her health; she was convinced that the Virgin had caused her fall, her suffering and her ultimate release.

Like many good mothers, the Virgin had a strong, penetrating voice. Angèle Lesbroussart, in midst of her terrible suffering and the horrible remedies she suffered for treatment of a spinal ailment, explained how she read Lasserre's history and heard 'une voix secrète' that told her to go to Lourdes.[83] Hermine Jumeau knew that she had to make the journey when she received direct communication: '"Go," she told me, "go to Lourdes; you will be cured there."'[84] In these recitals, women used all their willpower to obey, often having to overcome the opposition of relations and friends fearful that the journey to Lourdes might kill them. Marcelline Duchesne said, 'but trusting in Mary I gave myself up to the will of God',[85] a thought echoed by Elise Delahaye: 'I place myself in the hands of Our Lady, may her will be done.'[86] The narratives thus reveal an apparent paradox in which surrender brought power as opposed to defeat; the acceptance of the momentary loss of self was an avenue towards the assertion and definition of a healed and rejuvenated wholeness.

Such surrender could bring sufferers close to death. Before her cure, Blanche Meurat said that her body was shivering and cracking until she met the Virgin:

> 'Good Saint Virgin Mary, if I am still useful on earth, cure me, since I am your child, and if I am not useful, take me! I am yours.'
>
> Then, turning my eyes towards Our Good Mother of Heaven, I saw her smiling and repeating to me, three times, 'Leave! My child! Do not hesitate, you are indeed cured,' and, as I still hesitated, an invincible force that I cannot describe pushed me powerfully out of my stretcher from which I stepped.[87]

It is not clear if she was referring to the statue in the Grotto or to a vision, nor does she say how she interpreted the smile – as forgiveness, reassurance, encouragement or a combination of all these qualities. She none the less emphasized the sense of presence, both close and authoritative, which physically moved her off her stretcher, to the astonishment of those looking on.

Meurat's account of what she saw, heard and felt shows how she tried to give voice to the relationship between her imaginative encounter with the Virgin and the way it was translated into physical action. It provides a perfect example of the way the 'self' – a totality of imagination, sensation, posture and bodily motion – was reorientated through an existential process that depended entirely on a belief in the presence of the Virgin and the maternal force associated with her.[88] The encounter was so powerful precisely because it contrasted her finite humanity and its bodily limitations with a sense of the infinite and its supernatural possibility. This conception was not Cartesian; it preferred a vision of human wholeness and rejected the restrictions of mentalist preoccupations – *cogito ergo sum* – that favoured mind over body and thought over being, in favour of a unified conception of the self. The process could not be explained by reference to a precise physiological or psychological mechanism; rather the undefined nature of the transformation within the 'self' gave it unimagined strength.

In their encounters with the Virgin, others found grace by emulating her maternal solicitude. Jacques Pittet, one of the few men in the sample of 1897, was reportedly 'so very moved to see oneself surrounded by all these invalids, he no longer thought to ask the Very Blessed Virgin for his own cure; he had but one desire, but one cry in the depths of his heart: *Our Lady, cure them*'.[89] Camille Meslard 'asked for her cure, which she had great need of, but accepted that, if God preferred, another should be cured in her stead'.[90] At work here was more than Christian self-effacement, or a maternalist legacy in Catholic spirituality rooted in the Middle Ages.[91] There was also an innovative dimension, for in these cases, the sick – so in need of help themselves – acted as 'good mothers' and compassionate intercessors who sought to alleviate the suffering around them. Suffering thus became a creative act bringing rebirth and rejuvenation, demonstrating how, at least among some of the faithful, the 'religion of fear' had been superseded by that of love.[92]

Other narratives show how imagination and physical experience were inseparable, particularly in the way that certain rituals were followed at the Grotto. Marie Rocher, for example, went to the fountain and drank eighteen glasses of water, thereby invoking Bernadette's eighteen apparitions; she insisted that the healing occurred while she drank, the physicality of the experience being invested with the holiness of the water and the significance of the number eighteen.[93] Although only a few of the rural poor who came to the shrine wrote memoirs, such accounts as exist often underline the importance they attached to saints, special waters and oils as physical and spiritual intercessors. Elzire Gronnier, who suffered from a debilitating but unspecified 'seizure' as well as a 'uric gravel', was devoted to the Sacred Heart, Notre-Dame de Lourdes, Saint Joseph, and especially her beloved patron Saint Martin. So great was her humility that she asked an Assumptionist father to address him, rather than doing so herself, and was rewarded with a complete cure after an immersion in the pools. The nature of her belief was demonstrated when she later hurt her hand: 'Our Lady will cure me if she wishes, I shall put only the water of Our Lady of Lourdes on it, and the oil of Saint Martin, many say you should heat the water, that would make things worse . . . No, the water of Our Lady cures, but it should not be heated.'[94] For her, oil had anointing power, while the holy water was seen as purifying; neither could be transformed without undermining its essential properties. Such 'sacramentals' were part of a process whereby God's power, both physical and spiritual, was focused, enabling sufferers to cure themselves.

While such accounts illustrate the range of curative rituals, the most important of all was to bathe in the pools. Bathing at Lourdes was yet another rite that built a bridge between the physical and the spiritual, but in this case the style and manner were borrowed from nineteenth-century hygienic and curative preoccupations. For a brief moment in 1858 Mayor Lacadé had hoped to make the fountain into a spa and had to abandon his project only after the most up-to-date hydrological analysis showed that the water possessed no special mineral quality.[95] But while the thermalist option was defeated, and Lourdes unable to compete with nearby Cauterets and Bagnères-de-Bigorre, the *fin de siècle* world of the sanctuary was still affected by its proximity to such spas. Lourdes is virtually unique among pilgrimage centres in the investment it made in *piscines*, hotels and hospitals, developments that were to some extent modelled after these residential and touristic centres. In a way entirely different to the approach of the poor, rural pilgrims who came to the Grotto soon after the apparitions, the *malades* of the later period often approached their immersion in the waters as a kind of discipline, a daily activity with healthful possibilities, testing their endurance with each passing day.

In making this point, however, I am not suggesting that Lourdes was an example of the developing nineteenth-century leisure industry garbed in religious apparel, although this was the kind of specious comparison that opponents used when attacking it.[96] The miraculous reigned supreme, and the spiritual preparation required attests to a very *different* attitude. However, when confronted with the problem of having to deal with ever greater numbers of people in the late nineteenth and twentieth centuries, the denizens of the town received them in a manner that undoubtedly drew on the example of more prosaic neighbours.

The primitive installations of the 1850s, hastily constructed by local masons, were only slowly superseded by more sophisticated facilities. Until 1880 there were only two provisional pools, still filled by a manual pump; not until that year was a wooden structure built to house fourteen pools. The changing rituals of bathing are difficult to establish, although in 1880 *Le Pèlerin* published a dramatic image of two Assumptionists submerging a distressed pilgrim (see illus. 71). While they worked, another said a blessing and the *malade* sat in a halo of light streaming in through the windows. The spirituality of the moment was offset by the primitive installations, more reminiscent of public baths in a state of disorder than of a Marian shrine. Under these difficult conditions – here given, paradoxically, an almost Zolaesque quality in their lurid naturalism – it is hard to know how the pilgrim responded to the experience.

The next set of *piscines*, completed in 1891, sought to enhance the ritual of bathing. Tiled in the Virgin's blue – a donation from a Portuguese woman – the interior was broken into several different compartments, two for each *malade*. The first was a kind of antechamber for dressing and undressing, the second contained a black marble bath two metres long, with enough space for the helpers to submerge the *malade*. These improvements were matched by the focused spirituality of the new central pavilion that housed a statue

71. 'Vue intérieure de la piscine provisoire des hommes à Lourdes', Le Pèlerin, *11 September 1880*

of the Virgin. Rather than having the statue gaze heavenwards, embodying the moment that preceded the declaration – 'I am the Immaculate Conception' – the sculptor captures the Virgin directing Bernadette to find the fountain, with the inscription reading: 'Go and drink of the fountain and wash yourself in it.'

Pilgrims seemed to associate bathing with a fantasy of a maternal, oceanic and protective presence. But it was also perilous, a trial that plunged vulnerable and expectant pilgrims into icy mountain water. Naked, wet, cold and ill, the pilgrims depended on the helpers to assist them in a moment of great physical and psychic vulnerability. During the immersion, the following standard prayer was recited three times:

Blessed be the Holy and Immaculate Conception of the Blessed Mary,
Mother of God,
Our Lady of Lourdes, pray for us,
Mother, have pity on us,
O Mary, conceived without sin, pray for us who call upon you.[97]

The faithful never tried to wipe away the illness of previous occupants – the water in the baths was changed only twice daily – and tried to keep the special liquid on their skins as long as possible. The *malade* was then dressed again, rebandaged and any orthopaedic appliances put back in place.

Bathing, therefore, required help from others and an acceptance that any cure was as much a collective as a personal phenomenon. Those who were crippled were placed in the pools by the *hospitalières*, contravening the conventional boundaries of nineteenth-century bodily decorum.[98] By laying the surface of the body open to cold, nakedness and the touch of others, the bathing rituals at Lourdes prepared sufferers for a moment of dramatic intensity:

On contact with the water, the sick woman said: 'Lord, may your will be done.' It seemed to her that her limbs were relaxing, that their strength was returning. But she dared not yet believe and went on repeating: 'Saint Mary, pray for me! Blessed Virgin, cure me!' The women who assisted her were moved to the depths of their souls. At their suggestion, and without any indication of difficulty or suffering, Mme Gordet took a few steps in the *piscine*, then, alone, submerged herself a second time. 'But you are cured!' exclaimed the ladies. 'Ah! Help me, mesdames, to thank the Blessed Virgin!'[99]

Then the woman, Virginie Gordet, reportedly walked up the three steps of the pool alone, holding her crutches, and, while she threw herself at the feet of the statue of the Virgin with her 'visage transfiguré', onlookers in the bathhouse began to say the *Magnificat*.

As significant as immersion in the water was the procession of the Holy Sacrament. Like their medieval forebears, the sick identified the Eucharist as the food of sustenance and an important consolation. Women took communion frequently during the pilgrimage, and, for those who suffered from acute digestive and other conditions, the act of swallowing the wafer was itself both a torment *and* a life-sustaining feat. While bathing evoked a sense of security and love, the taking of communion offered a different form of comfort. The former was a ritual of immersion and the latter emphasized incorporation, both physical acts indissolubly bound to spiritual content. However, at the moment of the Eucharistic procession Christ was more than a nurturer; he was also a healer, and in the host the assembled beheld his power to transform sickness into health. The various steps of his human life and divine passage meant that they were assured of both his human empathy and supernatural transcendence.

Miracles tales at Lourdes thus centred time and again on the Eucharist's beneficent qualities, through sight, ingestion and touch, the last especially common when the monstrance was laid upon them as a form of blessing. Mlle Bedogni, referred to earlier, bathed in the waters and was even able to kneel before the Holy Sacrament when it passed. But she felt spiritually uncertain and unable to ask for a cure until she saw the procession again two days later:

> Then I thought that the paralysis was invading every part of me, and, making a sacrifice of my life, I asked God for the grace needed by those who love me so that they could bear the pain of my death with Christian submission . . .
>
> During this time the procession was advancing slowly, coming from the Grotto, where several invalids had risen on Christ's passage.
>
> Two stretcher-bearers helped me to get out of the little carriage: Jesus was coming forward, blessing and curing the souls and the bodies! A supernatural force made me walk, part the crowd and place myself behind the platform! . . . Then, upright and steady, without a trace of suffering or fatigue, I followed the procession, imbued with love and gratitude, for Him whose single glance had restored me to life!'[100]

In this tale were elements often associated with such miracles. Mlle Bedogni felt the living God in the elevated host, his healing power and care for her and her affliction. Time and again, sick pilgrims mentioned how the presence of the Eucharist made them move, forced by a 'je ne sais quoi' to get up and follow.[101] On a rare occasion the *malade* even heard a voice. Elise Delahaye, who prayed for those sicker than she during the procession and tried three times to follow the Eucharist, fell back helplessly on her stretcher each time she tried to rise. On the fourth attempt she explained how 'a voice said, "Follow me"; I ran like a thief towards the monstrance borne by Father Bailly, saying "Lord cure me." I lost my petticoat en route. I cried out, "I am cured, I no longer have a belly."'[102]

Whether the cure was in the pools or near the Eucharist, sufferers related their experience as radical and instantaneous. This belief, however, was often contradicted by the rest of their statements, which showed how the emerging sense of well-being often extended over several days and many encounters. Despite this, most indicated a certain moment of miraculous transformation, even if full implementation took longer. A memoir of Sœur Marie de Sainte-Anne, written by a fellow nun, described the cure of her chronic stomach ulcer: 'All at once, she felt in her stomach something like a divine touch at the same time as a celestial perfume replaced in her breath the unbearable foulness.'[103] Another woman simply said: 'And thus towards the end of the procession of the Holy Sacrament I felt an extraordinary well-being.'[104]

Narratives that referred to these moments as in some way pleasurable were greatly outnumbered by those that talked of pain and torment. Sœur Marie de Sainte-Anne's was the sole example of perfumed emanations, while the smiling Virgin of Blanche Meurat represented the only visionary experience. Far more typical was a perception of cure as an expulsion, with the illness spoken about almost as a kind of demon. When plunged into the *piscine*, for example, the sick often felt atrocious suffering. Sœur Marie Eugène du Saint Cœur, with advanced tuberculosis, explained how 'I felt as though my entire body were being torn to pieces', and went on to describe how, when she put her head in the water, 'I felt as though an iron skull-cap had been removed', a vision that suggested the removal of an instrument of torture.[105]

The account of Mme Vermont described the disappearance of her ulcer and her paralysis: 'Then cracks were heard, first in the stomach, then in the right arm, in the whole side and leg.'[106] Another had a similar feeling of 'a great shudder and a cracking of my entire being'.[107] One described her moment of cure as 'internal pains and a tearing as though a paper envelope had been torn'.[108] Using the modern technical imagery, or one derived from popular magnetism, Jeanne Delasalle with her tubercular arthritis felt 'as if electrified, an internal strength drove me to rise' before she was cured.[109] More dramatically, Marie Lemarchand, famous for her inclusion in Zola's novel as the young girl with horrible, disfiguring lupus, said of her experience in the pools: 'I was suffering tortures all through my body, it felt as though my bones were being crushed, and then Oh Miracle no more suffering.'[110] Burning as well as tearing was part of the sensual repertoire. Aurélie Heuprelle felt 'her chest was torn by a constriction, she felt an anguish that she could not define, a burning pain transpierced her, as she often repeated, it was as if thousands of iron teeth were tearing [her] breast'.[111] Others described this physical sensation as a kind of difficult labour: 'I felt my belly diminish, then suddenly swell. I placed myself in the hands of Our Lady, her will be done. I felt the swellings but smaller, it was if I were being cut, in little places, I can't explain the work it caused me.'[112]

These many descriptions, vivid and even brutal in their imagery, provide a vision of illness as a kind of alien force, with the cure not dissimilar from exorcism. The language of expulsion was associated, above all, with the baths, which may have been seen as a kind of baptism and thus having overtones of the exorcism that was part of the sacrament. Baptism was a kind of spiritual and physical rebirth; the parallel with the moment of the cure was hard to ignore, although at Lourdes the priest was often absent, and the 'exorcism' was as painful as that which adults had to undergo when possessed. Perhaps most significant was the way the pain of exorcism (expulsion) and baptism (cleansing) was associated with childbirth; women felt torn, shaken, their whole bodies 'working' towards the ultimate expulsion, another vision of cure that united suffering and renewal.

The cures from mid century contrast sharply in style with those of the 1880s and 1890s. The former show a greater cultural diversity, a world in which the 'self' is elusive, if not almost silent, and subsumed under collective beliefs and rituals. The later cures were also enmeshed in a collective repertoire, this time of more strictly orthodox Catholicism and patterned story-telling, but the women of the 1897 pilgrimage are clearly preoccupied with the 'self' and their imaginative encounter with the compassionate presence of both Mary and Jesus. The 'self' in the women's view of themselves and in my analysis did not privilege spirit over body; on the contrary, both bathing and taking the Eucharist were rituals that broke down the boundaries between the two. Additionally, their narratives expressed a range of painful physical experience that is absent from the earlier tales. For women of the later century the release of pain required more pain; without it, the healing was seen as somehow insubstantial.

Many often poor and very sick women irrevocably transformed their lives by going to Lourdes, but I am hardly suggesting they all would have passed a medical tribunal. For a large number the improvements enabled them to live more fruitful and active lives, while others may have died after only a few years. (Unfortunately, rarely do the records allow us to follow their future path.) But medicine now counts those who survive for five years after treatment for cancer as 'cured', a definition that suggests the cultural relativity of the notion of cure. Rather than seeing the transformations at Lourdes as the effects of suggestion on women who were psychologically impoverished and susceptible, the cures of Lourdes raise a vision of the 'self' as actively engaged and resourceful, able to overcome afflictions that all other therapies had failed to alleviate. Such healings deserve to be seen as having something of the 'miraculous' about them.

10

Religion and Science in the Third Republic

The sort of claims and counter-claims about cures documented in the previous chapter gave the Lourdes of the *fin de siècle* its reputation for unseemly, even vicious dispute between religious advocates and anti-clerical opponents. On one level this was true, especially when Emile Zola in 1893 unleashed his polemical genius in his novel *Lourdes*, painting the shrine in the lurid colours of hysteria, suggestion and crowd madness, and forcing its defenders to sharpen their arguments. The innumerable battles that culminated in French anti-clerical laws dissolving religious congregations, closing Catholic schools and finally separating Church and state in 1905 led to further scientific assaults on the sanctuary. Clinicians attacked Lourdes for fostering an atmosphere of mass hysteria, while hygienists saw the sanctuary as little more than a breeding ground for infection.

At another level, however, the relationship between religion and science was far more complex and ambivalent. Lourdes is the only major sanctuary in Christendom to possess a Medical Bureau of international renown, an institution founded in the belief that medicine might strengthen rather than undermine faith in miracles. Underneath the bitter polemic, intellectual currents of the *fin de siècle* show that the debate was more than two sides trading insults about superstition and modernity. Parisian physicians, impressed by therapeutic results they could neither deny nor duplicate, began to discuss the shrine as part of a broader debate over hypnotism, the 'unconscious' and mediumic power. Although these men never accepted the reality of supernatural intervention, they no longer dismissed what took place there as fraud. Instead of Lourdes being weakened by the attacks of positivism, the example of the inexplicable that it proffered led to the ultimate discrediting and abandonment in some scientific circles of much of the positivist ethos itself.

The Clerical and Medical Background

The novelty and significance of the Medical Bureau's foundation in 1883 can only be understood by comparison with what went before. The Episcopal Commission of Inquiry that originally deliberated on the claims of cure was composed entirely of clerics, with medical evaluation brought in as an afterthought; only two decades later such an approach seemed unprofessional. The early period was distinguished by a lack of defensiveness about what it was doing.[1] Comfortable in a diocese at the edge of France, unimpressed by scientific claims, the commissioners guided by the skilful Baradère did not yet feel the national spotlight upon them, and went about their business with ease and confidence, submitting dossiers to their medical consultant, Dr Vergez, in 1860. It chose twenty-nine cases for close examination and believed that twelve demonstrated the impact of supernatural intervention. The conclusion – modified by Vergez's more severe report – characterized only eight cases as miracles, and included Mlle Moreau of Tartas, the young woman from Bordeaux whose failing eyesight was cured in 1859.[2]

Baradère's report lacked any formal definition of the criteria that the sub-commission employed, but he obviously used those set forth in the future Benedict XIV's *De servorum Dei beatificatione et beatorum canonizatione* (1734–8). Designed to bring rigour to the adjudication of supernatural acts, this work reflected the changing worldview of Enlightenment philosophy, which undermined the ubiquity of the miraculous, and the Church's own concern with policing 'superstitious' excesses.[3] It put forward seven conditions for a cure to pass muster, focusing on the gravity and difficulty of treating the illness, and also requiring proof that either no medication had been used or that it had been entirely inefficacious. In addition, the cure had to be instantaneous, non-recurring, perfect in its completion and not improved by some earlier determinate cause.[4]

Straightforward enough in theory, these guidelines were rarely entirely adhered to in practice. Baradère and his colleagues certainly interpreted them flexibly, bending the rules most obviously over instantaneity, which was supposedly central to the theology of miracles, showing the special nature of God's compassion for humanity through his willingness to work prodigies. For example, when talking about the way in which Louis Bouriette recovered his sight, they were impressed by the rapidity of the cure, which 'happened almost instantly and rapidly progressed'.[5] At the same time they knew that he had continued to bathe his eye, and did not question whether these extra lotions undermined the claim to immediacy. Their discussions do not indicate vacillations, but instead show the widely held belief that instantaneous *improvement*, rather than a complete and immediate cure, was sufficient to prove miraculous intervention.

In line with the criteria required to prove supernatural intervention, the earlier commissioners, like the later sufferers who wrote to the *Annales*, revelled in the uselessness of medicine and contrasted it with the way intercession by the Virgin could produce a cure with ordinary water. Blaisette Soupène, whose infected and pustulant eyes had tormented her for years, had tried everything: 'the long years of suffering, the failure of the medication prescribed, the uselessness of spa waters replete with such powerful and energetic curative powers, more than suffice to prove that the infection was morbid to the highest degree'.[6] Only the water at the Grotto made a difference. They emphasized the way supplicants went *against* medical directives, showing how they were cured by faith rather than science; Henri Busquet, for instance, the young man with the tumour in his neck and chest, was expressly forbidden to apply cold water on his suppurating wound and deliberately ignored the command.[7]

While these *miraculés* showed the hopelessness of science, an equal number never had medical attention, inadvertently making it difficult for the commission to rule in favour of supernatural intervention. For example, Marcel Peyrègne was cured of the small tumour on his hand after only two lotions, but 'the absence of any care, and of any examination by a man of medical science, leaves us in complete ignorance on this none the less essential point'.[8] However, the commissioners were happy to be inconsistent when the cure seemed dramatic enough. Young Justin Bouhorts, who was plunged into the icy water for fifteen minutes, had been universally known for his ill-health, and the commissioners readily agreed with the popular assessment of a miracle, despite the absence of a medical diagnosis; in later years such a lack would prove a great obstacle.

A gentle faith pervades the report, as does a shrewd psychology that affirmed the narratives even when they were not considered miraculous. Baradère did not mock when Jeanne-Marie Arque, who had been deaf for twenty years because of wax in her ears, believed that syringing them with water had caused a miracle. Those who knew her were astonished and gladdened by the remarkable change, even if she did not fulfil the Church's criteria. Unwilling simply to dismiss her, as Vergez would in his report, Baradère remarked that the idea of using the water to such good effect, while not a miracle, might have been divinely inspired.[9]

Another show of delicacy was used to describe fifty-year-old Jeanne Crassus, whose wild and frequent nervous attacks dismayed her neighbours. Like others who used the waters over an extended period and felt themselves cured, she attributed her improvement to the Virgin. But Baradère and his colleagues suggested that the water had acted naturally, aiding her transition to the menopause, gently alluding to 'a new phase'. For Jeanne Crassus the 'cure' must have been all of a piece – spiritual renewal mixed with the evidence of a physiological transformation that brought the end to terrible suffering. Baradère and his fellow clerics were again keen not to undermine the importance of her transformation, even if it was not miraculous.

Vergez's list, in contrast, was smaller and contained some different cases.[10] But, despite divergences, he too believed passionately in miracles: 'by scrutiny of the most authentic facts, placed above the power of science and art, I have seen, I have touched the divine work, the miracle'.[11] Born in Esquièze in 1814, he studied at Saint-Pé, then at Tarbes and finally at Pau before moving to Montpellier. He was a Catholic physician who, like so many of his colleagues, defied the stereotype of the anti-clerical positivist seeking to bring enlightenment to the provincial hinterland. As the quintessential local notable with a large clientele in Barèges and Tarbes, he showed his political mettle in defiance of the anti-clerical Ferry laws in the 1880s, the legislation that made state primary education in France free, non-clerical and obligatory, by converting his garden into an *école libre*, or independent school, where Catholic brothers continued to teach.

His training at Montpellier, the most notable medical faculty in the country after Paris, indelibly marks the report, which was up to date and rigorous.[12] In speaking of those cases he did not find miraculous, he wrote: 'It will perhaps be thought that, if we exclude them, we are acting with excessive reserve, and displaying too severe a conscience. Far from complaining about this reproach, we shall congratulate ourselves thereon, because we are convinced that in such matters prudence itself requires severity.'[13]

In the case of Mlle Massot-Bordenave, whose weak hands could not even cut bread, Vergez saw only a 'convalescent weakness' transformed 'under the influence of strong moral excitement'.[14] Mme Daube's rheumatic, swollen legs were already getting better, while Jeanne Crassus's twisted and wounded hands were insufficiently investigated before bathing to confirm a result. Vergez also disagreed with the clerics when he discussed the disfiguring 'dartre laiteuse' of Mlle Garrot, a skin condition looking like a milky eczema, which for him was a disorder that could disappear at any moment, hence excluding it also from the supernatural category.[15]

This pervasive scepticism gave the report its analytical power and demonstrates a psychology different from that of the priests. As much as his clerical colleagues, Vergez emphasized the relationship between the physical and the moral, and for that reason acknowledged the power of the psyche in transforming the bodily economy. But, however impressive, such cures were for him natural. For example, in examining two children afflicted with 'quartan fever', both spontaneously cured after two visits to the Grotto, he took into account their 'strong sentiments of the soul, hope, joy, expectation'. He acknowledged the importance of such cures, but insisted that, rather than Mary's grace, the children's suggestible natures and their 'limited intellect' were more important.[16]

The priests were thus more ready than Vergez to entertain the claims of the poor and illiterate. He saw women too as susceptible to the effects of placebos, and argued that Mlle Abadie's use of the water on her rheumatic knees produced a cure based on nothing more than suggestion:

> This influence is so exaggerated in certain constitutions that it has been possible for doctors to produce surprising effects with insignificant agents; abundant purgation with bread crumb pills, suppression of certain sudden nervous crises with potato flour, etc., the patients having previously been assured that they were about to take a powerful medicine.[17]

What for Baradère was supernatural intervention, for Vergez was the result of 'a lively imagination'. Their assessments never differed more than in this case, despite the similarity of the evidence each considered. As a physician, Vergez believed he could help the sick with placebos, but had a low opinion of those who responded to such devices. There is no such cynicism in Baradère's assessment, in which the psychology of grace predominated even when the cure was natural.

The Medical Personnel and the Bureau

Baron Dunot de Saint-Maclou, a noble of elite, Norman extraction, brought an entirely different tone to the proceedings when in the early 1880s he began to take over from Vergez as the leading, if unofficial, medical consultant at the sanctuary.[18] Of a military family – his ancestors had fought during the Wars of Religion – Saint-Maclou had been destined for Saint-Cyr and the officer training course. He found a means of avoiding family tradition through an unspecified illness, but compensated by marrying one of the granddaughters of a page of Charles X, a woman of impeccable aristocratic credentials and a deep love for the Virgin. Living in his chateau in Calvados, Saint-Maclou occupied himself with Thomist philosophy, physiology and charity, showing how a young man of good family could remain entirely within a Catholic intellectual and spiritual orbit, seemingly untouched by secular cultural currents. When he began to study medicine at Caen, he published on medical abortion, a work acknowledged with an honorary doctorate by the University of Louvain, one of Europe's foremost Catholic institutions. The thesis, which combined theology and medicine, 'conferred on him an authority recognized in canon law in the matter of examining cures', giving him a unique qualification, ultimately put to use at Lourdes.[19] Later he engaged with the conflicts of his century, and became a champion of the dogma of papal infallibility and commander of the Order of Saint Sylvestre in recognition of his services to the papacy.

He was moved to take on his special role at Lourdes because from 1877 he repeatedly accompanied his sick wife there. She did not recover, but the couple none the less became notable personalities at the shrine, with Peyramale giving her the last rites. After her death, Saint-Maclou withdrew to study the relations between theology and medicine, while also studying Benedict XIV on the canonization of the saints and miraculous healing, intellectual interests that led him to think of himself as a 'worker of the Grotto'.

The initiative that created the Medical Bureau in 1883 seems to have come from the Garaison Fathers, although no documents exist to explain why they deemed it necessary.[20] Initially it was temporarily housed in the order's residence at Lourdes, and the very basic facilities veiled the quiet revolution that brought as many as forty physicians during the pilgrimage season to discuss the frontier between natural and supernatural causation.[21] Five physicians attested to the cure of Marie-Anne Beduchaud in September 1883, with the attendance of an Assumptionist father and a missionary father, a presence that demonstrates the happy collaboration of physicians and clerics in a situation where the former were just beginning to enjoy an ascendancy.[22]

While 143 cures were recorded in 1883, the number dropped to 83 the following year, a diminution perhaps attributable to the greater medical presence.[23] As a distinguished canonist, Saint-Maclou believed passionately in the power and presence of the supernatural in human affairs, but was also wary of the dangers of enthusiasm, and increasingly insisted on the need for a medical certificate to testify to the pilgrim's previous state. He was as conscious as any positivist about the role played by suggestion, especially in cases of potential hysteria. As one English observer explained, 'Then he told me how a sudden emotion, a lively faith, a powerful imagination or a state of religious exaltation were often the occasion for at least a temporary cessation of the most marked and inveterate symptoms of hysteria.'[24]

That the Medical Bureau was established at the same moment that Parisian medicine was at the height of its international fame for its work on hysteria was perhaps not coincidental.[25] For much of the slant of the Parisian approach was anti-clerical: the hysteria investigations were dominated by Jean-Martin Charcot, appointed in 1882 by the republican anti-clerical establishment to the chair of diseases of the nervous system. Once established, he targeted Catholic hospitals and belief through a concerted campaign to laicize their staff, a direct assault on the nursing sisters who had traditionally fulfilled this role.[26] More importantly, his Ecole Salpêtrière devoted itself to showing how the saints and martyrs of past ages were nothing more than neurotics who could now be treated by people like himself.[27] It is not surprising that he and his associates held similarly dismissive views of modern miracles as well. Although Charcot was hardly the only eminent Parisian to take such a line, his prestige and the persistence of his attacks made him a uniquely important opponent, whose assaults could not be ignored by either medical or lay believers in the miraculous.

In contrast to the hierarchies of the Parisian clinics that the Salpêtrière and especially Charcot exemplified, Saint-Maclou envisaged a different kind of medical collegiality, inviting physicians accompanying *malades* and later doctors of all creeds or religions to his bureau. This 'republic of physicians', however, had the effect of increasingly excluding non-medical personnel, especially priests who had for so long been responsible for recording cures. This change showed the penetration of medical epistemology despite the shrine's pervasive miraculous mood. A photograph of the 1880s continued to show the *malade*, physicians and priests together (see illus. 72), but in a later image of 1900 only one priest is left among the assembly of doctors (see illus. 73).

Even so, the contrast in style between the Medical Bureau's approach

72. *'Le Bureau des Constatations des guérisons miraculeuses', photograph from the 1880s reproduced in Gustave Boissarie,* Les Grandes Guérisons de Lourdes, *1900*
73. *'Le Bureau des Constatations des guérisons miraculeuses',* Le Pèlerin, *26 August 1900*

and that of the Parisian Charcot remains. In the earlier image the woman is a devout peasant, in the second she is urbane and elegant, but both are calm and at ease as they answer questions. The imagery of Charcot at work is strikingly different, for pictures such as André Brouillet's famous representation of his clinic (see illus. 74) often

74. *Pierre-André Brouillet,* Une leçon de Charcot à la Salpêtrière, *1887*

portray the women being studied in distress or ready to perform wildly for a male audience.[28] The assemblage seems more interested in the pathology on show than in the suffering woman before them. Deliberately or not, one set of images portrays the Catholic doctors as humane and sympathetic, while the other highlights the coldness of scientific rationalism. Underneath this contrast, both sides show women's experiences as subject to male adjudication.

Saint-Maclou died in 1891 and was succeeded by Gustave Boissarie, whose reign until 1914 saw the Medical Bureau enter a new and more professional phase of its existence. Boissarie was a man of the south-west, a native of Sarlat and a physician's son, a man destined to return from Paris to take his place among the local elite. But he long resisted a return to provincial life because of the capital's allure as a centre for research; unlike Saint-Maclou, his private papers demonstrate a fascination with Charcot and the world of Parisian medicine that he ultimately abandoned.[29] He even passed the taxing *concours*, or competitive examination, for the Internat des Hôpitaux, a position granted by the dean of the faculty of medicine, Paul Brouardel, a famous hygienist and Pasteurian. His ultimate rejection of this world may in part explain the intensity of his later assault upon it.

Like Saint-Maclou, he too came to Lourdes for personal reasons, in 1872 because of one son's cholera, and again in 1886 to thank the Virgin for sparing another from tuberculosis. It was in this year that he wrote his first article for the *Annales de Notre-Dame de Lourdes* and was, in a sense, head-hunted by the Garaison Fathers. He reached a vast audience with his *L'Histoire médicale de Lourdes* (1891) and, from provincial obscurity, was launched into the limelight, his work winning a papal 'brief of approval and congratulations'.[30] He took up his post when the development of the two Hospitalités seemed to ensure the care and provision of the *malades* on a full-time, yearly basis, guaranteeing the future of his medical bureau *cum* clinic.

In his era the Medical Bureau became another diocesan institution, devoted to using science to back up religious belief and aiming to force physicians to confront the special happenings at the Grotto.[31] This more important role was reflected in its physical location, for it became literally built into the fabric of the sanctuary. Saint-Maclou had sat on a few boards under a tile roof near the pools to examine the *malades*, while Boissarie received his patients in a permanent building under the right ramp of the Basilica of the Rosary. The community of physicians that Saint-Maclou had hoped to create finally developed: between 1899 and 1913 apparently 6,313 physicians passed through Lourdes, and there were many professors – often of an entirely atheistic bent – whose curiosity would ultimately bring them to the shrine.[32]

Opinion diverged over Boissarie's philosophy and clinical style. For the anti-clerical opposition he was credulous, but for believing Catholics his scepticism was notorious:

Besides, it has to be acknowledged that he seemed rather unprepossessing, had a tendency to dash all enthusiasm, and seemed inclined to discourage the sick who claimed to have been cured. The story is told that a woman who had been miraculously cured was one day telling a *hospitalière* about the examination she had just undergone at the Medical Bureau. One of the investigating doctors, she said, had concluded that her cure was the product of a supernatural intervention. 'Do you know the name of the doctor?' asked the *hospitalière*. 'I think his name is Boissarie,' answered the young woman. 'Oh, no, it's not him,' was the reply. 'Boissarie doesn't believe in miracles.'[33]

But of course Boissarie did believe in miracles, and hoped to prove the power of the supernatural through scientific confirmation, popularization and proselytization. He battled against Zola, publicized the cures in print and at conferences, and was the force behind the second wave of episcopal rulings on miracles in the first decade of the twentieth century. He willingly took up the cudgels against secularists and doubters, unabashedly sought to convert physicians to Catholicism, and developed lasting relationships with the *miraculés*. Something of his strong personality can be seen in a letter by Marie-Ange Clément, cured in 1904 of a 'coxalgia, with bone lesions':

> What first struck me about him was his apostolic need . . . He liked to follow those who had been miraculously cured and would make them feel the need for gratitude to God. He always knew the most telling word to say, the one that brought the cured face to face with themselves and their consciences; he pointed out the new duties that God expected of them.[34]

The *miraculé* could not return to a life of peaceful obscurity but rather had to join Boissarie's fight; in this respect, at least, he was remarkably similar to the often authoritarian Parisian physicians he opposed.

Zola's Lourdes

Zola's *Lourdes* was not only his most successful novel, it did more than any other publication to bring the sanctuary, Boissarie's *miraculés*, and the debate over the nature of healing to the wider public. In his Rougon-Macquart series of novels, he had sought to forge a new positivistic truth in literature by applying the experimental method of the nineteenth-century physiologist Claude Bernard, whose work sought to establish the centrality of ideas in scientific investigation, and the need for repetitive experiments on living organisms to confirm hypotheses.[35] Zola believed that he could apply these ideas to literature, and intended his fiction to operate as a *roman expérimental* in which the characters and conditions of social life would be observed, analysed and assessed.[36] His central experimental proposition was the interplay of heredity and environment; this he intended to examine by charting the lives and loves of one family through the course of the Second Empire. Like living organisms under a microscope, Zola intended to dissect the law-like processes of their development.

This literary philosophy differed significantly from Bernard's strictures, for in Zola's novels there was no possibility of repeating the experiment, nor were the subjects living. Literary vivisection was in fact little more than a metaphor, but the use of Bernard's terminology appealed to the scientism of his generation and, despite the speciousness of the parallels, the approach had an enormous impact on both the literary establishment and the reading public. The idea of an 'objective' novel treating matters of biology, sexuality and social conditions, without regard to the delicacies of bourgeois sensibility, created a sensation. His positivism, the self-conscious loss of a spiritual dimension to his characters, as well as his anti-clericalism and left-leaning political views, were all of a piece, making him a radical among his literary contemporaries.

Despite his extravagant success, his star had already passed its zenith by the early 1890s, as the 'religious revival' in letters,[37] the 'discovery' of the Russian novel, the conversion to Catholicism of erstwhile naturalists such as Paul Bourget[38] and Joris-Karl Huysmans,[39] as well as the literary criticism of Ferdinand Brunetière,[40] all undermined the appeal of his literary method. To varying degrees, these authors and critics sought the Christian and the spiritual rather than the atheistic and the materialistic, the beautiful rather than the brutal, the investigation of subjectivity rather than the display of objectivity.[41] Zola, in contrast, remained wedded to his own philosophy and determined to fight back against what he considered a retrograde trend.

To do this he revisited an old idea, for as early as 1872 he had described Lourdes as a 'miracle show'. He was appalled by the Grotto as a place for fairy-tales and right-wing politics masquerading as religion, and saw the displays of Catholic penitence as nothing more than the 'death rattle of the clerical party'.[42] Shocked and grieved by the humiliation of defeat, he had nothing but contempt for the legitimist bid for monarchical restoration and hoped instead for a republican ascendancy. His chance encounter with the shrine on a journey from Cauterets to Tarbes in September 1891 surprised him, however:

> I came to Lourdes, as it happened, in the rain – driving rain – and to a hotel where all the good rooms were taken. And with the mood I was in, I felt like leaving again the following morning! . . . But I went out for a moment . . . and the sight of the ill . . . of the dying children brought before the statue, of people lying flat on the ground, prostrate and praying . . . the sight of this town of faith, born of the hallucination of a little girl of fourteen, the sight of this mystical city in the century of scepticism . . . the sight of the Grotto, of the processions in the scenery, of this flood of pilgrims . . . This stirring of souls should be painted . . . Well, yes! The spectacle gripped me to such an extent that, having left for Tarbes, I spent two entire nights writing about Lourdes.[43]

For Zola the picture of the praying and distraught masses gave him the chance to come to grips with the pressing problem both of the 'revolt against science' prevalent among his literary colleagues and what he saw as a popular need for supernatural comfort. He acknowledged and sought to understand this need, even if he saw it as regressive.

Although still firmly wedded to his naturalist creed, his reactions were more complex when he came to Lourdes a second time to witness pilgrimage in August 1892, showing once again how, despite the scepticism of his conscious position, Zola was no crude cynic.[44] On the first few days of his stay he tried to remain unnoticed, until news of his arrival spread among the notability of the shrine. They believed that even he could be converted, and warmed to the gravity of his tone and his constant reiteration that he was a man of good faith by graciously welcoming him. Zola's journal shows how impressed he was by the energy and intelligence of Père Picard, and how ordinary in comparison was Père Bordelat, the leader of the Garaison Fathers in 1892, a view of the sanctuary's guardians that he put into his novel. The lack of defensiveness among the officials meant that he was positively encouraged to see everything on offer: he was taken by a member of the Hospitalité de Notre-Dame de Salut to the *piscines* and saw the devotion of the *dames hospitalières*. He visited the Medical Bureau and was greeted courteously by Boissarie; he even met Lasserre, who took him to the *cachot*. Zola was moved enough to describe this miserable dwelling as another Bethlehem, but not enough to be shaken in his conviction that Bernadette's apparitions were hallucinations, suggestible influences received from the local priest of Bartrès, Ader, who recalled how she resembled the children of La Salette.[45]

Despite his criticisms and his disdain for the shrine's commercialism and ugliness, the suffering at Lourdes disturbed and upset him. The continual chanting and endless supplication revealed yearnings that he had hoped – or believed – the nineteenth century had eradicated. Zola's journal shows how his journey produced in him powerful emotions and an intense ambivalence, feelings that he would repress once he returned to the familiar philosophical, literary and political world of the capital. The resulting book returned to the terrain of literary naturalism, and many of the ambiguities of his experience were stripped away.

The novel he produced was structured around the five days of national pilgrimage and highlighted a frustrated love affair between a priest, Pierre Froment, who has lost his faith and become a secret *libre-penseur*, and Marie de Guersaint, the playmate of his youth, cruelly crippled by a riding accident. Froment is painted as a tragic and paradoxical figure, for he is both manly and emasculated all at once. Although no longer a believer, he is unable to leave the priesthood and endures his celibacy because he believes Marie's illness is hysterical, induced by the trauma of her accident. Although confined to a kind of rolling coffin, Marie, he believes, will be cured at Lourdes as long as knowledge of his own scepticism does not weaken her faith.

The plot and characterization thus deploy the entire arsenal of anti-clerical weaponry: priests were sexually frustrated, while the women cured at Lourdes were unknowing hysterics, for Zola was a great believer in the thesis advanced by Charcot in his 1892 article 'La Foi qui guérit' ('Faith healing').[46] This famous piece was written shortly before the great neurologist died; it was effectively the physician's last word on the subject, a more considered survey of the question of healing and hysteria that had occupied him for much of his career. The article was an important shift in Charcot's stance, for although he held firmly to his belief that anyone who could be cured in such a way was an hysteric, he recognized that religious faith might produce a stronger suggestible effect on such people than medical authority, and he willingly admitted that he himself recommended pilgrimage to Lourdes in certain circumstances. Zola thus made Marie, the central character, a classic hysteric, emphasizing the point with a scene in which the young and intelligent physician recommends pilgrimage and notes the pain produced by light pressure on Marie's ovaries, an indication of undiagnosed hysteria.[47]

Her cure is the emotional centrepiece of the novel, considered by many Catholics to be a 'false' miracle that Zola intentionally highlighted in order to undermine the healings of 'real', 'organic' illness. Like so many 'real-life' healings, Marie is not cured on her first visit to the Grotto, but must wait until night when she is transfigured by her silent communion with the statue, who has spoken to her and smiled to indicate that her redemption is near; she becomes convinced she will be cured at four o'clock during the procession of the Holy Sacrament. Zola describes the cure as a kind of frenzy, a 'folie sacrée', and like a sexual initiation. When the Eucharist passes her, Marie de Guersaint

> [was seen to] rise suddenly, stand bolt upright in her cart . . . Great tremors ran through her virginal body . . . It was her legs that first came free of the fetters imprisoning them . . . an enormous weight . . . ran from her belly up to her throat. Only this time, it did not stop, she was not choked, it burst out of her open mouth, swelling into a cry of sublime joy: 'I'm cured! I'm cured!'[48]

Marie expels her illness, after its convulsive path up her body, like a demon spat out through the mouth. When the crowd follows her to the Medical Bureau, intoning the *Magnificat*, Marie explained:

> It was my legs the Blessed Virgin freed first . . . I could feel clear as anything the irons that bound them sliding over my skin, like broken chains . . . Then the weight that was always stifling, here, in my left side, rose up my body . . . But it went right past my throat, I had it in my mouth and I spat it out as hard as I could . . . That was it, my illness was gone – flown away.[49]

In language, tone and content Zola is thus utterly loyal to the healing narratives described in the last chapter, emphasizing spiritual preparation, the centrality of the Eucharistic procession, and the overriding preoccupation with expulsion, bodily torment and spasm. But while women saw these harsh encounters in creative and existential terms, Zola regarded them as the result of pathology, of susceptibility, degeneration and cultural anachronism. His assessment is summed up by Pierre, who is reminded of a passing remark: 'It was the devil she spat out.'[50] Marie's experience connects her to the old world of madness and superstition; and Zola's obsession with her virginity means he describes her cure as the closest she will ever come to sexual experience.

With Marie's 'cure', Zola acknowledged the occasional efficacy of suggestion, but went on to analyse other instances of apparently organic illness where the effect was ephemeral. Central to this part of the novel was La Grivotte, in real life Marie Lebranchu, grotesquely thin and wracked with coughs from pulmonary tuberculosis, who lived a shadowy existence in Paris hospitals for the five years before coming to Lourdes. Zola described her brilliant eyes and the belief that she was cured, only to find herself on the returning train 'as if she were again emaciated, her face livid and pain-racked . . . she spat blood copiously . . . This devastating relapse filled the carriage with terror.'[51] As has been said, however, Marie Lebranchu did not relapse, and Catholics never forgave him for the deceit.[52]

Clémentine Trouvé, alias Sophie Couteau, also appeared in the novel as a returning pilgrim cured in 1891 of a 'caries of the heel bone'. No one suggested a nervous element in the case of this child, and so her apparently instantaneous cure was significant. However, Zola was not convinced, maintaining that the clinical control – and above all a photograph of the wound before the bath – was inadequate; he gave little credence to the view that the bandage, pus and blood had fallen away, leaving only fresh skin.[53]

Zola thus made his central figure an hysteric, turned Lebranchu's cure into a relapse, and undermined the Trouvé case by claiming shoddy clinical procedure. He also assaulted the cure of Elise Rouquet, the fictional representation of Marie Lemarchand, of her terrible facial lupus: 'Her head elongated like the muzzle of a dog, with her bristly hair and great round eyes, had become repulsive.'[54] In the face of believers who maintained she emerged from the baths with a fresh, intact, albeit pink, skin, Zola insisted that there was no immediate change but rather a gradual amelioration, implying a longer-term process of suggestive therapy at work rather than an instantaneous miraculous healing.

For Zola this suggestive force could only operate through the powerful medium of the crowd, described as attaining such states as 'fury, exaltation, delirium'. In the process, he revealed the uncertainties of current scientific thought by using such phrases as an 'unknown force', 'vital fluid', 'power of auto-suggestion', 'extreme exaltation', 'an agent of the governing will forcing matter to obey',[55] terms that covered all the ambient theories of the day – magnetism, suggestion and various spiritualist hypotheses. Untroubled by this epistemological vagueness, he none the less condemned the crowd's irrationality, although he acknowledged the sincerity of the praying hordes. His concern with crowd psychology derived from the wider discussion of collective behaviour during the period.[56] The most famous advocate in the new field, Gustave Le Bon, would have agreed with his overall assessment, although he would have lumped all crowds, Catholic or anti-clerical, into the same dangerous state of thraldom.[57]

Zola also made much of the inadequacies of the Medical Bureau, maintaining a need for greater clinical control before immersion in the pools and implying that Dr Bonamy (Dr Boissarie), despite his rigorous tone, permitted all kinds of misdiagnoses. He also attacked the way pilgrims were treated at the hospitals, with the rudimentary conditions opening up a field for exploitation, arguing that the physicians were mainly concerned not with medical care but rather with the verification of cures. The hospitals at Lourdes did not pretend to offer conventional therapeutic treatment and hence doctors refrained from the administration of medicines.

Typical of this medical insouciance was the way the fictional Bonamy and his like permitted and encouraged immersion in the pools. Zola made much of the dirtiness of the water and, in characteristic style, embellished the horror for his readers, already now accustomed to thinking in a Pasteurian mode:

And the water was not exactly inviting. The Grotto Fathers were afraid that the output of the spring would be insufficient, so in those days they had the water in the pools changed just twice a day. As some hundred patients passed through the same water, you can imagine what a horrible slop it was at the end. There was everything in it: threads of blood, sloughed-off skin, scabs, bits of cloth and bandage, an abominable soup of ills . . . the miracle was that anyone emerged alive from this human slime.[58]

So while Picard drank this infected water as Mary's gift, Zola led the assault later taken up by others who tried to shut down the shrine on hygienic grounds.

For Catholics, all Zola's views thereafter were contaminated by his attack on Lourdes.[59] He became an emblem of the satanic nature of anti-clericalism (see illus. 75). Devotees saw nothing to identify with in his depiction of the shrine, which they considered an inappropriate

75. *'Echos infernaux'*, Le Pèlerin, *2 September 1894*
Two devils, one carrying Zola's Lourdes, *look at the crowds before the Grotto and wonder why their attempts to undermine the shrine have met with so little success*

application of a naturalist literary template to entirely different and spiritual phenomena. His defence of Dreyfus in 1898 in the press was seen not as an idealistic mission to uphold the Rights of Man and revise an unjust verdict, but rather as an intemperate desire to besmirch the military by defending a Jewish traitor. In their eyes his campaign for Dreyfus was another betrayal similar to the one he had perpetrated against Lourdes.[60]

The massive success of the novel suggests that, despite his many detractors, Zola and his vision of Lourdes had somehow triumphed. Certainly no one can deny the impact of the work, especially on the shrine and its officials, who thereafter viewed other famous, non-Catholic visitors with suspicion. But on another level the novel was a failure: it did not convince believers that they had been duped or that their faith was an anachronism. Nor did it have the effect on the literary milieu that Zola had sought. For example, despite all his misgivings, Huysmans in *Les Foules de Lourdes* (1906) utterly rejected Zola's naturalist vision and was astounded and moved by the spirituality of Lourdes, by the extraordinary mixture of horror and grace he saw there:

> It must be confessed that this hospital is at once a bodily hell and a spiritual paradise. Nowhere have I seen such appalling illnesses, so much charity and so much good grace. From the point of view of human mercy, Lourdes is a wonder; there, more than anywhere else, you see the Gospels put into practice.[61]

The Debate

In the short term Zola's novel perpetuated and intensified the polemic between the two sides, with Boissarie replying by organizing a conference at the Cercle de Luxembourg, to which he brought several *malades* cured at the sanctuary. The auditorium was packed; on the dais stood 'these simple persons, their faces modest, almost fearful, often very poorly dressed; you realize at once that this is something serious, which has nothing to do with theatre or staging'.[62] Despite this disclaimer, Boissarie's aim was to reach a broader public and to display God's works to the disbelieving world. In sum, the move denoted the seriousness of the counter-assault, and the willingness to take on Zola on his home turf.

Boissarie had tried to keep the moral high ground, but had made a dangerous bargain with Zola by enabling him to enter the Medical Bureau in the first place: 'How could I interrogate women and young girls before the novelist and his court of journalists? How could I lay bare their infirmities?'[63] But, of course, he had done precisely that, violating professional confidence in his vain attempt to convert the novelist. He paid a heavy price, for Zola had been unconvinced and argued instead for an adjudicatory commission elected by universal suffrage, and including the mayor, councillors and functionaries complete with a new 'exhibition hall of the sick'. Like many Catholic physicians, Boissarie was shocked by the suggestion of this indiscreet exhibition, wishing to maintain such discussions within a clinical context.

However, by presenting the *malades* to his Paris conference, Boissarie tottered even closer to the moral precipice. Although he had received the permission of the patients concerned, they were none the less there on show as part of his desire to cultivate a 'public' for his cause (see illus. 76). In an image showing the Virgin of Lourdes at the apex, Boissarie stood beside his *miraculés* before an adoring throng, some so excited that they leaped uncontrollably from their chairs. He retold the story of Clémentine Trouvé and her diseased foot and of Marie Lebranchu and her recovery from her lung condition, but reserved the full force of his dramatic talents for the character of Elise Rouquet. After reading out the novel's description of her lupus, he asked the real person, Marie Lemarchand, to stand up and face the audience: 'The poor little woman obeyed, and, instead of the "face of a dog with a slice taken out of it, a sort of gaping hole from which flowed a greenish purulence", etc., there stood the pale figure of a young woman, ideally beautiful beneath her black clothes.'[64] Marie Lemarchand claimed not to know of the horrid description of her illness and began to cry, while Boissarie, famous for his coldness, also began to weep. The physician reportedly felt strongly about the injury done to this young woman, and to all believers whose hopes Zola sought to destroy. His polemic contrasted the novelist's moral pitilessness and the simple, pious beauty of Lemarchand's ignorant soul:

76. The presentation of Dr Boissarie, Le Pèlerin, *9 December 1894*

Yes, Monsieur Zola . . . here is Marie Lemarchand! She is cured and she is beautiful in our sight. Yet there is a greater beauty in her that you did not see, could not guess at, a beauty of which you had not the least notion . . . And that is – her soul! You dwelt on her wounds, but one thing you forgot: the poor child worked – worked so hard! – to feed her mother and father. She was the eldest of five children and their only support . . . Forgot? It never so much as occurred to you to seek out this inner beauty![65]

Boissarie used the same dramatic style as Zola to carry his point, angry no doubt that the author had impugned both his clinical rigour and the faith of the poor. Both sides faced each other like distorting mirrors, reflecting back an idealism increasingly betrayed by bitterness. If Zola saw himself as the righteous unmasker of miraculous fraud, then Boissarie was the knight who defended the weak against the republican establishment.

Zola's book created a sense among Catholics of conspiratorial persecution. One undated letter to Boissarie from a certain Pierre Lauras in Paris warned the physician of an imminent subterfuge to be perpetrated by Dr Ballet, one of the leading Parisian alienists. Lauras had apparently heard from a student in Ballet's clinic that the great physician intended to place a hospital record card on a patient, claiming an organic paraplegia, knowing full well that the young woman from Calvados was afflicted by nothing more than an hysterical coxalgia.[66] He would then denounce her 'cure' to the world, if her pilgrimage was successful. The story – it is uncertain whether or not it was true – reinforced the Catholic view of anti-clerical duplicity and cruelty.

While anti-clericals felt they shared nothing with their religious opponents and *vice versa*, they had in common the breaking of professional confidences, the public display of patients, and an imposing, even authoritarian attitude. Like Charcot, Boissarie was not a distant clinician but an 'homme de combat', in his case seeking greater acknowledgement of the miraculous by initiating a campaign for episcopal recognition of cures. While Laurence's episcopal declaration confirmed the first series of miracles in 1862, the next three and a half decades brought not a single official verification, despite the multitude of healing narratives.[67] The movement to change this state of affairs developed ostensibly to commemorate the fiftieth anniversary of Bernadette's apparitions, but larger political issues infused the campaign.[68] For Boissarie had begun to work in earnest for this goal as early as 1901, the year of legislation against unauthorized Catholic religious orders in France executed under Emile Combes's anti-clerical ministry. To Leo XIII, Boissarie reportedly remarked, 'I have long desired to obtain for the Medical Bureau of Lourdes the blessing and encouragement of your Holiness', and he was subsequently given permission to proceed.[69]

Boissarie's communications with the papal emissary Dr Lapponi show how this campaign was officially orchestrated at the moment when the 1801 Concordat between Napoleon and the papacy – which had conferred state recognition, funds and property on the Church in exchange for giving the government the right to nominate bishops

– was being torn asunder. In response to the separation of Church and state in 1905, the Church sought to demonstrate God's power by focusing on the miracles of Lourdes, an emphasis perhaps heightened by the fact that the new bishop of Tarbes and Lourdes, Mgr Schoepfer, was having to struggle to keep the shrine going after the confiscation of much of its land and property.[70] After lengthy inquiries among bishoprics across Catholic Europe, but especially in France, twenty-four cures that took place between 1875 and 1905 were deemed miraculous, and another nine between 1905 and 1911. In sum, this process produced thirty-three of the sixty-five of the miracles recorded to date, demonstrating the perceived need to prove to the world the reality of such extraordinary events in the midst of trying political circumstances.

Remarkable cures that defied the arguments of the *libres-penseurs* flooded in, the most famous that of a labourer named Pierre de Rudder who lived on an aristocratic estate in Jabbeke, in the Flemish part of Belgium. When helping two men clear a fallen tree in 1868, the trunk had fallen on his leg and pulverized it. Two bones were broken and a gangrenous wound formed at the opening of the fracture, while another ulceration formed at the back. So bad did the condition become that one physician took out a bone fragment from the diseased tissues, an unhelpful expedient that only confirmed that a three-centimetre gap separated the unset bones from one another. After a year in bed with horrible pain, de Rudder limped on crutches, defying the advice of his many physicians who insisted that the only course left was amputation.

Catholic believers appreciated this story because of its extensive documentation and the morality tale that accompanied it. Vicomte de Bus, the owner of the estate, charitably paid de Rudder's medical expenses and supported his family but, as a liberal anti-cleric of atheistic bent, blocked his pilgrimage to Oostakker, near Gand, where there was a replica of the Grotto. It was only when his nephew inherited some property that the crippled man was able to make his journey.

In this instance the Church had a good case, because, just before he left, de Rudder was examined once again by various physicians, and his horrible deformity was witnessed both by the young *châtelaine* and another woman who bandaged his leg. Others testified to the purulence of the wound, while those unfortunate enough to share his railway compartment on the way to the shrine were appalled by the odour. His state was even remarked upon by the omnibus driver, a big man who helped him at the pilgrimage site.

De Rudder, unable to walk around the Grotto three times as he had planned for his penitential exercise, instead only pleaded with Notre-Dame de Lourdes to enable him to work: 'He felt himself shaken, agitated, overwhelmed; he was beside himself, as it were.'[71] And, without knowing how or why, he got up and went to kneel before the statue of the Virgin. His wife fainted when she saw him walk without difficulty and, to make sure she was seeing straight, sought the testimony of the Marquise de Courtebourne, who confirmed the extraordinary result. The wounds had disappeared, the bones were rejoined, and, above all, the two legs were the same length, especially significant because of the piece of bone removed and the distance confirmed between the fragments.

Like all 'great' cures, de Rudder's experience moved his neighbours: between 1,500 of the 2,000 inhabitants of Jabbeke came to church to celebrate a novena of masses, and no one, it was claimed, remained an unbeliever. De Rudder himself was a model of piety thereafter. The Church was fortunate to have a Belgian physician who in 1892 began an inquiry into the events while the major participants were still alive, a process central to de Rudder's later designation as a *miraculé* in 1908. In this instance the inquiry went even further than usual, with 'Dr Van Hoestenberghe, the very man whom the miracle had converted to the supernatural', intent on examining the bones of de Rudder's legs after he died in 1898.[72] The exhumation revealed that his legs were of the same length, the only trace of long invalidity being the line of fracture.

For the apologists of the shrine, de Rudder's cure was the closest to a medieval tale, a distant relation of stories of amputated limbs that re-emerged whole and extended. It was the only one of its kind, for the repair of the bones seemed to go beyond natural law. Almost like relics, the bones are held at Lourdes in a glass case next to the Medical Bureau, and bronze replicas are proudly displayed in the museum, supplying the necessary *physical* proof that Zola had always insisted upon. Of all the many marvels that Lourdes produced, de Rudder's cure shows the limits of historical explanation: while so many other healings *could* be the result of misdiagnosis – even in the apparently 'certain' realm of cancer, tuberculosis or paralysis – the case of de Rudder dismays and perplexes. Even if the bones in the glass case were somehow the result of a complicated fraud, de Rudder still walked on his shattered leg after years of incapacity and the complete failure of everything medicine had to offer (see illus. 77).

77. *Pierre de Rudder,* Le Pèlerin, *13 July 1893*

Another famous case concerned Mme Rouchel, a fifty-year-old woman whose face was virtually eaten away by tubercular lupus. Here, as always, the descriptions of her martyrdom were hideously detailed. The nose, lips and interior of her mouth were affected, creating holes in her palate and right cheek. She was, by her own admission, a horror to behold, and her wounds also gave off a foul-smelling suppuration. Her life became unbearable, both for herself and her family, and, although a believer, she was in such despair that she thought of suicide. She went on pilgrimage to Lourdes, hoping for a cure, and on the second day hid herself in the Basilica of the Rosary, waiting for the Eucharist. As Georges Bertrin, one of the great defenders of the shrine, tells it, the bishop of Saint-Dié came in the church carrying the monstrance after the procession, and Mme Rouchel felt her protective bandage fall away on to her book of prayers.[73] After readjusting the material, she found it fell off again while drinking from the taps near the Grotto. When she returned to the Hôpital des Sept Douleurs, one of the nursing sisters saw the transformation in her face, and she went off to the Medical Bureau at the behest of the bishop.

The first crippled, the second as deformed as a leper – both give some sense of the transformations that were claimed for the power of Notre-Dame de Lourdes. Both had sought extensive medical treatment, had given up hope and were instantaneously cured. De Rudder became especially famous because his transformation was so spectacular and because, as one of the rare men to be cured, he was less prone to being labelled an hysteric. The fact that he went to a facsimile of the Grotto rather than to the Grotto itself made his cure even more significant. The Virgin intervened without the crowds, the fountain or the holy site, detaching his cure from suggestion and all animistic associations at the same time that it confirmed the efficacy of prayer. Mme Rouchel's case was as significant for the way long suffering and despair ended in immediate relief. Although increasingly rare, such occurrences were frequent enough to make believers confident, if not serene; they defied the general materialist flow of nineteenth-century educated opinion, and provided material for intellectuals increasingly interested in varieties of religious experience.

Opponents of the shrine were far from being convinced by such claims. Apart from the proponents of suggestion, Lourdes was also subject to assault by hygienists, another group of anti-clerical sceptics with science on their side. While the former concentrated on the dangerous hypnotic effect of the crowds and religious belief, the latter focused on the horrors of uncleanliness, the dirtiness of the bathing pools and the unsanitary conditions in the trains and hospitals. The standard-bearer in this campaign was Jean de Bonnefon, who sent out letters to over 11,000 physicians, many of whom agreed that both the water and the long train journeys were unhygienic. These arguments showed the growing belief in public health more generally and signalled the rising credibility of microbiological reasoning.[74] Although hygienists had struggled for decades to ensure clean water supplies, the 'Pasteurian revolution' from the 1870s gave them a scientific basis for their sometimes draconian struggles against the pervasiveness of dangerous microbes.

Bonnefon sought to stamp out the 'pious audacities' of men like Picard through a pamphlet that mingled hygienic arguments with political condemnation, wheeling out the most scurrilous anti-clerical stereotypes: Lourdes was the worst sort of confidence trick, the revenge of the merchants in the Temple, a place where priests and nuns were intimate, and nuns conducted lesbian affairs.[75] He saw the shrine as a dangerous site of right-wing politics and a propagandistic centre of the Church militant, a case he undermined by the insulting images he included from the satirical *L'Assiette au beurre*. The worst made it clear that the Assumptionist press had no monopoly on distasteful venom and combined a virulent anti-clericalism with an equally poisonous anti-Semitism, showing, for example, a greedy Jew selling objects of piety and complaining that his business could not compete with that of an equally avaricious priest (see illus. 78).

The pamphlet argued that Boissarie, rather than being a therapist, was nothing more than 'the miracle-counter in the great Lourdes bazaar'.[76] The shrine was 'a ghetto, almost a charnel house',[77] a place of disorder and of death that the officials sought to conceal: 'When death passes and chooses a victim among the pilgrims driven here like sheep, the corpse is urgently disposed of, to avoid frightening the living during this triumphant pilgrimage.'[78] Physical infestation was linked to a vision of moral contamination, made all the more powerful by the view of a hidden, secretive world of clerical conspiracy and deception.

However, the doctors whose letters Bonnefon excerpted were not all as doctrinaire or as sanctimonious as he, one even concluding: 'In short, in my opinion, Lourdes is no more dangerous than a theatre or a race-course.'[79] This opinion, which reflected rather more honestly on the hygienic conditions in other public places in France, was

78. 'Well, Father Abraham, is business good?' 'Not as good as yours, M'sieur l'abbé!': illustration for L'Assiette au beurre *reproduced in 'Faut-il fermer Lourdes?',* Les Paroles françaises et romaines, *1906*

relatively rare. Keen to agree with Charcot and with the Parisian medical elite, most believed Lourdes might benefit people with 'functional' disorders, but rejected any therapeutic role for the weak and chronically ill who might simply expire in the icy water. Lourdes was seen as 'a Mecca for cholera',[80] the train journey a bouillon for breeding tuberculosis. The sanctuary was the site *par excellence* of infection: 'If I wished you harm, I would advise you to take a bath in this foul, stagnant water.'[81] Physicians suggested that Lourdes be disinfected by fire, a cleansing holocaust that others seconded by calling for a pasteurization at 120 degrees.

In this dispute there seemed little idealism and few ideas of any great merit, just a bitter repartee in the wake of the larger struggle over the separation of Church and state; ultimately it reached a stalemate and the campaign to close Lourdes lost momentum. Boissarie, certainly, was no more original in his formulations than the man he opposed, convinced that the assault was a conspiracy of the worst sort instigated by Protestants, Jews and republican politicians. He replied that many of the critics had never been to Lourdes, in contrast to the 300 physicians who attended the bureau each year, among whom were 'doctors who were faculty professors, hospital doctors and members of the Académie', as well as many visitors from abroad.[82] He never even sought to justify his colleagues' lack of therapeutic intervention because, like the clerics and the *malades*, he saw the sanctuary as a spiritual rather than a medical centre. Medical partisans of the Grotto repeatedly maintained that, contrary to Bonnefon's assertions, Lourdes was very far from a charnel house. Only twenty *malades* had died since records of the national pilgrimage had begun, fewer, it was argued, than in the wards of the Paris hospitals.[83] Despite such claims, Bonnefon was not the first – nor the last – to criticize the sanctuary for its clinical insouciance, an attitude of resignation that permitted what he saw as the maintenance of sub-standard conditions in the hospitals and in the pools.

Lourdes and the Disintegration of Positivism

The polemic masked a changing intellectual climate, with the likes of Bonnefon obscuring a growing amount of common ground between the two sides.[84] To begin with, there were a substantial number of Catholic doctors who had never accepted the dogmatic assertions of the Parisian medical establishment and had sent patients to Lourdes long before Charcot embraced the practice. Such people did not believe that there was a necessary and inevitable conflict between their healing art and miraculous intervention. Physicians in rural France often worked side by side with sisters from nursing orders, jointly providing medical expertise and the solace of religion.[85]

A substantial number of physicians, therefore, were open to accepting the benefits of pilgrimage, even if there remained an area of dispute about why such practices were sometimes effective. While the Catholic doctors could countenance the possibility of supernatural intervention, secular medical men who engaged in the study of the 'unconscious' were obliged to construct alternative explanations for the power of religious belief on bodily states that the healings at Lourdes forced to their attention. Charcot's 'La Foi qui guérit' noted cures for a host of disorders – including ulcers, tumours and fevers – that he had not previously considered to be hysterical in origin. They should, therefore, have been impervious to the suggestive forces thought to be operating in places like Lourdes.

Rather than reconsidering his idea of hysteria, however, he merely extended it. Thus, while Boissarie attacked the idea that Lourdes operated purely through the effects of suggestion on hysterics by pointing to cures of 'organic' illness, Charcot concluded that such conditions could be hysterical in origin, the proof being that Lourdes had an effect on them. While seen by Catholic opponents as nothing more than a more subtle, and therefore more dangerous, elaboration of the hysteria hypothesis that denied supernatural intervention, Charcot's reorientation at least recognized the limits of his therapies, if not of his diagnoses. In this conclusion he was seconded by Hippolyte Bernheim, a pioneer in hypnotherapy from the Nancy School in eastern France, whose work influenced Freud. In contrast to Charcot, Bernheim argued that suggestion worked on many kinds of conditions, even such disorders as arthritis. And, while he still believed that '*Suggestion does not kill microbes, it does not certify tubercles*, it does not heal the round stomach ulcer'[86] (no doubt an indirect assault on Boissarie and the Medical Bureau), he none the less also recognized the limits to his clinical practice and emphasized the power of religious faith, the most potent of all suggestions: 'Faith moves mountains, faith performs miracles, because faith is blind, because it does not reason, because it suppresses control and impresses itself directly upon the imagination, without moderating second thoughts.'[87] So strong was faith, and so limited medical authority in comparison, that Dumontpallier, another eminent medical hypnotist in the capital, described the case of a woman with an hysterical paralysis who went to Lourdes precisely because she resisted the hypnotic treatments offered by her physicians, Drs Jules and Pierre Janet, the latter a major figure in French psychoanalysis.[88]

Such findings led some physicians like Félix Régnault to ethnology.

He went to Paray-le-Monial for the celebration of the bicentenary of Marguerite-Marie Alacoque's visions of the Sacred Heart between 1673 and 1675, journeyed to Kalighat (Calcutta), and argued for the 'marked superiority' of Lourdes as a healing shrine. Sensitive to cultural difference, he recognized the crowds' often rural and provincial origin and noted how they 'chant the hymns in their patois, which is obviously more suggestive for them than the national language'. Through native dialect, the crowds were enthused by poetry, music and the Grotto's illuminations. He asked, almost enviously, 'What medical hypnotist can produce a stage set like this', especially when the religious ecstatics – with arms outstretched and spread out on the ground in the shape of the cross – heightened the emotional tension.[89] Régnault reiterated a view of suggestion, but one that was far more respectful. The confrontation with Lourdes and 'faith healing' forced positivist physicians to rethink their position and, by increasingly acknowledging the pragmatic therapeutic effects of religion, rendered the idea of suggestion elastic beyond definition.

Others went even further and sought a new framework for understanding such phenomena in the twentieth century. Inspired by A. T. and F. Myers's *Mind-cure, Faith-cure and the Miracles of Lourdes* (1903), Marcel Magnin argued that the occurrences at Lourdes could not be judged as suggestion or auto-suggestion in the clinical sense, for the forces unleashed were too powerful to be dismissed in this way.[90] Instead, he sought a greater appreciation of the 'subliminal unconscious', a force as powerful as a mediumic trance.[91] He used the famous case of Gabriel Gargam, a man injured in a train accident, crippled and physically destroyed for years, and later radically cured at Lourdes. Although one of the most famous cures of the late century, Gargam never became a *miraculé* because of a lingering weakness in the back. He none the less became a symbol of the Grotto's therapeutic possibilities, as he popularized the shrine and became a dedicated *hospitalier* who worked in the pools.[92] Magnin carefully analysed Gargam's narrative, paying attention to the moment when he took communion at the Grotto. Suddenly, the young man who did not believe in miracles felt an irresistible yearning to pray and was soon stifled by sobs. For apologists, Gargam's lack of religious feeling was proof that suggestion had played no role and that the miraculous had intervened. Magnin insisted that natural causes were at work, that

Gargam had been in touch with his 'subliminal unconscious': 'In the deepest layers of his mind a silent activity had been accomplished, unknown to normal consciousness, and the physiological metamorphosis had to be complete before the new mentality could erupt into the supraliminal consciousness.'[93] Thus, although a vague psychophysiological mechanism – more than suggestion, but not divine – was posited to account for the cure, Lourdes and some form of religious sentiment were none the less recognized as the means to attain it.

Catholic apologists, however, responded with increasing confidence to such sophisticated critics. For them, Gargam's case showed how Régnault was wrong, that faith in the cure was not essential to cure itself. Jean de Beaucorps explained how pilgrims made an essential distinction that lay medical men could not appreciate:

> [their] only blind absolute faith . . . is the faith they have in the existence of God and the revealed truths. But they are [also] said to have a blind faith that they will be cured, and this neither their consciences nor their religious learning permit. They may, and they do, believe that God can cure them; but they must not, and, without exception, they do not believe that God will necessarily cure them, that they will, in the terms reported by Charcot, be 'unfailingly', or as, Bernheim puts it, 'certainly' cured.[94]

Others, like Henry Berteaux in 1895, even mocked anti-clericals for wanting miracles that defied nature in a manner that mimicked the stories of the Middle Ages and early-modern period. Lourdes would not supply examples of amputated limbs that regenerated, but rather the '*instantaneous* fusion of the two bone fragments of a purulent tibia, the no less instantaneous and complete cure of suppurating osseous tuberculosis and of pulmonary cavities'.[95] In his view, physical transformations could not be attributed to 'imagination or willpower or a sufficiently powerful mediating force', since such an argument contravened scientific principles. Scars and vestiges of treatment testified to the illness's disappearance, hence demonstrating that miracles were not a transgression of natural law, but rather 'a planned divergence, freely willed from the usual functioning of the universe; a phenomenon discernible outside the grasp of science because it is independent of secondary causes, though consistent with the higher idea of order and purpose'.[96]

In advancing this idea, Berteaux showed he believed in the conservation of energy and of mass, but suggested that Helmholtz's law, which stated that no energy was lost in the manifold changes that nature undergoes, might not necessarily apply in the case of curing phenomena. Experimental evidence normally proved that chemical actions produced in the organic world could be accounted for by examining the products of metabolic processes, but nothing indicated their absolute conservation.[97] In line with the scientific and philosophical speculation of his era, he believed in an 'edge of contingency' and argued for placing the miraculous more comfortably within the natural order.[98] Catholics, Berteaux insisted, did not pray to change the divine plan but rather 'to obtain something whose achievement is, at this level, conditional on prayer'.[99] In this view, God does not interrupt general laws but executes them, by responding to the efficacy of prayer. With such subtle arguments, Berteaux, like Boissarie, sought to use science to press the case for the miraculous.

Thus, both sides in the debate used science, at the same time that both sides recognized science's limitations. Between them stood a middle ground that, in the case of Lourdes, was exemplified by Dr Noriogof's preoccupation with a 'physiological magnetism' defined as the 'occult influence of man on his fellows and, by extension, on other beings'.[100] This force explained the power of the 'effluvia emanated by a multitude in a state of exaltation, as it presses forward . . . before the pools of Lourdes' with one unifying thought: 'Lord, heal our sick!' He maintained that all the rays united into one enormous energy field that enveloped the sick person and brought healing. He went even further when he suggested that it was not only the crowd that exercised this magnetic influence, but the Grotto and the water itself: 'The water is magnetized by the laying on of hands and the action of breath and eyes', healing gestures that mimicked the action of priests during baptism.[101] In order to be cured, the subject had to be a *sensitif*, a trait that denoted a special aptitude or sensibility – 'magnetic perceptivity'. Like his medical colleagues, he believed that hysterics were highly susceptible to the curative effects of the shrine, and that others with functional disorders might also find significant improvement.

These theories gained greater credibility as the century turned, and were widely publicized by the psychiatrist Hippolyte Baraduc, who, in a course given at the School of Medicine in Paris in 1904/5, described the 'forces' that enveloped the Grotto. For Baraduc, they were intermediate entities between the unknowable supernatural and knowable realm of visible physical dimension. Like Noriogof, he was concerned to demonstrate their reality through photographic plates doubly wrapped against sunlight in radiographic papers. Against all expectation, he maintained that all the plates showed the shape of the baths, 'a burning trace of the passage of the Holy Sacrament', and a 'globular form', an independent entity that went out to greet the *malades* in procession.[102] He argued that cure did not come from suggestion, auto-suggestion or the subliminal self, but from this exterior force attracted to the enormous energy produced by supplicating individuals. So intrigued was he, that he asked for a laboratory to conduct experiments to observe the forces exchanged between heaven and the imploring earth.

Received with varying degrees of belief and derision, such hypotheses exemplified the rise of the 'revolt against science', of philosophical contingency and of pragmatism that William James's *Varieties of Religious Experience* (1902) made famous. The Harvard philosopher investigated the overwhelming impact of religious experience and was uninterested in its origins or causes, taking instead a 'pragmatic' approach to such phenomena. Despite the more respectful tone of such investigators, for a man like Boissarie, who died in 1919, their ideas expressed their persistent and perverse unwillingness to admit the role of the supernatural. He combated these newer formulations with the same ferocity as the earlier ones, seeing them as nothing more than new 'occult' theories that required opposition. In contrast, for those engaged in the new inquiries, the healing phenomena of Lourdes were significant in a process of reorientation in which the links between mind and body were irrevocably changed.

Lourdes survived the onslaught of positivism even though it had to face the genius of Emile Zola and the 'enlightened' public who avidly accepted his account of the shrine. The magnitude of his assault and the defensive stance that it generated among such men as Boissarie suggest that the sanctuary was fighting a rearguard action against the 'new' ideas of the impending twentieth century. In fact, it was Zola who was losing ground, as his naturalistic approach declined in the face of new forms of literature preoccupied with the self, spirituality and identity. Even the scientists whom he used as authorities were beginning to change their views on similar questions. Indeed, the transformations in literature, science and philosophy were all of a piece. The struggles of the 1860s, 1870s and 1880s to dethrone superstition and magic – manifesting itself even in religious studies, as exemplified by the works of men as different as Renan and Cros – were almost everywhere superseded by intellectual currents preoccupied with understanding the significance of all kinds of religious, spiritual and occult experience.

Such an intellectual shift made Lourdes an envied object of study, not a quarry to be hunted down and destroyed as a man like Bonnefon desired. Yet this intellectual interest, even approval, probably meant little to the faithful, and was indeed only half-consciously noticed by the shrine's officials, who instead remained ambivalent to the growing authority of those medical men they had invited into their midst. Boissarie's rigour underpinned the miraculous at Lourdes at the same time that his presence demonstrated that religious faith unaided was no longer enough to convince the world. In an age of anti-clericalism, when science and religion were deemed antithetical to one another, Lourdes generated an unusual relationship between them. Both gave some ground, and neither remained untouched by the other. But from the perspective of the shrine this accommodation was perhaps a Mephistophelean bargain. For by continuing to limit the domain of the supernatural, science had the effect of undermining the judgements of Catholic believers. The subjective assessments of pilgrims, as well as the empirical evaluations of relatives, neighbours and friends, became of less value than those of medical experts.

Both sides in the debate sought to further an understanding of the relationship between mind and body. And although they took opposing sides to the question, they were both fascinated by the same object, the hysterical or suffering woman. They provide an almost comforting vision of curative phenomena as a suggestion, a seemingly rational explanation for bodily transformations that could not otherwise be understood. But although they pioneered new forms of psychotherapy and grew increasingly open to the examination of phenomena beyond their positivist purview, they none the less remained strangely uninterested in the 'self'. Their scientific and cultural instincts all pushed them to underestimate the women they examined; the word hysteria dismissed as much as it explained. Like the mechanism of suggestion, hysteria became a catch-all phrase that explained everything and nothing all at once, pinning upon the subject the taint of pathology or susceptibility.

For the women (and sometimes men) under discussion were religious, as opposed to hysterical. They had a worldview that focused unflinchingly on spiritual and physical pain, and it is perhaps shocking to contemporary sensibilities precisely because it celebrated suffering. This dolourism was one of the defining features of the pilgrimage movement, with organizers speaking about *nos chers malades*, a vision of the sick that prized their vulnerability but also strangely patronized them. As much as their anti-clerical counterparts, the clergy who ran this movement could not hope to appreciate entirely the dilemmas that such women faced. Sometimes they might advocate the journey to Lourdes when all else seemed to fail. They did not, perhaps, realize that the desire to visit the Grotto was also potentially a means of escaping from priestly influence. For at Lourdes such women were able to encounter Mary and Jesus sometimes without mediation, to use the imaginative resources that their religious universe afforded without recourse to the hierarchy. In both therapeutic and in religious terms, therefore, Lourdes offered unique possibilities.

Epilogue

Bernadette Soubirous's apparitions at the Grotto of Massabieille and the development of the shrine at Lourdes followed in a long tradition of the miraculous in the Pyrenees. At the same time these extraordinary phenomena revealed something particular about the religious aspirations of the nineteenth century. The story of Lourdes demonstrates how the religion of the rural poor and the tale of a shepherdess in a grotto was eagerly embraced by both laity and clergy, rural and urban. They romanticized and sentimentalized its details, contributed to the construction of the sanctuary, embarked on massive pilgrimages and made Lourdes the best-known shrine in modern Christendom.

The history of the shrine shows the mingling of different currents of Catholic belief and also offers a rare glimpse of a France normally hidden from view. For the history of the nineteenth century is still seen as the inevitable triumph of the republican ethos of secularization; even today historians are influenced by a stripped-down version of the model of religious belief and political modernization associated with the German sociologist Max Weber. With notable and growing exceptions, modern history has been understood as a process of 'disenchantment' in which school, ballot box and barracks ultimately triumph over superstition and backwoods provincialism, with peasant belief studied only to see the process of its eradication.[1] In such an overarching scheme, the apparitions at Lourdes seem nothing more than a 'survival', a lingering cultural manifestation of a remote, impoverished and illiterate world. In this guise the development of the sanctuary is nothing more than an example of 'revival', of a mass, 'modernized' form of piety facilitated by package pilgrimage, a view that reduces the phenomenon to a form of right-wing leisure activity and ignores the widespread appeal of its devotional novelty and the unique, psychological dimensions of nineteenth-century Marianism.

This view is wrong, for it was the living and evolving religious tradition of the early cultists of Lourdes that stimulated the world's imagination and transformed the story of their apparitions into the model for contemporary Marian pilgrimage. Their judgement of the miraculous was hardly based on some naïve misunderstanding, or the need to find solace in the supernatural to compensate for the miseries of their daily life. Certainly, the Lourdais *were* comforted by their conviction that the Virgin had chosen their *bourg* as the site for her appearance, but this sense of blessing was matched by the sophistication of the mythical and legendary apparatus they used to assess Bernadette's experience. French peasants were neither gullible nor superstitious; such pejorative adjectives make more difficult the necessary process of understanding a magical and religious universe as much detached from secularism as it often was from orthodoxy. The beliefs of the Lourdais can best be understood as building on the traditions of older centuries and borrowing from more recent nineteenth-century cultural trends. Dismissing them as 'irrational' explains nothing, and perpetuates a complacent and inaccurate assessment of the 'rationality' of the contemporary era.

Lourdes shows the continued vibrancy of peasant belief and the sustained appeal and evolution of modern Catholicism. The classic stereotype of nineteenth-century Catholicism shows a reactionary and fossilized institution on the defensive, unable to adapt and destined to lose adherents and influence in a changing world. Through Lourdes, however, we can see something of its remarkable resilience and strength, and the shrewd ability of its supporters to build new social and political alliances. The likes of a layman like Veuillot blended a potent brew of populism, militancy and devotional innovation that linked religion to a novel form of politics. Within the episcopate too there were men like Laurence, who seized the new opportunities that changing political alliances offered. In the history of Lourdes it was a churchman, rather than an activist and secularizing prefect, who brought a peripheral and poverty-stricken region into the national mainstream. Laurence, despite his ultramontanist religious sensibility and his natural conservatism, defies the conventional portrait of episcopal reaction.

Young girls and women were central to this story. Girls like Bernadette were seen as appropriate vessels to encounter the divine and women the proper judges of their experiences. Later, pious women of more genteel and educated background joined in supervising and educating the visionary, enhancing their status in the community by their access to the humble but all-important seer. Despite the crucial mediation of such men as Peyramale – who wrote, organized, cajoled, repressed – and Laurence, who worked to overcome all bureaucratic obstacles, women defended the miraculous and forced the men to take account of it. What is astonishing throughout is how little impact male figures of authority actually had, as examining physicians, the police commissioner, the prefect, the imperial prosecutor and many others came up against this resolute phalanx of women believers determined to see the apparitions sanctified. This image of serried ranks of female devotees remained a central feature of Lourdes right up to the First World War. They came in peasant costume, in the humble dress of the poor, with the veils and headdresses of Catholic orders and in the flowing robes of the aristocratic elite. A photograph of the national pilgrimage of 1897 shows a crowd of women (and men too) with umbrellas shielding themselves from the rain, a black-and-white image of a believing multitude in the *fin de siècle* reminiscent of an Impressionist painting (see illus. 79).

Their presence at the shrine was not fortuitous. They came to pay homage to the Virgin and to express their hope for a revitalized, hierarchical and re-Christianized France. In contrast to the egalitarian tendencies of the republic, which in their view broke down local, regional and especially religious networks of charity and devotion, they sought instead a world in which personal connection was paramount. Against a vision of republican citizenship infused by an ethos of anti-clericalism and rationalism,[2] they insisted on the organic links between men and women, between rich and poor, relationships contained under the protective umbrella of Christian fellowship and patronage. Harking back to the Middle Ages, they favoured the chivalry of gentlemen over the vulgarity of republican parvenus, the charity of *grandes dames* over the welfare of a faceless municipality. All of these oppositions idealized a world that did not exist – and never had existed – but it was still the stuff of which their social and cultural dreams were made. They tried to turn these ideals into reality through the priority they placed on intimate relationships, as the stacks of letters between women activists and Assumptionist priests,

79. *'Dimanche soir, la procession sous la pluie', from Anon.,* Pèlerinage national du jubilé de 1897, *1897*

and between nuns and lay women, reveal. At the heart of such encounters was love in its earthly form, sanctified by the work they did in the name of Mary and Jesus.

In pilgrimage, they sought to care for the sick in a way that showed the same psychological focus manifested in their other relationships. They laboured at Lourdes to be like Mary and Jesus, to succour the dying and heal the sick through elaborate rituals of touch, consolation and care. The secular republic lacked the emotional and historical resources to challenge the power of this vision as effectively as it wished, hence, perhaps, its hurried efforts to build new traditions and elevate alternative heroes capable of channelling the public imagination and capturing its loyalties. In these efforts one can see the brief reversal of the traditional pattern of Catholicism constantly reacting defensively to secular incursion.

The resolution of women activists in this movement had little to do with feminism, a largely secular creed associated with the emancipation of women. Studies have shown how unlike the English or American models French feminism was, for activists were largely unconcerned with the political questions – especially suffrage – that so exercised their sisters across the Channel and the Atlantic.[3] To explain why feminism failed to find a wide audience in France, historians focus on the political culture of the early Third Republic, which feared a clerical backlash in the wake of women's suffrage; and on the importance of 'familialism', which placed women's duty as wives and mothers ahead of the rights of individuals.[4] While these explanations touch the truth, apart from a few notable exceptions,[5] they present Catholicism as a set of moribund social values that retarded the forward march of feminism.

In contrast, the experience of women in the history of Lourdes suggests that the calls of feminism went unheeded not because the Church sought to block women's aspirations, but because it was so effective at channelling them in spiritual and practical directions outside the republican mainstream. Simple though it would be to see Catholicism as a monolithic bloc representing paternalist repression, the story is, in fact, very much more complicated. The Church did encourage the subordination of women; at the same time, however, it offered them a world of opportunity and found a means of cultivating their loyalty and energies. The hundreds of thousands of Catholic women in the religious orders, mainly working in nursing and teaching,[6] and the untold legions of lay women active in fundraising and charity,[7] show how comparatively small were the republican initiatives in similar fields.[8] The strength of such activism perhaps explains why even moderate French feminists of the nineteenth century accepted Michelet's view and feared giving women the vote.[9]

Even within the Catholic world, however, the sick, and especially sick women, could be objectified. At Lourdes their designation as 'nos chers malades' highlighted their helpless and victimized status at the same time that it underscored the charitable and compassionate impulses of the helpers. The sick were often expected to fulfil the redemptive role that the strong and healthy had devised for them, and in this respect they seem to parallel the plight of the hysterical subjects in Parisian clinics at the end of the century. They were passive objects of the clinicians' gaze rather than suffering individuals actively seeking relief. The *mémoires* of Lourdes remove one layer of that abstraction and allow the *malades* – often precisely the sort of people that doctors failed to take seriously – to testify to their emotional and physical quest for relief. In this they escaped their physicians' ministrations as well as the well-meaning condescension of other Catholic women and male clerics.

At first glance the shrine seems a strange place to find a commitment to an active, engaged 'self', since so much of nineteenth-century Catholic sensibility, especially among women, depended on an ethos of resignation. It is even stranger that such a commitment required a rejection of the secular world and its ideology of individualism. None the less, what is remarkable about the cured individuals of Lourdes is how, despite personal histories of obedience and spiritual submission, they often circumvented both medical and priestly authority in their efforts to make personal contact with the divine. Perhaps it is the strangest paradox of all that, at Lourdes, the full realization of 'self' came only through its surrender. This abandonment was made possible through a richly imaginative relationship with the Mother of God and the Queen of Heaven, the ministering, merciful but also firm maternal presence that commanded and consoled. Jesus inhabited their religious universe also, as vulnerable humanity and as miracle worker.

As the experience of cure enabled the sick to discover a new sense of 'self', so lay and religious helpers alike went on similar voyages of self-discovery when they became involved in the movement. Spiritual direction released feelings of jealousy, anger and bitterness, as well as self-doubt and religious torment. Despite the venting of the entire range of negative emotions, the process also revealed the capacity for love. Through the anguish of such intense relationships, women, and sometimes men, found spiritual and personal serenity, and the strength to undertake new projects. Whether it was the women of Notre-Dame de Salut, Père Pernet or the Petites-Sœurs, the meticulous, even sometimes morbid attention to issues of conscience, emotion and spirituality released tremendous energy.

Lourdes would seem to cast the debate between science and religion as a battle between irredeemable opposites. And yet, at the very moment that science seemed supreme, intellectuals and physicians appeared at the shrine to question their investigative techniques, therapeutic procedures and the philosophical foundations of their work. On the whole they were not reconverted, but they were impressed, moved and forced to take account of what they saw. Alexis Carrel came as a physician to Lourdes in 1902, tending a patient, Marie Bailly, with a tubercular peritonitis, and wrote later of her cure, even though at the time he refused to confirm it for Boissarie. So appalled were his secular colleagues by his 'betrayal' that he emigrated to America, earning there one of France's first Nobel prizes in 1912 for his work in suturing blood vessels.[10] Although condemned for his outspoken testimony concerning the reality of this cure, he was none the less typical of many in his generation. For him, part of his scientific mission was a willingness to entertain new possibilities, to question the reigning positivism of the previous generation.

In larger terms, scientists taking such intermediate positions and investigating religious, magical and spiritualist experiences were central to developing notions of the unconscious and the discipline of psychoanalysis. By stripping away clerics and confessions and disposing of religious belief in favour of a therapeutic relationship and the investigation of fantasy, psychoanalysis seems to typify the secular vision of the twentieth century. And yet, psychoanalysis is built on religious foundations, on the nineteenth-century attempt to reinterpret the physical and psychological dimensions of the religious imagination.[11] Charcot's evocation of hysteria was indebted to early-modern models of religious ecstasy and iconography.[12] Anti-clerical physicians examined nineteenth-century stigmatics and constructed the pathological lexicon of hysteria out of the bodily manifestations of spiritual rapture and suffering,[13] while founding researches in psychoanalysis centred on the mystical preoccupations of 'Madeleine Lebouc', the devoutedly Catholic subject of Pierre Janet.[14] While Vienna and other European cities contributed a well-known and distinctive blend of scientific and religious preoccupations to the developing study of the 'self', the Catholic and anti-clerical alignments of France offered their own particular set of traditions.

Concentration on the anti-clerical/clerical divide at the end of the nineteenth century in France tends to obscure the close and enduring relationship between Catholicism and psychoanalysis specifically in France, and between religion and science more generally. This is not to suggest that the passions generated by the political struggle were unimportant. Every programme of state 'persecution' brought more crowds to the Grotto, the first years of the anti-clerical laws between 1878 and 1881 coinciding with the consolidation of the special mission of pilgrimage to heal the sick. The Dreyfus Affair badly damaged attempts to reconcile Catholics with the republic and encouraged the Assumptionist leadership to intensify its dissident and anti-Semitic activities. Although the order was expelled for plotting against the republic in 1900, the right-wing, militant leadership of the pilgrimage movement survived in new forms. The Hospitalités harboured the Action Française, famous for its anti-Semitic, monarchist, some would say even proto-fascist creed. The radicalism and elitism of many of its members remained a potent force until the First World War and beyond, causing tensions between the Hospitalités and the direction of Notre-Dame de Salut.[15] The Vatican proscribed the Action Française in 1926 after years of disquiet,[16] and the Hospitalités apparently acquiesced in the ban. However, there seems little doubt that they remained havens for right-wing sentiment for years after.[17]

On the heels of the Assumptionists' expulsion came the anti-clerical laws that dissolved congregations, closed Catholic schools and finally separated Church and state in 1905, ending over a hundred years of concordatory regime. As far as Lourdes was concerned, the results were at first glance disastrous. From 1903 the Garaison Fathers were no longer able to live in community and those who ministered to pilgrims had to do so as secular clergy. The sanctuary's property was transferred to the town in 1910, although Mgr François-Xavier Schoepfer, the bishop of Tarbes and Lourdes, refused to accept this loss as legitimate. Compromise followed, and the sanctuary won the right to rent back its domain for eighteen years and to continue, largely unperturbed, until the First World War.[18]

The bitterness of these struggles had not been forgotten when another military catastrophe in 1940 offered the opportunity to redress the balance. Lourdes came to symbolize the partnership between the Catholic Church and the new Vichy regime, which reasserted the phantom of conspiratorial links between Jews, Freemasons and republicans. At Lourdes the ascendency of Philippe Pétain meant the revenge of the sanctuary: almost immediately its officials successfully petitioned him for the restitution of their property. As early as 20 April 1941 Pétain came to Lourdes and, although privately a lukewarm Catholic, became publicly the Catholic grandfather of a renewed Christian nation. Special thanks were literally inscribed on the white marble side doors of the Basilica of the Rosary. While the left-hand side referred to the law separating Church and state in 1905, the right read '*In Memoriam*, 1940–41, on the morrow of our disasters, France is trying to rediscover her soul under the government of Maréchal Pétain.'[19] When many of the anti-clerical laws were reversed under his leadership and Catholic institutions experienced a revival, most of the hierarchy seemed content to accept the anti-Semitic and anti-masonic persecutions almost as part of the overall package, with some welcoming them as the long-delayed implementation of policies they had desired for more than half a century. For many, the struggles at the beginning of the century were only a lost battle in a larger war, which they now seemed to have won in the midst of disaster and defeat.

During the Liberation, the inscription of the basilica bore testimony to Lourdes's dangerous passage during the 'Franco-French' civil war. But, as has always been the case with Lourdes, the tale of political reaction and even hatred does not tell the whole story. For the sanctuary town has also been a way-station for fleeing refugees. Franz Werfel, the Jewish Viennese novelist, found refuge there *en route* to safety in America, gratefully hiding from the National Socialists. He vowed to write *The Song of Bernadette* (1942), the story that had inspired him in those moments of dire peril. His mission clearly indicated how aspects of the shrine could transcend the malevolence of politics; it moved him to 'magnify the divine mystery and the holiness of man – careless of a period which has turned away with scorn and rage and indifference from these ultimate values of our mortal lot'.[20] And while the bishop of Tarbes and Lourdes during the Occupation, Georges Choquet, continued to condemn de Gaulle's government as illegitimate well into 1944, he was succeeded in 1946 by Mgr Pierre-Marie Théas, the bishop of Montauban, who had become in 1942 one of the rare members of the French hierarchy publicly and indefatigably to denounce the persecution of the Jews.[21] With his arrival the shrine began a new period in which it would later share in the hopes and initiatives of Vatican II.

The history of Lourdes in the twentieth century thus continued to exhibit the many different strands of an evolving Catholicism at the same time that its fortunes reflected the inescapable interaction between religion and politics in the history of France. From its foundation Lourdes has derived some sustenance from the campaign for legitimist restoration, the anti-Semitic hatreds of the Dreyfus Affair and the resentments of the extreme right. But above all it was sustained by the piety of the poor and the yearnings of the sick, all drawn by the simplicity of Bernadette's message, a simplicity that matched her own character. Her ignorance uncannily protected her from vicious anti-clerical assault, for she could be seen by many as the prototype of Rousseauian innocence untainted by doctrine. The same characteristic, perhaps, also made her immune from co-option as a symbol of resurgent Catholicism. Bernadette's enigmatic figure perhaps partly explains the sanctuary's capacity to attract so many people of divergent spiritual inclinations, for on to her frail form could be projected the many different longings of different eras. It was her simplicity that attracted Henri Lasserre and led him to construct a story of Lourdes that seized the imaginations of millions. The same qualities led Werfel to sing the song of Bernadette and attracted Hollywood to turn his book into a movie. For, despite the attempts by some to romanticize, by others to politicize and by more still to medicalize, throughout the history of Lourdes there has always remained one fixed point: the essential image of a young, poverty-stricken and sickly girl kneeling in ecstasy in a muddy grotto.

Notes

Abbreviations

AAR	Archives des Assomptionnistes, Rome
AN	Archives Nationales, Paris
APSA	Archives de la Congrégation des Petites-Sœurs de l'Assomption, Paris
Archives Cros	manuscripts and notebooks of Léonard Cros, held at the Archives de la Grotte
Archives de la Grotte	Archives of the Sanctuary, Lourdes
LDA	René Laurentin and Bernard Billet, *Lourdes: Documents authentiques*, 7 vols. (Paris, P. Lethielleux, 1957–66)
LHA	René Laurentin, *Lourdes: Histoire authentique des apparitions*, 6 vols. (Paris, P. Lethielleux, 1961–4)
PA Nevers	Procès apostolique de Nevers, Archives Nevers, 8 vols.
PO Nevers	Procès ordinaire de Nevers, Archives Nevers, 6 vols.

Part One *The Lourdes of the Apparitions*

1. Town, Region, Family

1. *LDA*, vol. 4, no. 590, p. 87.
2. *LDA*, vol. 1, pp. 51–2.
3. Nor were the Pyrenees the only region to suffer such a crisis well into the nineteenth century; see P. Vigier, *La Seconde République dans la région alpine. Etude politique et sociale* (Paris, PUF, 1963); A. Armengaud, *Les Populations de l'Est-Aquitaine au début de l'époque contemporaine.*

Recherches sur une région moins développée, vers 1845–1871 (Paris, La Haye, 1961); Maurice Agulhon, *Un mouvement populaire au temps de 1848. Histoire des populations du Var dans la première moitié du XIXe siècle* (thèse d'Etat, Paris-Sorbonne, 1969); Alain Corbin, *Archaïsme et modernité en Limousin au XIXe siècle 1845–1880* (Paris, M. Rivière, 1975); Geneviève Gavignaud-Fontaine, *La Propriété en Roussillon. Structures et conjonctures agraires XVIIIe–XIXe siècles* (Lille, ANRT, 1984). For specifics of the region, see Jean-François Soulet, *Les Pyrénées au XIXe siècle* (Toulouse, Eché, 1987), vol. 2, pp. 11–29.

4. Jean Fourcassié, *Le Romantisme et les Pyrénées* (Toulouse, ESPER, n.d.), pp. 61, 64.

5. Bernard Billet, 'Lourdes et les Lourdais au temps de Bernadette', in *La Vie quotidienne dans les Hautes-Pyrénées au temps de Bernadette* (Lourdes, Exposition Musée Pyrénéen, 1979), p. 10.

6. Jean Fourcassié, *Le Romantisme et les Pyrénées*, pp. 145–97.

7. For a summary of the different representations, see Jean-François Soulet, *Les Pyrénées au XIXe siècle* (Toulouse, Eché, 1987), vol. 1, pp. 1–49; see also Jean Fourcassié and Anne Lasserre-Vergne, *Les Pyrénées centrales dans la littérature française* (Toulouse, Eché, 1985), pp. 113–34.

8. Jean-François Le Nail, 'L'Age d'or du château fort (XI–XVe siècle)', in Stéphane Baumont, ed., *Histoire de Lourdes* (Toulouse, Privat, 1993), pp. 25–76.

9. José-Ramón Cubero, *La Révolution en Bigorre* (Toulouse, Privat, 1989).

10. José-Ramón Cubero, 'Des lumières à la Seconde République', in *Histoire de Lourdes*, Stéphane Baumont, ed., pp. 117–38.

11. For an analysis of the census, see Bernard Billet, 'Lourdes et les Lourdais au temps de Bernadette', pp. 10–13.

12. See ch. 9.

13. Jean-François Soulet, *Les Pyrénées au XIXe siècle*, vol. 2, p. 31.

14. ibid., pp. 126–49.

15. ibid., pp. 11–29.

16. For more on the recurring trauma of this disease, see Richard J. Evans, 'Blue Funk and Yellow Peril: Cholera and Society in Nineteenth-century France', *European History Quarterly*, vol. 20 (1990), pp. 111–26.

17. Jean-François Soulet, *Les Pyrénées au XIXe siècle*, vol. 2, pp. 39–46.

18. Léonard Cros, *Lourdes 1858: Témoins de l'événement* (Paris, P. Lethielleux, 1957), p. 84; see also *LDA*, vol. 5, no. 912, p. 327; on Bernadette's asthma, 'Rapport des médecins, 31 mars, 1858', *LDA*, vol. 1, no. 104, pp. 297–8.

19. Archives Cros, BXII, pp. 12–13.

20. *LHA*, vol. 2, p. 56.

21. The case against him was not proven, but the episode confirmed the

widespread view that this was a family that needed to steal to survive. *LDA*, vol. 1, no. X, pp. 131–5.

22. Jean-François Soulet, *Les Pyrénées au XIXe siècle*, vol. 2, pp. 88–92.

23. ibid., vol. 1, p. 62; see also Peter Sahlins, *Boundaries: The Making of France and Spain in the Pyrenees* (Berkeley and Los Angeles, University of California Press, 1989), pp. 238–40.

24. See René Laurentin, *Lourdes: Le Récit authentique des apparitions* (P. Lethielleux, Œuvre de la Grotte, 1966), pp. 172–3, for the clerical attempts to question Bernadette and their mutual misunderstandings.

25. Jean-François Soulet, *Les Pyrénées au XIXe siècle*, vol. 2, pp. 309–37; indeed, local languages and costumes were often elaborated in defiance of the attempt to assimilate the Pyreneans into a wider French culture.

26. For more on the intensified policing of the boundary during the period of delimitation and the negative impact on the poor, see Peter Sahlins, *Boundaries: The Making of France and Spain in the Pyrenees*, pp. 240–46.

27. Jean-François Soulet, *Les Pyrénées au XIXe siècle*, vol. 2, pp. 443–63, 471–501.

28. Isaure Gratacos, *Fées et gestes – femmes pyrénéennes: Un statut social exceptionnel en Europe* (Toulouse, Editions Privat, 1987), pp. 113–16.

29. See ch. 4.

30. Jean-François Soulet, *Les Pyrénées au XIXe siècle*, vol. 1, pp. 84–6; vol. 2, pp. 142–5.

31. For this background, see ibid., vol. 2, pp. 149–71; for the forest's importance in one commune, see Edouard Lynch, *Entre la commune et la nation: Identité communautaire et pratique politique en vallée de Campan (Hautes-Pyrénées) au XIXe siècle* (Tarbes, Association Guillaume Mauran, 1992), pp. 41–61.

32. See Peter Sahlins, *Forest Rites: The War of the Demoiselles in Nineteenth-century France* (Cambridge, MA, Harvard University Press, 1994); F. Baby, *La Guerre des Demoiselles en Ariège 1829–1872* (Paris, Montbel, 1972); Jean-François Soulet, *Les Pyrénées au XIXe siècle*, vol. 2, pp. 471–536, 602–15.

33. Jean-François Soulet, *Les Pyrénées au XIXe siècle*, vol. 2, p. 502.

34. Jean-François Soulet, 'La Société Lourdaise vue par Eugène Cordier', *Catalogue de l'exposition du Musée Pyrénéen de Lourdes* (Lourdes, Exposition Musée Pyrénéen, juin 1987), pp. 140–48.

35. Archives Cros, AIII(3), Frère Cérase, no. 27, para. 27.

36. For the importance of Montserrat and Compostela for the people of the Bigorre, see Abbé E. Lafforgue, *Les Anciens Pèlerinages de la Bigorre* (Lourdes, Optima, n.d.), pp. 9–25; he guessed that the pilgrimages to these two sites only ended in 1869; see also Jean Francez, 'Notre-Dame de Montserrat et les Hautes-Pyrénées', *Studia Monastica*, vol. 15 (1973), pp. 65–101.

37. For the special significance of this witness/chronicler, see Therese Taylor, 'So many extraordinary things to tell – Letters from Lourdes, 1858', *Journal of Ecclesiastical History*, vol. 46, no. 3 (1995), pp. 457–81.
38. *LDA*, vol. 1, no. 42, p. 225.
39. X. Recroix, *Récits d'apparitions mariales (Pyrénées centrales)* (extrait de la *Revue de Comminges*, 3ème trimestre 1986 à 3ème trimestre 1988), pp. 38–9.
40. *LDA*, vol. 2, n. 50, pp. 19–20.
41. In his work *Traditions et réformes religieuses dans les Pyrénées centrales au XVIIe siècle (Le diocèse de Tarbes de 1602 à 1716)* (Pau, Marrimpouey jeune, 1974), Jean-François Soulet makes the case for the strong resistance to orthodox Catholic teaching.
42. Jean-François Soulet, *Les Pyrénées au XIXe siècle*, vol. 1, pp. 457–8.
43. See Judith Devlin, *The Superstitious Mind: French Peasants and the Supernatural in the Nineteenth Century* (New Haven, Conn., Yale University Press, 1987), for an overview of peasant belief and the way 'orthodox' Christianity was constantly threatened by the vitality of more 'popular' conceptions.
44. Olivier de Marliave, *Trésor de la mythologie pyrénéenne* (Toulouse, ESPER, 2nd ed., 1989), pp. 107–64, 215–70.
45. ibid., pp. 133–63; for the medieval background, see Jean-Claude Schmitt, *Le Saint Lévrier: Guinefort, guérisseur d'enfants depuis le XIIe siècle* (Paris, Flammarion, 1979); for the classic, if outdated, examination of such cults in peasant France, see Paul Sébillot, *Le Folklore de France* (Paris, Guilmoto, 1905), vol. 2, pp. 216–303; vol. 3, pp. 367–442.
46. See ch. 2.
47. See ch. 9.
48. Jean-François Soulet, *Traditions et réformes religieuses dans les Pyrénées centrales au XVIIe siècle*, p. 354.
49. Léonard Cros, *Lourdes 1858: Témoins de l'événement*, p. 64.
50. For more on the collective nature of the search for the supernatural, see Jean-François Le Nail and Jean-François Soulet, eds., *Le Pays de Bigorre et les quatre vallées* (Paris, Société nouvelle d'éditions régionales et de diffusion, 1981), p. 203.
51. Jean-François Soulet, *Les Pyrénées au XIXe siècle*, vol. 1, p. 250.
52. For more on this world, see Jean-François Soulet, 'Pèlerinage et sociabilité dans les Pyrénées aux XVII et XVIII siècles', in *Catalogue de l'exposition: Pèlerins et pèlerinages dans les Pyrénées françaises* (Lourdes, Musée Pyrénéen, juin–octobre 1975), pp. xi–xxi; for an example of the kind of raucousness that could prevail, see Norbert Rosapelly, *Traditions et coutumes des Hautes-Pyrénées* (Tarbes, Société académique des Hautes-Pyrénées, 1990), p. 48.
53. For an invaluable description of Carnival rituals, see Arnold Van Gennep, *Manuel de folklore français contemporain* (Paris, A. et J. Picard, 1949); for

the theoretical appreciation of the riotous and transgressive dimension of Carnival, see Mikhail Bakhtin, *Rabelais and His World*, H. Iswolsky, tr. (Cambridge, MA, MIT Press, 1968), as well as an appreciative critique of this work, Peter Stallybrass and Allon White, *The Politics and Poetics of Transgression* (London, Methuen, 1986). See Isaure Gratacos for the resilience of such rituals in *Calendrier pyrénéen: Rites, coutumes et croyances dans la tradition orale en Comminges et Couserans* (Toulouse, Privat, 1995), pp. 85–104.

54. See chs. 7 and 8.

55. See A.-J.-M. Hamon, *Notre-Dame de France, ou histoire du culte de la Sainte Vierge en France depuis l'origine du christianisme jusqu'à nos jours* (Paris, Henri Plon, 1863), pp. 443–62, for the shrines to the Virgin in the diocese of Tarbes and Lourdes.

56. T.-M.-J.-T. Azun de Bernétas, *La Grotte des Pyrénées ou manifestation de la Sainte Vierge à la Grotte de Lourdes (Diocèse de Tarbes, précéde d'une notice sur les Pyrénées)* (Tarbes, J.-P. Larrieu, 1861), pp. 97–8.

57. Christian Desplat, *Notre-Dame de Sarrance* (Pau, Les Amis des Eglises anciennes du Béarn, 1980), pp. 3–4; see also G. B. de Lagrèze, *Les Pèlerinages des Pyrénées* (Paris, Jacques Lecoffre, 1858), pp. 18–22.

58. See Archives de la Grotte, VIII 01. G., Anon., 'Courte notice sur Notre-Dame de Héas', juillet, 1889, p. iv.

59. G. B. de Lagrèze, *Les Pèlerinages des Pyrénées* (Paris, Jacques Lecoffre, 1858), pp. 152–3.

60. ibid., pp. 176–7.

61. William A. Christian, *Apparitions in Late Medieval and Renaissance Spain* (Princeton, Princeton University Press, 1981), p. 209.

62. See Abbé E. Lafforgue, *Les Ermites de la Bigorre* (Lourdes, Optima, 1922).

63. Brigitte Caulier, *L'Eau et le sacré: Les Cultes thérapeutiques autour des fontaines en France du Moyen Age à nos jours* (Paris, Beauchesne, 1990), p. 39.

64. Norbert Rosapelly, *Traditions et coutumes des Hautes-Pyrénées*, pp. 135–6.

65. G. B. de Lagrèze, *Les Pèlerinages des Pyrénées*, p. 22.

66. ibid., p. 138.

67. Archives de la Grotte, VIII 01. G., Anon., 'Courte notice sur Notre-Dame de Héas', juillet 1889, p. iv.

68. For this topographical dimension to peasant memory, see J. Fentress and C. Wickham, *Social Memory* (Oxford, Blackwell, 1992), p. 93; for the larger question of space in relation to the sacred, see Michel Crépu and Richard Figuier, eds., *Hauts Lieux: Une Quête de racines, de sacré, de symboles* (Paris, Autrement, 1990), especially sections 2 and 3.

69. A. Dupront, 'Pèlerinage et lieux sacrés', *Mélanges F. Braudel* (Toulouse, Privat, 1973), pp. 190–91.
70. Joel Perrin and Jean-Claude Lasserre, *Notre-Dame de Bétharram* (Pau, Les Amis des Eglises anciennes du Béarn, 1980), pp. 7–8.
71. For the full scholarly treatment, see X. Recroix, *Anglèze de Sagazan et la chapelle de Garaison* (Pau, Marrimpouey jeune, 1982).
72. For the significance of food miracles, see Caroline Walker Bynum, *Holy Feast and Holy Fast: The Religious Significance of Food to Medieval Women* (Berkeley, University of California Press, 1987), especially pp. 73–142.
73. Léonard Cros, *Histoire de Notre-Dame de Lourdes* (Paris, Beauchesne, 1957), vol. 1, p. 62, testimony of Jeanne Verdère.
74. For its impact on neighbouring Spanish Catalonia, see Henry Kamen, *The Phoenix and the Flame: Catalonia and the Counter-Reformation* (New Haven, Yale University Press, 1993).
75. Jean-François Soulet, *Les Pyrénées au XIXe siècle*, vol. 1, p. 242; for more information on the significance of such organizations, see Marie-Hélène Froeschlé-Chopard, *Espace et sacré en Provence, XIVe–XXe siècles, cultes, images, confréries* (Paris, Cerf, 1994), pp. 435–81.
76. See Philippe Boutry, 'Marie, la grande consolatrice de la France au XIXe siècle', *L'Histoire*, no. 50 (1982), pp. 31–9.
77. Léonard Cros, *Histoire de Notre-Dame de Lourdes*, vol. 1, p. 28.
78. For the piety of the Soubirous, see *LHA*, vol. 2, no. 145, pp. 49–50.
79. *LDA*, vol. 1, no. II, pp. 75–83.
80. René Laurentin, *Lourdes: Le Récit authentique des apparitions*, pp. 9–10.
81. René Laurentin, *Vie de Bernadette* (Paris, Desclée de Brouwer, 1978), p. 28.
82. Jean-François Le Nail and Jean-François Soulet, eds., *Le Pays de Bigorre et les quatre vallées*, pp. 177–81; see also the chapters by Rolande Bonnain and Georges Augustins in Georges Augustins, et al., *Les Baronnies des Pyrénées* (Paris, Editions des hautes études en sciences sociales, 1981), pp. 63–214. For the maintenance of these traditions in the twentieth century, see Isaure Gratacos, *Fées et gestes – femmes pyrénéennes: Un statut social exceptionnel en Europe*, pp. 78–81.
83. The primacy of the household, and the notion of successorial integrity that underpinned it, fascinated nineteenth-century sociological investigators. Ethnographers wondered if the Pyreneans were the ancestors of primitive Europeans who practised matriarchy, while Frédéric Le Play, the famous conservative sociologist, used the example of the Dulmo family from nearby Cauterets to demonstrate the social importance of the *famille souche*, maintaining that such patriarchal clans (he concentrated on the eldest *male* in any given family) represented tradition and stability, while those based on

partible inheritance and the revolutionary legacy fostered individualism and social disintegration. See Frédéric Le Play, *L'Organisation de la famille selon le vrai modèle signalé par l'histoire de toutes les races et de tous les temps* (Paris, Téqui, 1871); see also Emmanuel Le Roy Ladurie, *Montaillou: Cathars and Catholics in a French Village 1294–1324*, Barbara Bray, tr. (Harmondsworth, Penguin Books, 1978), pp. 24–5, and William A. Douglass, 'The Famille Souche and Its Interpreters', *Continuity and Change*, vol. 8, no. 1 (1993), pp. 87–102.

84. Léonard Cros, *Lourdes 1858: Témoins de l'événement*, pp. 174, 180.

85. *LDA*, vol. 5, no. 912, p. 327.

86. See *LHA*, vol. 2, pp. 72–3.

87. René Laurentin, *Vie de Bernadette*, pp. 18–23.

88. See the varying testimonies and conclusions in *LHA*, vol. 2, pp. 76–80.

89. For the numerous and varying appreciations, see ibid., nn. 46, 47, p. 22; nn. 111, 112, 113, 114, p. 39.

90. Léonard Cros, *Lourdes 1858: Témoins de l'événement*, p. 45.

91. Léonard Cros, *Histoire de Notre-Dame de Lourdes*, vol. 1, pp. 45–50.

92. *LHA*, vol. 2, see pp. 25–49.

93. Jean-François Soulet, *Les Pyrénées au XIXe siècle*, vol. 1, pp. 144–8. These people were now seen as competition for meagre jobs and resources, and were often hated by the local population. Indeed, one of the ways a notion of Frenchness was forged was in contradistinction to the Spaniards, seen as opposing the local interests of the poor on the French side of the border; see Peter Sahlins, *Boundaries: The Making of France and Spain in the Pyrenees*, *passim*.

94. Archives Cros, AVII, A. Sajous. no. 813, p. 122.

95. There was never agreement over the formative role that the time in Bartrès played in the experience of the apparitions. The work of Jean Barbet, *Bernadette Soubirous: Sa naissance, sa vie, sa mort, d'après des documents inédits* (Pau, G. Les Cher, 1909), p. 16, suggested that Abbé Ader, the curé of Bartrès, had already predicted Bernadette's special vocation as a visionary when he likened her to the seers of La Salette, seeing in all of the children a divine simplicity that predisposed them to an encounter with the divine.

96. *LHA*, vol. 2, p. 29.

97. Léonard Cros, *Lourdes 1858: Témoins de l'événement*, p. 181.

98. René Laurentin, *Vie de Bernadette*, p. 28.

99. Bernadette always sought to retain her prerogatives and tried to direct the fortunes and spiritual lives of siblings from faraway Nevers; she did so with varying success and was highly sensitive to any slight on her position, especially if she thought they were hiding things from her. See André Ravier, ed., *Les Ecrits de sainte Bernadette et sa voie spirituelle* (Paris, P. Lethielleux, 2nd ed., 1980), pp. 284–8, 301–6, for some examples among many.

100. *LHA*, vol. 2, p. 54, n. 157, p. 55.
101. Léonard Cros, *Histoire de Notre-Dame de Lourdes*, vol. 1, p. 125.
102. For the various testimonies of her piety, see *LHA*, vol. 3, p. 50. It seems likely that Bernadette learned these prayers from other women, especially her Aunt Bernarde; in this she was shaped in an old tradition that dated at least to the Tridentine reforms. See Marcel Bernos, 'La Catéchèse des filles par les femmes aux XVIIe et XVIIIe siècles', in Jean Delumeau, ed., *La Religion de ma mère: Le Rôle des femmes dans la transmission de la foi* (Paris, Cerf, 1992), pp. 269–87.
103. Léonard Cros, *Lourdes 1858: Témoins de l'événement*, p. 160.
104. For the importance of the rosary for the illiterate who could use it to pray without a church, see Olwen Hufton, *The Prospect before Her: A History of Women in Western Europe 1500–1800* (London, HarperCollins, 1995), vol. 1, pp. 393–4.
105. For these trials, see ch. 5.
106. René Laurentin, *Lourdes: Le Récit authentique des apparitions*, pp. 37, 51, 53.
107. See *LDA*, vol. 1, no. 3, pp. 160–65, for the first, all-important interrogation. See also Léonard Cros, *Lourdes 1858: Témoins de l'événement*, p. 47. Jacomet reportedly shouted at her, 'Tu veux devenir une petite coquine et une petite putain!' Pierre Callet made this statement virtually twenty years after the events. Another witness of the interrogation, Emmanuélite Estrade, denied that the word 'whore' was used, while the word 'coquine', if uttered, was said in her view without harmful intent.
108. See ch. 6.
109. See ch. 5.
110. *LHA*, vol. 3, n. 44, p. 19.
111. ibid., n. 102, p. 33; p. 34.
112. Cros describes the development of this communal pasturing from the beginning of the sixteenth century on p. 37, vol. 1, while Laurentin cites local archives in *LHA*, vol. 3, n. 95, p. 31.
113. Archives Cros, AVII, p. 38; AVIII, pp. 8, 11.
114. *LHA*, vol. 3, 101, p. 33.
115. Archives Cros, AVIII, pp. 761–2.
116. P. Forneau, 'La Vierge immaculée et le culte de la Sainte Eucharistie . . .' *Annales de Notre-Dame de Lourdes*, vol. 32 (1900), p. 160. Fourneau was the superior of the Garaison Fathers at the Grotto and made reference to old people in the community who saw this custom; cited in X. Recroix, 'Un aspect de la piété populaire dans les Pyrénées centrales: La Dévotion mariale', *Revue de Comminges*, no. 102 (1989), p. 128.
117. *LDA*, vol. 1, no. 42, p. 229.
118. Christian Desplat, *Sorcières et diables en Béarn (fin XIVe–début XIXe*

siècles) (Pau, Imprimerie Graphique Marrimpouey Succ., 1988), p. 65.
119. Archives Cros, AVIIe, p. 194.
120. *LHA*, vol. 3, p. 31.

2. *The Apparitions and Their Interpretation*

1. Léonard Cros, *Lourdes 1858: Témoins de l'événement*, pp. 61–2.
2. ibid., p. 77.
3. According to the majority of witnesses, this remark was made by the intelligent and severe Mère Ursule Fardes; see *LHA*, vol. 2, no. 10, p. 282, no. 22, p. 285, no. 27, p. 287.
4. See ch. 5.
5. For background, see Jacques Le Goff, *La Naissance du Purgatoire* (Paris, Gallimard, 1981), pp. 180–316; on the characteristics of revenants, see Jean-Claude Schmitt, *Les Revenants: Les Vivants et les morts dans la société médiévale* (Paris, Gallimard, 1994), especially pp. 223–49.
6. Thomas A. Kselman, *Death and the Afterlife in Modern France* (Princeton, Princeton University Press, 1993), pp. 111–24.
7. Charles Joisten, 'Les Etres fantastiques dans le folklore de l'Ariège', *Via Domitia*, vol. 9 (1962), pp. 25–48.
8. *LDA*, vol. 1, no. XVI, p. 144.
9. For the background and a discussion of priestly attendance and burial rites, see Thomas A. Kselman, *Death and the Afterlife in Modern France*, pp. 88–94.
10. For the continuation of such traditions, see Jean-Pierre Pinies, *Figures de la sorcellerie languedocienne* (Paris, CNRS, 1983), especially pp. 205–41.
11. Abbé Dambielle, *La Sorcellerie en Gascogne* (Nîmes, Collection Rediviva, C. Lacour, ed., 1992; reprint of ed. first pub. Auch, Léonce Cocharux, 1907), p. 17.
12. See Nicole Edelman, *Voyantes, guérisseuses et visionnaires en France 1785–1914* (Paris, Albin Michel, 1995), especially pp. 109–58, and Thomas A. Kselman, *Death and the Afterlife in Modern France*, pp. 125–62.
13. For more on *spiritisme*, see Thomas A. Kselman, *Death and the Afterlife in Modern France*, pp. 143–62, and Henri F. Ellenberger, *The Discovery of the Unconscious: The History and Evolution of Dynamic Psychiatry* (New York, Basic Books, 1970), p. 84. Hippolyte Rivail, alias Allan Kardec, became famous for his *Livre des esprits, contenant les principes de la doctrine spirite* (Paris, Dentu, 1857).
14. The interest of spiritualists in the case of Lourdes can be seen from the interventions of the *La Revue des spiritualistes*; see *LDA*, vol. 2, no. 307,

pp. 351–2; vol. 3, no. 476, pp. 240–41; vol. 4, no. 616, pp. 117–18, no. 725, pp. 217–22. See also the intervention of Marquis Jules-Eudes de Mirville, who wrote to Mgr Laurence, trying to convince the prelate of the need to reconcile Catholicism with spiritualism, *LDA*, vol. 4, nos. 662, 662a, pp. 155–60. For some of the background to the Church's generally hostile reaction to spiritualist arguments, see Nicole Edelman, *Voyantes, guérisseuses et visionnaires en France 1785–1914*, pp. 165–71.

15. For the importance of market day, see Jean-François Soulet, *Les Pyrénées au XIXe siècle*, vol. 1, p. 247. In Lourdes in January 1856 the police commissioner recorded the arrival of 621 horses, 1,760 sheep, 1,270 cows, 898 pigs and 629 mules, an indication of the mass of people and livestock that could descend on the town on such days.

16. Sandra L. Zimdars-Swartz, *Encountering Mary: Visions of Mary from La Salette to Medjugorje* (New York, Avon Books, 1992), pp. 27–34.

17. For Bernadette's secrets, see ch. 5, and *LHA*, vol. 3, pp. 250–58. For the contrasting and very different handling of their secrets, see Sandra L. Zimdars-Swartz, *Encountering Mary: Visions of Mary from La Salette to Medjugorje*, pp. 165–89.

18. See Louis Borel, *Notre-Dame de La Salette* (Paris, Letouzey et Ané, 1923), pp. 18–24.

19. J.-P. Bertier, *Notre-Dame de La Salette. Son apparition, son culte* (Paris, Haton, n.d.), p. 14.

20. Arnold Van Gennep, *Le Folklore du Dauphiné (Isère)* (Paris, Maisonneuve, 1932), p. 202.

21. See Jean-François Le Nail and Jean-François Soulet, eds., *Le Pays de Bigorre et les quatre vallées*, illustration after p. 204.

22. X. Recroix, 'Un aspect de la piété populaire dans les Pyrénées centrales: La Dévotion mariale', *Revue de Comminges*, no. 102 (1989), p. 121; this lateness distinguishes it from its pre-Counter-Reformation flowering in the fifteenth century under the impetus of the Dominicans in other parts of France; see Olwen Hufton, *The Prospect before Her: A History of Women in Western Europe 1500–1800*, vol. 1, pp. 393–4.

23. *LDA*, vol. 1, no. 12, p. 179.

24. ibid., no. 30, p. 211.

25. ibid., no. 36, p. 211.

26. ibid., no. 104, pp. 299–300.

27. ibid., p. 300.

28. In using such a term, Dr Balencie and his colleagues were demonstrating their knowledge of an important debate within medical and, particularly, psychiatric circles in the 1850s. See Tony James, *Dream, Creativity and Madness in Nineteenth-century France* (Oxford, Oxford University Press, 1995), pp. 69–73, 145–50.

29. Léonard Cros, *Lourdes 1858: Témoins de l'événement*, p. 62.
30. ibid., p. 320.
31. ibid., p. 108; for the various testimonies of this event, see *LHA*, vol. 4, n. 75, p. 215.
32. See Michel de Certeau, ed., *La Possession de Loudun* (Paris, Gallimard, 2nd ed., 1990), p. 245.
33. See Georges Didi-Huberman, *Invention de l'hystérie: Charcot et l'iconographie photographique de la Salpêtrière* (Paris, Editions Macula, 1982), illus. 66 and 77, pp. 176 and 194.
34. Léonard Cros, *Lourdes 1858: Témoins de l'événement*, pp. 45, 164.
35. *LHA*, vol. 3, no. 84, p. 102; later medical investigators, however, would argue that sensible tasks like these could be conducted during an hypnotic trance; such objections would not, however, have convinced the crowd at the Grotto.
36. Léonard Cros, *Lourdes 1858: Témoins de l'événement*, p. 83.
37. ibid., p. 111.
38. ibid., p. 56.
39. ibid., p. 85.
40. For an excellent overview, see *LHA*, vol. 3, pp. 57–80.
41. For an analysis of the different classes in evidence, see ibid., pp. 64–7.
42. *LDA*, vol. 1, p. 174, editorial note.
43. ibid., p. 184.
44. ibid., p. 268.
45. Archives Cros, AIII(1).
46. William A. Christian, *Apparitions in Late Medieval and Renaissance Spain*, pp. 186–7.
47. Archives Cros, AIII(3), Frère Cérase, 'On disait que Bernadette avait eu quelques visions chez elle', no. 38, p. 8.
48. William A. Christian, *Apparitions in Late Medieval and Renaissance Spain*, pp. 25, 62–3.
49. *LDA*, vol. 1, p. 172, editorial note.
50. Françoise Loux, *Le Jeune Enfant et son corps dans la médecine traditionnelle* (Paris, Flammarion, 1978), pp. 196–7.
51. Olivier de Marliave, *Trésor de la mythologie pyrénéenne*, pp. 150–51.
52. Léonard Cros, *Lourdes 1858: Témoins de l'événement*, p. 186, from the testimony of Jeanne Védère.
53. For an introduction to such ideas, see Joyce McDougall, *Theatres of the Mind: Illusion and Truth on the Psychoanalytic Stage* (London, Faber, 1985), *passim*.
54. Archives Cros, AVIII, p. 231.
55. Archives Cros, AVIII, p. 97.
56. Archives Cros, AVIII, p. 57.

57. Archives Cros, AVIII, pp. 7–8.
58. Archives Cros, AVIII, pp. 181–2.
59. Archives Cros, AVII, pp. 85–6.
60. Archives Cros, AVIII, p. 18. Martin Tarbès also described her as an infant in the cradle, although he did not see her as dead. AVIII, p. 157.
61. Archives Cros, AVIII, p. 147.
62. Léonard Cros, *Lourdes 1858: Témoins de l'événement*, p. 115.
63. Archives Cros, AVIII, pp. 181–2.
64. René Laurentin, *Lourdes: Le Récit authentique des apparitions*, p. 124.
65. ibid., p. 125.
66. *LDA*, vol. 1, p. 172, editorial note.
67. See the important critical work of Paul Connerton, *How Societies Remember* (Cambridge, Cambridge University Press, 1989), pp. 72–104, in which he none the less overemphasizes the notion of a single 'social memory'. See also Jan Bremmer and Herman Roodenburg, eds., *A Cultural History of Gesture* (Ithaca, Cornell University Press, 1991).
68. *LHA*, vol. 3, p. 151, Dr Balencie in 1879.
69. ibid., p. 153.
70. *LDA*, vol. 1, no. 5, p. 169. The newspaper in question was *Le Lavedan*; the recitation of events was highly fanciful, suggesting that Bernadette said, 'Voyez, voyez cette Dame, de blanc habillée, elle vient de me parler: c'est la Mère des anges.' For a thorough description of the transformation of Bernadette's early words, and the way even she on later occasions may have slipped into the trap, see *LHA*, vol. 3, n. 58, p. 146.
71. For example, Père Sempé, the head of the Garaison Fathers, described her as fifteen in the *Annales de Notre-Dame de Lourdes*, pp. 103–6, while Pène in his written statement to Cros in 1879 put her at between eighteen and twenty years of age.
72. *LHA*, vol. 3, no. 58, p. 205.
73. For more on its canons and inspirations, see Bruno Foucart, *Le Renouveau de la peinture religieuse en France (1800–1860)* (Paris, Arthena, 1987), and Ruth Butler, 'Religious Sculpture in Post-Christian France', in *The Romantics to Rodin: French Nineteenth-century Sculpture from North American Collections*, Peter Fusco and H. W. Janson, eds. (Los Angeles, Los Angeles County Museum of Art and George Braziller, Inc., 1980), pp. 83–95.
74. Seen as immodest and potentially corrupting to the poor *femmes de chambre* who attended them, women who wore such fashions to local Lent balls were even denied absolution by a condemnatory clergy. *LDA*, vol. 1, no. 59, n. 1, p. 241.
75. René Laurentin, *Vie de Bernadette*, pp. 81–2.
76. Léonard Cros, *Histoire de Notre-Dame de Lourdes*, vol. 1, p. 103.
77. *La Vierge dans l'art et la tradition populaire des Pyrénées* (Exposition

France–Espagne, avril–octobre 1958), see especially nos. 1–26 for the Bigorre, the area in which Lourdes was situated.
78. X. Recroix, *Récits d'apparitions mariales*, pp. 117–32; for more on the smallness of the apparitions, see William A. Christian, *Apparitions in Late Medieval and Renaissance Spain*, pp. 133, 157–8, 210.
79. Léonard Cros, *Histoire de Notre-Dame de Lourdes*, vol. 2, p. 226.
80. William A. Christian, *Apparitions in Late Medieval and Renaissance Spain*, pp. 133, 157–8, 210.
81. Quoted in Léonard Cros, *Histoire de Notre-Dame de Lourdes*, vol. 1, n. 1, p. 102, from her *Vida*, ch. 33, 'Era grandisima la hermosura que vi en Nuestra Señora . . . vestida de blanco, con grandisimo resplandor . . . Pareciame Nuestra Señora *muy niña*.'
82. See the classic by W. Y. Evans, *The Fairy Faith in Celtic Countries* (New York, Carol Publishing Group, 1990), especially section 3.
83. Quoted in M. L. Delville, *Croyances populaires. Fées. – Esprit Follet. Une Légende pyrénéenne* (Tarbes, Th. Telmon, n.d.), p. 2.
84. For Pyrenean varieties of fairies, see Charles Joisten, 'Les Etres fantastiques dans le folklore de l'Ariège', pp. 17–36.
85. See Eugène Cordier, *Les Légendes des Hautes-Pyrénées*, Jean-François Le Nail and X. Recroix, eds. (Tarbes, Centre départemental de documentation pédagogique, 1986; reprint of 1878 ed.), pp. 55–6.
86. Léonard Cros, *Lourdes 1858: Témoins de l'événement*, p. 39.
87. *LDA*, vol. 1, p. 170, editorial note.
88. Yvonne Verdier, *Façons de dire, façons de faire: La Laveuse, la couturière, la cuisinière* (Paris, Gallimard, 1979), pp. 83–156.
89. Léonard Cros, *Lourdes 1858: Témoins de l'événement*, p. 117.
90. Catherine Rosenbaum-Dondaine, ed., *L'Image de piété en France 1814–1914* (Paris, Musée-Galerie de la Seita, 1984), *passim*.
91. *LDA*, vol. 1, no. XIII, p. 139.
92. X. Recroix, *Anglèze de Sagazan et la chapelle de Garaison*, p. 13.
93. *LDA*, vol. 5, no. 842, pp. 168–9; no. 898, 263–4.
94. Léonard Cros, *Lourdes 1858: Témoins de l'événement*, p. 117.
95. ibid., p. 103.
96. See Abbé Jean Francez, 'La Dévotion à l'Immaculée Conception et thèmes iconographiques dans le diocèse de Tarbes et Lourdes (XIV–XVIIIe siècles)', Archives départementales des Hautes-Pyrénées, 8BR 436. Even such imagery, however, showed the Immaculate Virgin in presentations that rejected a vision of the Virgin in first youth or in adolescence. For example, the Virgin was shown coming out of the tree of Jesse, her purity evident from the way she emerged without trace from a race soiled with crimes; this representation, however, showed her with the infant Jesus, once again reiterating the maternal references that were absent in Bernadette's vision. The famous Vierge aux

Litanies in Monléon-Magnoac showed her with fifteen mystical emblems; although she stood without child, she was a large and rounded figure, a woman in her early twenties, but hardly the girl that Bernadette claimed to see. For more on the cult of the Immaculate Virgin, see Archives Cros, AV(5), 'Fondation Soubies'; this native son who had made his fortune in Spain wanted to build a chapel, but, because of lack of space, instead left money for masses and the instruction of Latin to children.

97. See Hilda Graef, *Mary: A History of Doctrine and Devotion* (London, Sheed & Ward, 1994), vol. 1, pp. 215–21, 250–53, 298–305, 310–14; vol. 2, pp. 78–83; Marina Warner, *Alone of All Her Sex: The Myth and Cult of the Virgin Mary* (London, Picador, 1976), pp. 236–54; Jaroslav Pelikan, *Mary through the Centuries: Her Place in the History of Culture* (New Haven, Yale University Press, 1996), pp. 189–200.

98. René Laurentin, *Vie authentique de Catherine Labouré: Voyante de la rue du Bac et servante des pauvres (1806–1876)* (Paris, Desclée de Brouwer, 1980), pp. 73–94, 100–109.

99. Indeed, the cult of the Immaculate Conception grew widely among the faithful in the first half of the nineteenth century, with the Pope's promulgation merely confirming a growing devotion. See Stéphane Michaud, *Muse et madone: Visages de la femme de la Révolution française aux apparitions de Lourdes* (Paris, Seuil, 1985), pp. 17–78.

100. *LDA*, vol. 1, no. 85, n. 4, p. 285.

3. After-visions: Cultists and Seers

1. For examples, see David Blackbourn, *Marpingen: Apparitions of the Virgin Mary in Bismarckian Germany* (Oxford, Clarendon Press, 1993); for several examples and more interpretations, see Sandra L. Zimdars-Swartz, *Encountering Mary: Visions of Mary from La Salette to Medjugorje*; Michael P. Carroll, *The Cult of the Virgin Mary: Psychological Origins*, especially chs. 7, 8; René Masson, *La Salette, ou les larmes de Marie* (Paris, Editions SOS, 1982); James S. Donnelly, 'The Marian Shrine of Knock: The First Decade', *Éire/Ireland*, vol. 28 (1993), pp. 55–99; apparition experiences also often tend to be rejected when this kind of confirmation does not occur, as was the case in Ezkioga – see William A. Christian, *Visionaries: The Spanish Republic and the Reign of Christ* (Berkeley, University of California Press, 1996); see also his *Moving Crucifixes in Modern Spain* (Princeton, Princeton University Press, 1992); and Maggie Parham, 'With God on Our Side' [a report on Medjugorje], *The Independent Magazine*, (4 December 1993), pp. 35–40.

2. *LDA*, vol. 2, no. 167, pp. 208–9.

3. ibid., p. 209.
4. X. Recroix, 'Eugène Cordier et les légendes des Hautes-Pyrénées: Formation et sources du légendaire', in Eugène Cordier, *Les Légendes des Hautes-Pyrénées*, p. 15.
5. *LDA*, vol. 2, no. 117, p. 138.
6. ibid., no. 126, p. 149.
7. ibid., no. 146, p. 169.
8. ibid., no. 183, p. 234.
9. ibid., no. 185, p. 235.
10. Archives Cros, AVIIe, p. 176.
11. ibid., p. 237.
12. For a discussion of the difference between local and generalized devotions, see William A. Christian, *Person and God in a Spanish Valley* (New York, Seminar Press, 1972), ch. 2.
13. *LDA*, vol. 2, no. 189, p. 238.
14. Archives Cros, AVIIe, p. 191.
15. ibid., no. 146, p. 169, no. 183, p. 234.
16. Françoise Loux, *Le Jeune Enfant et son corps dans la médecine traditionelle*, p. 166; here she suggests that the cheeses were made from the milk of nursing mothers to ensure a plentiful supply. We have no way of knowing whether the cheese at the shrine was of this kind.
17. *LDA*, vol. 2, no. 189, p. 239.
18. Archives Cros, AVIIe, p. 188.
19. ibid., p. 231.
20. ibid., p. 244.
21. ibid., p. 190.
22. ibid., p. 192.
23. *LDA*, vol. 2, p. 246, editorial note.
24. Archives Cros, AVIIe, p. 244.
25. Léonard Cros, *Lourdes 1858: Témoins de l'événement*, p. 43.
26. *LDA*, no. 150, p. 176.
27. ibid., no. 168, pp. 215–16.
28. *LDA*, vol. 5, no. 820, pp. 133–5; no. 898, pp. 248–50.
29. *LDA*, vol. 2, no. 182, p. 233.
30. ibid., no. 193, pp. 243–4.
31. ibid., no. 209, p. 258.
32. Archives Cros, AVIIe, p. 214.
33. ibid., p. 167.
34. *LDA*, vol. 2, p. 267, editorial note.
35. The barriers were demolished on 17 June, reconstructed on the 18th, demolished again on the 27th, reconstructed on the 28th and demolished again on 4 July, only to be reconstructed for the last time on the 10th.

36. *LDA*, vol. 2, no. 155, pp. 185–91, for the details of their experience and the quotations.
37. See Jan Goldstein, '"Moral Contagion": A Professional Ideology of Medicine and Psychiatry in Eighteenth- and Nineteenth-century France', in Gerald L. Geison, ed., *Professions and the French State 1700–1900* (Philadelphia, University of Pennsylvania Press, 1984), pp. 181–222.
38. *LDA*, vol. 2, no. 142, p. 165.
39. ibid., no. 167, p. 210.
40. Despite his harsh remarks, she would once again appear in 1878 as an employee of the Grotto, either converted from sin or perhaps incorrectly accused by the official in 1858; see the testimony of Eléonore Pérard, Archives Cros, AIII, fol. 109, p. 13.
41. *LDA*, vol. 2, no. 156, p. 193.
42. ibid., no. 2, p. 59.
43. ibid., no. 174, p. 221.
44. ibid., n. 1.
45. Archives Cros, AVIIIe, p. 83.
46. Archives Cros, AIII, Eléonore Pérard, fol. 109, p. 14.
47. The most obvious example of an apparition predicting doom was the Virgin of La Salette, although she appeared majestic and in white, without the blackness of Joséphine's vision. Scenes of the passion, of blood and of foreboding were an important part of the visions of Ezkioga; see William A. Christian, *Visionaries: The Spanish Republic and the Reign of Christ, passim.*
48. *LDA*, vol. 2, no. 176, p. 223.
49. Archives Cros, AIII, Eléonore Pérard, fol. 109, p. 13.
50. This was second-hand testimony. Elfrida Lacrampe in a letter to Père Cros, 2 octobre 1878, recounted the words of Eléonore Pérard; see *LDA*, vol. 2, no. 2, p. 59.
51. See ch. 2, nn. 32, 33.
52. Nor was she the only one; clerical dislike of perceived dissembling could induce violent reactions. Chanoine Ribes described how he was once at the Grotto with a colleague and saw a young girl between twelve and fourteen seeming to imitate Bernadette. 'Ses traits étaient contractés et repoussants. Mon compagnon lui cria: "Sors de là, tu fais l'œuvre du diable." L'enfant . . . continua ses opérations: "Sors de là," lui répéta une voix de tonnerre, "ou la main de Dieu va te frapper"'. Archives Cros, AIII(3).
53. Archives Cros, AVIIe, pp. 126–7.
54. ibid., p. 202.
55. ibid., p. 177.
56. ibid., pp. 148–9.
57. ibid., p. 153.
58. ibid., p. 154.

59. ibid., pp. 151–2.
60. ibid., p. 178.
61. ibid., pp. 150, 152. She describes how he interrogated her on both occasions, but then describes her confessor on p. 152 without specifying his identity.
62. *LDA*, vol. 2, no. 18, p. 69.
63. Archives Cros, AVIIe, p. 153.
64. ibid., p. 179.
65. ibid.
66. ibid., p. 180.
67. ibid., p. 179.
68. Archives Cros, AVIIe, p. 155, for both quotations.
69. ibid., p. 273.
70. ibid., p. 183.
71. *LDA*, no. 18, vol. 2, p. 67, testimony of Dominiquette Cazenave.
72. ibid., no. 209, p. 258.
73. ibid., no. 18, p. 69, see testimony of Jeanne-Marie Trézères.
74. Archives Cros, AIII(2), p. 9.
75. For examples of this belief, see *LDA*, vol. 2, no. 18, p. 68, quoting testimony of Justine Cassou; for others with the same opinion, see the testimony of Jean-Pierre Gesta, Jeanne Montat and Eléonore Pérard, p. 70.
76. Norbert Rosapelly, *Traditions et coutumes des Hautes-Pyrénées*, p. 79.
77. See Olivier de Marliave, *Trésor de la mythologie pyrénéenne*, pp. 50–54, and Norbert Rosapelly, *Traditions et coutumes des Hautes-Pyrénées*, pp. 125–9; Isaure Gratacos, *Calendrier pyrénéen: Rites, coutumes et croyances dans la tradition orale en Comminges et Couserans*, pp. 161–218.
78. Jean-François Soulet, *Les Pyrénées au XIXe siècle*, vol. 1, pp. 209–17.
79. Yves-Marie Bercé, *Fête et révolte: Des mentalités populaires du XVIe au XVIIIe siècle* (Paris, Hachette, 1976), p. 21; Saint John's Day increasingly began to resemble Carnival in the nineteenth century; for more on the relationship between disorder, revolt and festival, see Natalie Davis, 'Charivari, Honor and Community in Seventeenth-century Lyon and Geneva', in J. MacAloon, ed., *Rite, Drama, Festival, Spectacle: Rehearsals toward a Theory of Cultural Performance* (Philadelphia, Institute for the Study of Human Issues, 1984), pp. 42–57; for a vision of Carnival as a form of popular religion, see Claude Gaignebet and Marie Claude Florentin, *Le Carnaval: Essai de mythologie populaire* (Paris, Payot, 1974); for an appreciative historical critique of their work, see Daniel Fabre, 'Le Monde du carnaval', *Annales: Economies, sociétés, cultures*, vol. 31 (1976), pp. 389–407.
80. Léonard Cros, *Lourdes 1858: Témoins de l'événement*, p. 145. This communal solidarity was reinforced in Ségus on their patron saint's day – Saint Peter's Day – at the end of June. Friends and relatives came from afar

to walk to the cave of Massabieille, headed by their local visionaries, as if to demonstrate their solidarity against the Lourdais.

81. Archives Cros, AVIIIe, pp. 113–14.

82. ibid., p. 256.

83. ibid., p. 128.

84. See Olivier de Marliave, *Trésor de la mythologie pyrénéenne*, p. 161 in particular, pp. 148–55; for the folkloric associations surrounding trees more generally, see Paul Sébillot, *Le Folklore de France* (Paris, Imago, 1985, repr. of Guilmoto, 1904–6), vol. 6, pp. 19–103, and Arnold Van Gennep, *Manuel de folklore français contemporain*, vol. 1(iv) (Paris, A. et J. Picard, 1949), pp. 1,729–2,130.

85. Archives Cros, AVIIe, p. 114.

86. *LDA*, vol. 2, no. 15, pp. 61–2.

87. Archives Cros, AVIIe, p. 222.

88. ibid., p. 115, both quotations.

89. ibid., pp. 223–4; in this deposition Julien Cazenave admitted to dipping the rosaries in the fountain but not the river.

90. See ch. 5, pp. 144–5.

91. Archives Cros, AVIIe, p. 211.

92. Léonard Cros, *Lourdes 1858: Témoins de l'événement*, pp. 133–4.

93. Archives Cros, AVIIe, p. 283.

94. Léonard Cros, *Lourdes 1858: Témoins de l'événement*, p. 134.

95. Archives Cros, AVIIe, p. 299.

96. André Palluel-Guillard, et al., *La Savoie de la Révolution à nos jours, XIXe–XXe siècles* (Rennes, Ouest France, 1986), pp. 150–54.

97. For more on the religious life of the region, see Roger Devos, 'Quelques aspects de la vie religieuse dans le diocèse d'Annecy au milieu du XIXe siècle (d'après une enquête de Mgr Rendu)', *Cahiers d'histoire* (1966), pp. 49–83.

98. For this interpretation and all the details of the different peasant worlds of the Alps, see my 'Possession on the Borders: The "mal de Morzine" in Nineteenth-century France', *Journal of Modern History*, vol. 69 (1997), pp. 451–78; see also C. L. Maire, *Les Possédées de Morzine 1857–1873* (Lyon, Presses Universitaires de Lyon, 1981) and Jacqueline Carroy, *Le Mal de Morzine: De la Possession à l'hystérie* (Paris, Solin, 1981).

4. *The Bishop, the Nanny and the Journalist: Lourdes Emerges on to the National Scene*

1. See J. Merriman, *The Agony of the Republic: The Repression of the Left in Revolutionary France 1848–51* (New Haven, Yale University Press, 1978); Ted W. Margadant, *French Peasants in Revolt: The Insurrection of 1851*

(Princeton, Princeton University Press, 1979); Peter McPhee, *The Politics of Rural Life: Political Mobilization in the French Countryside 1846–1852* (Oxford, Oxford University Press, 1992); Thomas R. Forstenzer, *French Provincial Police and the Fall of the Second Republic: Social Fear and Counter-revolution* (Princeton, Princeton University Press, 1981); Howard C. Payne, *The Police State of Louis Napoleon Bonaparte 1851–1860* (Seattle, WA, University of Washington Press, 1966).

2. Jean-François Soulet, *Les Pyrénées au XIX*[e] *siècle*, vol. 2, pp. 615–34.

3. On these new powers, see Sudhir Hazareesingh and Vincent Wright, 'Le Second Empire: Enjeu politique de la Commune et la commune comme enjeu politique', in *Histoire des communes de France* (Paris, Editions du CNRS, 1998), forthcoming.

4. See Theodore Zeldin, *The Political System of Louis Napoleon Bonaparte* (London, Macmillan, 1958) for the pre-eminent role of the prefects in establishing the regime, pp. 10–27; Guy Thuillier and Jean Tulard, *Histoire de l'administration française* (Paris, PUF, 1984); and Pierre-François-Gustave de La Gorce, *Histoire du Second Empire* (Paris, Henri Plon, 1894–1905), especially vol. 1, for the establishment of the regime and the way it was modelled on the First Empire. See also F. Burdeau, *Histoire de l'administration française du 18*[ème] *au 20*[ème] *siècles* (Paris, Montchrestien, 1989).

5. Matthew Truesdell, *Spectacular Politics: Louis Napoleon Bonaparte and the Fête Impériale 1849–1870* (New York, Oxford University Press, 1997), pp. 156–72; and Rupert Christiansen, *Tales of the New Babylon: Paris in the Mid Nineteenth Century* (London, Minerva, 1996), pp. 17–37.

6. For the variety and importance of these journeys, see Ernest du Barrail, *Voyage de L. Napoléon, Président de la République dans l'est de la France et dans la Normandie* (1850); J.-M. Poulain-Corbion, *Récit du voyage de l'Empereur et de l'Impératrice en Normandie et en Bretagne* (Paris, Amyot, 1858); Anon., *Voyage de LL MM l'Empereur et l'Impératrice dans les départements du sud-est, de la Savoie, de la Corse et de l'Algérie* (1860); F. Laurent, *Voyage de Sa Majesté Napoléon III, Empereur des Français, dans les départements de l'est, du centre et du midi de la France* (Paris, S. Raçon, 1853); C.-L. Cormont, *Voyage de Leurs Majestés Impériales en Auvergne* (Clermont-Ferrand, P. Hubler, 1862); see also A. Méjean, 'Utilisation politique d'une catastrophe: Le Voyage de Napoléon III en Provence durant la grande crise', *Revue historique*, vol. 597 (1996), pp. 133–52.

7. For a concise analytical account, see R. Gildea, *The Past in French History* (London, Yale University Press, 1994), pp. 62–111.

8. Maurice Agulhon, *The Republican Experiment 1848–1852* (Cambridge, Cambridge University Press, 1983), pp. 149–65; Ted W. Margadant, *French Peasants in Revolt*, especially pp. 302–35; James McMillan, *Napoleon III* (Harlow, Longman, 1991), pp. 47–8; P. McPhee, *The Politics of Rural*

Life: Political Mobilization in the French Countryside 1846–1852, pp. 227–59.

9. Bernard Ménager, *Les Napoléon du peuple* (Paris, Aubier, 1988), chronicles the story well, especially in his summary remarks on pp. 355–66; see Alain Corbin, in *Le Village des Cannibales* (Paris, Aubier, 1990), pp. 17, 39–40, 43–56, for the struggles in the Dordogne.

10. For an example, see David M. Luebke, '"Naïve Monarchism" and Marian Veneration in Early-Modern Germany', *Past & Present*, no. 154 (1997), pp. 71–106.

11. *LDA*, vol. 2, cited on p. 45; for the relaying of the messages at the oven, see Léonard Cros, *Histoire de Notre-Dame de Lourdes*, vol. 2, p. 152.

12. Archives Cros, AVIIe, p. 336.

13. ibid., p. 330.

14. ibid., p. 315.

15. *LDA*, vol. 3, no. 357a, pp. 120–21; by 2 January 1859 the condemned had paid neither the fine nor the costs.

16. Archives Cros, AVIIe, p. 316.

17. ibid., p. 334.

18. *LDA*, vol. 3, no. 431a, pp. 188–90.

19. Archives Cros, AVIIe, p. 338.

20. ibid., p. 337.

21. *LDA*, vol. 3, no. 424, p. 179.

22. For this argument in forceful and clear terms, see S. Hazareesingh and Vincent Wright, 'Le Second Empire: Enjeu politique de la Commune et la commune comme enjeu politique', in *Histoires des communes de France*.

23. See for example Jacques Lafon, *Les Prêtres, les fidèles et l'état: Le Ménage à trois du XIXe siècle* (Paris, Beauchesne, 1987), pp. 189–232, charts these changes and makes a clear distinction between the period before and after 1860; see the now classic piece by Roger Magraw, 'The Conflict in the Villages: Popular Anti-clericalism in the Isère (1852–1870)', in Theodore Zeldin, *Conflicts in French Society: Anti-clericalism, Education and Morals in the Nineteenth Century* (London, George Allen & Unwin, 1970), pp. 169–237; for an example of earlier anti-clericalism in rural communes and parishes, see also Barnett Singer, *Village Notables in Nineteenth-century France: Priests, Mayors, Schoolmasters* (Albany, State University of New York Press, 1983), especially pp. 67–88. For other examples of anti-clericalism in rural communes and parishes, Maurice Agulhon, *La République au village: Les Populations du Var de la Révolution à la Seconde République* (Paris, Henri Plon, 1970), pp. 172–88, and Alain Corbin, *Archaïsme et modernité en Limousin au XIXe siècle 1845–1880*, vol. 1, pp. 647–52.

24. Jean-François Soulet, *Les Pyrénées au XIXe siècle*, vol. 2, pp. 220–22.

25. Jean-Clément Martin, *La Vendée et la France* (Paris, Seuil, 1987) and his

La Vendée de la mémoire (Paris, Seuil, 1989); see also R. Gildea, *The Past in French History*, pp. 26–31.

26. The definitive biography is still by his brother Eugène Veuillot and his son François, *Louis Veuillot* (Paris, P. Lethielleux, 1899–1913); see also 'Louis Veuillot et son temps: colloque historique organisé à l'occasion du 100ème anniversaire de sa mort', *Revue de l'Institut Catholique de Paris*, no. 10 (avril–juin 1984); Benoît Le Roux, *Louis Veuillot: Un homme, un combat* (Paris, Téqui, 1984); see the excellent chapter in Austin Gough, *Paris and Rome: The Gallican Church and the Ultramontane Campaign* (Oxford, Oxford University Press, 1986), pp. 81–102; Jacques Gadille, 'Autour de Louis Veuillot et de *L'Univers*', *Cahiers d'histoire* (1969), pp. 275–88.

27. Austin Gough, *Paris and Rome: The Gallican Church and the Ultramontane Campaign*, p. 86.

28. ibid., p. 96.

29. R. Aubert, *Le Pontificat de Pie IX* (Paris, Bloud & Gay, 1963), pp. 262–3; Jacques Lafon, *Les Prêtres, les fidèles et l'état: Le Ménage à trois du XIXe siècle*, pp. 149–87; Philippe Boutry, *Prêtres et paroisses au pays du Curé d'Ars* (Paris, Cerf, 1986), pp. 280–303; Pierre Pierrard, *La Vie quotidienne des prêtres au XIXème siècle 1801–1905* (Paris, Hachette, 1986), pp. 36–8; Jean-Baptiste Duroselle, 'L'Abbé Clavel et les revendications du bas-clergé sous Louis-Philippe', *Etudes d'histoire moderne et contemporaine*, vol. 1 (1947), pp. 99–126.

30. Jean-René Derré, *Lamennais, ses amis et le mouvement des idées à l'époque romantique (1824–1834)* (Paris, Librairie C. Klincksieck, 1962), pp. 385–459, 679–99; P. Bénichou, *Le Temps des prophètes. Doctrines de l'âge romantique* (Paris, Gallimard, 1977), pp. 121–73; and Jean-Baptiste Duroselle, *Les Débuts du catholicisme social en France 1822–1870* (Paris, PUF, 1951), pp. 36–40.

31. Gaston Bordet, 'Emmanuel d'Alzon et la crise mennaisienne 1828–1835', in *Emmanuel d'Alzon dans la société et l'Eglise du XIXe siècle* (Colloque d'histoire sous la direction de René Rémond et Emile Poulat, décembre 1980) (Paris, Editions du Centurion, 1982), p. 45.

32. Austin Gough, *Paris and Rome: The Gallican Church and the Ultramontane Campaign*, especially pp. 26–33; Adrien Dansette, *Religious History of Modern France. Vol. 1: From the Revolution to the Third Republic* (Edinburgh and London, Nelson, 1961), pp. 7–21.

33. For more on Lacordaire, see P. Spencer, *The Politics of Belief in Nineteenth-century France* (London, Faber, 1954), pp. 35–115; and José Cabanis, *Lacordaire et quelques autres: Politique et religion* (Paris, Gallimard, 1982), pp. 278–309.

34. See C. Johnson, *Prosper Guéranger (1805–1875), a Liturgical Theologian:*

An Introduction to His Liturgical Writings and Work. Studio Anselmiana 89 (Rome, Pontifico Ateneo S. Anselmo, 1984); Austin Gough, *Paris and Rome: The Gallican Church and the Ultramontane Campaign*, pp. 127–8, 166–70, 176–80.

35. Denis-Auguste Affre (1793–1848) was a supporter of Lacordaire and academic freedom who recognized the republic in February 1848. The circumstances of his death remain unclear; however, the likelihood that his shooting was an accident did not prevent him becoming an example for the religious right of the uselessness of attempting a reconciliation with the political left. See R. Limouzin-Lamothe and J. Leflon, *Mgr Denis-Auguste Affre, archevêque de Paris 1793–1848* (Paris, J. Vrin, 1971).

36. For Louis Napoleon's often double-dealing role in Italy's changing destiny, see William E. Echard, *Napoleon III and the Concert of Europe* (Baton Rouge, Louisiana State University Press, 1983), pp. 107–28, 141–50, 259–75.

37. Léonard Cros, *Histoire de Notre-Dame de Lourdes*, vol. 2, pp. 305–6.

38. *LDA*, no. 455, p. 220.

39. ibid., no. 434, p. 195.

40. *LDA*, vol. 3, p. 190, editorial note.

41. ibid., no. 432, p. 192.

42. ibid., no. 447, p. 209.

43. For more on his life and work, Gaëtan Bernoville, *Un saint basque: Le Bienheureux Michel Garicoïts* (Paris, J. de Gigord, 1936).

44. *LDA*, vol. 3, no. 448, pp. 209–10.

45. *LDA*, vol. 3, p. 42.

46. On their role, see Howard C. Payne, *The Police State of Louis Napoleon Bonaparte 1851–1860*, pp. 244–7.

47. Archives Cros, AVIIe, p. 143.

48. The uniform was an oddity; while in theory these men carried sabres, and a firearm if their superiors thought it necessary, they were not required to wear a uniform, a fact that further defined their low status.

49. *LDA*, vol. 3, no. 452, p. 217.

50. Archives Cros, AVIIe, p. 146.

51. *LDA*, vol. 3, no. 452, p. 218.

52. Léonard Cros, *Histoire de Notre-Dame de Lourdes*, p. 301.

53. Archives Cros, AVIIe, p. 145.

54. Matthew Truesdell, *Spectacular Politics: Louis Napoleon Bonaparte and the Fête Impériale 1849–1870*, pp. 121–35.

55. Archives Cros, AVIIe, p. 146.

56. See the articles strewn throughout *LDA*, vol. 4; for a reproduction of Veuillot's initial article on 28 August, see the first pages of the volume.

57. For a history of the diocese before, during and after Laurence, see

Jean-Baptiste Laffon, ed., *Le Diocèse de Tarbes et Lourdes* (Paris, Letouzey et Ané, 1971).

58. Laurence had initially supported the 1848 revolution, but, like many in the Church, turned to Louis Napoleon to safeguard and restore order. For aspects of this story, see Edward Berenson, *Populist Religion and Left-Wing Politics in France 1830–1852* (Princeton, Princeton University Press, 1984), especially pp. 36–73.

59. For the plight of the Church in the Revolutionary period, see Timothy Tackett, *Religion, Revolution and Regional Culture in Eighteenth-century France: The Ecclesiastical Oath of 1791* (Princeton, Princeton University Press, 1986); Michel Vovelle, *The Revolution against the Church: From Reason to the Supreme Being*, A. José, tr. (Cambridge, Polity Press, 1991); Ralph Gibson, *A Social History of French Catholicism 1789–1914* (London, Routledge, 1989), pp. 30–35; on de-Christianization, Richard Cobb, *The People's Armies: The Armées Révolutionnaires – Instrument of the Terror in the Departments April 1793 to Floréal Year II*, Marianne Elliot, tr. (New Haven and London, Yale University Press, 1987), pp. 442–79.

60. Gaëtan Bernoville, *L'Evêque de Bernadette* (Paris, Grasset, 1955), pp. 19–20.

61. ibid., pp. 26–68.

62. ibid., p. 117.

63. For the perceived links between patois and Catholic practice, see Caroline Ford, *Creating the Nation in Provincial France: Religion and Political Identity in Brittany* (Princeton, Princeton University Press, 1993), pp. 19, 24–8. She explains how in 1903 a decree banned the use of Breton, Basque, Flemish and Provençal in religious instruction. Regional dialects in the Pyrenees resisted the state's attempt to usurp them well into the nineteenth century; the clergy encouraged these native languages as a means of reaching the faithful, especially women; see Jean-François Soulet, *Les Pyrénées au XIXe siècle*, vol. 2, p. 321. For an introduction to the history of linguistic politics in France, see Michel de Certeau, Dominique Julia, Jacques Revel, *Une politique de la langue: La Révolution française et les patois – l'enquête de Grégoire* (Paris, Gallimard, 1974).

64. Gaëtan Bernoville, *De Notre-Dame de Garaison à Notre-Dame de Lourdes. Jean-Louis Peydessus: Apôtre marial de la Bigorre 1807–1882* (Paris, Grasset, 1959), p. 38.

65. From their perspective, the apparitions at Lourdes were the end of a process rather than a new beginning. Notre-Dame de Héas, founded in the fifteenth century and then destroyed during the Revolution, reopened, and, at the great festivals of Marian piety, the Assumption, the Nativity and the Rosary, hundreds would make their way on the difficult tracks to the mountain chapel. Near the town of Arrens, Notre-Dame de Poueylaün was

resuscitated, a church built and a small college established. Notre-Dame de Piétat, situated on a hill only six kilometres from Tarbes, became once again an important site of pilgrimage in 1861. See Gaëtan Bernoville, *L'Evêque de Bernadette*, pp. 161–4.

66. ibid., pp. 11–27.

67. ibid., p. 38.

68. Gaëtan Bernoville, *De Notre-Dame de Garaison à Notre-Dame de Lourdes. Jean-Louis Peydessus: Apôtre marial de la Bigorre 1807–1882*, p. 70.

69. Timothy Tackett, in his *Priest and Parish in Eighteenth-century France* (Princeton, Princeton University Press, 1977), p. 151, describes men of a different social standing and education from their nineteenth-century successors, in which the clergy were often as much the representatives of the Enlightenment as they were of the Church. See general works such as W. J. Callahan and D. Higgs, eds., *Church and Society in Catholic Europe in the Eighteenth Century* (Cambridge, Cambridge University Press, 1979), pp. 138–54, and G. R. Cragg, *The Church and the Age of Reason 1648–1789* (London, Pelican, 1984), pp. 174–93, for the impact of the Enlightenment on the outlook of the higher clergy; K. O. Aretin, *The Papacy in the Modern World* (London, Weidenfeld & Nicolson, 1970), pp. 15–20, describes the strengthening of Jansenism and reform movements in the Church. For the declining fortunes of the Jesuits and with them many of the 'Baroque' devotional practices that they had promoted since the Counter-Reformation, see L.-J. Rogier, *Siècle des lumières, révolutions, restaurations* (Paris, Seuil, 1966), pp. 107–22.

70. See Ralph Gibson, *A Social History of French Catholicism*, pp. 138–45. For an overview of this general movement across France, see Gérard Cholvy, Yves-Marie Hilaire, *Histoire religieuse de la France contemporaine. Vol. 1: 1800–1880* (Paris, Privat, 1985), pp. 153–93.

71. Archives de la Grotte, IO24; see also William H. C. Smith, *Eugénie: Impératrice et femme (1826–1920)* (Paris, Olivier Orban, 1989), which gives the flavour of the life and roles of the empress.

72. Archives de la Grotte, IO24, 'Allocution au Préfet et aux autorités à l'occasion de l'inauguration de la chapelle Saint-Sauveur près de Luz'.

73. *LDA*, vol. 2, no. 135, p. 159.

74. Gaëtan Bernoville, *L'Evêque de Bernadette*, p. 170, and *LDA*, vol. 6, p. 136, editorial note.

75. The struggle over the Grotto took place at the same time as a seemingly trivial jurisdiction dispute over where to build stables. While the dispute over the Grotto raged, this more banal affair simmered in the background and showed, once again, the importance of local struggles in the national deliberations; see, for example, *LDA*, vol. 2, pp. 378–80; vol. 3, pp. 60–63.

76. See for example *LDA*, vol. 4, nos. 607, 607a, 608, pp. 109–10.
77. ibid., p. 21.
78. ibid., pp. 232–3, excerpt from C. Sylvain, *Vie du P. Hermann, en religion, Augustin-Marie du Très-Saint-Sacrement, Carme déchaussé* (Tours, Mame, 1880; 5th ed., 1924), pp. 325–7.
79. *LDA*, vol. 4, no. 750, p. 250.

5. Bernadette

1. *LDA*, vol. 7, pp. 74–7. For the significance of this construction, see the Prologue to the second half of this volume.
2. For the magnitude of the festival, see *LDA*, vol. 7, pp. 55–60.
3. PO Nevers 5, Sœur Court, fol. 1243^{v}.
4. *LDA*, vol. 7, n. 448, pp. 75–6.
5. PO Nevers 5, Sœur Court, fol. 1243^{v}.
6. PO Nevers 4, Sœur Carrière, fol. 909. Witnesses report how upset she was to be shown to the crowd like a 'bête curieuse'. See PO Nevers 2, Sœur Fabre, fol. 293, PA Nevers, Abbé Perreau, 153.
7. *LDA*, vol. 6, no. 921, p. 110.
8. For example, the Saint Bernadette Chapel was inaugurated only in 1927, and a statue of the visionary in ecstasy in 1932 in the Basilica of the Rosary; the statue of Saint Bernadette as a child appeared outside the train station in 1934.
9. Archives de la Grotte, A20; see the declarations from her family probably drafted by the head of the Garaison Fathers, Père Sempé, contained in this dossier.
10. Père André Ravier, *Le Corps de sainte Bernadette d'après les archives du couvent Saint-Gildard, du diocèse et de la ville de Nevers* (Paris, n.p., 1991), pp. 14–15; see also Archives de la Grotte, A49, 'Châsse de Bernadette conservée à la Maison-Mère des Sœurs de la Charité de Nevers'.
11. She spoke not infrequently of the pressure of visits, as in a letter to the demoiselles Lacour, 'Je suis accablée tous les jours par les visites, cela me fatigue beaucoup.' See Père André Ravier, ed., *Les Ecrits de sainte Bernadette et sa voie spirituelle* (Paris, P. Lethielleux, 2nd ed., 1980), p. 156.
12. Archives Cros, AVIIe, pp. 204–5.
13. For more on the activities of Antoinette, who taught Bernadette for free and corresponded with Rome at an early juncture about the wonders at the Grotto, see *LDA*, vol. 6, dossier Tardhivail, pp. 99–106; for the love between Bernadette and the sisters, see Archives Cros, AVIIe, p. 72.
14. ibid., p. 68.
15. ibid., p. 73, a story repeated in PA Nevers 2, M. T. Bordenave, fol. 379^{v}.

16. ibid., p. 68.
17. ibid. Her companion Sœur Victorine described her agonizing illnesses in many parts of her body and her stoicism in the face of such extreme suffering.
18. Archives Cros AVIIe, p. 55.
19. Père André Ravier, ed., *Les Ecrits de sainte Bernadette*, insists on this point on p. 41, showing how neither the curé of Bartrès nor Pomian even knew who she was.
20. *LDA*, vol. 1, no. 35, p. 218.
21. *LDA*, vol. 1, no. 75*bis*, p. 269.
22. Archives Cros, AVIIe, Jeanne-Marie Poueyto, pp. 139–40.
23. *LDA*, vol. 2, no. 168, pp. 215–16, Adélaïde Monlaur; see n. 28, ch. 3.
24. ibid., vol. 1, no. 75*bis*, p. 270.
25. ibid., no. 33, p. 215.
26. ibid., no. 68, pp. 256–7.
27. ibid., no. 69, p. 258; the editorial note explains that the authorship of this 'procès-verbal' is uncertain, but it seems that Dutour, Jacomet and Lacadé were all present.
28. ibid., no. 69, p. 259.
29. ibid., vol. 1, no. 69, pp. 259–60.
30. ibid., no. 69, p. 259.
31. ibid., no. 76, pp. 273–4.
32. Laurentin explains her purpose in no. 69, n. 7, p. 259.
33. Archives de la Grotte, A20, Houzelot to Peyramale, 12 mai 1873, and Archives Cros, AIII28(39).
34. Archives Cros, AVIIe, p. 74.
35. ibid., André Sajous, pp. 323–4.
36. ibid., Sœur Victorine, pp. 75–6.
37. Archives Cros, AXIV, Abbé Pène, pp. 26–7.
38. Archives Cros, AVIIe, p. 59.
39. ibid., Antoinette and Marie Tardhivail, p. 73.
40. See René Laurentin, *Visage de Bernadette* (Paris, P. Lethielleux, 1978); see the Introduction in vol. 1, pp. 15–19.
41. The apparitions took place in winter, hence the probability that Bernadette was wearing the garments of uncarded wool that were made within her household and typical of the working poor. Calico *was* purchased by rich farmers in mid century to make the dresses and aprons of women, although it is unlikely that the Soubirous would have been able to afford such luxuries. For more on local costume, see Jean-François Soulet, *Les Pyrénées au XIXe siècle*, vol. 2, pp. 310–14, and especially p. 311. See also Therese Taylor, 'Images of Sanctity: Photography of Saint Bernadette of Lourdes and Saint Thérèse of Lisieux', unpub. article.

42. For the photographic trend, see André Rouillé, *L'Empire de la photographie: Photographie et pouvoir bourgeois (1839–1870)* (Paris, Le Sycamore, 1982), pp. 172–4.
43. *LDA*, vol. 7, no. 1777, p. 467.
44. Jean Fourcassié, *Le Romantisme et les Pyrénées*, especially pp. 325 and 339.
45. See Anne Lasserre-Vergne, *Les Pyrénées centrales dans la littérature française*, p. 126.
46. Lettre de l'Abbé M. U. Similien, *LDA*, vol. 6, no. 1273, p. 343.
47. J.-B. Courtin, *Lourdes: Le Domaine de Notre-Dame de Lourdes de 1858 à 1947* (Rennes, Aux éditions franciscaines, 1947), pp. 65–6.
48. For this interpretation of Bernadette's plight, see Therese Taylor, 'Images of Sanctity: Photography of Saint Bernadette of Lourdes and Saint Thérèse of Lisieux'. I thank Dr Taylor for allowing me to cite unpublished work.
49. Archives Cros, AVIIe, p. 44.
50. ibid., pp. 55–6.
51. Letter to Mgr Laurence, *LDA*, vol. 1, no. 65, pp. 248, 249.
52. See ch. 1, p. 33, for Peyramale's belief in divine protection from wolves. *LDA*, vol. 2, n. 50, pp. 19–20.
53. ibid., no. 315, p. 358.
54. *LDA*, vol. 3, p. 31.
55. ibid., no. 455, p. 220.
56. Archives Cros, AIII(5), Chanoine Baudassé.
57. Archives Cros, AVIIe, p. 343a.
58. *LDA*, vol. 2, no. 132, p. 155.
59. Archives Cros, AIII(26)(2), Dr Balencie, at this time the physician at the hospice.
60. Archives Cros, AIII(1), Frère Léobard.
61. Archives Cros, AIII(2).
62. Archives Cros, AVIIe, p. 82.
63. Both letters of self-justification to be found in Archives Cros, AVI(9).
64. Archives Cros, AVI, mémoire de Justin Nereci, p. 3.
65. *LDA*, vol. 7, p. 433.
66. *LDA*, vol. 6, n. 240, pp. 87–8.
67. Archives de la Grotte, A21, mémoire de l'Abbé Montauzé.
68. René Laurentin, *Bernadette vous parle, Lourdes (1844–1866)* (Lourdes, Œuvre de la Grotte, 1972), vol. 1, p. 201.
69. *LDA*, vol. 7, p. 81.
70. *LDA*, vol. 3, n. 244, p. 74.
71. Archives Cros, AVIIe, pp. 45–6.
72. ibid., pp. 72–3.

73. For this critical apparatus, see Père André Ravier, ed., *Les Ecrits de sainte Bernadette et sa voie spirituelle*, pp. 8–9; for the following interpretations of her writings I rely on his judgement.
74. ibid., pp. 116–28.
75. ibid., p. 166.
76. ibid., pp. 154–5.
77. ibid., pp. 159–63.
78. See for example Elizabeth Rapley, *The* Dévotes*: Women and the Church in Seventeenth-century France* (Montreal/London, McGill/Queen's University Press, 1990), pp. 35–40, 79–92; see also Colin Jones, *The Charitable Imperative: Hospitals and Nursing in Ancien Régime and Revolutionary France* (London, Routledge, 1989).
79. See ch. 7.
80. See the controversial and often unsympathetic account of Jean-François Six, *La Véritable Enfance de Thérèse de Lisieux: Névrose et sainteté* (Paris, Seuil, 1972).
81. Jacques Maître, *L'Orpheline de la Bérésina: Thérèse de Lisieux (1873–1897)* (Paris, Cerf, 1995); for the extraordinary circumstances of her life, milieu and the composition of the manuscript, see pp. 81–144.
82. *LHA*, vol. 3, p. 262. For the secrets of La Salette, see Sandra L. Zimdars-Swartz, *Encountering Mary: Visions of Mary from La Salette to Medjugorje*, pp. 165–89.
83. For the popularity of such themes in the nineteenth century, see Caroline Ford, 'Female Martyrdom and the Politics of Sainthood in Nineteenth-century France: The Cult of Sainte Philomène', in Frank Tallett and Nicholas Atkin, eds., *Catholicism in Britain and France since 1789* (London, Hambledon Press, 1996), pp. 115–34.
84. See Frances Beer, *Women and Mystical Experience in the Middle Ages* (London, Boydell Press, 1992), for reflections on Hildegard of Bingen, Mechtild of Magdeburg and Julian of Norwich. For a wider analysis, see Grace M. Jantzen, *Power, Gender and Christian Mysticism* (Cambridge, Cambridge University Press, 1995). See also Gillian T. W. Ahlgren, *Theresa of Avila and the Politics of Sanctity* (Ithaca, Cornell University Press, 1996) and Jodi Bilinkoff, *The Avila of Saint Theresa: Religious Reform in a Sixteenth-century City* (Ithaca, Cornell University Press, 1989), especially pp. 116–23, 140–45, for the social, political and ecclesiastical milieu of the great saint, and Alison Weber, *Theresa of Avila and the Rhetoric of Femininity* (Princeton, Princeton University Press, 1993), which reveals the strategic ambiguities of the Spanish saint's mystical writings; see Jacques Maître, *L'Orpheline de la Bérésina*, for this tradition of writing, especially pp. 49–80, and its impact on Thérèse de Lisieux.
85. For an excellent evocation of this world, see Jacqueline Carroy, *Hypnose,*

suggestion et psychologie: L'Invention de sujets (Paris, PUF, 1991), especially pp. 65–96.
86. See René Laurentin, *Bernadette vous parle, Lourdes (1844–1866)*, vol. 2.

Part Two *The Lourdes of Pilgrimage*

Prologue

1. For a summary of these disastrous beginnings, see *LDA*, vol. 7, pp. 32–40.
2. J.-B. Courtin, *Lourdes: Le Domaine de Notre-Dame de Lourdes de 1858 à 1947*, p. 159.
3. For more on this story, see ch. 8.
4. Joris-Karl Huysmans, *Les Foules de Lourdes* (Grenoble, Jérôme Millon, 1993), pp. 121, 125.
5. *LDA*, vol. 7, pp. 17–27.

6. The Battle of the Books

1. See David C. J. Lee, *Ernest Renan: In the Shadow of Faith* (London, Duckworth, 1996), pp. 187–206; Antoine Albalat, *La Vie de Jésus d'Ernest Renan* (Paris, Société française d'éditions littéraires et techniques, 1933), pp. 43–54; H. W. Wardman, *Ernest Renan: A Critical Biography* (London, Athlone Press, 1964), pp. 72–90; and Charles Rearick, *Beyond the Enlightenment: Historians and Folklore in Nineteenth-century France* (Bloomington, Indiana University Press, 1974), pp. 152–7.
2. Vytas V. Gaigalas, *Ernest Renan and His French Catholic Critics* (North Quincy, MA, Christopher Publishing House, 1972), pp. 33–55.
3. Henri Lasserre, *L'Evangile selon Renan* (Paris, Victor Palmé, 12th ed., 1863), p. 23.
4. *LDA*, vol. 7, dossier annexe no. 1, pp. 129–40.
5. Archives de la Grotte, CII, Léonard Cros, 'M. Henri Lasserre et son livre', unpub. manuscript, pp. 5–7; from here on 'M. Henri Lasserre et son livre'.
6. Victor Palmé, the editor, explained that there were 91 editions in 18mo, 42 editions of the *Mois de Marie* (an abridged version) and 9 editions in octavo with or without engravings.
7. *LDA*, vol. 7, dossier annexe no. 1, p. 129.

8. Henri Lasserre, *Notre-Dame de Lourdes* (Paris, Victor Palmé, 3rd ed., 1878), p. 9.
9. For more on Michelet, see Jean Walch, *Les Maîtres de l'histoire 1815–1850: Augustin Thierry, Mignet, Guizot, Thiers, Michelet, Edgard Quinet* (Geneva and Paris, Editions Slatking, 1986), pp. 193–233; and Ceri Crossley, *French Historians and Romanticism: Thierry, Guizot, the Saint-Simonians, Quinet, Michelet* (London, Routledge, 1993).
10. Henri Lasserre, *Notre-Dame de Lourdes*, p. 173.
11. ibid., p. 85.
12. Indeed, this was the conviction of E. Artus, a devotee of Lasserre and a man dedicated to upholding his account. See his 'Mémoire de Mr Artus, pour Mr Lasserre' in the Archives de la Grotte, in which he insisted that during long conversations with Peyramale, the priest had confirmed the '*exactitude absolue*' of Lasserre's history (p. 22). In subsequent writings on the subject, Artus called Lasserre's work a kind of gospel and accused Cros of being a 'fou'. See Archives de la Grotte, A47, 'Le Livre du Père Cros'.
13. Henri Lasserre, *Notre-Dame de Lourdes*, pp. 351–5.
14. ibid., pp. 64–5.
15. ibid., p. 117.
16. ibid., p. 326.
17. See Henri Lasserre, *Le Curé de Lourdes: Mgr Peyramale* (Paris, Bloud & Barral, 10th ed., 1898).
18. Henri Lasserre, *Notre-Dame de Lourdes*, p. 326.
19. ibid., p. 19.
20. ibid., p. 27.
21. René Laurentin, *LHA*, vol. 1, p. 103.
22. Henri Lasserre, *Notre-Dame de Lourdes*, p. 144.
23. See Jean Walch, *Les Maîtres de l'histoire 1815–1850 . . .*, pp. 137–92 and Ceri Crossley, *French Historians and Romanticism . . .*, pp. 30–35. Lasserre particularly admired Thiers's *Histoire du Consulat et de l'Empire* (Paris, Paulin, 21 vols., 1845–69), although it is perhaps surprising that he was not more critical of the historian's anti-clericalism.
24. Henri Lasserre, *Notre-Dame de Lourdes*, p. 466.
25. ibid., pp. 543, 544.
26. Pierre-Rémi Sempé and Jean-Marie Duboë, reprinted as *Notre-Dame de Lourdes* (Paris, Letouzey et Ané, 1868; 12th ed., 1931); see, for example, p. 76, where Bernadette scolds her younger sister for not praying enough. For the role of Laurence, see pp. 156–68, 197–214.
27. See Stéphane Baumont, 'La Réinvention de Lourdes (1858–1993)', in *Histoire de Lourdes* (Toulouse, Privat, 1993), p. 251; and P. A. Larrouy, *Petite histoire de Notre-Dame de Garaison (1510 environ–1923)* (Garaison, Notre-Dame de Garaison, 1933), pp. 73–83.

28. See ch. 10.
29. For the bishop's unhappiness over the characterization of the officials, see 'M. Henri Lasserre et son livre', p. 69.
30. ibid., p. 22.
31. ibid., pp. 55, 74.
32. ibid., pp. 45–8.
33. ibid., p. 48; see Abbé Fourcade's honourable but inaccurate account, *L'Apparition à la Grotte de Lourdes* (Tarbes, chez Fouga, 1862).
34. Archives de la Grotte, A38, Henri Lasserre, 'Très-humble supplique et mémoire adressé par M. Henri Lasserre à la sacrée congrégation du Saint-Office romain sur certains abus très préjudiciable à la religion', pp. 8–9.
35. Forcade did not know about the tension between Lasserre and the sanctuary officials, and was later to regret publicly having authorized the meeting. See 'M. Henri Lasserre et son livre', pp. 117–19.
36. Archives de la Grotte, A39, 'Lettre de Pierre-Rémi Sempé à Monseigneur Pierre-Anastase Pichenot en réponse aux accusations de M. Henri Lasserre', pp. 11–14.
37. Archives Cros, DXIV, 'Notre histoire de l'événement de Lourdes' (avril 1864–décembre 1892); see, for example, pp. 22, 28, 39–40, 42, 45–54. From here on this will be cited as 'Notre histoire de l'événement de Lourdes'.
38. See ch. 2.
39. See ch. 10.
40. Henri Lasserre, 'Très-humble supplique . . . la religion', p. 43.
41. ibid., p. 49.
42. Archives de la Grotte, A39, 'Lettre de Pierre-Rémi Sempé à Monseigneur Pierre-Anastase Pichenot en réponse aux accusations de M. Henri Lasserre', p. 11.
43. ibid., p. 18.
44. ibid., p. 23.
45. Archives de la Grotte, A42, 'Mémoire confidentiel présenté au Saint Siège par l'Evêque de Tarbes', p. 10.
46. Archives de la Grotte, A42, 'Mémoire confidentiel présenté au Saint Siège par l'Evêque de Tarbes', pp. 6–7, and J.-B. Courtin, *Lourdes: Le Domaine de Notre-Dame de Lourdes de 1858 à 1947*, pp. 5–6.
47. 'M. Henri Lasserre et son livre', p. 172.
48. For this story, see Philippe Boutry, *Prêtres et paroisses au pays du Curé d'Ars*, pp. 117–32; Peyramale's dilemmas and desires were common; see Jean-Michel Leniaud, 'Les Constructions d'églises sous le Second Empire: Architecture et prix de revient', *Revue d'histoire de l'église de la France*, vol. 55 (1979), pp. 267–78.
49. Archives de la Grotte, VO2, Anon. [A. Peyramale], *L'Eglise nouvelle de*

Lourdes et Monseigneur Peyramale (Pau, Imprimerie-Stéréotypie Garet, 2nd ed., 1890).
50. Archives de la Grotte, A42, 'Mémoire confidentiel présenté au Saint Siège par l'Evêque de Tarbes', p. 14.
51. ibid., p. 16.
52. ibid., pp. 16–17.
53. Archives Cros, CII(V), 'Mémoire confidentiel communiqué à nos seigneurs les évêques de France', p. 21.
54. 'M. Henri Lasserre et son livre', p. 212.
55. *LDA*, vol. 7, no. 1611, p. 352.
56. ibid., no. 1,777, p. 467.
57. ibid., p. 470.
58. ibid., p. 469.
59. See editorial note in *LDA*, vol. 7, no. 1,777, pp. 465–6.
60. 'M. Henri Lasserre et son livre', p. 227.
61. 'Notre histoire de l'événement de Lourdes', p. 14.
62. G. Cubitt, *The Jesuit Myth: Conspiracy Theory and Politics in Nineteenth-century France* (Oxford, Clarendon Press, 1993), pp. 143–81.
63. Léonard Cros, *Histoire de Notre-Dame de Lourdes* (Paris, Beauchesne, 3 vols., 1925–7), Père Ferdinand Cavallera, ed.
64. Léonard Cros, *Histoire de Notre-Dame de Lourdes* (Paris, Beauchesne, 3 vols., 1957) and *Lourdes 1858: Témoins de l'événement* (Paris, P. Lethielleux, 1957), Père M. Olphe-Galliard, ed.
65. 'M. Henri Lasserre et son livre', pp. 232–4.
66. See, for example, the differences between Archives Cros, AVII, 'Journal d'enquête du Père Cros (minutes de dépositions et notes de voyages 1878–1881)' and AVIII, 'Témoins de l'apparition', which largely appeared in book form edited by Père M. Olphe-Galliard, *Lourdes 1858: Témoins de l'événement*.
67. *LDA*, vol. 2, no. 130, p. 153.
68. Léonard Cros, *Lourdes 1858: Témoins de l'événement*, p. 358.
69. Henri Lasserre, *Notre-Dame de Lourdes*, pp. 225–6.
70. Léonard Cros, *Histoire de Notre-Dame de Lourdes. Vol. 1: Les Apparitions* (Paris, Beauchesne, 1957), pp. 479–99; for a summary, see pp. 496–8.
71. *LHA*, vol. 6, pp. 173–201, especially p. 174. Laurentin seems to be in the same tradition when he in turn demolishes Cros's argument by recourse to the original documents.
72. Léonard Cros, *Histoire de Notre-Dame de Lourdes. Vol. 1: Les Apparitions*, pp. 44–50.
73. ibid., pp. 271–88.
74. ibid., pp. 96–135.

75. ibid., pp. 392–8; see also Léonard Cros, *Histoire de Notre-Dame de Lourdes. Vol. 2: Les Luttes*, pp. 33, 38, 471.
76. ibid. This interpretation of the people unwittingly doing Satan's work surfaces throughout the work; see, for example, ibid., pp. 35, 48, 99–100, 103, 158, 172–3, 188, 219.
77. ibid., p. 35.
78. ibid., vol. 2, see for example pp. 8–9, 26. Peyramale is implicitly criticized for believing too early in the apparitions and for being on the look-out for miracles; see also pp. 17–18 for Cros's judgement that both Pène and Peyramale unjustly accused their bishop of lack of courage. Cros believed that Laurence showed prudence rather than pusillanimity; the work is littered with these cautionary notes about the behaviour of the local clergy.
79. 'M. Henri Lasserre et son livre', p. 234.
80. ibid., pp. 234–5.
81. ibid., pp. 235–6.
82. For this extraordinary tale, see *LDA*, vol. 1, pp. 25–31; for the failure of Sempé to achieve better results with the Massy clan by not securing the papal nobility they wanted for their eldest son, pp. 28–9. For Cros's continued efforts to regain access to the papers after once seeing them, see 'Notre histoire de l'événement de Lourdes', pp. 330–37; they were in his possession for only a few days and he did his best to copy the manuscripts. These are now the only remains of Massy's papers, which were later lost.
83. 'Notre histoire de l'événement de Lourdes', pp. 84–6.
84. ibid., p. 131.
85. ibid., p. 154.
86. ibid., p. 188.
87. ibid., p. 226.
88. ibid., p. 197.
89. ibid., p. 198.
90. ibid., p. 223.
91. ibid., p. 189.
92. ibid., pp. 253–83.
93. Jean-Baptiste Estrade, *Les Apparitions de Lourdes: Souvenirs intimes d'un témoin* (Tours, Mame, 1899).
94. 'Notre histoire de l'événement de Lourdes', p. 277; for the larger story, see pp. 265–73.
95. ibid., p. 305.
96. See *LHA*, vol. 1, p. 135.
97. Archives Cros, DXIV, manuscript by Père Ferdinand Cavallera, 'Histoire de Notre-Dame de Lourdes du Père Cros', 31 août 1924. See also Abbé Georges Bertrin, *Histoire critique des événements de Lourdes: Apparitions et guérisons* (Paris, Librairie Gabalda, 1905).

98. Archives Cros, DXIV, 'Memorandum on *Histoire de Notre-Dame de Lourdes* du Père Cros', written by 'F.C.', undoubtedly Père Ferdinand Cavallera, 31 août 1924.
99. ibid., p. 298.
100. *La Source* (revue de Lourdes), décembre 1927, janvier 1928 and février 1928.

7. The Assumption and the Foundations of Pilgrimage

1. See *Annales de Notre-Dame de Lourdes*, vol. 1 (1868), pp. 28–32, for the unformed nature of pilgrimage coming from mainly regional, rather than distant, centres.
2. For a broad social analysis of legitimism, see Steven D. Kale, *Legitimism and the Reconstruction of French Society (1852–1883)* (Baton Rouge and London, Louisiana State University Press, 1992), especially pp. 263–328.
3. For a classic scholarly account, see R. Aubert, *Le Pontificat de Pie IX (1846–1878)* (Paris, Bloud & Gay, 2nd ed., 1963), pp. 72–106, for background, for doctrinal disputes and the triumph of the ultramontanist current, pp. 311–67; and pp. 369–73 for a newer interpretation.
4. See Eamon Duffy, *Saints and Sinners: A History of the Popes* (London, Yale University Press, 1997), pp. 222–35.
5. E. Larkin, 'The Devotional Revolution in Ireland 1850–1875', *American Historical Review*, vol. 77 (1972), pp. 625–52; see Jonathan Sperber, *Popular Catholicism in Nineteenth-century Germany* (Princeton, Princeton University Press, 1984), pp. 55–79, 91–8; F. Lannon, *Privilege, Persecution and Prophecy: The Catholic Church in Spain 1875–1975* (Oxford, Oxford University Press, 1987), pp. 59–88; and Ralph Gibson, *A Social History of French Catholicism 1789–1914*, pp. 134–57.
6. Claude Langlois, *Le catholicisme au féminin: Les Congrégations françaises à supérieure générale au XIXe siècle* (Paris, Cerf, 1984). For more on the wide scope for activism that such communities afforded to women, see Yvonne Turin, *Femmes et religieuses au XIXe siècle: Le Féminisme 'en religion'* (Paris, Nouvelle Cité, 1989); and Jacques Léonard, 'Femmes, religion et médecine: Les Religieuses qui soignent, en France au XIXe siècle', *Annales ESC*, vol. 32 (1977), pp. 887–907; and for the pace and nature of their spirituality, see Odile Arnold, *Le Corps et l'âme: La Vie des religieuses au XIXe siècle* (Paris, Seuil, 1984).
7. For this institutional efflorescence and the special role of feminine spirituality in its development, see Olwen Hufton, *The Prospect before Her: A History of Women in Western Europe 1500–1800*, vol. 1, pp. 366–96; for a pioneering examination of the spiritual wellsprings of this movement and

its intellectual bases, see Linda Timmermans, *L'Accès des femmes à la culture (1598–1715)* (Paris, Honoré Champion, 1993), pp. 393–811.

8. See nn. 69, 70, ch. 4.

9. Bonnie Smith, in her pathbreaking *Ladies of the Leisure Class: The Bourgeoises of Northern France* (Princeton, Princeton University Press, 1981), demonstrates the ideological divide between the sexes that Catholicism created within elite families.

10. This caricatural view has been promoted by Ralph Gibson, *A Social History of French Catholicism 1789–1914*; see especially his remarks pp. 134–57, 180–90; for sympathetic portrayals of women's devotion to religion in the face of revolutionary persecution, see Olwen Hufton, *Women and the Limits of Citizenship during the French Revolution* (Toronto, Toronto University Press, 1992) and Suzanne Desan, *Reclaiming the Sacred: Lay Religion and Popular Politics during the French Revolution* (Ithaca, Cornell University Press, 1990).

11. For the enduring impact of such modes of thought on French political culture, see Paul Smith, *Feminism and the Third Republic: Women's Political and Civil Rights in France 1918–1945* (Oxford, Oxford University Press, 1996), pp. 63–162, especially. This work demonstrates the left's continued refusal to countenance the vote for women on anti-clerical grounds right through the inter-war period. For a more interpretive account, see Pierre Ronsanvallon, *Le Sacre du citoyen: Histoire du suffrage universel en France* (Paris, Gallimard, 1992), pp. 393–412.

12. For the authoritative biography, see Siméon Vailhé, *La Vie du Père Emmanuel d'Alzon* (Paris, Maison de la Bonne Presse, 2 vols., 1926–34). For the relationship to his region, see Gérard Cholvy, 'Emmanuel d'Alzon: Les Racines', in *Emmanuel d'Alzon dans la société et l'Eglise du XIXe siècle*, René Rémond and Emile Poulat, eds. (Paris, Le Centurion, 1982), pp. 15–41.

13. See Louis Secondy, 'Aux origines de la maison de l'Assomption à Nîmes (1844–1853)', in ibid., pp. 233–56; on the importance of the papal military forces in ultramontanist circles, see 'Cinquantième anniversaire de la création du régiment des Zouaves pontificaux: Allocution de Monseigneur de Cabrières', Montmartre, 5 juin 1910 (Montpellier, Imprimerie de la Manufacture de la Charité).

14. AAR, d'Alzon to the Clergy of the Diocese of Nîmes, 23 août 1873; d'Alzon initiated this pilgrimage as early as 1845, taking with him the young students from his college in Nîmes, and only those concerned with sincere religious conversion. See Claude Softens, 'Le Père d'Alzon, les Assomptionnistes et les pèlerinages', in *Emmanuel d'Alzon dans la société et l'Eglise du XIXe siècle*, p. 303.

15. For this fascinating story of change and continuity, see Michel Vovelle,

Les Métamorphoses de la fête en Provence de 1750 à 1820, pp. 269–84 in particular.
16. E. Lacoste, *Le Père François Picard* (Paris, Maison de la Bonne Presse, 1932), n., p. 2. In his native village of Saint-Gervasy, an eighteenth-century bishop erected a cross as 'une réparation des outrages que les protestants, les "camisards", avaient infligés à la croix dans tout le Midi'.
17. Maurice Larkin, *Religion, Politics and Preferment in France since 1890:* La Belle Epoque *and Its Legacy* (Cambridge, Cambridge University Press, 1995), p. 23.
18. E. Lacoste, *Le Père François Picard*, pp. 440–44.
19. This man went twice to Compostela, Our Lady of Pilar, once to Saint Nicholas of Bari, twice to Jerusalem, and to Lourdes and La Salette every year.
20. Père Rémi Kokel, *Le Père Vincent de Paul Bailly: Journaliste et pèlerin (1832–1912)* (Paris, Maison de la Bonne Presse, 1943), p. 22.
21. For the history of this newspaper, see Pierre Sorlin, *'La Croix' et les juifs 1880–1899: Contribution à l'histoire de l'antisémitisme contemporain* (Paris, B. Grasset, 1967).
22. AAR, Père d'Alzon to Père Picard, 29 janvier 1870.
23. G. Miegge, *The Virgin Mary: The Roman Catholic Marian Doctrine* (London, Lutterworth Press, 1955), pp. 83–106.
24. AAR, Père d'Alzon to Père Picard, 3 septembre 1877.
25. For a discussion of the shift from rigourism to the confessional philosophy of Alphonse de Liguori in the early decades of the century, see Philippe Boutry, *Prêtres et paroisses au pays du Curé d'Ars*, pp. 405–22.
26. See Gérard Cholvy, 'Emmanuel d'Alzon: Les Racines', in *Emmanuel d'Alzon dans la société et l'Eglise du XIXe siècle*, p. 33.
27. Claude Savart, 'Le Père d'Alzon et la direction spirituelle des laïques d'après sa correspondance', in ibid., p. 265.
28. See ch. 3.
29. For the classic account, see Dom Cuthbert Butler, *The Vatican Council 1869–1870* (London, Fontana, 1962, repr. of 1930 edition).
30. For d'Alzon's specific contribution, see Père Pierre Touveneraud, 'La Participation du Père d'Alzon à la défense des états pontificaux 1859–1863', *Pages d'archives*, no. 12 (octobre 1960), pp. 385–410.
31. See AAR, Père Désiré Deraedt, 'Le Père d'Alzon et les droits de Dieu sur la société', unpub. manuscript, for the impact of de Bonald's thought on d'Alzon.
32. For the orchestration of many symbols and commemorations, see Pierre Nora, ed., *Les Lieux de mémoire: La République* (Paris, Gallimard, 1984), vol. 1.
33. None the less, as time went on, the success of this initiative would surprise even him, and he worried lest the national pilgrimage take too much of his priests' limited energies. For an example of his doubts, and of his desire to leave pilgrimage to the bishops, see his letter to Père Picard, AAR, 8 septembre 1875.

34. Père Charles Monsch, AAR, 'Comment, dans les pèlerinages, les disciples du Père d'Alzon sont-ils restés fidèles à l'affirmation, par leur fondateur, des droits de Dieu?', unpub. manuscript.
35. AAR, Père Bailly to Père d'Alzon, no. 1,066, 20 juillet 1870; Vincent de Paul Bailly spoke of the thousands of men departing from the Gare de l'Est and the Gare du Nord, the sound of the 'Marseillaise', the tearful but brave partings and the concern for the wounded.
36. AAR, Père Picard to Père d'Alzon, no. 791, 10 février 1871.
37. AAR, Père d'Alzon to Père Victorin Galabert, another of his priests, 24 septembre 1870.
38. For the Assumptionists in Germany, see AAR, Père Bailly to Père d'Alzon, no. 1,077, 7 novembre 1870; and for more on *Rerum novarum* and social Catholicism, see pp. 372–3.
39. Père Rémi Kokel, *Le Père Vincent de Paul Bailly: Journaliste et pèlerin*, p. 41.
40. AAR, Père Picard to Père d'Alzon, no. 797, 10 avril 1871.
41. AAR, Père Bailly to Père d'Alzon, no. 1,151, 12 avril 1871.
42. AAR, Père Bailly to Père d'Alzon, no. 1,143, 23 mars 1871.
43. AAR, Père Bailly to Père d'Alzon, no. 1,155, 12 mai 1871.
44. AAR, Père Bailly to Père Alzon, no. 1,159, 31 mai 1871.
45. AAR, Père Bailly to Père d'Alzon, no. 1,151, 12 avril 1871. He was particularly impressed by those who were 'furieuses contre la Commune, ayant appelé Versailles à grands cris de femmes, bonnes chrétiennes indignées des églises fermées etc., etc.; viennent et encore ce matin nous apporter des malédictions contre Versailles, ils n'ont pas eu, disent-elles, tant de courage pour nous délivrer des Prussiens et le reste.'
46. AAR, Père Picard to Père d'Alzon, no. 804, 25 mai 1871.
47. AAR, Père Picard to Père Bailly, no. 854, 29 juin 1871.
48. See Susanna Barrows, *Distorting Mirrors: Visions of the Crowd in Late Nineteenth-century France* (New Haven, Yale University Press, 1981), especially pp. 7–92.
49. Père Picard, 'Notre-Dame de Salut', *Sermons et allocutions*, vol. 5, no. 490, pp. 190–200.
50. AAR, Sœur Thérèse Maylis, 'Marie-Eugénie et le Père d'Alzon: Intuitions communes, influence réciproque?', unpub. manuscript, p. 31. Her order lived by the following principles: 'Vous faites partie d'une Congrégation dont l'amour doit aller, en toutes choses, jusqu'à l'adoration . . . Marie en qui tout a été l'adoration . . . Adoratrices et zélatrices des droits de Dieu . . . Adoratrices et apôtres des droits de Dieu.'
51. AAR, Père Picard to Père Alexis Dumazer, no. 967, 30 mai 1872.
52. For a copy of the manifesto, see A. Pépin, 'Le Père François Picard, directeur de l'association de Notre-Dame de Salut et des pèlerinages nationaux', *Pages d'archives*, no. 3 (novembre 1963), pp. 183–4.

53. Benjamin F. Martin, *Count Albert de Mun: Paladin of the Third Republic* (Chapel Hill, University of North Carolina Press, 1978), pp. 13–20.
54. For d'Alzon's doubts, see AAR, Charles Monsch, 'Comment, dans les pèlerinages, les disciples du Père d'Alzon sont-ils restés fidèles à l'affirmation, par leur fondateur, des droits de Dieu?', pp. 2, 4.
55. 'Madame de la Rochefoucauld, Duchesse d'Estissac, née de Ségur, présidente du conseil de Notre-Dame de Salut', *Hospitalité de Notre-Dame de Salut: Membres décédés* (Toulouse, Imprimerie catholique Saint-Cyprien, 1906), pp. 24–6; 'Mme La Duchesse d'Estissac', *Bulletin de Notre-Dame de Salut*, no. 36 (1905), pp. 115–20.
56. AAR, Père d'Alzon to Père Picard, 21 novembre 1874.
57. Olwen Hufton, *The Prospect before Her: A History of Women in Western Europe 1500–1800*, pp. 375–9; see also her unpublished lecture, 'The Widow's Mite and Other Strategies: Funding the Catholic Reformation', read 2 July as the Prothero Lecture, Royal Historical Society, London 1997.
58. For a copy of the manifesto, see A. Pépin, 'Le Père François Picard, directeur de l'association de Notre-Dame de Salut et des pèlerinages nationaux', *Pages d'archives*, p. 185; Père Bailly, *Association de Notre-Dame de Salut, rapport général* (Paris, Au Sécretariat, rue François 1er, 1874), pp. 11–12.
59. Père Bailly, *Association de Notre-Dame de Salut, rapport général*, p. 11.
60. ibid., p. 12.
61. ibid., pp. 11–12.
62. Her more limited circumstances also come through when she wrote to Picard of the labour of decorating her new apartment in Boulogne-sur-Mer, a kind of work that the most elevated might not have needed to attend to personally; see AAR, FF66, 10 mars 1885.
63. AAR, UB209, Mme Laforest to Père Picard, 2 novembre 1874.
64. AAR, UB210, Mme Laforest to Père Picard, 31 novembre 1874.
65. AAR, UB193, Mme Dumont to Père Bailly, 1874, no specific date.
66. AAR, UB195, Mme Dumont to Père Bailly, 1874.
67. AAR, Père Picard to Père Bailly, no. 1,019, 17 juillet 1873.
68. AAR, Père Picard to Père Bailly, no. 1,039, 28 août 1873. He wrote:

Je joins à votre lettre un petit mot pour Mme La Forest. Remettez-le lui après l'avoir lu. Avec les femmes il faut réclamer avec autorité, autrement on n'a rien. Dites carrément que vous voulez les lettres tous les soirs, que je vous ai écrit d'y tenir. Ne vous étonnez pas, lorsqu'on ne voit pas le côté large et juste des choses, montrez-le et tenez à ce que vous avez dit. Laissez Mme Gossin avec ses petits mots; s'il le faut, arrêtez-les au passage ou, mieux encore, écrivez un mot à cette brave dame pour lui dire que, lorsqu'on a la besogne à faire, on a besoin de toute son initiative. Je ne dis rien de cet incident, je me contente de la correspondance et me garde bien de mettre en fureur contre vous.

69. See Claude Savart, 'Le Père d'Alzon et la direction spirituelle des laïques d'après sa correspondance', in *Emmanuel d'Alzon dans la société et l'Eglise du XIXe siècle*, pp. 259–72; for the most famous of these interactions – which included a 'spiritual friendship' that lasted decades and involved the establishment of the sister order of the Religieuses de l'Assomption, see Sœur Thérèse Maylis, 'Marie-Eugénie et le Père d'Alzon: Intuitions communes, influence réciproque?' AAR, unpub. manuscript. For more on her life, see Gaëtan Bernoville, *Les Religieuses de l'Assomption: Eugénie Milleret* (Paris, Grasset, 1948).
70. AAR, Père d'Alzon to Mlle Valentine Chaudordy, 15 juillet 1873.
71. See the classic discussion in Caroline Walker Bynum's *Holy Feast and Holy Fast: The Religious Significance of Food to Medieval Women*, especially pp. 189–218, 245–59, as well as the more recent Elizabeth Alvilda Petroff, *Body and Soul: Essays on Medieval Women and Mysticism* (New York, Oxford University Press, 1994).
72. AAR, UB213, Mme Laforest to Père Picard, 7 décembre 1874.
73. AAR, GT541, Mme Dumont to Père Bailly, 1876, no specific date.
74. AAR, UB203, Mme Laforest to Père Picard, 14 février 1874.
75. AAR, UB205, Mme Laforest to Père Picard, 1874, no specific date.
76. AAR, FF62/1, Mme Laforest to Père Picard, 10 septembre 1873.
77. AAR, FF63/1, Mme Laforest to Père Picard, 23 octobre 1874.
78. AAR, UB206, Mme Laforest to Père Picard, 26 octobre 1874.
79. AAR, FF65, Mme Laforest to Père Picard, 25 octobre 1874.
80. AAR, UB211, Mme Laforest to Père Picard, 2 décembre 1874.
81. AAR, UB192, Mme Dumont to Père Bailly, 1874, no specific date.
82. AAR, UB190, Mme Dumont to Père Bailly, 1874, no specific date.
83. AAR, UB196, Mme Dumont to Père Bailly, 1874, no specific date.
84. See, for example, the following letters between Picard and Mme la Baronne de Bastard: AAR, no. 865, 12 avril 1871; no. 1,059, 6 août 1873; no. 1,060, 21 octobre 1873. Their relationship lasted for years, and was interspersed with mutual consolation over the political turn of events and Mme la Baronne de Bastard's frequent contributions to the Assumption. As she sank increasingly into solitary invalidism, he praised her willingness to embody the passion of France in her own person; see his remarks in no. 865, especially: 'Crucifiez-vous dans les détails de la vie et faites abnégation complète de votre volonté . . . C'est le meilleur moyen d'ajouter votre goutte de sang à ces flots répandus pour la régénération de notre patrie et le triomphe de l'Eglise.' A distinguished woman of fortune from a distinguished house, she sought only anonymity when she offered funds (see another letter to Père Alexis Dumazer, AAR, no. 965, 8 mai 1872), an embodiment of Christian humility and physical suffering that gained Picard's true loyalty. Both priest and penitent gained much from their emotional interaction, the former the

edifying spectacle of a 'good death', the latter a firm belief in her ultimate heavenly reward.

85. AAR, FF66, Mme Laforest to Père Picard, 10 mars 1885.

86. Sœur M. Humberte, 'La Famille d'Etienne Pernet: Sa mère', in *Le Père Etienne Pernet: Hier et aujourd'hui, Pages d'archives*, 4th series, vol. 1 (1966), pp. 21–7.

87. Père Pierre Touveneraud, 'Aux origines de la vocation personnelle d'Etienne Pernet: "Une période de quatorze années de rude souffrance"', ibid., pp. 29–69.

88. AAR, Père d'Alzon to Père Pernet, *c.* 9 décembre 1857.

89. AAR, Père d'Alzon to Père Pernet, 29 avril 1859.

90. Père Pierre Touveneraud, 'Aux origines de la vocation personnelle d'Etienne Pernet: "Une période de quatorze années de rude souffrance"', Père Pernet to Père d'Alzon quoted on p. 60.

91. Claude Savart, 'Pour une sociologie de la ferveur religieuse: L'Archiconfrérie de Notre-Dame des Victoires', *Revue d'Histoire Ecclésiastique [Belgium]*, vol. 59 (1964), pp. 823–44.

92. For a quick summary of her life, see Anon., *Mère Marie de Jésus: Marie-Antoinette Fage, cofondatrice avec le Père Pernet, AA, des Petites-Sœurs de l'Assomption* (Paris, 57 rue Violet, 1983); for the definitive account, see Anon., *La Mère Marie de Jésus: Fondatrice des Petites-Sœurs de l'Assomption, gardes-malades des pauvres à domicile* (Paris, Maison de la Bonne Presse, 1908).

93. APSA, Marie-Antoinette Fage to Père Pernet, 14 juin 1864.

94. APSA, Marie-Antoinette Fage to Père Pernet, 26 juin 1864.

95. APSA, Marie Antoinette Fage to Père Pernet, 26 novembre 1864.

96. APSA, Marie-Antoinette Fage to Père Pernet, 1865, no specific date.

97. APSA, Marie-Antoinette Fage to Père Pernet, 3 novembre 1867.

98. APSA, Père Pernet to Marie-Antoinette Fage, 21 juillet 1864.

99. APSA, Père Pernet to Marie-Antoinette Fage, 5 novembre 1864.

100. APSA, Père Pernet to Marie-Antoinette Fage, 29 septembre 1864.

101. See for example Père Pernet to Marie-Antoinette Fage, 14 janvier 1865.

102. Père Pernet to Marie-Antoinette Fage, 29 octobre 1866.

103. Père Pernet to Marie-Antoinette Fage, 2 novembre 1866.

104. Père Pernet to Marie-Antoinette Fage, 26 juillet 1865.

105. Both citations from Père Pierre Touveneraud, 'Mère Marie de Jésus', unpub. manuscript; n.d., APSA, quotations from her contemporaries.

106. For this developing spirituality, see Jacques Maître, *L'Orpheline de la Bérésina*, especially pp. 363–79.

107. Luisa Accati, 'Explicit Meanings: Catholicism, Matriarchy and the Distinctive Problems of Italian Feminism', *Gender and History*, vol. 7 (1995), pp. 241–59.

108. APSA, Mère Marie de Jésus to Sœur Marie de la Croix, 28 novembre 1866.
109. APSA, Mère Marie de Jésus 'à une de ses filles', 1872, no specific date.
110. APSA, Mère Marie de Jésus to Sœur M. Stéphanie, 15 juin 1870.
111. Anon., *La Mère Marie de Jésus: Fondatrice des Petites-Sœurs de l'Assomption, gardes-malades des pauvres à domicile*, pp. 254–5.
112. APSA, C. Bizinard to Mère Marie de Jésus, 28 juin 1880.
113. See n. 78, ch. 5.
114. Anon., *La Mère Marie de Jésus: Fondatrice des Petites-Sœurs de l'Assomption, gardes-malades des pauvres à domicile*, p. 295.

8. The Past, the Present and the Rituals of Modern Pilgrimage

1. A. Pépin, 'Le Père François Picard: directeur de l'association de Notre-Dame de Salut et des pèlerinages nationaux', *Pages d'archives*, no. 3 (novembre 1963), p. 225.
2. Caroline Walker Bynum, *Holy Feast and Holy Fast: The Religious Significance of Food to Medieval Women*, pp. 115–86.
3. See Bruno Latour, *Les Microbes* (Paris, A. M. Métailié, 1984) and C. Salomon-Bayet, *Pasteur et la révolution pasteurienne* (Paris, Payot, 1986) for changes in microbiological and hygienic perceptions. See also Gerald L. Geison, *The Private Science of Louis Pasteur* (Princeton, Princeton University Press, 1995), pp. 35–45, for more on Pasteur and the germ theory.
4. Thomas A. Kselman, *Miracles and Prophecies in Nineteenth-century France* (New Brunswick, NJ, Rutgers University Press, 1983), pp. 164–5.
5. Eric Hobsbawm and Terry Ranger, *The Invention of Tradition* (Cambridge, Cambridge University Press, 1983).
6. For how such symbols were advanced and past events commemorated, see Pierre Nora, ed., *Les Lieux de mémoire: La République*, vol. 1; for Marianne, see Maurice Agulhon, *Marianne into Battle: Republican Imagery and Symbolism in France 1789–1880* (Cambridge, Cambridge University Press, 1981) and his *Marianne au pouvoir: L'Image et la symbolique républicaine* (Paris, Flammarion, 1989); for the memorialization of republican heroes see 'La "statuomanie" et l'histoire', in Agulhon's *Histoire vagabonde* (Paris, Gallimard, 1988), vol. 1, pp. 137–85, and William Cohen, 'Symbols of Power: Statues in Nineteenth-century Provincial France', *Comparative Studies in Society and History*, vol. 31 (1989), pp. 491–513.
7. See Steven D. Kale, *Legitimism and the Reconstruction of French Society (1852–1883)* (Baton Rouge, Louisiana, University of Louisiana Press, 1992), pp. 175–80, and Robert R. Locke, *French Legitimists and the Politics of Moral Order in the Early Third Republic* (Princeton, Princeton University

Press, 1974), especially pp. 10–52, for the difficulties of the legitimist project.
8. See Raymond A. Jonas, 'Monument as Ex-Voto, Monument as Historiography: The Basilica of Sacré-Cœur', *French Historical Studies*, vol. 18 (1993), pp. 482–502.
9. ibid., n. 11, p. 485.
10. René Laurentin and A. Durand, *Pontmain – Histoire authentique: Un signe dans le ciel* (Paris, P. Lethielleux, 1970), pp. 22-43.
11. David Blackbourn, *Marpingen: Apparitions of the Virgin Mary in Bismarckian Germany* (Oxford, Oxford University Press, 1993), pp. 35–6; for an example of the response in France, see *Le Pèlerin*, no. 34 (28 février 1874), which describes a vision of the Virgin who appeared first in the position of the Immaculate Conception, then accompanied by a vision of Pius IX and, finally, as a weeping Notre-Dame des Douleurs, pp. 671–7.
12. Abbé J.-M. Curique, *Voix prophétiques ou signes, apparitions et prédictions modernes touchant les grands événements de la chrétienté au XIX siècle et vers l'approche de la fin des temps* (Paris, Victor Palmé, 1872), pp. 254–73.
13. Vincent de Paul Bailly, 'Apparition de la Sainte Vierge à deux écoliers', *Revue de l'enseignement chrétien*, vol. 5 (1873), pp. 49–56, quotation p. 49.
14. 'Les Visions', *Le Pèlerin*, no. 23 (13 décembre), p. 3.
15. For this fascinating tale, see Jean-Marie Mayeur, 'Mgr Dupanloup et Louis Veuillot devant les "prophéties contemporaines" en 1874', *Revue de l'histoire de la spiritualité*, vol. 48 (1972), pp. 193–204.
16. For the vicissitudes of the shrine, see AAR, UD 185, Père Pierre Touveneraud, 'Le Premier Pèlerinage national à La Salette de passage à Grenoble, en août 1872', unpub. manuscript, pp. 9–11.
17. AAR, Père Picard to Père Alzon, no. 882, 13 mai 1872.
18. AAR, Père Alzon to Mère Marie de Jésus, 16 août 1868.
19. AAR, Père Picard to Père Bailly, no. 921, 21 juillet 1872.
20. AAR, Père Pierre Touveneraud, 'Le Premier Pèlerinage national à La Salette de passage à Grenoble, en août 1872', p. 27.
21. ibid., p. 30.
22. ibid., pp. 41–2.
23. Archives de la Grotte, 12E1, Anon. [Un des missionnaires gardiens de la Grotte], *Les Bannières de la France à Notre-Dame de Lourdes* (Lourdes, Bertrand Pujo, 1873), p. 6.
24. See Leonard von Matt and Francis Trochu, *Saint Bernadette: A Pictorial Biography*, p. 76, for the engraving of the event.
25. 'Le Pèlerinage national', *Le Pèlerin*, no. 1 (12 juillet 1873), p. 4.
26. ibid., p. 3.
27. ibid.
28. ibid., 'Partie officielle', no. 2, p. 33.

29. ibid., 'Pèlerinage national de Pontmain et de Saint-Michel', no. 4, p. 62.
30. For more on Laurence's 'reinvention' of Marian piety in the Pyrenees, for example, see Gaëtan Bernoville, *De Notre-Dame de Garaison à Notre-Dame de Lourdes. Jean-Louis Peydessus: Apôtre marial de la Bigorre 1807–1882*, pp. 11–27 and ch. 4.
31. Archives de la Grotte, 12E1, report from Père Miegeville on the 'Pèlerinage de Loubajac', p. 3.
32. ibid., p. 5.
33. 'Pèlerinage national à Tours, à Saint Vincent de Paul et à Notre-Dame de Lourdes', *Le Pèlerin*, no. 4 (2 août 1873), p. 72.
34. Anon., *Le Jubilé du pèlerinage national à Lourdes* (Paris, Maison de la Bonne Presse, 1897), n. 1, p. 27.
35. Père Picard, 'Pèlerinage de Notre-Dame de Salut à Lourdes du 19 au 27 août 1879', in *Association de Notre-Dame de Salut, rapport général, lu à l'assemblée du 2 février 1881* (Paris, Au secrétariat, rue François Ier, 1881), p. 2.
36. Austin Gough, 'The Conflict in Politics: Bishop Pie's Campaign against the Nineteenth Century', in Theodore Zeldin, ed., *Conflicts in French Society: Anti-clericalism, Education and Morals in the Nineteenth Century*, p. 98.
37. Père Picard, 'Pèlerinage de Notre-Dame de Salut à Lourdes du 19 au 27 août 1879', p. 2.
38. ibid., p. 6.
39. ibid., p. 7.
40. ibid.
41. ibid., p. 8.
42. ibid., pp. 8–9.
43. For this process, see ch. 10.
44. Quoted in A. Pépin, 'Le Père François Picard . . .', p. 214.
45. AAR, Père Bailly to Père Galabert, 2 août 1878.
46. Quoted in A. Pépin, 'Le Père François Picard . . .', pp. 212–13.
47. For the history of this field, see Robert A. Nye, *The Origins of Crowd Psychology: Gustave Le Bon and the Crisis of Mass Democracy in the Third Republic* (London, Sage, 1975), especially pp. 59–82, and Susanna Barrows, *Distorting Mirrors: Visions of the Crowd in Late Nineteenth-century France*, *passim*.
48. Evelyn Martha Acomb, *The French Laic Laws (1879–1889): The First Anti-clerical Campaign of the Third French Republic* (New York, Octagon Books, 1967), p. 77.
49. Even d'Alzon, always suspicious of the effort that pilgrimage demanded, and moreover often critical of the populist agenda of *Le Pèlerin*, none the less became enthused by the miracles of Lourdes. In a letter to Picard he related a cure of a female novice who was at death's door, and was only

resuscitated with a few drops of Lourdes water. In a letter written on 30 August 1877 to Père Galabert after the pilgrimage, he was convinced that the Assumptionists had been chosen for special favours. 'La Sainte Vierge nous a comblés à Lourdes, nous avons 32 miracles bien constatés. Ce sont de grandes grâces pour la Congrégation, qui a fourni les directeurs du pèlerinage. Dieu se plaît à se montrer que nous devons soigner les pauvres, puisque nous en avions amené environ 200, dont on avait payé le voyage.' He was so moved that he stayed behind a day after the pilgrimage to see if the Virgin would confirm his desire 'pour travailler à la conversion des schismatiques orientaux. La guérison de mon oblate [a woman dying of anaemia] consacrée précisément à cette œuvre, ne serait-elle pas le signe accordé?' (Père d'Alzon to Père Picard, 3 septembre 1877). D'Alzon answered the question by beginning his mission in Bulgaria, where the Assumptionists became famous for converting the gypsies to Catholicism.

50. AAR, Père d'Alzon to Père Picard, 26 août 1878: 'les pèlerinages ... mettent en fureur une telle masse d'évêques, qu'il est impossible qu'une tempête n'éclate pas. Il faut des pèlerinages, mais il s'en fait assez sans vous, et croyez que le monopole des miracles aura des inconvénients.'

51. Archives de la Grotte, 5H19, Père Picard to Père Burosse, Paris, 3 mars 1880.

52. Quoted in A. Pépin, 'Le Père François Picard ...', p. 213.

53. Père Picard, 'Pèlerinage de Notre-Dame de Salut à Lourdes du 19 au 27 août 1879', p. 1.

54. Gaëtan Bernoville, *Le Père Pernet: Fondateur des Petites-Sœurs de l'Assomption* (Paris, Grasset, 1944), pp. 117–18.

55. Olwen Hufton, *The Prospect before Her: A History of Women in Western Europe 1500–1800*, pp. 369–70.

56. Gaëtan Bernoville, *Le Père Pernet: Fondateur des Petites-Sœurs de l'Assomption*, p. 127.

57. Association de Notre-Dame de Salut, *Hospitalité de Notre-Dame de Salut: Documents, statuts, coutumiers, historique* (Paris, 4 Avenue de Breteuil, 1921), p. 120.

58. For more on the story of the nursing sisters who ran this hospital and its Pyrenean character, see Gaëtan Bernoville, *Mère Saint-Jean Baptiste (Marie Saint-Frai) et le Père Ribes: Fondateurs de la Congrégation hospitalière-missionnaire des Filles de Notre-Dame des Sept Douleurs* (Paris, Grasset, 1958), especially pp. 113–36.

59. APSA, Sœur Gisèle Marchand, 'Extraits de "Une page de l'histoire de Lourdes"', p. 3.

60. APSA, Mère Marie de Jésus to Père Pernet, 22 août 1877.

61. APSA, Sœur Gisèle Marchand, 'Extraits de "Une page de l'histoire de Lourdes"', p. 2.

62. APSA, Mère Emmanuel Marie to Mère Marie de Jésus, 25 août 1878.
63. APSA, Mère Marie de Jésus to Père Pernet, 13 août 1877.
64. Archives de la Grotte, 5H19, Mme Laforest to Père Burosse, Paris, complete date illegible, 1879.
65. Archives de la Grotte, 5H19, Mme Laforest to Père Burosse, Paris, 11 juillet 1880.
66. ibid.
67. *Hospitalité de Notre-Dame de Salut: Documents, statuts, coutumiers, historiques*, pp. 121–2.
68. A. Rebsomen, *Souvenirs d'un brancardier de Lourdes* (Paris, Editions Alsatia, 1936), p. 14.
69. Archives de la Grotte, 5H19, illegible name to Père Burosse, Lourdes, 20 septembre 1882.
70. Archives de la Grotte, 5H20, Claudius Morel to Père Burosse, Lourdes, 8 mai 1885.
71. Archives de la Grotte, 5H19, Le Président du Comité, name illegible, Dijon, 7 juillet 1884. For a contemporary anthropological gloss on the potentially exploitative relationship between *brancardiers* and pilgrims, see John Eade, 'Order and Power at Lourdes: Lay Helpers and the Organization of a Pilgrimage Shrine', in John Eade and Michael J. Sallnow, eds., *Contesting the Sacred: The Anthropology of Christian Pilgrimage* (London, Routledge, 1991), pp. 51–76.
72. Archives de la Grotte, 5H6, Père Burosse to Père Picard, 12 octobre 1885.
73. Archives de la Grotte, 5H19, Combettes de Luc to Père Burosse, 23 février 1883; for more on the feelings of the members of the Hospitalité de Notre-Dame de Salut during this period of change, see especially AAR, SV33, M. Blondel to Combettes de Luc, 22 février 1883, and SV34, M. de l'Epinois to Père Picard, 6 avril 1883.
74. The preponderance of elite women can be seen in *Hospitalité de Notre-Dame de Salut: Membres décédés* (Toulouse, Imprimerie Catholique Saint-Cyprien, 1904).
75. Anon., *Le Petit Manuel des Dames Hospitalières de Notre-Dame de Lourdes* (Lourdes, Imprimerie de la Grotte, 1896), p. 11.
76. *Hospitalité de Notre-Dame de Salut: Documents, statuts, coutumiers, historiques*, p. 106.
77. Adrien Dansette, *Histoire religieuse de la France contemporaine sous la troisième république* (Paris, Flammarion, 1951), p. 200.
78. Pierre Pierrard, *L'Eglise et les ouvriers en France (1840–1940)* (Paris, Hachette, 1984), pp. 357–412, for the many different ways of following the Pope's directions.
79. A. Rebsomen, *Souvenirs d'un brancardier de Lourdes*, p. 16.

80. Archives de la Grotte, 5H19, Combettes de Luc to Père Burosse (Rabastans, Tarn), 25 février 1883.
81. Jean-Marie Mayeur, 'Catholicisme intransigeant, catholicisme social, démocratie chrétienne', *Annales ESC*, vol. 27 (1972), pp. 483–99.
82. John McManners, *Church and State in France 1870–1914* (London, SPCK, 1972), pp. 64–80; Benjamin F. Martin, *Count Albert de Mun: Paladin of the Third Republic*, pp. 86–128.
83. Archives de la Grotte, 5H16, 'Notices concernant les membres de l'Hospitalité de Notre-Dame de Salut'. Obituary notices spoke of men taught by Jesuits and Carmelites, active in the *cercles* associated with Saint Vincent de Paul, of landowners who applied their social and political vision in a world still governed by hierarchy and deference. A similar compilation is found in AAR, E48, in *Hospitalité de Notre-Dame de Salut: Pèlerinage national à Notre-Dame de Lourdes* (Toulouse, Imprimerie Catholique Saint-Cyprien, 1904). See also the sections on France interspersed throughout for the maintenance of the elites and their pre-revolutionary attitudes in Arno J. Mayer, *The Persistence of the Old Regime in Europe to the Great War* (New York, Pantheon Books, 1981), pp. 102–9.
84. Maurice Larkin, *The Church and State after the Dreyfus Affair: The Separation Issue in France* (London, Macmillan, 1974), p. 67.
85. Maurice Larkin, *Religion, Politics and Preferment in France since 1890:* La Belle Epoque *and Its Legacy*, p. 23.
86. See Emile Zola, 'La Vérité en marche', in *Œuvres complètes*, vol. 14, Henri Mitterand, ed. (Paris, Cercle du livre précieux, 1966–9).
87. The bibliography in this area is enormous. For summaries of the affair, see Douglas Johnson, *France and the Dreyfus Affair* (London, Blandford, 1966); H. R. Kedward, *The Dreyfus Affair: Catalyst for Tension in French Society* (London, Longman, 1969); Jean-Denis Bredin, *L'Affaire* (Paris, Julliard, 1983); for the special role of the intellectuals, see Géraldi Leroy, ed., *Les Ecrivains et l'Affaire Dreyfus: Actes du colloque organisé par le Centre Charles Péguy et l'université d'Orléans (29–31 octobre 1981)* (Paris, PUF, 1983); Pascal Ory and Jean-François Sirinelli, *Les Intellectuels en France de l'Affaire Dreyfus à nos jours* (Paris, Colin, 1986); see also Stephen Wilson, *Ideology and Experience: Anti-Semitism in France at the Time of the Dreyfus Affair* (Madison, NJ, Fairleigh Dickinson University Press, 1982); Michael Burns, *The Dreyfus Family 1789–1945* (London, Chatto & Windus, 1992).
88. Miri Rubin, *Gentile Tales*, forthcoming with Yale University Press, describes these narratives in some detail. I thank her for sharing her unpublished work with me.
89. He was the son of an important Jewish Alsatian family; his elder brother, Théodor, had already converted in 1825 and created an order to convert others.

90. See Robert A. Nye, 'Degeneration and the Medical Model of Cultural Crisis in the Belle Epoque', in S. Drescher, D. Sabean, and A. Sharlin, eds., *Political Symbolism in Modern Europe* (New Brunswick, NJ, Rutgers University Press, 1982), pp. 19–41, and his larger volume, *Crime, Madness and Politics in Modern France: The Medical Concept of National Decline* (Princeton, Princeton University Press, 1984), pp. 132–70; and Daniel Pick, *Faces of Degeneration: A European Disorder* c. *1848–1918* (Cambridge, Cambridge University Press, 1989), pp. 74–106.
91. See *Eucharistia* (Paris, 1934), p. 934–43 for the growing centrality of Eucharistic devotion in France in the nineteenth century. I thank Père Charles Monsch at the AAR for this citation.
92. A. Pépin, 'Le Père François Picard . . .', p. 220.
93. AAR, Père d'Alzon, 'Méditations, seizième méditation Eucharistie', *Ecrits spirituels*, text 13.
94. ibid., text 24.
95. AAR, Père d'Alzon, textes divers parus dans les *Ecrits Spirituels*, 'Méditation sur l'Eucharistie', text 26.
96. AAR, Père Picard, 'Jésus-Christ, notre modèle dans l'Eucharistie', *Ecrits divers dactylographiés*, Tome XV, B52/15.
97. AAR, Père Picard, editorial in *La Croix*, 3 juin 1888.
98. Miri Rubin, *Corpus Christi: The Eucharist in Late Medieval Culture* (Cambridge, Cambridge University Press, 1991), p. 114; for a larger discussion, see pp. 108–28.
99. *Eucharistia* (Paris, 1934), p. 820, quoting Veuillot. I thank Père Charles Monsch at the AAR for this citation.
100. Anon., *Le Jubilé du pèlerinage national à Lourdes*, p. 162.
101. ibid., p. 168.
102. A. Pépin, 'Le Père François Picard . . .', p. 223.
103. See ch. 9 for the curing narratives of the poor.
104. Barbara Corrado Pope, 'Immaculate and Powerful: The Marian Revival in the Nineteenth Century', in *Immaculate and Powerful: The Female in Sacred Image and Social Reality*, Clarissa W. Atkinson, et al., eds. (Boston, Beacon Press, 1985), p. 189.
105. See *Le Pèlerin* (17 août 1885).
106. G. Miegge, *The Virgin Mary: The Roman Catholic Marian Doctrine*, Waldo Smith, tr. (London, Lutterworth Press, 2nd ed., 1961), p. 143.
107. Marina Warner, *Alone of All Her Sex: The Myth and Cult of the Virgin Mary*, pp. 192–205.
108. Anon., *Le Jubilé du pèlerinage national à Lourdes*, pp. 162–3.
109. See, for example, Victor Turner and Edith L. B. Turner, *Image and Pilgrimage in Christian Culture: Anthropological Perspectives* (Oxford, Blackwell, 1978), pp. 1–39. In this introductory chapter the authors discuss

the concept of liminality and, perhaps, exaggerate the distinction between Christian individual pilgrimage and rites of passage associated with tribal groups. As I suggest, the feelings of social solidarity were an integral part of nineteenth-century pilgrimage. For a recent critique of the thesis of liminality and the feelings of 'communitas' that such journeys engendered, see John Eade and Michael J. Sallnow, eds., *Contesting the Sacred: The Anthropology of Christian Pilgrimage*, *passim*.

110. For the way Carnival mixed these themes, see Peter Stallybrass and Allon White, *The Politics and Poetics of Transgression*; see also Mikhail Bakhtin, *Rabelais and His World*.

111. The differentials in this domain were extraordinary. In 1894, to pick a year at random, the women were obliged to give 36,070 baths, while the men accomplished their task after only 18,023 immersions; see A. Rebsomen, *Souvenirs d'un brancardier de Lourdes*, p. 75.

9. The Cures

1. For the most famous and one of the more authoritative, see Ruth Cranston, *The Miracle of Lourdes* (New York, Doubleday, 1988); Philippe Aziz, *Les Miracles de Lourdes: La Science face à la foi* (Paris, Robert Laffont, 1981); for the miracles between 1947 and 1989, see Alphonse Oliviéri and Bernard Billet, *Y-a-t-il encore des miracles à Lourdes?* (Paris, P. Lethielleux, 5th ed., 1989).

2. For the distribution of fountains, see Brigitte Caulier, *L'Eau et le sacré*, pp. 15–21.

3. For the origins, see L. W. B. Brockliss, 'The Development of the Spa in Seventeenth-century France', in Roy Porter, ed., *The Medical History of Waters and Spas* (London, Wellcome Institute for the History of Medicine, 1990), pp. 23–47. For more on the history and significance of thermalism to the region, see Jean-François Soulet, *Les Pyrénées au XIX*[e] *siècle*, vol. 1, pp. 84–6. For more on the industry, see Société d'études des Sept Vallées, *Thermalisme et climatisme dans les Pyrénées* (Actes du congrès des sociétés académiques et savantes, 1984, published in 1985), and Jean Fourcassié, *Le Romantisme et les Pyrénées*, pp. 79–93.

4. See Paul Sébillot for the variety of beliefs and practices associated with fountains and the classical ethnological approach, 'La Puissance des fontaines', in *Le Folklore de France* (Paris, Editions G.-P. Maisonneuve & Larose, repr. 1968), pp. 216–303.

5. For the many testimonies of the presence of water on the spot, *LDA*, vol. 5, p. 24, 'note-clé'.

6. Brigitte Caulier, *L'Eau et le sacré*, p. 113.

7. See ch. 5 for the crowd's perception of Bernadette as a living thaumaturge.
8. Brigitte Caulier, *L'Eau et le sacré*, p. 108.
9. Olivier de Marliave, *Trésor de la mythologie pyrénéenne*, p. 139.
10. Henri Charbonneau, *Chapelles et saints guérisseurs basques et béarnais* (Hélette, Editions Harriet, 1995), p. 83.
11. ibid., p. 81.
12. See ch. 2.
13. For the proper way to conduct a devotion in the Charentais in western France, see Paul Leproux, *Dévotions et saints guérisseurs* (Paris, PUF, 1957), pp. 90–93.
14. ibid., p. 102.
15. Brigitte Caulier, *L'Eau et le sacré*, p. 102.
16. For more on the 'tireuses des saints', see Brigitte Caulier, *L'Eau et le sacré*, p. 97.
17. Olivier de Marliave, *Trésor de la mythologie pyrénéenne*, pp. 135–6.
18. ibid., p. 143.
19. Jean-Pierre Goubert, *The Conquest of Water: The Advent of Health in the Industrial Age*, A. Wilson, tr. (London, Polity Press, 1989), pp. 214, 217–18.
20. Brigitte Caulier, *L'Eau et le sacré*, p. 96.
21. For a discussion, see François Laplantine, *Anthropologie de la maladie: Etude ethnologique des systèmes de représentations étiologiques et thérapeutiques dans la société occidentale contemporaine* (Paris, Payot, 1992), pp. 383–8.
22. Olivier de Marliave, *Trésor de la mythologie pyrénéenne*, pp. 143–4.
23. See Ronald C. Finucane, *Miracles and Pilgrims: Popular Beliefs in Medieval England* (London, Macmillan, 1995), pp. 63–7, for the disdain for human healing among the monks or canons responsible for setting down the records of miracles; priests held preference over physicians, who were seen as overpriced and ineffective. René Taveneaux, *Le catholicisme dans la France classique 1610–1715* (Paris, SEDES, 1980), vol. 2, pp. 382–9, explains how the post-Tridentine Church tightened up on procedures for the verification of miracles; although physicians were included on such commissions, their role was clearly subordinate to the task of determining the spiritual enhancement of the *miraculés*. See finally David Gentilcore, 'Contesting Illness in Early-Modern Naples: Miracolati, Physicians and the Congregation of Rites', *Past & Present*, no. 148 (1995), pp. 117–48, for the ambivalent role of the medical man in such adjudications.
24. For more on the history of the man, see *LDA*, vol. 1, no. 7, pp. 95–128; see also Archives de la Grotte, 6H2.
25. Nor was this the only investigation. Twenty years later an attempt was made to confirm events and to follow up others who claimed cures. See

Archives de la Grotte, 6H4, 'Enquête Sempé sur les guérisons obtenues en 1858 (1878–1879)'.

26. *LDA*, vol. 2, no. 314, p. 358, especially n. 1.

27. Quoted in Annie Quartararo-Vinas, *Médecins et médecine dans les Hautes-Pyrénées au XIXe siècle* (Tarbes, Association Guillaume Mauran, 1982), p. 228.

28. See Anne Lasserre-Vergne, *Les Pyrénées centrales dans la littérature française*, pp. 124–5; for an excellent analysis of the genre of this travel literature, see Stéphane Gerson, 'Travellers on Mission in the French Provinces: Domestic Journeys and the Construction of National Unity', *Past & Present*, no. 151 (1996), pp. 141–73.

29. Only a few cures were ever investigated, but those that were merely recorded and ultimately discarded supply an equally interesting history of local epidemiology. People who went to the fountain had every imaginable illness, but especially chronic conditions for which they had all but given up hope.

30. *LDA*, vol. 2, no. 138, p. 161.

31. Auguste Borde came in a wagon, Benoîte Cazau with a stick and Marie Daube enveloped her swollen legs in her skirt and made her way down to the Grotto on her bottom; *LDA*, vol. 5, no. 860, pp. 171, 198, 199.

32. As in the case of Louis Bouriette, whose daughter fetched the water. *LDA*, vol. 5, no. 820, p. 133.

33. ibid., the case of B. Soubies, no. 860, p. 201; D. Bouchet, no. 842, p. 170; and Jean-Marie Tambourré, no. 884, pp. 228–9.

34. ibid., no. 820, pp. 136–40.

35. ibid., no. 820, p. 136.

36. ibid., no. 833, pp. 155–6.

37. See, for example, the way one Petite-Sœur explained how Pernet had to explain to the assembled nuns that 'les guérisons en général ne s'étaient pas effectuées par l'action de l'eau; mais par celles de la prière et de la Sainte Communion'; see APSA, letter from Mère Emmanuel Marie to Mère Marie de Jésus, Paris, 25 août 1878.

38. See the next ch. for the tale of Pierre de Rudder, in which a 'great' cure occurred even when the sufferer was far from the Grotto and never drank the fountain's water.

39. For the varieties of prayer in the nineteenth century, see Guy Thuillier, *L'Imaginaire Quotidien du XIXe siècle* (Paris, Economica, 1985), pp. 31–59.

40. J. Gélis, '"De la mort à la vie": Les "Sanctuaires à répit"', *Ethnologie française*, vol. 11 (1981), pp. 211–24, and his 'Miracle et médecine aux siècles classiques: Le Corps médical et le retour temporaire à la vie des mort-nés', *Historical Reflections*, vol. 9 (1982), pp. 85–101.

41. *LDA*, vol. 2, no. 143, p. 166.

42. *LDA*, vol. 5, no. 820, p. 137.
43. For the critical notes, see ibid., pp. 137–8, which suggest the reasons for her probable misremembering.
44. *LDA*, vol. 5, no. 840, pp. 165–6.
45. ibid., no. 842, pp. 170–71.
46. ibid., no. 820, p. 135.
47. ibid., no. 827, p. 146.
48. ibid., no. 827, p. 147.
49. ibid., no. 797, p. 103; includes both quotations.
50. ibid., no. 833, p. 155.
51. See this ch., pp. 317–18.
52. For the late introduction of her case in early 1859, see no. 838, pp. 160–62; nos. 853–6, pp. 191–3; nos. 874, 876, pp. 215–16; no. 913, p. 338.
53. *LDA*, vol. 5, no. 836, p. 159.
54. See, for example, Louis Chatellier, 'Le Miracle baroque', in *Actes de la sixième rencontre d'histoire religieuse tenue à Fontevraud les 8 et 9 octobre organisée par le Centre de recherches d'histoire religieuse et d'histoire des idées* (Angers, Presses de l'Université d'Angers, 1983), pp. 85–93, and Jacques Virgerie, 'Le Miracle dans la France du XVIIe siècle', *Dix-Septième siècle*, vol. 35 (1983), no. 3, pp. 313–31. Paul Leproux, *Dévotions et saints guérisseurs*, describes how in the Charentais mothers vowed to dress their children each succeeding year first in white, in blue and then in grey, pp. 96–7.
55. See ch. 10.
56. Théodore Mangiapan, *Les Guérisons de Lourdes: Etude historique et critique depuis l'origine à nos jours* (Lourdes, Œuvre de la Grotte, 1994), p. 67.
57. ibid., p. 68.
58. 'Une guérison', *Annales de Notre-Dame de Lourdes*, vol. 1 (1868), p. 18.
59. ibid.
60. ibid., p. 38.
61. This can be seen in *Annales de Notre-Dame de Lourdes*, vol. 2 (1869), pp. 61–7, in the case of Madeleine Latapie with a 'phthisie du second degré'. The narrator focused on the impotence of science and the astonishment of her hapless physician: 'les ressources de l'art étaient impuissantes à enrayer le mal, ainsi que l'ont déclaré plusieurs médecins d'accord avec moi. Sans savoir par quelle cause, je la revois subitement guérie: j'affirme que cette guérison excite mon étonnement au plus haut degré, ainsi que celui de toute la commune.' p. 67.
62. *Annales de Notre-Dame de Lourdes*, vol. 6 (1873/4), p. 69.
63. The certificate came from a certain Dr Labbé; see Théodore Mangiapan, *Les Guérisons de Lourdes*, p. 69.
64. See ch. 10.

65. See ch. 7.
66. Théodore Mangiapan, *Les Guérisons de Lourdes*, p. 71.
67. See for example the congratulatory certificate of the doctor who had failed in his treatment in *Annales de Notre-Dame de Lourdes*, vol. 13 (1880/81), p. 15; see also evidence of Dr Vergez's reassuring if seemingly rigorous presence on p. 19 and an example of the growing medical information on p. 285.
68. For these insights, see Thomas J. Csordas, *The Sacred Self: A Cultural Phenomenology of Charismatic Healing* (Berkeley, University of California Press, 1994), particularly pp. 2–3.
69. Joyce MacDougall, *Theatres of the Body: A Psychoanalytic Approach to Psychosomatic Illness* (London, Free Association Books, 1989), *passim*, but especially pp. 119–39.
70. See ch. 8.
71. Archives de la Grotte, 6H22, 'Relations de guérisons (1873–1897)' (from here on will be abbreviated as 6H22). Stéphanie Vermersch, Roubaix, diocèse de Cambrai, aphonie incurable, guérie en 1890, pèlerinage diocésain de Cambrai.
72. 6H22, Léonide Calmels, Villefranche-de-Rouergue [Aveyron], diocèse de Rodez, guérie en 1879, pèlerinage local.
73. 6H22, Léontine Aubain, Paris, diocèse de Paris, moëlle épinière, guérie en 1882, à l'âge de 35 ans, au pèlerinage national. She insisted that it was not the cold water of the baths that had cured her – such expedients in the past had done nothing – but rather the impact of the prayers offered by people on her behalf: 'Au moment de mon départ pour Lourdes, un nombre incalculable de parents, d'amis, d'élèves, de simples relations, des communautés entières commençaient à mon intention la neuvaine du Pèlerinage.'
74. 6H22, Annappes [Nord], diocèse de Cambrai, hystérie, guérie en 1887, à l'âge de 32 ans, au pèlerinage national.
75. 6H22, Paris, diocèse de Paris, paralysie aphonie et muette, guérie en 1890, au pèlerinage de Séez. Age missing.
76. 6H22, Château de Capiguet, près de Caen [Calvados], diocèse de Bayeux, myélite chronique, guérie en 1890 à l'âge de 27 ans, au pèlerinage national.
77. 6H22, Saint-Valéry-sur-Somme [Somme], diocèse d'Amiens, tumeur fibreuse, guérie en 1887, à l'âge de 26 ans, au pèlerinage national.
78. 6H22, Paris, diocèse de Paris, moëlle épinière, guérie en 1882, à l'âge de 35 ans, au pèlerinage national.
79. 6H22, Rethel [Ardennes], diocèse de Reims, myélite, paralysie, guérie en 1893, à l'âge de 32 ans, au pèlerinage national.
80. 6H22, Paris, diocèse de Paris, paralysie aphonie et muette, guérie en 1890, au pèlerinage de Séez. Age missing.

81. 6H22, Paris, diocèse de Paris, astigmatismes dans les 2 yeux, guérie en 1895, à l'âge de 17 ans, au pèlerinage national.
82. 6H22, Jeanne Delasalle, Tourcoing [Nord], diocèse de Cambrai, arthrite tuberculeuse, guérie en 1893 [*sic*], à l'âge de 19 ans, au pèlerinage national.
83. 6H22, Auneuil [Oise], diocèse de Beauvais, moëlle épinière, guérie en 1874, à l'âge de 21 ans, au pèlerinage national.
84. 6H22, La Loupe [Eure-et-Loir], diocèse de Chartres, ulcère de l'estomac, guérie en 1896, à l'âge de 19 ans, au pèlerinage national.
85. 6H22, femme Duchesne, La Marolle [Loir-et-Cher], diocèse de Blois, paralysie des deux jambes, guérie en 1895, à l'âge de 43 ans, au pèlerinage national.
86. 6H22, à l'Hospice de Beauvais [Oise], hypertrophie du foie et de la rate, guérie en 1893, à l'âge de 23 ans, au pèlerinage national.
87. 6H22, Lille, diocèse de Cambrai, bronchite chronique, guérie en 1887, à l'âge de 30 ans, au pèlerinage national.
88. Thomas J. Csordas, *The Sacred Self: A Cultural Phenomenology of Charismatic Healing*, especially pp. 57–140.
89. 6H22, Messery [Haute-Savoie], diocèse d'Annecy, gastralgie, hypertrophie du cœur, guérie en 1896, à l'âge de 22 ans, au pèlerinage national. Narrative written in third person by unnamed author.
90. 6H22, Orléans, diocèse d'Orléans, coxalgie congénitale, guérie en 1894, à l'âge de 34 ans, au pèlerinage national. Narrative written in third person by unnamed author.
91. See Caroline Bynum, *Holy Feast and Holy Fast: The Religious Significance of Food to Medieval Women*, pp. 166, 172–80, for example, and *Jesus as Mother: Studies in the Spirituality of the High Middle Ages* (Berkeley, University of California Press, 1982), *passim*, but especially pp. 110–69.
92. Once again, see Jacques Maître, *L'Orpheline de la Bérésina*, for the development of a spirituality normally associated with Thérèse de Lisieux, but which had much wider resonance among the Catholic faithful, especially women.
93. 6H22, Paris, diocèse de Paris, congestion pulmonaire, guérie en 1894, à l'âge de 28 ans, au pèlerinage national.
94. 6H22, Trefcon, par Vermand [Aisne], diocèse de Soissons, gravelle urique et hystérie, guérie en 1890, à l'âge de 33 ans, au pèlerinage national.
95. For the final and definitive analysis by the leader of 'modern' hydrology in France, see Filhol's conclusions in *LDA*, vol. 3, no. 498, pp. 259–62.
96. See, for example, Félix de Backer, *Lourdes et les médecins* (Paris, J. Maloine, 1905), pp. 46–7: 'Bref, je trouvais une sorte de grande ville d'eaux où le casino et les jeux étaient remplacés par une basilique et une crypte souterraine.'
97. For the history of the pools, see J.-B. Courtin, *Lourdes: Le Domaine de*

Notre-Dame de Lourdes de 1858 à 1947, pp. 46–54, quotation on p. 49.
98. See Terence Turner, 'The Social Skin', in J. Cherfas and R. Lewin, eds., *Not Work Alone: A Cross-cultural View of Activities Superfluous to Survival* (London, Maurice Temple Smith, 1980), pp. 112–40, for the importance of the surface of the body as a 'frontier' zone between the biological and psychological self on the one hand and the social self on the other.
99. 6H22, Virginie Gordet, Henrichemont [Cher], diocèse de Bourges, ovaro-salpingite, guérie en 1892, à l'âge de 32 ans, au pèlerinage de Berrichon.
100. 6H22 Château de Capiguet, près de Caen [Calvados], diocèse de Bayeux, myélite chronique, guérie en 1890, à l'âge de 27 ans, au pèlerinage national.
101. See 6H22, Sœur Marie du Saint Sacrement, Paris, diocèse de Paris, affection de la moëlle épinière, guérie en 1891, à l'âge de 27 ans, au pèlerinage national.
102. 6H22, L'Hospice de Beauvais [Oise], hypertrophie du foie et de la rate, guérie en 1893, à l'âge de 23 ans, au pèlerinage national.
103. 6H22, Blois, diocèse de Blois, ulcère de l'estomac, guérie en 1894, à l'âge de 34 ans, au pèlerinage national. Narrative signed by S. S. B., *religieuse* de Notre-Dame de Providence.
104. 6H22, Mme Crosmier, Paris, diocèse de Paris, astigmatisme dans les 2 yeux, guérie en 1895, à l'âge de 17 ans, au pèlerinage national.
105. 6H22, Paris, diocèse de Paris, tuberculose, guérie en 1880, à l'âge de 36 ans, pèlerinage Lorraine joint au pèlerinage national.
106. 6H22, Liévin [Pas-de-Calais], diocèse d'Arras, ulcère intérieur, guérie en 1882, à l'âge de 35 ans, au pèlerinage diocésain de Cambrai, narrative told by *religieuse*.
107. 6H22, Blanche Meurat, Lille, diocèse de Cambrai, bronchite chronique, guérie en 1887, à l'âge de 30 ans, au pèlerinage national.
108. 6H22, Zulma Ranson, Saint-Valéry-sur-Somme [Somme], diocèse d'Amiens, tumeur fibreuse, guérie en 1887, à l'âge de 26 ans, au pèlerinage national.
109. 6H22, Tourcoing [Nord], diocèse de Cambrai, arthrite tuberculeuse, guérie en 1893 [*sic*], à l'âge de 19 ans, au pèlerinage national.
110. 6H22, Lion-sur-Mer et Caen, diocèse de Bayeux, lupus de la face et de la jambe, guérie en 1893, à l'âge de 19 ans, au pèlerinage national.
111. 6H22, Saint-Martin-le-Nœud [Oise], diocèse de Beauvais, poitrinaire au dernier degré, guérie en 1895, à l'âge de 26 ans, au pèlerinage national. Narrative written by curé, name illegible.
112. 6H22, Elise Delahaye, demeurant à l'Hospice de Beauvais [Oise], hypertrophie du foie et de la rate, guérie en 1893, à l'âge de 23 ans, au pèlerinage national.

10. Religion and Science in the Third Republic

1. For a summation of the value of the report, see *LDA*, vol. 5, pp. 33–49. It is important to realize, however, these cures were never 'l'objet d'un jugement canonique en forme'; rather they were used by Laurence to underpin the divine character of the apparitions. See *LDA*, vol. 6, n. 320, p. 280.
2. See ch. 9.
3. For a discussion of both the Church and secular critiques, see Louis Trénard, 'Les Miracles raillés par Voltaire', in *Actes de la sixième rencontre d'histoire religieuse tenue à Fontevraud les 8 et 9 octobre organisée par le Centre de recherches d'histoire religieuse et d'histoire des idées*, pp. 95–109.
4. Paul Miest, *Les 54 Miracles de Lourdes au jugement du droit canon* (Paris, Editions Universitaires, 1958), p. 9.
5. *LDA*, vol. 5, no. 898, p. 249.
6. ibid., p. 253.
7. ibid., no. 827, pp. 146–7. Perhaps the best example was Mme Rizan, who had tried all the remedies that science could muster, so that 'les médecins perdirent tout espoir et déclarèrent que la veuve Rizan était absolument incurable'. See ibid., no. 898, p. 257.
8. ibid., no. 898, p. 262. This argument was once again made in the case of Jeanne Crassus, who had frequent nervous attacks and violent convulsions. No one contradicted the veracity of her statement, confirmed by her entourage; rather, it was the lack of a diagnosis that disturbed them; see ibid., p. 267.
9. ibid.
10. Some of the cases, such as Louis Bouriette and Justin Bouhort, moved from the second class – 'faits sur lesquels la commission inclinerait à admettre du surnaturel' – into the first class, while Mlle Moreau belatedly received the same privilege.
11. Archives de la Grotte, A7, 'Le Docteur Henri Vergez, Professeur agrégé de la Faculté de Montpellier (1814–1888)'.
12. See Elizabeth A. Williams, *The Physical and the Moral: Anthropology, Physiology and Philosophical Medicine in France 1750–1850* (Cambridge, Cambridge University Press, 1994), for a discussion of Montpellier's development of the doctrine of vitalism in the eighteenth century and its continued significance into the nineteenth.
13. *LDA*, vol. 5, no. 916, p. 357.
14. ibid., p. 358.
15. ibid.
16. ibid., p. 359.
17. ibid., p. 360.

18. 'M. Le Docteur Baron Dunot de Saint-Maclou', *Annales de Notre-Dame de Lourdes*, vol. 24 (1891), pp. 117–24, provides this information.
19. ibid., p. 119.
20. ibid., p. 77.
21. For the uncertain chronological and documentary beginnings of this institution, see Théodore Mangiapan, *Les Guérisons de Lourdes*, p. 78.
22. *Annales de Notre-Dame de Lourdes*, vol. 16 (1883/4), p. 196.
23. Théodore Mangiapan, *Les Guérisons de Lourdes*, p. 82.
24. Père Richard Clarke, SJ, quoted in ibid., p. 83.
25. For this elaboration, see Georges Didi-Huberman, *Invention de l'hystérie: Charcot et l'iconographie photographique de la Salpêtrière*.
26. See Jan Goldstein's classic article, 'The Hysteria Diagnosis and the Politics of Anti-clericalism in Late Nineteenth-century France', *Journal of Modern History*, vol. 54 (1982), pp. 209–39, and her *Console and Classify: The French Psychiatric Profession in the Nineteenth Century* (Cambridge, Cambridge University Press, 1987), pp. 322–77.
27. Jean-Martin Charcot and Paul Richer, *Les Démoniaques dans l'art*, P. Fédida and Georges Didi-Huberman, eds. (Paris, Editions Macula, 1984).
28. For a fuller interpretation of the medical representation of the hysteric, see Sander L. Gilman, 'The Image of the Hysteric', in Sander L. Gilman, Helen King, Roy Porter, G. S. Rousseau and Elaine Showalter, *Hysteria beyond Freud* (Berkeley, University of California Press, 1993), pp. 345–452.
29. Alfred van den Brule, SJ, *Le Docteur Boissarie. Président du Bureau des Constatations médicales de Lourdes* (Paris, J. de Gigord, 1919), p. 69.
30. ibid., p. 148.
31. ibid., p. 208.
32. ibid., pp. 211–12.
33. ibid., quoted on p. 279.
34. ibid., p. 377.
35. Claude Bernard, *L'Introduction à la médecine expérimentale* (Paris, J.-B. Ballière et fils, 1865).
36. For Zola's treatise, see *Le Roman expérimental* (Paris, Flammarion, 1971).
37. For more on this literary background, see the illuminating thesis of Jean Marsal, *Lourdes: Un roman d'Emile Zola, genèse et signification* (Université des sciences humaines de Strasbourg, Faculté de théologie catholique, 1992), pp. 11–17; see also the classic R. Griffiths, *The Reactionary Revolution: The Catholic Revival in French Literature 1870–1914* (London, Constable, 1966), pp. 3–20, for an introduction to the literary context of the period.
38. Bourget's intellectual trajectory began to change when he wrote *Le Disciple* in 1889, a work concerned with a young man who slavishly accepts

the positivist creed of his intellectual master, only to be awakened, after disaster, to the Catholic ethics of his youth.

39. See Huysmans's pathbreaking *A Rebours* (Paris, G. Charpentier, 1882) and *Là-bas* (Paris, Tresse & Stock, 1891), works that put forward the new aestheticism against Zola's naturalism.

40. For more on Brunetière's ideas, see Harry W. Paul, 'The Debate over the Bankruptcy of Science in 1895', *French Historical Studies*, vol. 5 (1968), pp. 298–327.

41. This point is made in Jean Marsal, *Lourdes: Un Roman d'Emile Zola, genèse et signification*, pp. 18–33. They were preoccupied also by decadence. See, for example, J. Pierrot, *The Decadent Imagination 1880–1900*, D. Coltman, tr. (Chicago, University of Chicago Press, 1981); M. Praz, *The Romantic Agony*, A. Davidson, tr. (London, Oxford University Press, 2nd ed., 1951); A. E. Carter, *The Idea of Decadence in French Literature 1830–1900* (Toronto, University of Toronto Press, 1958), pp. 62–122; and Koenraad W. Swart, *The Sense of Decadence in Nineteenth-century France* (The Hague, Martinus Nijhoff, 1964), pp. 139–92.

42. 'La Grotte de Lourdes et les miracles', in *La Cloche*, 29 décembre 1872, in *Œuvres complètes*, vol. 14, pp. 177, 178.

43. Edmond and Jules de Goncourt, *Mémoires de la vie littéraire 1891–1892* (Paris, 1956–9), vol. 18, 26 juillet 1892, p. 220.

44. Emile Zola, *Mes Voyages: Lourdes, Rome, journaux inédits*, René Ternois, ed. (Paris, Fasquelle éditeurs, 1958), pp. 9–118. For more on the same themes, see René Ternois, *Zola et son temps: Lourdes, Rome, Paris* (Paris, Société des belles lettres, 1961), pp. 193–250; for the polemics and criticism, see pp. 363–78.

45. See n. 95, ch. 1.

46. Jean-Martin Charcot, 'La Foi qui guérit', *Revue Hebdomadaire* (3 décembre 1892), pp. 112–32.

47. *Lourdes* (Paris, Bibliothèque Charpentier, 1912), p. 40.

48. ibid., pp. 405–6.

49. ibid., p. 410.

50. ibid., p. 411.

51. ibid., pp. 555, 556.

52. Indeed, the story told is that Zola went so far as to visit Marie Lebranchu, to take her away from her poverty-stricken circumstances and to remove her to the heart of the Belgian countryside, where her presence would not destroy his reputation. See Philippe Aziz, *Les Miracles de Lourdes: La Science face à la foi*, p. 209.

53. See *Lourdes*, pp. 66–72, for the initial introduction of Sophie's tale on the train, and especially pp. 191–4.

54. ibid., p. 16.

55. Quoted in Jean Marsal, *Lourdes: Un roman d'Emile Zola*, p. 129.
56. Susanna Barrows, *Distorting Mirrors: Visions of the Crowd in Late Nineteenth-century France*, *passim*.
57. Robert A. Nye, *The Origins of Crowd Psychology: Gustave Le Bon and the Crisis of Mass Democracy in the Third Republic*, especially pp. 59–82.
58. *Lourdes*, p. 175.
59. Henri Lasserre, for example, repudiated Zola in *Lettres de Henri Lasserre à l'occasion du roman de M. Zola* (Paris, Dentu, 1894).
60. Emile Zola, *La Vérité en marche*, in *Œuvres complètes*, vol. 14, pp. 861–1,104.
61. Joris-Karl Huysmans, *Les Foules de Lourdes*, p. 105.
62. Gustave Boissarie, *Zola: Conférence du Luxembourg* (Paris, Maison de la Bonne Presse, 1895), p. xi.
63. ibid., p. 8.
64. Gustave Boissarie, *Zola: Conférence du Luxembourg*, p. 70.
65. ibid., p. 71.
66. Archives de la Grotte, 6H32, letter dated 1 juillet, no year, to Boissarie from Pierre Lauras.
67. For the text of the 'mandement', see *LDA*, vol. 6, no. 1,044, pp. 237–45.
68. For how this process worked, see Archives de la Grotte, 6H7, 'Lettres adressées au médecin président au Bureau des Constatations et autres personnages au sujet des enquêtes canoniques à faire au sujet des guérisons miraculeuses (1906–1911)'.
69. Paul Miest, *Les 54 Miracles de Lourdes au jugement du droit canon*, pp. 10–11.
70. For more on this story, see the Epilogue. For the difficulties and polemics of this period, see Archives Nationales, F19 2,374, 2,375, 2,376.
71. Georges Bertrin, *Histoire critique des événements de Lourdes: Apparitions et guérisons*, p. 250.
72. ibid., p. 262.
73. ibid., p. 361.
74. For a good introduction to water and cleanliness, see Georges Vigarello, *Concepts of Cleanliness: Changing Attitudes in France since the Middle Ages*, Jean Birrel, tr. (Cambridge, Cambridge University Press, 1988), especially chs. 5, 7, 8, 12. See also Jean-Pierre Goubert, *The Conquest of Water: The Advent of Health in the Industrial Age*, *passim*.
75. Jean de Bonnefon, 'Faut-il fermer Lourdes?', *Les Paroles françaises et romaines* (1 juillet 1906), p. 9.
76. ibid., p. 32.
77. ibid., p. 36.
78. ibid., p. 37.

79. ibid., p. 61.
80. ibid., p. 41.
81. ibid., p. 43.
82. Archives de la Grotte, 6H32, Affaire Bonnefon, p. 2 of manuscript.
83. Félix de Backer, *Lourdes et les médecins* (Paris, J. Maloine, 1905), p. 98; these statistics were apparently mentioned in a quoted discussion between Abbé Bertrin, one of the shrine's chief apologists, and Edgar Bérillon, one of Paris's leading hypnotherapists.
84. See Mark Micale's excellent work on the changing discussion of hysteria and the centrality of Lourdes in the debate, *Approaching Hysteria: Disease and Its Interpretations* (Princeton, Princeton University Press, 1995), pp. 260–84; for more on the polemic between medicine and the Church in the nineteenth century and the merging common ground in the twentieth, see Pierre Guillaume, *Médecins, église et foi* (Paris, Aubier, 1990).
85. Jacques Léonard, 'Femmes, religion et médecine: Les Religieuses qui soignent, en France au XIXe siècle', *Annales ESC*, vol. 32 (1977), pp. 887–907.
86. Hippolyte Bernheim, *Hypnotisme, suggestion et psychothérapie: Etudes nouvelles* (Paris, Doin, 1891), p. 209.
87. ibid., pp. 50–51.
88. Félix Régnault, 'De l'hypnotisme dans le genèse des miracles', *Revue de l'Hypnotisme* (1894), p. 277 in discussion.
89. ibid., p. 270.
90. Marcel Magnin, 'Les Guérisons de Lourdes et les phénomènes métapsychiques', *Annales des sciences psychiques* (décembre 1907), pp. 816–66.
91. See Adam Crabtree, *From Mesmer to Freud: Magnetic Sleep and the Roots of Psychological Healing* (New Haven, Yale University Press, 1993), pp. 333–5.
92. For the classic apologetic account of Gargam, see Georges Bertrin, *Histoire critique des événements de Lourdes: Apparitions et guérisons*, pp. 543–50; see Anon., 'Les Merveilles de Lourdes: Gabriel Gargam, son accident de chemin de fer, sa vie d'hôpital, sa guérison miraculeuse, notice publiée à l'occasion de sa conférence donnée à Toulouse le 28 juin 1914', (n.p., n.d.).
93. Marcel Magnin, 'Les Guérisons de Lourdes et les phénomènes métapsychiques', p. 842.
94. Jean de Beaucorps, *Lourdes: Les Guérisons* (Paris, Bloud & Cie, 1913), vol. 2, p. 146.
95. Henry Berteaux, 'Lourdes et la science', séance du 16 juillet, *Revue de l'hypnotisme*, vol. 9 (1895), p. 214.
96. ibid., p. 215.
97. ibid., p. 216.
98. Harry Paul, *The Edge of Contingency: French Catholic Reaction to*

Scientific Change from Darwin to Duhem (Gainesville, University Presses of Florida, 1979), especially pp. 6–21.
99. Henry Berteaux, 'Lourdes et la science', p. 217.
100. Dr Noriogof, *Notre-Dame de Lourdes et la science de l'occulte* (Paris, Chaumel, 2nd ed., 1898), p. 88.
101. ibid., p. 91, both quotations.
102. Hippolyte Baraduc, *La Force curatrice à Lourdes et la psychologie du miracle* (Paris, Bloud, 1907).

Epilogue

1. For the most compelling and eloquent statement of this view, see Eugen Weber, *Peasants into Frenchmen: The Modernization of Rural France* (London, Chatto & Windus, 1977); many other excellent studies focus on the disintegration of local cultures, such as P. M. Jones, *Politics and Rural Society: The Southern Massif Central* c. *1750–1880* (Cambridge, Cambridge University Press, 1985) and Maurice Agulhon, *La République au village: Les Populations du Var de la Révolution à la Seconde République*, which none the less imply a model of modernization. For a revision of some of his 'modernizing' preoccupations, see Eugen Weber, 'Religion and Superstition in Nineteenth-century France', *Historical Journal*, vol. 32 (1988), pp. 399–423. See Judith Devlin for a wide-ranging attempt to unravel the cosmology of rural France, *The Superstitious Mind: French Peasants and the Supernatural in the Nineteenth Century* (New Haven, Yale University Press, 1987); for new approaches, see Peter Sahlins, *Forest Rites: The War of the Demoiselles in Nineteenth-century France* and his *Boundaries: The Making of France and Spain in the Pyrenees*, Caroline Ford, *Creating the Nation in Provincial France: Religion and Political Identity in Brittany* and J. Lehning, *Peasant and French: Cultural Contact in Rural France during the Nineteenth Century* (New York, Cambridge University Press, 1995) and my 'Possession on the Borders: The "mal de Morzine" in Nineteenth-century France', *Journal of Modern History*, vol. 69 (1997), pp. 451–78.
2. See Claude Nicolet, *L'Idée républicaine en France: Essai d'histoire critique* (Paris, Gallimard, 1982), pp. 187–385.
3. For the story of such timidity, see for example, P. K. Bidelman, *Pariahs Stand UP! The Founding of the Liberal Feminist Movement in France 1858–1889* (Westport, CT, and London, Greenwood, 1982); for the extent of the suffrage movement, see Steven C. Hause, *Hubertine Auclert: The French Suffragette* (New Haven, Yale University Press, 1987), and his more wide-ranging (with Anne R. Kenny), *Women's Suffrage and Social Politics in the French Third Republic* (Princeton, Princeton University Press, 1984); on the

fundamental difficulties between socialist feminists and their liberal sisters, see Charles Sowerwine, *Sisters or Citizens? Women and Socialism in France since 1876* (Cambridge, Cambridge University Press, 1982). For a good survey of French feminism, see L. Klejman and F. Rochefort, *L'Egalité en marche* (Paris, Presses de la fondation nationale des sciences politiques, 1989). See also J. Waelti-Walters and Steven C. Hause, *Feminisms of the Belle Epoque: A Historical and Literary Anthology* (Lincoln, Nebr., University of Nebraska Press, 1994), for the range of ideological strands.

4. Karen Offen, 'Depopulation, Nationalism and Feminism in the *Fin de Siècle*', *American Historical Review*, vol. 89 (1984), pp. 648–76.

5. Steven C. Hause and A. Kenny, 'The Development of the Catholic Women's Suffrage Movement in France 1896–1922', *Catholic Historical Review*, vol. 68 (1981), pp. 11–30, and their *Women's Suffrage and Social Politics*, pp. 81–6; see also James McMillan, 'Religion and Gender in Modern France: Some Reflections', in Frank Tallett and Nicholas Atkin, *Religion, Society and Politics in France since 1789* (London, Hambledon Press, 1991), pp. 55–66. Indeed, as these selections show, Catholic women, such as Marie Maugeret, supported the suffrage in an attempt to defend the Church and reform the republic and were hence viewed warily by their anti-clerical sisters.

6. Claude Langlois, *Le catholicisme au féminin: Les Congrégations françaises à supérieure générale au XIXe siècle*, Yvonne Turin, *Femmes et religieuses au XIXe siècle: Le Féminisme 'en religion'*, Jacques Léonard, 'Femmes, religion et médecine: Les Religieuses qui soignent, en France au XIXe siècle' and Odile Arnold, *Le Corps et l'âme.*

7. See Sylvie Fayet-Scribe, *Associations féminines et catholicisme XIXe–XXe siècles* (Paris, Les Editions ouvrières, 1990), not only for the wide range of organizations but also, once again, for the importance of 'catholicisme intransigeant' in shaping their vision of social Catholicism, pp. 187–90; see also Hazel Mills, 'Negotiating the Divide: Women, Philanthropy and the "Public Sphere" in Nineteenth-century France', in Frank Tallett and Nicholas Atkin, *Religion, Society and Politics in France since 1789*, pp. 29–54.

8. For an example of their inspiring story, see Jo Burr Margadant, *Madame le Professeur: Women Educators in the Third Republic* (Princeton, Princeton University Press, 1990).

9. See P. K. Bidelman, *Pariahs Stand UP! The Founding of the Liberal Feminist Movement in France 1858–1889.*

10. For more, see Théodore Mangiapan, *Les Guérisons de Lourdes*, pp. 124–6; see also Alexis Carrel, *The Voyage to Lourdes*, Virgilia Peterson, tr. (Fraser, Michigan, Real-View Books, 1994).

11. For a first foray into investigating the relations between religion and hysteria in late nineteenth- and early twentieth-century France and Italy,

see Cristina Mazzoni, *Saint Hysteria: Neurosis, Mysticism and Gender in European Culture* (Ithaca, Cornell University Press, 1996).

12. See for one example among many Jean-Martin Charcot and Paul Richer, *Les Démoniaques dans l'art*.

13. D.-M. Bourneville, *Science et miracle: Louise Lateau ou la stigmatisée belge* (Paris, A. Delahaye, 1875), and for the eloquent and compendious response of a Catholic neurologist, see Antoine-Imbert Gourbeyre, *La Stigmatisation, l'extase divine et les miracles de Lourdes: Réponse aux libres-penseurs*.

14. P. Janet, *De l'angoisse à l'extase: Etudes sur les croyances et les sentiments* (Paris, Alcan, 2 vols., 1926–8). For the extraordinary discovery of Madeleine's real identity as Pauline Lair, see Jacques Maître, *Une inconnue célèbre: La Madeleine Lebouc de Janet* (Paris, Anthropos, 1993).

15. Père Charles Monsch, archivist, AAR, in correspondence, and AAR, SW1-231, 'Lettres 1912–32, Question de l'Action française', which show the disputes arising from these political loyalties.

16. For more on the organization's widespread influence on the Catholic right, see Eugen Weber, *Action Française, Royalism and Reaction in Twentieth-century France* (Stanford, Stanford University Press, 1964), pp. 219–39; Michael Sutton, *Nationalism, Positivism and Catholicism: The Politics of Charles Maurras and French Catholics 1890–1914* (Cambridge, Cambridge University Press, 1982).

17. On the female side of the Hospitalité, Germain Féron-Vrau, for example, was a founder of the Ligue patriotique des femmes, while her husband Paul became the proprietor of La Bonne Presse, the media empire of the Assumptionists.

18. Stéphane Baumont, 'La Réinvention de Lourdes', in *Histoire de Lourdes*, p. 252.

19. ibid., p. 276.

20. Franz Werfel, *The Song of Bernadette* (London, Hamish Hamilton, 1942), p. 6.

21. André Latreille, 'Un évêque résistant: Mgr Pierre-Marie Théas, évêque de Montauban, 1940–1946', *Revue d'histoire ecclésiastique* [Belgium], 1980, vol. 75, pp. 284–321.

Dramatis Personae

The Family

Bernadette Soubirous, visionary
François Soubirous, her father
Louise Castérot Soubirous, her mother
Toinette, her sister
Bernarde Castérot, her aunt
Marie Laguës, her wet nurse
André Sajous, a relation who helped the Soubirous family

Officials and Notables

Captain Adolphe d'Angla, captain of the gendarmes
Pierre Callet, *garde champêtre*
Romain Capdevielle, editor of the local paper
M. A. Clarens, director of the Ecole supérieure de Lourdes
Dr Pierre-Romain Dozous, doctor and believer
Marie Dufo, Capdevielle's fiancée
Vital Dutour, the imperial prosecutor
Jean-Baptiste Estrade, the tax collector
Emmanuélite Estrade, his pious sister
Dominique Jacomet, the police commissioner
Alexandre Joanas, the mayor's secretary
Anselme Lacadé, the mayor
Baron Oscar Massy, prefect of the department
Clément-Dominique Pailhasson, the pharmacist
Marie-Rosella Pailhasson, his wife
Comte Albert de Rességuier, legitimist deputy
Jean Vergès, *garde champêtre*

The Clergy

Mgr Antoine de Salinis, archbishop of Auch
Mgr Bertrand-Sévère Mascarou Laurence, bishop of Tarbes and Lourdes
Mgr César-Victor Jourdan, Laurence's successor
Mgr Ignace-Armand de Garsignies, bishop of Soissons
Mgr Charles-Thomas Thibault, bishop of Montpellier
Abbé Marie-Jean-Gualbert-Antoine Fourcade, secretary of Episcopal Commission of Inquiry
Abbé Dominique Peyramale, curé of Lourdes
Abbé Marie-Bertrand Pomian,

Bernadette's confessor at the hospice
Abbé Antoine Dézirat, priest who witnessed one of the apparitions
Abbé Jean-Matthieu-Joseph Serres, one of the priests at Lourdes
Abbé Pierre-Jean-Bertrand Pène, a priest of Lourdes and defender of the apparitions
Abbé Pierre-Marcel Montauzé, interrogator of Bernadette
Frère Marie Léobard, the schoolteacher
Père Burosse, of the Episcopal Commission of Inquiry
Canon Germain Baradère, head of subcommittee investigating cures
Chanoine Dominique Ribes, director of the seminary at Tarbes
Père Michel Garicoïts, missionary
Jean-Louis Peydessus, superior of the Garaison Fathers
Pierre-Rémi Sempé and
Jean-Marie Duboë, Peydessus's successors
Mère Ursule Fardes, superior of the Hospice–Ecole des Sœurs de Nevers
Père Nègre, Jesuit and sceptic
Père Justin Nereci, curé of Estipou
Père Charles Bouin, correspondent of Bernadette
'Père Hermann', or Hermann Cohen, Jewish convert to Catholicism who leads a procession at Lourdes

Townspeople and Villagers

Jeanne Abadie
Josèphe Barinque
Louis Bouriette
Justine Cassou
Laurentine Cazeau
Dominiquette Cazenave
Marie-Madeleine Courrade
Anna Dupin
Antoinette Garros
Cyprine Gesta
Catherine Labayle
Jacques Laborde
Jean-Marie Laborde
Elfrida Lacrampe
Elisa Latapie
Léon Latapie
Catherine Latapie-Chouat
Paul Layrisse
Jeanne-Marie Milhet
Adélaide Monlaur
Fanny Nicolau
Eléonore Pérard
Antoinette Peyret
Marie Tardhivail
Antoinette Tardhivail
Etienne Théas
Eugénie Troy

The 'False Visionaries'

Joséphine Albario
Madeleine Cazaux
Julien Cazenave
Marie Cazenave
Marie Courrech
Jean Labayle
Marie Labayle
Honorine Lacroix

Suzette Lavantès
Marie Poujol
Jeanne-Marie Poueyto

Outsiders

Henri Lasserre, journalist
Léonard Cros, Jesuit historian
Louis-François Veuillot, Catholic polemicist
Joseph Fabisch, sculptor
Amirale Bruat, imperial nanny
Achille Fould, minister of state
Comte de Broussard, atheist converted by Bernadette
Mme Joseph, Protestant converted by Bernadette
Hippolyte Duran, architect of the basilica

Assumptionists and Others

Père Emmanuel d'Alzon, founder of the Assumptionists
Père François Picard, his successor
Père Vincent de Paul Bailly, editor of *La Croix*
Père Etienne Pernet, spiritual director of Antoinette Fage and co-founder of the Petites-Sœurs
Mère Marie-Eugénie Milleret, friend and confidante of d'Alzon and superior of the Petites-Sœurs de l'Assomption
Antoinette Fage, Mère Marie de Jésus, superior of the Petites-Sœurs
Madame de la Rochefoucauld, Duchesse d'Estissac, president of Notre-Dame de Salut
Mme Laforest, secretary of Notre-Dame de Salut
Mme Dumont, activist in Notre-Dame de Salut
Mme Gossin, activist in Notre-Dame de Salut
Abbé Thédenat, originator of first national pilgrimage to La Salette in 1872
Abbé Chocarne, organizer of pilgrimage of the banners to Lourdes
M. de Combettes de Luc, one of the founders of the Hospitalité de Notre-Dame de Salut
M. de l'Epinois, one of the founders of the Hospitalité de Notre-Dame de Salut

Doctors and Critics

Dr Henri Vergez, medical consultant to the Episcopal Commission of Inquiry
Baron Dunot de Saint-Maclou, first head of the Medical Bureau
Gustave Boissarie, his successor after 1891
Hippolyte Baraduc, physician
Emile Zola, novelist
Jean-Martin Charcot, neurologist
Hippolyte Bernheim, psychiatrist and hypnotist
Jean de Bonnefon, hygienist
Félix Régnault, physician
Pierre Janet, psychoanalyst

Bibliography

Manuscript Sources

Archives Cros at the Archives de la Grotte, Lourdes
Archives de la Congrégation des Petites-Sœurs de l'Assomption, Paris
Archives de la Grotte, Lourdes
Archives Nationales, Paris
Archives de Notre-Dame de Salut, Paris
Archives départementales des Hautes-Pyrénées, Tarbes
Archives des Assomptionnistes, Rome
Archives du Couvent de Saint-Gildard, Nevers

Primary Printed Sources

Anon. [Un des missionnaires gardiens de la Grotte], *Les Bannières de la France à Notre-Dame de Lourdes* (Lourdes, Bertrand Pujo, 1873)

Anon., 'Cinquantième anniversaire de la création du régiment des Zouaves pontificaux: Allocution de Monseigneur de Cabrières', Montmartre, 5 juin 1910 (Montpellier, Imprimerie de la Manufacture de la Charité, 1910)

Anon., [A. Peyramale], *L'Eglise nouvelle de Lourdes et Monseigneur Peyramale* (Pau, Imprimerie-Stéreótypie Garet, *c.* 1890)

Anon., *L'Eglise du Rosaire de Notre-Dame de Lourdes* (Lourdes, Bertrand Pujo, n.d.)

Anon., *Hospitalité de Notre-Dame de Salut: Pèlerinage national à Notre-Dame de Lourdes* (Toulouse, Imprimerie Catholique Saint-Cyprien, 1904)

Anon., *Le Jubilé du pèlerinage national à Lourdes* (Paris, Maison de la Bonne Presse, 1897)

Anon., *Manuel: Pèlerinage national des hommes à Lourdes* (Tarbes, n.p., 1903)

Anon., *La Mère Marie de Jésus: Fondatrice des Petites-Sœurs de l'Assomption, gardes-malades des pauvres à domicile* (Paris, Maison de la Bonne Presse, 1908)

Anon., *Notes et historique de l'hôpital de Notre-Dame de Salut: Lourdes durant le National* (Toulouse, Imprimerie Catholique Saint-Cyprien, 1913)

Anon., *Le Petit Manuel des Dames Hospitalières de Notre-Dame de Lourdes* (Lourdes, Imprimerie de la Grotte, 1896)

Anon., *Voyage de LL MM l'Empereur et l'Impératrice dans les départements du sud-est, de la Savoie, de la Corse et de l'Algérie* (n.p., 1860)

Association de Notre-Dame de Salut, *Hospitalité de Notre-Dame de Salut: Documents, statuts, coutumiers, historiques* (Paris, 4 avenue de Breteuil, 1921)

Association de Notre-Dame de Salut, *Rapport Général lu à l'assemblée le 5 février 1873* (Paris, rue François Ier, 1873)

Azun de Bernétas, T.-M.-J.-T., *La Grotte des Pyrénées ou manifestation de la Sainte Vierge à la Grotte de Lourdes (Diocèse de Tarbes, précédé d'une notice sur les Pyrénées)* (Tarbes, J.-P. Larrieu, 1861)

Backer, Félix de, *Lourdes et les médecins* (Paris, J. Maloine, 1905)

Bailly, Vincent de Paul, 'Apparition de la Sainte Vierge à deux écoliers', *Revue de l'Enseignement chrétien*, vol. 5 (1873), pp. 49–56

Baraduc, Hippolyte, *La Force curatrice à Lourdes et la psychologie du miracle* (Paris, Bloud, 1907)

Barrail, Ernest du, *Voyage de L. Napoléon, Président de la République dans l'est de la France et dans la Normandie* (1850)

Beaucorps, Jean de, *Lourdes: Les Guérisons* (Paris, Bloud & Cie, 1913)

Bernard, Claude, *L'Introduction à la médecine expérimentale* (Paris, J.-B. Ballière et fils, 1865)

Bernheim, Hippolyte, *Hypnotisme, suggestion et psychothérapie: Etudes nouvelles* (Paris, Doin, 1891)

Berteaux, Henry, 'Lourdes et la science', *Revue de l'hypnotisme*, no. 9 (1895), pp. 210–17

Bertier, J.-P., *Notre-Dame de La Salette: Son apparition, son culte* (Paris, Haton, n.d.)

Bertrin, Abbé Georges, *Histoire critique des événements de Lourdes: Apparitions et guérisons* (Paris, Librairie Gabalda, 1905)

Boissarie, Gustave, *Zola: Conférence du Luxembourg* (Paris, Maison de la Bonne Presse, 1895)

Bonnefon, Jean de, 'Faut-il fermer Lourdes?', *Les Paroles françaises et romaines* (1 juillet 1906), pp. 3–64

Bourneville, D.-M., *Science et miracle: Louise Lateau ou la stigmatisée belge* (Paris, A. Delahaye, 1875)

Carrel, Alexis, *The Voyage to Lourdes*, Virgilia Peterson, tr. (Fraser, Michigan, Real-View Books, 1994)

Charcot, Jean-Martin, and Richer, Paul, *Les Démoniaques dans l'art*, P. Fédida and G. Didi-Huberman, eds. (Paris, Edition Macula, 1984)

Copéré, P. Louis, *Cause de Béatification et de Canonisation de Sœur Marie Bernard Soubirous de l'Institut des Sœurs de la Charité* (Rome, Imprimerie Pontificale, 1908)

Cordier, Eugène, *Les Légendes des Hautes-Pyrénées*, Jean-François Le Nail and X. Recroix, eds. (Tarbes, Centre départemental de documentation pédagogique, 1986; reprint of 1878 ed.)

Cormont, C.-L., *Voyage de Leurs Majestés Impériales en Auvergne* (Clermont-Ferrand, P. Hubler, 1862)

Cros, Léonard, *Histoire de Notre-Dame de Lourdes*, Ferdinand Cavallera, ed. (Paris, Beauchesne, 3 vols., 1925–7)

— *Histoire de Notre-Dame de Lourdes*, Père M. Olphe-Galliard, pref. (Paris, Beauchesne, 3 vols., 1957)

— *Lourdes 1858: Témoins de l'événement*, Père M. Olphe-Galliard, ed. (Paris, P. Lethielleux, 3 vols., 1957)

Curique, Abbé J.-M., *Voix prophétiques, ou signes, apparitions et prédictions modernes touchant les grands événements de la chrétienté au XIX siècle et vers l'approche de la fin des temps* (Paris, Victor Palmé, 1872)

Dambielle, Abbé, *La Sorcellerie en Gascogne* (Nîmes, Collection Rediviva, C. Lacour, ed., 1992; reprint of ed. first pub. Auch, Léonce Cocharux, 1907)

Dozous, Dr Pierre-Romain, *La Grotte de Lourdes, sa fontaine, ses guérisons* (Auch, Thibaut, 1874)

Estrade, Jean-Baptiste, *Les Apparitions de Lourdes: Souvenirs intimes d'un témoin* (Tours, Mame, 1899)

Fourcade, Abbé M. J. G. A., *L'Apparition à la Grotte de Lourdes* (Tarbes, chez Fouga, 1862)

Gourbeyre, Antoine-Imbert, *La Stigmatisation, l'extase divine et les miracles de Lourdes: Réponse aux libres-penseurs* (Clermont-Ferrand, Librairie Catholique, and Paris, Belle, 1894)

Granier de Cassagnac, A., *Souvenirs du Second Empire* (Paris, E. Dentu, 1879–82)

Hamon, A.-J.-M., *Notre-Dame de France, ou histoire du culte de la Sainte Vierge en France depuis l'origine du christianisme jusqu'à nos jours* (Paris, Henri Plon, 3 vols., 1863)

Hospitalité de Notre-Dame de Salut, *Membres décédés* (Toulouse, Imprimerie Catholique Saint-Cyprien, 1904–10)

Huysmans, Joris-Karl, *Là-bas* (Paris, Tresse & Stock, 1891)

— *Les Foules de Lourdes* (Grenoble, Jérôme Millon, 1993)

— *A Rebours* (Paris, G. Charpentier, 1882)

Janet, P., *De l'angoisse à l'extase: Etudes sur les croyances et les sentiments* (Paris, Alcan, 2 vols., 1926–8)

Lagrèze, G. B. de, *Les Pèlerinages des Pyrénées* (Paris, Jacques Lecoffre, 1858)

Lamennais, Felicité Robert de, *Des progrès de la révolution et de la guerre contre l'église* (Paris, Délun, Mander & Devaux, 1829)

Lasserre, Henri, *Le Curé de Lourdes: Mgr Peyramale* (Paris, Bloud & Barral, 10th ed., 1898)

— *L'Evangile selon Renan* (Paris, Victor Palmé, 12th ed., 1863)

— *Notre-Dame de Lourdes* (Paris, Victor Palmé, 3rd ed., 1878)

— 'Très-humble supplique et mémoire adressé par M. Henri Lasserre à la sacrée congrégation du Saint-Office romain sur certains abus très préjudiciables à la religion' (Archives de la Grotte, A38)

Laurent, F., *Voyage de Sa Majesté Napoléon III, Empereur des Français, dans les départements de l'est, du centre et du midi de la France* (Paris, S. Raçon, 1853)

Magnin, Marcel, 'Les Guérisons de Lourdes et les phénomènes métapsychiques', *Annales des sciences psychiques* (décembre 1907), pp. 816–66

Moniquet, Abbé Poulain, *Le Cas de M. Henri Lasserre, Lourdes–Rome* (Paris, Arthur Savaète, 1897)

Noriogof, Dr, *Notre-Dame de Lourdes et la science de l'occulte* (Paris, Chaumel, 1898)

Pie X, *Paroles Pontificales en faveur de l'association [de Notre-Dame de Salut]: Discours de S. S. Pie X de 1908 à 1912* (Paris, 4 avenue de Breteuil, 1914)

Pierrebourg, Patrice de, *La Psychologie du brancardier de Lourdes* (Paris, Association de Notre-Dame de Lourdes, 1954)

Poulain-Corbion, J.-M., *Récit du voyage de l'Empereur et de l'Impératrice en Normandie et en Bretagne* (Paris, Amyot, 1858)

Rebsomen, A., *Souvenirs d'un brancardier de Lourdes* (Paris, Editions Alsatia, 1936)

Régnault, Félix, 'De l'hypnotisme dans la genèse des miracles', *Revue de l'hypnotisme* (1894), pp. 270–77

Renan, Ernest, *Vie de Jésus* (Paris, Gallimard, 1974)

Rivail, Hippolyte, alias Allan Kardec, *Livre des esprits, contenant les principes de la doctrine spirite* (Paris, Dentu, 1857)

Sébillot, P., *Le Folklore de France* (Paris, Guilmoto, 1905)

Sempé, P., 'Lettre à Monseigneur Pierre-Anastase Pichenot en réponse aux accusations de M. Henri Lasserre' (Lourdes, 1872)

Veuillot, François, *Les Hommes de France à Lourdes (Souvenirs du pèlerinage national d'hommes)* (Paris, Bloud & Barral, 1899)

Veuillot, Louis, *Œuvres complètes* (Paris, P. Lethielleux, 1923–39)

Zola, Emile, *Œuvres complètes*, Henri Mitterand, ed. (Paris, Cercle du livre précieux, 15 vols., 1966–9)

— *Mes Voyages: Lourdes, Rome, journaux inédits*, René Ternois, ed. (Paris, Fasquelle éditeurs, 1958)

Journals

Annales de Notre-Dame de Lourdes
Annuaire de l'Hospitalité de Notre-Dame de Salut
L'Assiette au Beurre
Bulletin de l'Association de Notre-Dame de Salut
La Croix
Journal de la Grotte de Lourdes
Journal de Lourdes
Le Pèlerin
Revue de l'hypnotisme
Revue de Lourdes
Semaine Catholique de Toulouse
La Source
Souvenirs de l'Hospitalité de Notre-Dame de Salut
L'Univers

Unpublished Works

Deraedt, Père Désiré, 'Le Père d'Alzon et les droits de Dieu sur la société', typescript, 17pp. and notes, AAR

Marchand, Sœur Gisèle, 'Extraits de "Une page de l'histoire de Lourdes"', typescript, APSA

Maylis, Sœur Thérèse, 'Marie-Eugénie et le Père d'Alzon: Intuitions communes, influence réciproque?', typescript, AAR

Monsch, Père Charles, 'Comment, dans les pèlerinages, les disciples du Père d'Alzon sont-ils restés fidèles à l'affirmation, par leur fondateur, des droits de Dieu?', typescript, 5pp. and 8pp. of interventions, AAR

— 'Essai de portrait du Père Vincent de Paul Bailly', typescript, 3pp., AAR

Taylor, Therese, 'Images of Sanctity: Photography of Saint Bernadette of Lourdes and Saint Thérèse of Lisieux', typescript, 40pp.

Touveneraud, Père Pierre, 'Chronologie des premières années de l'association de Notre-Dame de Salut', typescript, 3pp., AAR, UW322

— 'Le Premier Pèlerinage national à La Salette de passage à Grenoble, en août 1872', typescript, AAR, UD185

— 'Le Séjour d'Etienne Pernet à Paris en 1849', typescript, 10pp., AAR

Secondary Printed Sources

Accati, Luisa, 'Explicit Meanings: Catholicism, Matriarchy and the Distinctive Problems of Italian Feminism', *Gender and History*, vol. 7 (1995), pp. 241–59

Acomb, Evelyn Martha, *The French Laic Laws (1879–1889): The First Anti-clerical Campaign of the Third French Republic* (New York, Octagon Books, 1967)

Agulhon, Maurice, *Marianne into Battle: Republican Imagery and Symbolism in France 1789–1880* (Cambridge, Cambridge University Press, 1981)

— *Marianne au pouvoir: L'Image et la symbolique républicaine* (Paris, Flammarion, 1989)

— *Un mouvement populaire au temps de 1848. Histoire des populations du Var dans la première moitié du XIXe siècle* (thèse d'Etat, Paris-Sorbonne, 1969)

— *The Republican Experiment, 1848–1852* (Cambridge, Cambridge University Press, 1983)

— *La République au village: Les Populations du Var de la Révolution à la Seconde République* (Paris, Henri Plon, 1970)

— 'La "statuomanie" et l'histoire', in *Histoire vagabonde* (Paris, Gallimard, 1988), vol. 1, pp. 137–85

Ahlgren, Gillian T. W., *Theresa of Avila and the Politics of Sanctity* (Ithaca, NY, Cornell University Press, 1996)

Albalat, Antoine, *La Vie de Jésus d'Ernest Renan* (Paris, Société française d'éditions littéraires et techniques, 1933)

Anon., *De Notre-Dame de Garaison à Notre-Dame de Lourdes. Jean-Louis Peydessus: Apôtre marial de la Bigorre 1807–1882* (Paris, Grasset, 1959)

Anon., *Mère Marie de Jésus: Marie-Antoinette Fage, cofondatrice avec le Père Pernet, AA, des Petites-Sœurs de l'Assomption* (Paris, 57 rue Violet, 1983)

Aretin, K. O., *The Papacy in the Modern World* (London, Weidenfeld & Nicolson, 1970)

Armengaud, A., *Les Populations de l'Est-Aquitaine au début de l'époque contemporaine. Recherches sur une région moins développée, vers 1845–1871* (Paris, La Haye, 1961)

Arnold, Odile, *Le Corps et l'âme: La Vie des religieuses au XIXe siècle* (Paris, Seuil, 1984)

Atkinson, Clarissa W., et al., eds., *Immaculate and Powerful: The Female in Sacred Image and Social Reality* (Boston, Beacon Press, 1985)

Aubert, R., *Le Pontificat de Pie IX (1846–1878)* (Paris, Bloud & Gay, 1963)

Augustins, G., et al., *Les Baronnies des Pyrénées* (Paris, Editions des hautes études en sciences sociales, 1981)

Aziz, Philippe, *Les Miracles de Lourdes: La Science face à la foi* (Paris, Robert Laffont, 1981)

Baby, F., *La Guerre des Demoiselles en Ariège 1829–1872* (Paris, Montbel, 1972)

Bakhtin, Mikhail, *Rabelais and His World*, H. Iswolsky, tr. (Cambridge, MA, MIT Press, 1968)

Barbet, Jean, *Bernadette Soubirous: Sa naissance, sa vie, sa mort, d'après des documents inédits* (Pau, G. Les Cher, 1909)

Barrows, Susanna, *Distorting Mirrors: Visions of the Crowd in Late Nineteenth-century France* (New Haven, Yale University Press, 1981)

Baud, Henri, 'Le Défi protestant et les débuts de la contre-réforme (1536–1622)', in Henri Baud, ed., *Le Diocèse de Genève-Annecy* (Paris, Beauchesne, 1985), pp. 98–128

Baumont, Stéphane, ed., *Histoire de Lourdes* (Toulouse, Privat, 1993)

Bénichou, P., *Le Temps des prophètes: Doctrines de l'âge romantique* (Paris, Gallimard, 1977)

Bercé, Yves-Marie, *Fête et révolte: Des mentalités populaires du XVIe au XVIIIe siècle* (Paris, Hachette, 1976)

Berenson, Edward, *Populist Religion and Left-Wing Politics in France 1830–1852* (Princeton, Princeton University Press, 1984)

Bernos, Marcel, 'La Catéchèse des filles par les femmes aux XVIIe et XVIIIe siècles', in Jean Delumeau, ed., *La Religion de ma mère: Le Rôle des femmes dans la transmission de la foi* (Paris, Cerf, 1992), pp. 269–87

Bernoville, Gaëtan, *L'Evêque de Bernadette* (Paris, Grasset, 1955)

— *Mère Saint-Jean Baptiste (Marie Saint-Frai) et le Père Ribes: Fondateurs de la Congrégation hospitalière-missionnaire des Filles de Notre-Dame des Sept Douleurs* (Paris, Grasset, 1958)

— *De Notre-Dame de Garaison à Notre-Dame de Lourdes. Jean-Louis Peydessus: Apôtre marial de la Bigorre 1807–1882* (Paris, Grasset, 1959)

— *Le Père Pernet: Fondateur des Petites-Sœurs de l'Assomption* (Paris, Grasset, 1944)

— *Les Religieuses de l'Assomption: Eugénie Milleret* (Paris, Grasset, 1948)

— *Un saint basque: Le Bienheureux Michel Garicoïts* (Paris, J. de Gigord, 1936)

Bertier, J.-P., *Notre-Dame de La Salette. Son apparition, son culte* (Paris, Haton, n.d.)

Bidelman, P. K., *Pariahs Stand UP! The Founding of the Liberal Feminist Movement in France 1858–1889* (Westport, CT, and London, Greenwood, 1982)

Bilinkoff, Jodi, *The Avila of Saint Theresa: Religious Reform in a Sixteenth-century City* (Ithaca, Cornell University Press, 1989)

Billet, Bernard, 'Lourdes et les Lourdais au temps de Bernadette', in *La Vie quotidienne dans les Hautes-Pyrénées au temps de Bernadette* (Lourdes, Exposition Musée Pyrénéen, 1979), pp. 9–24

Blackbourn, David, *Marpingen: Apparitions of the Virgin Mary in Bismarckian Germany* (Oxford, Oxford University Press, 1993)

Borel, Louis, *Notre-Dame de La Salette* (Paris, Letouzey et Ané, 1923)

Boutry, Philippe, 'Marie, la grande consolatrice de la France au XIXe siècle', *L'Histoire*, no. 50 (1982), pp. 31–9

— *Prêtres et paroisses au pays du Curé d'Ars* (Paris, Cerf, 1986)

— and Cinquen, Michel, *Deux Pèlerinages au XIXe siècle: Ars et Paray-le-Monial* (Paris, Beauchesne, 1980)

Bredin, Jean-Denis, *L'Affaire* (Paris, Julliard, 1983)

Bremmer, Jan, and Roodenburg, Herman, eds., *A Cultural History of Gesture* (Ithaca, Cornell University Press, 1991)

Brockliss, L. W. B., 'The Development of the Spa in Seventeenth-century France', in Roy Porter, ed., *The Medical History of Waters and Spas* (London, Wellcome Institute for the History of Medicine, 1990), pp. 23–47

Brown, Peter, *The Body and Society* (London, Faber, 1989)

Brule, Alfred van den, SJ, *Le Docteur Boissarie: Président du Bureau des Constatations médicales de Lourdes* (Paris, J. de Gigord, 1919)

Burdeau, F., *Histoire de l'administration française du 18ème au 20ème siècle* (Paris, Montchrestien, 1989)

Burns, Michael, *The Dreyfus Family 1789–1945* (London, Chatto & Windus, 1992)

Butler, Dom Cuthbert, *The Vatican Council 1869–1870* (London, Fontana, 1962, reprinted from 1930 ed.)

Bynum, Caroline Walker, *Holy Feast and Holy Fast: The Religious Significance of Food to Medieval Women* (Berkeley, University of California Press, 1987)

— *Jesus as Mother: Studies in the Spirituality of the High Middle Ages* (Berkeley, University of California Press, 1982)

— *The Resurrection of the Body in Western Christianity* (New York, Columbia University Press, 1995)

Cabanis, José, *Lacordaire et quelques autres: Politique et religion* (Paris, Gallimard, 1982)

Callahan, W. J., and Higgs, D., eds., *Church and Society in Catholic Europe in the Eighteenth Century* (Cambridge, Cambridge University Press, 1979)

Carroll, Michael P., *The Cult of the Virgin Mary: Psychological Origins* (Princeton, Princeton University Press, 1986)

Carroy, Jacqueline, *Hypnose, suggestion et psychologie: L'Invention des sujets* (Paris, PUF, 1991)

— *Le Mal de Morzine: De la Possession à l'hystérie* (Paris, Solin, 1981)

— *Les Personnalités doubles et multiples* (Paris, PUF, 1993)

Carter, A. E., *The Idea of Decadence in French Literature 1830–1900* (Toronto, University of Toronto Press, 1958)

Cattanéo, Bernard, *Montalembert: Un catholique en politique* (Chambray, CLD, 1990)

Caulier, Brigitte, *L'Eau et le sacré: Les Cultes thérapeutiques autour des fontaines en France du Moyen Age à nos jours* (Paris, Beauchesne, 1990)

Certeau, Michel de, *The Mystic Fable. Volume 1: The Sixteenth and Seventeenth Centuries*, Michael B. Smith, tr. (Chicago, University of Chicago Press, 1992)

— ed., *La Possession de Loudun* (Paris, Gallimard, 2nd ed., 1990)

— Julia, Dominique, and Revel, Jacques, *Une politique de la langue: La Révolution française et les patois – l'enquête de Grégoire* (Paris, Gallimard, 1974)

Charbonneau, Henri, *Chapelles et saints guérisseurs basques et béarnais* (Hélette, Editions Harriet, 1995)

Chatellier, Louis, 'Le Miracle baroque', in *Actes de la sixième rencontre d'histoire religieuse tenue à Fontevraud les 8 et 9 octobre organisée par le Centre de recherches d'histoire religieuse et d'histoire des idées* (Angers, Presses de l'Université d'Angers, 1983), pp. 85–93

Chélini, Jean, and Branthomme, Henry, *Les Chemins de Dieu: Histoire des pèlerinages chrétiens des origines à nos jours* (Paris, Hachette, 1982)

Cherfas, J., and Lewin, R., eds., *Not Work Alone: A Cross-cultural View of Activities Superfluous to Survival* (London, Maurice Temple Smith, 1980)

Chiron, Yves, *Enquête sur les apparitions de la Vierge* (Paris, Perrin-Mame, 1995)

— *Pie IX: Pape moderne* (Paris, Clovis, 1995)

Cholvy, Gérard, 'Emmanuel d'Alzon: Les Racines', in *Emmanuel d'Alzon dans la société et l'Eglise du XIXe siècle*, René Rémond and Emile Poulat, eds. (Paris, Le Centurion, 1982), pp. 15–41

— and Hilaire, Yves-Marie, *Histoire religieuse de la France contemporaine. Volume 1: 1800–1880* (Paris, Privat, 1985)

Christian, William A., *Apparitions in Late Medieval and Renaissance Spain* (Princeton, Princeton University Press, 1981)

— *Moving Crucifixes in Modern Spain* (Princeton, Princeton University Press, 1992)

— *Person and God in a Spanish Valley* (Cambridge, MA, Harvard University Press, 1972)

— *Visionaries: The Spanish Republic and the Reign of Christ* (Berkeley, University of California Press, 1996)

Christiansen, Rupert, *Tales of the New Babylon: Paris in the Mid Nineteenth Century* (London, Minerva, 1996)

Cobb, Richard, *The People's Armies: The Armées Révolutionnaires – Instrument of the Terror in the Departments April 1793 to Floréal Year II*, Marianne Elliot, tr. (New Haven and London, Yale University Press, 1987)

Cohen, William, 'Symbols of Power: Statues in Nineteenth-century Provincial France', *Comparative Studies in Society and History*, vol. 31 (1989), pp. 491–513

Connerton, Paul, *How Societies Remember* (Cambridge, Cambridge University Press, 1989)

Coquerel, R., 'Considérations sur la vie quotidienne dans les Hautes-Pyrénées vers le milieu du XIXe siècle', in *La Vie quotidienne dans les Hautes-Pyrénées au temps de Bernadette* (Lourdes, Exposition Musée Pyrénéen, 1979), pp. 33–50

Corbin, Alain, *Archaïsme et modernité en Limousin au XIXe siècle 1845–1880* (Paris, M. Rivière, 2 vols., 1975)

— *Le Village des Cannibales* (Paris, Aubier, 1990)

Courtin, J.-B., *Lourdes: Le Domaine de Notre-Dame de Lourdes de 1858 à 1947* (Rennes, Aux éditions franciscaines, 1947)

Crabtree, Adam, *From Mesmer to Freud: Magnetic Sleep and the Roots of Psychological Healing* (New Haven, Yale University Press, 1993)

Cragg, G. R., *The Church and the Age of Reason 1648–1789* (London, Pelican, 1984)

Cranston, Ruth, *The Miracle of Lourdes* (New York, Doubleday, 1988)

Crépu, Michel, Figuier, Richard, and Louis, René, eds., *Hauts Lieux: Une quête de racines, de sacré, de symboles* (Paris, Autrement, 1990)

Crossley, Ceri, *French Historians and Romanticism: Thierry, Guizot, the Saint-Simonians, Quinet, Michelet* (London, Routledge, 1993)

Csordas, Thomas J., *The Sacred Self: A Cultural Phenomenology of Charismatic Healing* (Berkeley, University of California Press, 1994)

Cubero, José-Ramón, 'Des lumières à la Seconde République', in *Histoire de Lourdes*, Stéphane Baumont, ed. (Toulouse, Privat, 1993)

— *La Révolution en Bigorre* (Toulouse, Privat, 1989)

Cubitt, G., *The Jesuit Myth: Conspiracy Theory and Politics in Nineteenth-century France* (Oxford, Clarendon Press, 1993)

Dansette, Adrien, *Religious History of Modern France. Volume 1: From the Revolution to the Third Republic* (Edinburgh and London, Nelson, 1961)

Dantin, Chanoine L., *L'Evêque des apparitions: Mgr Laurence, évêque de Tarbes 1845–1870* (Paris, Editions Spes, 1931)

Davis, Natalie, 'Charivari, Honor and Community in Seventeenth-century Lyon and Geneva', in J. MacAloon, ed., *Rite, Drama, Festival, Spectacle: Rehearsals towards a Theory of Cultural Performance* (Philadelphia, Institute for the Study of Human Issues, 1984), pp. 42–57

Delalande, Jean, *Les Extraordinaires Croisades d'enfants et de pastoureaux au Moyen Age: Les Pèlerinages d'enfants au Mont-Saint-Michel* (Paris, P. Lethielleux, 1962)

Delumeau, Jean, ed., *La Religion de ma mère: Le Rôle des femmes dans la transmission de la foi* (Paris, Cerf, 1992)

Delville, M. L., *Croyances populaires. Fées. – Esprit Follet. Une Légende pyrénéenne* (Tarbes, Th. Telmon, n.d.)

Derré, Jean-René, *Lamennais, ses amis et le mouvement des idées à l'époque romantique (1824–1834)* (Paris, Librairie C. Klincksieck, 1962)

Desan, Suzanne, *Reclaiming the Sacred: Lay Religion and Popular Politics during the French Revolution* (Ithaca, Cornell University Press, 1990)

Desplat, Christian, *Notre-Dame de Sarrance* (Pau, Les Amis des Eglises anciennes du Béarn, 1980)

— *Sorcières et diables en Béarn (fin XIVe–début XIXe siècle)* (Pau, Imprimerie Graphique Marrimpouey Succ., 1988)

Devlin, Judith, *The Superstitious Mind: French Peasants and the Supernatural in the Nineteenth Century* (New Haven, Yale University Press, 1987)

Devos, Roger, 'Quelques aspects de la vie religieuse dans le diocèse d'Annecy au milieu du XIXe siècle (d'après une enquête de Mgr Rendu)', *Cahiers d'histoire* (1966), pp. 49–83

Didi-Huberman, Georges, *Invention de l'hystérie: Charcot et l'iconographie photographique de la Salpêtrière* (Paris, Editions Macula, 1982)

Donnelly, James S., 'The Marian Shrine of Knock: The First Decade', *Éire/Ireland*, vol. 28 (1993), pp. 55–99

Douglass, William A., 'The Famille Souche and Its Interpreters', *Continuity and Change*, vol. 8, no. 1, (1993), pp. 87–102

Duffy, Eamon, *Saints and Sinners: A History of the Popes* (London, Yale University Press, 1997)

Dupront, A., 'Pèlerinage et lieux sacrés', *Mélanges F. Braudel* (Toulouse, Privat, 1973)

Duroselle, Jean-Baptiste, 'L'Abbé Clavel et les revendications du bas-clergé sous Louis-Philippe', *Etudes d'histoire moderne et contemporaine*, vol. 1 (1947), pp. 99–126

— *Les Débuts du catholicisme social en France 1822–1870* (Paris, PUF, 1951)

Eade, John, and Sallnow, Michael J., eds., *Contesting the Sacred: The Anthropology of Christian Pilgrimage* (London, Routledge, 1991)

Echard, William E., *Napoleon III and the Concert of Europe* (Baton Rouge, Louisiana State University Press, 1983)

Edelman, Nicole, *Voyantes, guérisseuses et visionnaires en France 1785–1914* (Paris, Albin Michel, 1995)

Ellenberger, Henri F., *The Discovery of the Unconscious: The History and Evolution of Dynamic Psychiatry* (New York, Basic Books, 1970)

Evans, W. Y., *The Fairy Faith in Celtic Countries* (New York, Carol Publishing Group, 1990)
Fabre, Daniel, 'Le Monde du carnaval', *Annales: Economies, sociétés, cultures*, vol. 31 (1976), pp. 389–407
Fayet-Scribe, Sylvie, *Associations féminines et catholicisme XIXe–XXe siècles* (Paris, Les Editions ouvrières, 1990)
Fentress, J., and Wickham, C., *Social Memory* (Oxford, Blackwell, 1992)
Finucane, Ronald C., *Miracles and Pilgrims: Popular Beliefs in Medieval England* (London, Macmillan, 1995)
Ford, Caroline, *Creating the Nation in Provincial France: Religion and Political Identity in Brittany* (Princeton, Princeton University Press, 1993)
— 'Female Martyrdom and the Politics of Sainthood in Nineteenth-century France: The Cult of Sainte Philomène', in Frank Tallett and Nicholas Atkin, eds., *Catholicism in Britain and France since 1789* (London, Hambledon Press, 1996), pp. 115–34
Forstenzer, Thomas R., *French Provincial Police and the Fall of the Second Republic: Social Fear and Counter-revolution* (Princeton, Princeton University Press, 1981)
Fourcassié, Jean, *Le Romantisme et les Pyrénées* (Toulouse, ESPER, n.d., reprinted from Gallimard, 1940)
Fraisse, Geneviève, and Perrot, Michelle, eds., *A History of Women in the West: Emerging Feminism from Revolution to World War*, Arthur Goldhammer et al., tr. (Cambridge, MA: Belknap/Harvard University Press, 1993), vol. 4
Francez, Abbé Jean, 'Notre-Dame de Montserrat et les Hautes-Pyrénées', *Studia Monastica*, vol. 15 (1973), pp. 65–101
Froeschlé-Chopard, Marie-Hélène, *Espace et sacré en Provence, XIVe–XXe siècles, cultes, images, confréries* (Paris, Cerf, 1994)
Gadille, Jacques, 'Autour de Louis Veuillot et de *L'Univers*', *Cahiers d'histoire* (1969), pp. 275–88
Gaigalas, Vytas V., *Ernest Renan and His French Catholic Critics* (North Quincy, MA, The Christopher Publishing House, 1972)
Gaignebet, Claude, and Florentin, Marie-Claude, *Le Carnaval: Essai de mythologie populaire* (Paris, Payot, 1974)
Gavignaud-Fontaine, Geneviève, *La Propriété en Roussillon: Structures et conjonctures agraires XVIIIe–XIXe siècles* (Lille, ANRT, 1984)
Geison, Gerald L., *The Private Science of Louis Pasteur* (Princeton, Princeton University Press, 1995)
Gélis, J., '"De la mort à la vie": Les "Sanctuaires à répit"', *Ethnologie française*, vol. 11 (1981), pp. 211–24
— 'Miracle et médecine aux siècles classiques: Le Corps médical et le retour

temporaire à la vie des mort-nés', *Historical Reflections*, vol. 9 (1982), pp. 85–101

Gentilcore, David, 'Contesting Illness in Early-Modern Naples: Miracolati, Physicians and the Congregation of Rites', *Past & Present*, no. 148 (1995), pp. 117–48

Gerson, Stéphane, 'Travellers on Mission in the French Provinces: Domestic Journeys and the Construction of National Unity', *Past & Present*, no. 151 (1996), pp. 141–73

Getrey, Gérard, *Les Apparitions mariales de Pellevoisin (1876)* (Paris, F.-X. de Guibert, 1994)

Gibson, Ralph, *A Social History of French Catholicism 1789–1914* (London, Routledge, 1989)

Gildea, R., *The Past in French History* (London, Yale University Press, 1994)

Gilman, Sander L., 'The Image of the Hysteric', in Sander L. Gilman, Helen King, Roy Porter, G. S. Rousseau and Elaine Showalter, *Hysteria beyond Freud* (Berkeley, University of California Press, 1993), pp. 345–452

Ginsburg, Carlo, 'Deciphering the Witches' Sabbath', in *Early-Modern European Witchcraft: Centres and Peripheries*, B. Ankarloo and G. Henningsen, eds. (Oxford, Oxford University Press, 1990), pp. 121–37

Goldstein, Jan, *Console and Classify: The French Psychiatric Profession in the Nineteenth Century* (Cambridge, Cambridge University Press, 1987)

— 'The Hysteria Diagnosis and the Politics of Anti-clericalism in Late Nineteenth-century France', *Journal of Modern History*, vol. 54 (1982), pp. 209–39

— '"Moral Contagion": A Professional Ideology of Medicine and Psychiatry in Eighteenth- and Nineteenth-century France', in Gerald L. Geison, ed., *Professions and the French State 1700–1900* (Philadelphia, University of Pennsylvania Press, 1984), pp. 181–222

Goubert, Jean-Pierre, *The Conquest of Water: The Advent of Health in the Industrial Age*, A. Wilson, tr. (London, Polity Press, 1989)

Gough, Austin, *Paris and Rome: The Gallican Church and the Ultramontane Campaign* (Oxford, Oxford University Press, 1986)

— 'The Conflict in Politics: Bishop Pie's Campaign against the Nineteenth Century', in Theodore Zeldin, ed., *Conflicts in French Society: Anti-clericalism, Education and Morals in the Nineteenth Century* (London, George Allen & Unwin, 1970), pp. 94–168

Graef, Hilda, *Mary: A History of Doctrine and Devotion* (London, Sheed & Ward, 1994)

Gratacos, Isaure, *Calendrier pyrénéen: Rites, coutumes et croyances dans la tradition orale en Comminges et Couserans* (Toulouse, Privat, 1995)

— *Fées et gestes – femmes pyrénéennes: Un statut social exceptionnel en Europe* (Toulouse, Privat, 1987)

Griffiths, R., *The Reactionary Revolution: The Catholic Revival in French Literature 1870–1914* (London, Constable, 1966)

Guillaume, Pierre, *Médecins, église et foi* (Paris, Aubier, 1990)

Guillet, Claude, *La Rumeur de Dieu: Apparitions, prophéties et miracles sous la Restauration* (Paris, Imago, 1994)

Guiraud, Jean, *Histoire de l'Inquisition au Moyen Age* (Paris, A. Picard, 2 vols., 1935)

Harris, Ruth, 'Possession on the Borders: The "mal de Morzine" in Nineteenth-century France', *Journal of Modern History*, vol. 69 (1997), pp. 451–78

— 'Gender and the Sexual Politics of Pilgrimage to Lourdes', in Judith Devlin and Ronan Fanning, eds., *Religion and Rebellion* (Dublin, University College, Dublin Press, 1997), pp. 152–73

Hause, Steven C., *Hubertine Auclert: The French Suffragette* (New Haven, Yale University Press, 1987)

— and Kenny, Anne R., *Women's Suffrage and Social Politics in the French Third Republic* (Princeton, Princeton University Press, 1984)

Hazareesingh, Sudhir, and Wright, Vincent, 'Le Second Empire: Enjeu politique de la Commune et la commune comme enjeu politique', in *Histoire des communes de France* (Paris, Editions du CNRS, forthcoming)

Hobsbawm, Eric, and Ranger, Terry, *The Invention of Tradition* (Cambridge, Cambridge University Press, 1983)

Hufton, Olwen, *The Prospect before Her: A History of Women in Western Europe 1500–1800* (London, HarperCollins, 1995), vol. 1

— *Women and the Limits of Citizenship during the French Revolution* (Toronto, Toronto University Press, 1992)

Humberte, Sœur M., 'La Famille d'Etienne Pernet: Sa mère', *Le Père Etienne Pernet, Pages d'archives*, 4th series, vol. 1 (1996), pp. 21–7

Institut Catholique de Paris, 'Louis Veuillot et son temps: Colloque historique organisé à l'occasion du 100ème anniversaire de sa mort', *Revue de l'Institut Catholique de Paris*, no. 10 (avril–juin 1984)

James, Tony, *Dreams, Creativity and Madness in Nineteenth-century France* (Oxford, Oxford University Press, 1995)

Jantzen, Grace M., *Power, Gender and Christian Mysticism* (Cambridge, Cambridge University Press, 1995)

Johnson, C., *Prosper Guéranger (1805–1875), a Liturgical Theologian: An Introduction to His Liturgical Writings and Work. Studio Anselmiana 89* (Rome, Pontifico Ateneo S. Anselmo, 1984)

Johnson, Douglas, *France and the Dreyfus Affair* (London, Blandford, 1966)

Joisten, Charles, 'Les Etres fantastiques dans le folklore de l'Ariège', *Via Domitia*, vol. 9 (1962), pp. 25–48

Jonas, Raymond A., 'Monument as Ex-Voto, Monument as Historiography:

The Basilica of Sacré-Cœur', *French Historical Studies*, vol. 18 (1993), pp. 482–502

Jones, Colin, *The Charitable Imperative: Hospitals and Nursing in Ancien Régime and Revolutionary France* (London, Routledge, 1989)

Jones, P. M., *Politics and Rural Society: The Southern Massif Central c. 1750–1880* (Cambridge, Cambridge University Press, 1985)

Kale, Steven D., *Legitimism and the Reconstruction of French Society (1852–1883)* (Baton Rouge and London, Louisiana State University Press, 1992)

Kamen, Henry, *The Phoenix and the Flame: Catalonia and the Counter-Reformation* (New Haven, Yale University Press, 1993)

Kedward, H. R., *The Dreyfus Affair: Catalyst for Tension in French Society* (London, Longman, 1969)

Klejman, L., and Rochefort, F., *L'Egalité en marche* (Paris, Presses de la fondation nationale des sciences politiques, 1989)

Kokel, Père Rémi, *Le Père Vincent de Paul Bailly: Journaliste et pèlerin (1832–1912)* (Paris, Maison de la Bonne Presse, 1943)

Kselman, Thomas A., *Death and the Afterlife in Modern France* (Princeton, Princeton University Press, 1993)

— *Miracles and Prophecies in Nineteenth-century France* (New Brunswick, NJ, Rutgers University Press, 1983)

Lacoste, E., *Le Père François Picard* (Paris, Maison de la Bonne Presse, 1932)

Ladurie, Emmanuel Le Roy, *Montaillou: Cathars and Catholics in a French Village 1294–1324*, Barbara Bray, tr. (Harmondsworth, Penguin Books, 1978)

Laffon, Jean-Baptiste, ed., *Le Diocèse de Tarbes et Lourdes* (Paris, Letouzey et Ané, 1971)

Lafforgue, Abbé E., *Les Anciens Pèlerinages de la Bigorre* (Lourdes, Optima, 1924)

— *Les Ermites de Bigorre* (Lourdes, Optima, 1922)

Lafon, Jacques, *Les Prêtres, les fidèles et l'état: Le Ménage à trois du XIXe siècle* (Paris, Beauchesne, 1987)

La Gorce, Pierre-François-Gustave de, *Histoire du Second Empire* (Paris, Henri Plon, 7 vols., 1894–1905)

Langlois, Claude, *Le catholicisme au féminin: Les Congrégations françaises à supérieure générale au XIXe siècle* (Paris, Cerf, 1984)

Lannon, F., *Privilege, Persecution and Prophecy: The Catholic Church in Spain 1875–1975* (Oxford, Oxford University Press, 1987)

Laplantine, François, *Anthropologie de la maladie: Etude ethnologique des systèmes de représentations étiologiques et thérapeutiques dans la société occidentale contemporaine* (Paris, Payot, 1992)

— *La Médecine populaire des campagnes françaises d'aujourd'hui* (Paris, Delarge, 1987)

Larkin, Maurice, *Church and State after the Dreyfus Affair: The Separation Issue in France* (London, Macmillan, 1974)

— *Religion, Politics and Preferment in France since 1890:* La Belle Epoque *and Its Legacy* (Cambridge, Cambridge University Press, 1995)

Larrouy, P. A., *Petite histoire de Notre-Dame de Garaison (1510 environ–1923)* (Notre-Dame de Garaison, 1933)

Lasserre-Vergne, Anne, *Les Pyrénées centrales dans la littérature française* (Toulouse, Eché, 1985)

Latour, Bruno, *Les Microbes* (Paris, A. M. Métailié, 1984)

Latreille, André, 'Un évêque résistant: Mgr Pierre-Marie Théas, évêque de Montauban, 1940–1946', *Revue d'histoire ecclésiastique* [Belgium], vol. 75 (1980), pp. 284–321

Laurentin, René, *Bernadette vous parle, Lourdes (1844–1866)* (Paris, Médiaspaul & Lethielleux, 1972)

— *Lourdes: Histoire authentique des apparitions* (Paris, P. Lethielleux, 6 vols., 1961–4)

— *Lourdes: Le Récit authentique des apparitions* (Paris, P. Lethielleux, 1966)

— *Vie authentique de Catherine Labouré: Voyante de la rue du Bac et servante des pauvres (1806–1876)* (Paris, Desclée de Brouwer, 2 vols., 1980)

— *Vie de Bernadette* (Paris, Desclée de Brouwer, 1978)

— *Visage de Bernadette* (Paris, P. Lethielleux, 2 vols., 1978)

— and Billet, Bernard, *Lourdes: Documents authentiques* (Paris, P. Lethielleux, 7 vols., 1957–66)

— and Durand, A., *Pontmain – Histoire authentique: Un signe dans le ciel* (Paris, P. Lethielleux, 1970)

Lee, David C. J., *Ernest Renan: In the Shadow of Faith* (London, Duckworth, 1996)

Le Goff, Jacques, *La Naissance du Purgatoire* (Paris, Gallimard, 1981)

Lehning, J., *Peasant and French: Cultural Contact in Rural France during the Nineteenth Century* (New York, Cambridge University Press, 1995)

Le Nail, Jean-François, 'L'Age d'or du château fort (XI–XVe siècles)', in Stéphane Baumont, ed., *L'Histoire de Lourdes* (Toulouse, Privat, 1993)

— and Soulet, Jean-François, eds., *Le Pays de Bigorre et les quatre vallées* (Paris, Société nouvelle d'éditions régionales et de diffusion, 1981)

Leniaud, Jean-Michel, 'Les Constructions d'églises sous le Second Empire: Architecture et prix de revient', *Revue d'histoire de l'église de la France*, vol. 55 (1979), pp. 267–78

Léonard, Jacques, 'Femmes, religion et médecine: Les Religieuses qui soignent, en France au XIXe siècle', *Annales ESC*, vol. 32 (1977), pp. 887–907

Le Play, Frédéric, *L'Organisation de la famille selon le vrai modèle signalé par l'histoire de toutes les races et de tous les temps* (Paris, Téqui, 1871)

Leproux, Paul, *Dévotions et saints guérisseurs* (Paris, PUF, 1957)

Le Roux, Benoît, *Louis Veuillot: Un homme, un combat* (Paris, Téqui, 1984)

Leroy, Géraldi, ed., *Les Ecrivains et l'Affaire Dreyfus: Actes du colloque organisé par le Centre Charles Péguy et l'université d'Orléans (29–31 octobre 1981)* (Paris, PUF, 1983)

Limouzin-Lamothe, R., and Leflon, J., *Mgr Denis-Auguste Affre, archevêque de Paris 1793–1848* (Paris, J. Vrin, 1971)

Locke, Robert R., *French Legitimists and the Politics of Moral Order in the Early Third Republic* (Princeton, Princeton University Press, 1974)

Longpré, Père Ephrem, *La Vierge Immaculée: Histoire et doctrine* (Paris, Aux éditions franciscaines, 1939)

Loux, Françoise, *Le Jeune Enfant et son corps dans la médecine traditionnelle* (Paris, Flammarion, 1978)

Luebke, David M., '"Naïve Monarchism" and Marian Veneration in Early-Modern Germany', *Past & Present*, no. 154 (1997), pp. 71–106

Lynch, Edouard, *Entre la commune et la nation: Identité communautaire et pratique politique en vallée de Campan (Hautes-Pyrénées) au XIXe siècle* (Tarbes, Association Guillaume Mauran, 1992)

MacAloon, J., ed., *Rite, Drama, Festival, Spectacle: Rehearsals towards a Theory of Cultural Performance* (Philadelphia, Institute for the Study of Human Issues, 1984)

McDougall, Joyce, *Theatres of the Body: A Psychoanalytic Approach to Psychosomatic Illness* (London, Free Association Books, 1989)

— *Theatres of the Mind: Illusion and Truth on the Psychoanalytic Stage* (London, Faber and Faber, 1985)

McManners, John, *Church and State in France 1870–1914* (London, SPCK, 1972)

McMillan, James, *Napoleon III* (Harlow, Longman, 1991)

— 'Religion and Gender in Modern France: Some Reflections', in Frank Tallett and Nicholas Atkin, eds., *Religion, Society and Politics in France since 1789* (London, Hambledon Press, 1991), pp. 55–66

McPhee, Peter, *The Politics of Rural Life: Political Mobilization in the French Countryside 1846–1852* (Oxford, Oxford University Press, 1992)

Magraw, Roger, 'The Conflict in the Villages: Popular Anti-clericalism in the Isère (1852–1870), in Theodore Zeldin, ed., *Conflicts in French Society: Anti-clericalism, Education and Morals in the Nineteenth Century* (London, George Allen & Unwin, 1970), pp. 169–237

Maire, C. L., *Les Possédées de Morzine 1857–1873* (Lyon, Presses Universitaires de Lyon, 1981)

Maître, Jacques, *Une inconnue célèbre: La Madeleine Lebouc de Janet* (Paris, Anthropos, 1993)

— *L'Orpheline de la Bérésina: Thérèse de Lisieux (1873–1897)* (Paris, Cerf, 1995)

Mangiapan, Théodore, *Les Guérisons de Lourdes: Etude historique et critique depuis l'origine à nos jours* (Lourdes, Œuvre de la Grotte, 1994)

Marcilhacy, C., *Le Diocèse d'Orléans au milieu du dix-neuvième siècle* (Paris, Henri Plon, 1964)

Margadant, Jo Burr, *Madame le Professeur: Women Educators in the Third Republic* (Princeton, Princeton University Press, 1990)

Margadant, Ted W., *French Peasants in Revolt: The Insurrection of 1851* (Princeton, Princeton University Press, 1979)

Marliave, Olivier de, *Trésor de la mythologie pyrénéenne* (Toulouse, ESPER, 1987)

Marsal, Jean, *Lourdes: Un roman d'Emile Zola, genèse et signification*, Diplôme d'études approfondies de théologie (Université des sciences humaines de Strasbourg, Faculté de théologie catholique, 1992)

Martin, Jean-Clément, *La Vendée et la France* (Paris, Seuil, 1987)

— *La Vendée de la mémoire* (Paris, Seuil, 1989)

Marx, Jean, *L'Inquisition en Dauphiné: Etude sur le développement et la répression de l'hérésie et la sorcellerie du XIVe siècle au début du règne de François Ier* (Paris, E. Champion, 1914)

Masson, René, *La Salette, ou les larmes de Marie* (Paris, Editions SOS, 1982)

Matt, Leonard von, and Tronchu, Francis, *Saint Bernadette: A Pictorial Biography*, Herbert Rees, tr. (London, Longman, 1957)

Mayer, Arno J., *The Persistence of the Old Regime in Europe to the Great War* (New York, Pantheon Books, 1981)

Mayeur, Jean-Marie, ed., *L'Histoire religieuse de la France 19e–20e siècles: Problèmes et méthodes* (Paris, Beauchesne, 1975)

— 'Mgr Dupanloup et Louis Veuillot devant les "prophéties contemporaines" en 1874', *Revue de l'histoire de la spiritualité*, vol. 48 (1972), pp. 193–204

Mazzoni, Cristina, *Saint Hysteria: Neurosis, Mysticism and Gender in European Culture* (Ithaca, Cornell University Press, 1996)

Méjean, A., 'Utilisation politique d'une catastrophe: Le Voyage de Napoléon III en Provence durant la grande crise', *Revue historique*, vol. 597 (1996), pp. 133–52

Ménager, Bernard, *Les Napoléon du peuple* (Paris, Aubier, 1988)

Merriman, J., *The Agony of the Republic: The Repression of the Left in Revolutionary France 1848–1851* (New Haven, Yale University Press, 1978)

Micale, Mark, *Approaching Hysteria: Disease and Its Interpretations* (Princeton, Princeton University Press, 1995)

Michaud, Stéphane, *Muse et madone: Visages de la femme de la Révolution française aux apparitions de Lourdes* (Paris, Seuil, 1985)

Miegge, G., *The Virgin Mary: The Roman Catholic Marian Doctrine*, Waldo Smith, tr. (London, Lutterworth Press, 1955)

Miest, Paul, *Les 54 Miracles de Lourdes au jugement du droit canon* (Paris, Editions Universitaires, 1958)

Mills, Hazel, 'Negotiating the Divide: Women, Philanthropy and the "Public Sphere" in Nineteenth-century France', in Frank Tallett and Nicholas Atkin, eds., *Religion, Society and Politics in France since 1789* (London, Hambledon Press, 1991), pp. 29–54

Mitterauer, Michael, *History of Youth*, G. Dunphy, tr. (Oxford, Blackwell, 1992)

Monter, E. William, *Witchcraft in France and Switzerland: The Borderlands during the Reformation* (Ithaca, Cornell University Press, 1976)

Morris, David B., *The Culture of Pain* (Berkeley, University of California Press, 1991)

Nicolet, Claude, *L'Idée républicaine en France: Essai d'histoire critique* (Paris, Gallimard, 1982)

Nolan, Mary Lee, and Nolan, Sidney, *Christian Pilgrimage in Modern Western Europe* (Chapel Hill, University of North Carolina Press, 1989)

Nora, Pierre, ed., *Les Lieux de mémoire: La République* (Paris, Gallimard, 1984), vol. 1

Nye, Robert A., *Crime, Madness and Politics in Modern France: The Medical Concept of National Decline* (Princeton, Princeton University Press, 1984)

— 'Degeneration and the Medical Model of Cultural Crisis in the Belle Epoque', in S. Drescher, D. Sabean and A. Sharlin, eds., *Political Symbolism in Modern Europe* (New Brunswick, NJ, Rutgers University Press, 1982), pp. 19–41

— *The Origins of Crowd Psychology: Gustave Le Bon and the Crisis of Mass Democracy in the Third Republic* (London, Sage, 1975)

Offen, Karen, 'Depopulation, Nationalism and Feminism in the Fin-de-siècle', *American Historical Review*, vol. 89 (1984), pp. 648–76

Oliviéri, Alponse, and Billet, Bernard, *Y-a-t-il encore des miracles à Lourdes?* (Paris, P. Lethielleux, 5th ed., 1989)

Ory, Pascal, and Sirinelli, Jean-François, *Les Intellectuels en France de l'Affaire Dreyfus à nos jours* (Paris, Colin, 1986)

Parham, Maggie, 'With God on Our Side' [a report on Medjugorje], *Independent Magazine*, 4 December 1993, pp. 35–40

Paul, Harry W., 'The Debate over the Bankruptcy of Science in 1895', *French Historical Studies*, vol. 5 (1968), pp. 298–327

— *The Edge of Contingency: French Catholic Reaction to Scientific Change from Darwin to Duhem* (Gainesville, University Presses of Florida, 1979)

Palluel-Guillard, André, et al., *La Savoie de la Révolution à nos jours, XIXe–XXe siècles* (Rennes, Ouest France, 1986)

Payne, Howard C., *The Police State of Louis Napoleon Bonaparte 1851–1860* (Seattle, WA, University of Washington Press, 1966)

Pelikan, Jaroslav, *Mary through the Centuries: Her Place in the History of Culture* (New Haven, Yale University Press, 1996)

Pépin, A., 'Le Père François Picard, directeur de l'association de Notre-Dame de Salut et des pèlerinages nationaux', *Pages d'archives*, 3rd series, no. 3 (1963)

— *Le Père François Picard: Directeur de Notre-Dame de Salut* (Rome, Ars Nova, 1964)

Perrin, Joel, and Lasserre, Jean-Claude, *Notre-Dame de Bétharram* (Pau, Les Amis des Eglises anciennes du Béarn, 1980)

Perry, Nicholas, and Echeverría, Loreto, *Under the Heel of Mary* (London, Routledge, 1988)

Petroff, Elizabeth Alvilda, *Body and Soul: Essays on Medieval Women and Mysticism* (New York, Oxford University Press, 1994)

Pick, Daniel, *Faces of Degeneration: A European Disorder* c. *1848–1918* (Cambridge, Cambridge University Press, 1989)

Pierrard, Pierre, *L'Eglise et les ouvriers en France (1840–1940)* (Paris, Hachette, 1984)

— *La Vie quotidienne des prêtres au XIXème siècle 1801–1905* (Paris, Hachette, 1986)

Pierrot, J., *The Decadent Imagination 1880–1900*, D. Coltman, tr. (Chicago, University of Chicago Press, 1981)

Pinies, Jean-Pierre, *Figures de la sorcellerie languedocienne* (Paris, CNRS, 1983)

Plessis, A., *The Rise and Fall of the Second Empire 1852–1871*, J. Mandelbaum, tr. (Cambridge, Cambridge University Press, 1985)

Pope, Barbara Corrado, 'Immaculate and Powerful: The Marian Revival in the Nineteenth Century', in *Immaculate and Powerful: The Female in Sacred Image and Social Reality*, Clarissa W. Atkinson, et al., eds. (Boston, Beacon Press, 1985)

Porter, Roy, ed., *The Medical History of Waters and Spas* (London, Wellcome Institute for the History of Medicine, 1990)

Praz, M., *The Romantic Agony*, A. Davidson, tr. (London, Oxford University Press, 2nd ed., 1951)

Proudfoot, Wayne, *Religious Experience* (Berkeley, University of California Press, 1985)

Quartararo-Vinas, Annie, *Médecins et médecine dans les Hautes-Pyrénées au XIXe siècle* (Tarbes, Association Guillaume Mauran, 1982)

Rapley, Elizabeth, *The* Dévotes*: Women and the Church in Seventeenth-*

century France (Montreal/London, McGill/Queen's University Press, 1990)

Ravier, Père André, SJ, *Le Corps de sainte Bernadette d'après les archives du couvent Saint-Gildard, du diocèse et de la ville de Nevers* (Paris, n.p., 1991)

— *ed., Les Ecrits de sainte Bernadette et sa voie spirituelle* (Paris, P. Lethielleux, Œuvre de la Grotte, 2nd ed., 1980)

Rearick, Charles, *Beyond the Enlightenment: Historians and Folklore in Nineteenth-century France* (Bloomington, Indiana University Press, 1974)

Recroix, X., *Anglèze de Sagazan et la chapelle de Garaison* (Pau, Marrimpouey jeune, 1982)

— 'Un aspect de la piété populaire dans les Pyrénées centrales: La Dévotion mariale', *Revue de Comminges*, no. 102 (1989), pp. 121–8

— 'Eugène Cordier et les légendes des Hautes-Pyrénées: Formation et sources du légendaire', in Eugène Cordier, *Les Légendes des Hautes-Pyrénées*, J.-F. Le Nail and X. Recroix, eds. (Tarbes, Association Guillaume Mauran, 1986)

— *Les Peintures du Narthex de la chapelle de Garaison* (Pau, Marrimpouey jeune, 1981)

— *Récits d'apparitions mariales (Pyrénées centrales)* (extrait de la *Revue de Comminges*, 3ème trimestre, 1986 à 3ème trimestre, 1988)

Rémond, René, and Poulat, Emile, eds., *Emmanuel d'Alzon dans la société et l'Eglise du XIXe siècle* (Paris, Le Centurion, 1982)

Rogier, L.-J., *Siècle des lumières, révolutions, restaurations* (Paris, Seuil, 1966)

Ronsanvallon, Pierre, *Le Sacre du citoyen: Histoire du suffrage universel en France* (Paris, Gallimard, 1992)

Rosapelly, Norbert, *Traditions et coutumes des Hautes-Pyrénées* (Tarbes, Société académique des Hautes-Pyrénées, 1990)

Rosenbaum-Dondaine, Catherine, ed., *L'Image de piété en France 1814–1914* (Paris, Musée-Galerie de la Seita, 1984)

Rouillé, André, *L'Empire de la photographie: Photographie et pouvoir bourgeois (1839–1870)* (Paris, Le Sycamore, 1982)

Rubin, Miri, *Corpus Christi: The Eucharist in Late Medieval Culture* (Cambridge, Cambridge University Press, 1991)

Sahlins, Peter, *Boundaries: The Making of France and Spain in the Pyrenees* (Berkeley and Los Angeles, University of California Press, 1989)

— *Forest Rites: The War of the Demoiselles in Nineteenth-century France* (Cambridge, MA, Harvard University Press, 1994)

Salomon-Bayet, C., ed., *Pasteur et la révolution pasteurienne* (Paris, Payot, 1986)

Savart, Claude, 'Cent ans après: Les Apparitions mariales en France au XIXe siècle, un ensemble?' *Revue de l'histoire de la spiritualité*, vol. 48 (1972), pp. 205–20

— 'Pour une sociologie de la ferveur religieuse: L'Archiconfrérie de Notre-Dame des Victoires', *Revue d'Histoire Ecclésiastique* [Belgium], vol. 59 (1964), pp. 823–44

Scarry, Elaine, *The Body in Pain: The Making and Unmaking of the World* (Oxford, Oxford University Press, 1985)

Schmitt, Jean-Claude, *Les Revenants: Les Vivants et les morts dans la société médiévale* (Paris, Gallimard, 1994)

— *Le Saint Lévrier: Guinefort, guérisseur d'enfants depuis le XIIe siècle* (Paris, Flammarion, 1979)

Scott, James, *Domination and the Arts of Resistance: Hidden Transcripts* (New Haven, Yale University Press, 1990)

Sébillot, Paul, *Le Folklore de France* (Paris, Imago, 8 vols., 1985, previously in Guilmoto, 1904–6)

Sedgwick, A., *The Ralliement in French Politics 1890–1898* (Cambridge, MA, Harvard University Press, 1965)

Sempé, Pierre-Rémi, and Duboë, Jean-Marie, *Petite histoire de Lourdes*, reprinted as *Notre-Dame de Lourdes* (Paris, Letouzey et Ané, 12th ed., 1931)

Sigal, Pierre-André, *L'Homme et le miracle dans la France médiévale (XIe–XIIe siècles)* (Paris, Cerf, 1985)

— *L'Image du pèlerin au Moyen Age et sous l'Ancien Régime* (Rocamadour, Association des amis de Rocamadour, 1994)

Singer, Barnett, *Village Notables in Nineteenth-century France: Priests, Mayors, Schoolmasters* (Albany, NY, State University of New York Press, 1983)

Six, Jean-François, *La Véritable Enfance de Thérèse de Lisieux: Névrose et sainteté* (Paris, Seuil, 1972)

Smith, Bonnie, *Ladies of the Leisure Class: The Bourgeoises of Northern France* (Princeton, Princeton University Press, 1981)

Smith, Paul, *Feminism and the Third Republic: Women's Political and Civil Rights in France 1918–1945* (Oxford, Oxford University Press, 1996)

Smith, William H. C., *Eugénie: Impératrice et femme (1826–1920)* (Paris, Olivier Orban, 1989)

Société d'études des Sept Vallées, *Thermalisme et climatisme dans les Pyrénées* (Actes du congrès des sociétés académiques et savantes, 1984, pub. 1985)

Soderini, E., *Leo XIII, Italy and France* (London, Burns, Oates & Washbourne, 1935)

Somerville, John, *The Rise and Fall of Childhood* (London, Sage, 1982)

Sorlin, Pierre, *'La Croix' et les juifs 1880–1899: Contribution à l'histoire de l'antisémitisme contemporain* (Paris, B. Grasset, 1967)

Soulet, Jean-François, 'Pèlerinage et sociabilité dans les Pyrénées aux XVIIe et XVIIIe siècles', in *Catalogue de l'exposition: Pèlerins et pèlerinages dans les Pyrénées françaises* (Lourdes, Exposition Musée Pyrénéen, juin–octobre 1975), pp. xi–xxi

— *Les Pyrénées au XIXe siècle* (Toulouse, Eché, 2 vols., 1987)

— 'La Société Lourdaise vue par Eugène Cordier', *Catalogue de l'exposition du Musée Pyrénéen de Lourdes* (Lourdes, Exposition Musée Pyrénéen, juin 1987)

— *Traditions et réformes religieuses dans les Pyrénées centrales au XVIIe siècle (Le Diocèse de Tarbes de 1602 à 1716)* (Pau, Marrimpouey jeune, 1974)

— *La Vie quotidienne dans les Pyrénées sous l'Ancien Régime* (Paris, Hachette, 1974)

— ed., *Le Pays de Bigorre et les quatre vallées* (Paris, Société nouvelle d'éditions régionales et de diffusion, 1981)

Sowerwine, Charles, *Sisters or Citizens? Women and Socialism in France since 1876* (Cambridge, Cambridge University Press, 1982)

Spencer, P., *The Politics of Belief in Nineteenth-century France* (London, Faber, 1954)

Sperber, Jonathan, *Popular Catholicism in Nineteenth-century Germany* (Princeton, Princeton University Press, 1984)

Stallybrass, Peter, and White, Allon, *The Politics and Poetics of Transgression* (London, Methuen, 1986)

Strenski, Ivan, *Religion in Relation: Method, Application and Moral Location* (London, Macmillan, 1993)

Sutton, Michael, *Nationalism, Positivism and Catholicism: The Politics of Charles Maurras and French Catholics 1890–1914* (Cambridge, Cambridge University Press, 1982)

Swart, Koenraad W., *The Sense of Decadence in Nineteenth-century France* (The Hague, Martinus Nijhoff, 1964)

Sylvain, C., *Vie du Père Hermann, en religion, Augustin-Marie du Très-Saint-Sacrement, Carme déchaussé* (Tours, Mame, 1st ed., 1880, 5th ed., 1924)

Tackett, Timothy, *Priest and Parish in Eighteenth-century France* (Princeton, Princeton University Press, 1977)

— *Religion, Revolution and Regional Culture in Eighteenth-century France: The Ecclesiastical Oath of 1791* (Princeton, Princeton University Press, 1986)

Tallett, Frank, and Atkin, Nicholas, eds., *Catholicism in Britain and France since 1789* (London, Hambledon Press, 1996)

—— *Religion, Society and Politics in France since 1789* (London, Hambledon Press, 1991)

Taveneaux, René, *Le catholicisme dans la France classique 1610–1715* (Paris, SEDES, 1980)

Taylor, Therese, 'So many extraordinary things to tell – Letters from Lourdes, 1858', *Journal of Ecclesiastical History*, vol. 46, no. 3 (1995), pp. 457–81

Ternois, René, *Zola et son temps: Lourdes, Rome, Paris* (Paris, Société des Belles Lettres, 1961)

Thuillier, Guy, *L'Imaginaire Quotidien du XIXe siècle* (Paris, Economica, 1985)

— and Tulard, Jean, *Histoire de l'administration française* (Paris, PUF, 1984)

Timmermans, Linda, *L'Accès des femmes à la culture (1598–1715)* (Paris, Honoré Champion, 1993)

Touveneraud, Père Pierre, 'Aux origines de la vocation personnelle d'Etienne Pernet: "Une période de quatorze années de rude souffrance"', *Pages d'archives*, 4th series, vol. 1 (1966), pp. 29–69

— 'La Participation du Père d'Alzon à la défense des états pontificaux 1859–1863', *Pages d'archives*, 3rd series, vol. 12 (1960), pp. 385–410

Trénard, Louis, 'Les Miracles raillés par Voltaire', in *Actes de la sixième rencontre d'histoire religieuse tenue à Fontevraud les 8 et 9 octobre organisée par le Centre de recherches d'histoire religieuse et d'histoire des idées* (Angers, Presses de l'Université d'Angers, 1983), pp. 95–109

Truesdell, Matthew, *Spectacular Politics: Louis Napoleon Bonaparte and the Fête Impériale 1849–1870* (New York, Oxford University Press, 1997)

Turin, Yvonne, *Femmes et religieuses au XIXe siècle: Le Féminisme 'en religion'* (Paris, Nouvelle Cité, 1989)

Turner, Terence, 'The Social Skin', in J. Cherfas and R. Lewin, eds., *Not Work Alone: A Cross-cultural View of Activities Superfluous to Survival* (London, Maurce Temple Smith, 1980), pp. 112–40

Turner, Victor, and Turner, Edith L. B., *Image and Pilgrimage in Christian Culture: Anthropological Perspectives* (Oxford, Blackwell, 1978)

Vailhé, Siméon, *La Vie du Père Emmanuel d'Alzon* (Paris, Maison de la Bonne Presse, 2 vols., 1926–34)

Van Gennep, Arnold, *Le Folklore du Dauphiné (Isère)* (Paris, Maisonneuve, 1932), vol. 1

— *Manuel de folklore français contemporain* (Paris, Editions A. et J. Picard, 4 vols., 1949)

Verdier, Yvonne, *Façons de dire, façons de faire: La Laveuse, la couturière, la cuisinière* (Paris, Gallimard, 1979)

Veuillot, Eugène, and Veuillot, François, *Louis Veuillot* (Paris, P. Lethielleux, 4 vols., 1899–1913)

Vidal, P., *Miracles et convulsions jansénistes au XVIII*ᵉ siècle (Paris, PUF, 1987)

Vigarello, Georges, *Concepts of Cleanliness: Changing Attitudes in France since the Middle Ages*, Jean Birrel, tr. (Cambridge, Cambridge University Press, 1988)

Vigier, P., *La Seconde République dans la région alpine: Etude politique et sociale* (Paris, PUF, 1963)

Virgerie, Jacques, 'Le Miracle dans la France du XVIIᵉ siècle', *Dix-Septième siècle*, vol. 35, no. 3 (1983), pp. 313–31

Vovelle, Michel, *Les Métamorphoses de la fête en Provence de 1750 à 1820* (Paris, Aubier–Flammarion, 1976)

— *The Revolution against the Church: From Reason to the Supreme Being*, A. José, tr. (Cambridge, Polity Press, 1991)

Waelti-Walters, J., and Hause, Steven C., *Feminisms of the Belle Epoque: A Historical and Literary Anthology* (Lincoln, Neb., University of Nebraska Press, 1994)

Walch, Jean, *Les Maîtres de l'histoire 1815–1850: Augustin Thierry, Mignet, Guizot, Thiers, Michelet, Edgard Quinet* (Geneva and Paris, Editions Slatking, 1986)

Wardman, H. W., *Ernest Renan: A Critical Biography* (London, Athlone Press, 1964)

Warner, Marina, *Alone of All Her Sex: The Myth and Cult of the Virgin Mary* (London, Picador, 1976)

Weber, Alison, *Theresa of Avila and the Rhetoric of Femininity* (Princeton, Princeton University Press, 1993)

Weber, Eugen, *Action Française: Royalism and Reaction in Twentieth-century France* (Stanford, Stanford University Press, 1964)

— *Peasants into Frenchmen: The Modernization of Rural France* (London, Chatto & Windus, 1977)

— 'Religion and Superstition in Nineteenth-century France', *Historical Journal*, vol. 32 (1988), pp. 399–423

Werfel, Franz, *The Song of Bernadette* (London, Hamish Hamilton, 1942)

Williams, Elizabeth A., *The Physical and the Moral: Anthropology, Physiology and Philosophical Medicine in France 1750–1850* (Cambridge, Cambridge University Press, 1994)

Wilson, Stephen, *Ideology and Experience: Anti-Semitism in France at the Time of the Dreyfus Affair* (Madison, NJ, Fairleigh Dickinson University Press, 1982)

Zeldin, Theodore, *The Political System of Louis Napoleon Bonaparte* (London, Macmillan, 1958)

— ed., *Conflicts in French Society: Anti-clericalism, Education and Morals in the Nineteenth Century* (London, George Allen & Unwin, 1970)
Zimdars-Swartz, Sandra L., *Encountering Mary: Visions of Mary from La Salette to Medjugorje* (New York, Avon Books, 1992)

Index

Note: Page numbers in *italics* refer to illustrations. Only those notes that give substantial further information are indexed.